MARI AND THE BIBLE

STUDIES IN THE HISTORY AND CULTURE OF THE ANCIENT NEAR EAST

EDITED BY

B. HALPERN AND M.H.E. WEIPPERT

VOLUME XII

MARI AND THE BIBLE

BY

ABRAHAM MALAMAT

TUTA SUB AEGIDE PALLAS · 1683 ·

BRILL
LEIDEN · BOSTON · KÖLN
1998

This book is printed on acid-free paper.

Library of Congress Cataloging-in-Publication Data

Malamat, Abraham.
Mari and the Bible / by Abraham Malamat.
p. cm.—(Studies in the history and culture of the ancient Near East, ISSN 0169-9024 ; v. 12)
Includes bibliographical references.
ISBN 9004108637 (alk. paper)
1. Mari (Extinct city). 2. Assyro-Babylonian literature—Relation to the Old Testament. I. Title. II. Series.
DS99.M3M343 1998
939'.4—dc21
97-18282
CIP

Die Deutsche Bibliothek – CIP-Einheitsaufnahme

Malāmāt, Avrāhām:
Mari and the Bible / by Abraham Malamat. - Leiden ; Boston ; Köln : Brill, 1998
(Studies in the history and culture of the ancient Near East ; Vol. 12)
ISBN 90-04-10863-7

ISSN 0169-9024
ISBN 90 04 10863 7

PRINTED IN THE NETHERLANDS

CONTENTS

PART THREE

CUSTOMS AND SOCIETY

PREFACE

The present volume contains twenty-two chapters, almost all originally published in journals or in books of different sorts, usually *Festschriften*. However, the articles have here undergone a major or minor revision and substantial updating, especially those of an earlier date (except for chapters 19, 20 and 21, which have remained practically unchanged). Two of the chapters have hitherto not been published in English (chs. 1 and 13) and a few others are still in the press elsewhere. The book frequently incorporates cross-references, so that the reader may easily find complementary material on issues dealt with. On the other hand, certain passages of the original papers which have now become redundant have been eliminated, although there still remains some overlap. There has not been any attempt throughout the book to conform to the technical apparatus, which remains in its original format.

The original articles span a period of over 25 years and have been selected from my entire output on the subject of Mari and the Bible, but the great majority of the papers included in the volume were composed in the 1990s. The papers have been arranged according to subject matter and divided into three parts. After an Introductory Chapter, which emphasizes method, the First Part deals with Mari and its variegated relations with Syria, Palestine and the Mediterranean. The Second Part deals with Mari "Prophecy" and its biblical counterpart, concluding that the former is a forerunner of biblical prophecy, but should not be conceived as its origin. The Third Part deals with customs, both religious and profane, and institutions and, in a way, social facets at large.

In short, the present book highlights the significance of Mari, not only for its time, but also for the later corpus of the Bible, as well as for biblical Israel, from the spiritual sphere to the material and mundane. Mari remains throughout the years, and perhaps increasingly, without doubt one of the most important external sources for illuminating the Bible and Early Israel.

Under the title of each chapter, the source of the original publication has been indicated. Here we express our thanks to the various publishers (in accordance with the chapter sequence) for granting permission to make use of the materials in the present book: Akademie Verlag (Berlin), MacMillan (England) and the Israel Academy of Sciences (Jerusalem), Sheffield University Press (Sheffield), Peeters (Leuven), the Israel Exploration Society (Jerusalem), Österreichische Akademie der Wissenschaften (Vienna), British Academy and Oxford University Press (London and Oxford), E.J. Brill (Leiden), S. Gitin for FS Frerichs (U.S.A.), De Gruyter (Berlin), Société Études du Proche Orient (Paris), Padaia (Brescia), Kohlhammer (Stuttgart), Eisenbrauns (Winona Lake, IN), Oriental Institute (Prague), CDL Press (Bethesda, MD), the American Oriental Society (Baltimore).

The work on a number of papers published in the 1990s has been generously supported (since 1990) by the Fund for Basic Research administered by the Israel Academy of Sciences and Humanities and I am deeply grateful to the Academy. My sincere thanks go also to the *équipe de Mari* in Paris and above all to its head, Prof. J.-M. Durand, who was of significant help in various ways. I cannot list here all the colleagues, assistants and students whose discourses with me were of considerable benefit to my endeavor. But a number of colleagues from whose stimulating contact throughout the many years I greatly profited should be mentioned: Prof. Pinhas Artzi (Ramat Gan) (who also co-authored two of the articles, chs. 19 and 20), Mr. Rafi Grafman (Jerusalem), Profs. Moshe Greenberg (Jerusalem), the late Jona Greenfield (Jerusalem), W.W. Hallo (New Haven), Baruch Levine (New York), Alan Millard (Liverpool) and Aaron Shaffer (Jerusalem).

My thanks also to Mrs. R. Nikolsky and Miss A. Lifshitz who assisted me in preparing the Indexes, and to Mrs. C.A. Bar-Yaacov for reading the last set of proofs.

Finally, I am much indebted to the Publishing House of E.J. Brill and especially to the Desk Editor for Ancient Near East and Asian Studies, Ms. Patricia Radder, for handling and taking care of the production of my book.

Jerusalem
November 1997

1

INTRODUCTORY ESSAY
MARI AND THE BIBLE: A COMPARATIVE PERSPECTIVE*

Among the various methodological approaches in research concerning culture or society, two methods shall be mentioned here: one was applied to the Babylonian world by the distinguished scholar Benno Landsberger in his seminal article of 1926 entitled: "Die Eigenbegrifflichkeit der babylonischen Welt" (translated into English as "The Conceptual Autonomy of the Babylonian World", 1976).[1] This approach to understanding an ancient culture has enjoyed acceptance among scholars bold enough to claim that their empathy enables them to reconstruct the past more or less accurately, and that they are capable of putting themselves in the shoes of the ancients.

A less presumptuous method, not necessarily in contrast to the previous one, has become widespread during the last generations. It aims at understanding the culture and social patterns, ancient as well as modern, of a society on the basis of comparative method.[2] This approach has gained favour in many of the humanities and social sciences, including history and religion, sociology and anthropology, as well as linguistics.[3] Critics of the comparative method claim that

---

* This study is a follow-up of the relevant passages in my book *Mari and the Early Israelite Experience* (cf. below, n. 5). I have tried, as much as possible, to adhere to new material from Mari, which has become known since the publication of my book.

[1] For the German original see B. Landsberger, *Islamica* 2 (1926), 355–72; the English translation is by Th. Jacobsen, B. Foster and H. von Siebenthal, published in *Sources and Monographs* (*on the Ancient Near East*), Undena Publications, Malibu 1976.

[2] See in general A. Etzioni and F.L. Dubow, eds., *Comparative Perspectives*, Boston 1970; I. Vallier, ed., *Comparative Methods in Sociology*, Berkeley etc. 1971; G. Sarana, *The Methodology of Anthropological Comparisons: An Analysis of Comparative Methods in Social and Cultural Anthropology*, Tucson 1975; L. Holy, ed., *Comparative Anthropology*, Oxford 1987; M. Malul, *The Comparative Method in Ancient Near Eastern and Biblical Legal Studies*, Neukirchen-Vluyn 1990.

[3] For bibliography see n. 2 and cf., e.g., I.J. Gelb, "Comparative Method in the Study of Society and Economy of the Ancient Near East," *Ročznik Orientalistyczny* 41 (1980), 29–36. Concerning the realm of history as such see M. Mandelbaum, "Some Forms and Uses of Comparative History," *American Studies International* 18 (1979/80), 19–34.

comparisons between cultures are trivial, that generalizations may be valid only with regard to a single culture, and that comparisons between different societies lead to distortions of reality.[4]

Notwithstanding these and similar real or imagined shortcomings, I have adopted a comparative study aimed at a more profound understanding and with potential for proffering new interpretations in my studies related to Mari and the Hebrew Bible.[5] A slogan often stressed, particularly by the great Russian thinker V. Bakhtin, conveys the idea that an in-depth understanding of a specific culture is only possible from the vantage point of a different one. What is required is a comparative study which presents not only similarities, parallels and analogies, but which also examines differences and contrasts, an endeavour sometimes neglected in research.

Such an approach, juxtaposing similarity and contrast, is by some referred to as the "contextual" approach.[6] A further reflection regarding Mari and the Bible: these are relatively distant from one another in both space and time (see below). Yet this fact does not necessarily invalidate the proposed methodology. It would appear to be accommodated inter alia by the French school as "comparative method on the grand scale", a concept employed by Marc Bloch.[7] Advocated are broad comparisons encompassing distant regions and considerable time-spans, indeed often far greater than the gap between Mari and the Bible, both of which belong, in essence, to the same cultural milieu.

By what means may we most satisfactorily and efficiently approach a comparative study of Mari and the Bible? It goes without saying that the comparison must be significantly relevant rather than inci-

---

[4] See A.J.F. Köbben, "Comparativists and Non-Comparativists in Anthropology," in R. Naroll and R. Cohen, eds., *A Handbook of Method in Cultural Anthropology*, Garden City, N.Y., 1970, 584 and ff.; L. Holy in *Comparative Anthropology* (above, n. 2), 1–21. For certain strictures against the comparative method concerning biblical studies see S. Talmon, "The 'Comparative Method' in Biblical Interpretation—Principles and Problems," *SVT* 29 (1977), 320–356. For the limitations of the comparative method see also M. Harris, *The Rise of Anthropological Theory*, New York 1968, 156 ff.

[5] For my latest treatment see my book on *Mari and the Early Israelite Experience* (the Schweich Lectures 1984), The British Academy and Oxford 1989, repr. 1992, and the more extended version in Hebrew, *Mari and Israel*, Jerusalem 1991.

[6] In ancient Near Eastern and biblical studies this has been stressed by W.W. Hallo in a series of articles, most recently in "The Context of Scripture, Ancient Near Eastern Texts . . .," *Eleventh World Congress of Jewish Studies* (Division A: *The Bible and its World*), Jerusalem 1994, 9–15.

[7] M. Bloch, "Two Strategies of Comparison," in Etzioni and Dubow, eds. (above, n. 2), 39–41.

dental, thereby leading to superficial conclusions. We must avoid romanticism in arriving at conclusions, and not draw any direct connection between Mari and the predecessors of Israel which would be suggestive of an erstwhile genetic link between them. This for example, was the path taken (mistakenly, in my opinion) by the first excavator of Mari, A. Parrot, and many others. I shall mention here only W.F. Albright, who went so far as to state that the First Old Babylonian dynasty at Babylon, south of Mari, was founded by the early Hebrews.[8]

Historical-genetic comparisons are thus to be avoided. One would be advised rather to rely upon the so-called typological approach, designating "typological" as suiting the existence of considerable distance in space and time between the entities being compared.[9] The typological or phenomenological approach rests upon comparison of typical phenomena, similar customs, related organizations and institutions and even analogous conceptual frameworks. When such parallels are viewed systematically, a relatively firm foundation is laid for comparison between Mari and the world of the Bible. Currently available data do not sustain the possibility of an erstwhile historical relationship between Mari and early Israel, and are insufficient to tip the balance in favor of such a connection.

On the basis of these assumptions and restrictions, we will now move to controlled empirical analysis of comparisons between Mari on the one hand and the Bible and Israel on the other. Such a cross-cultural study, if applied systematically, may prove highly productive.

Comparisons of a Technical Nature

First we shall deal with the chronological perspective.[10] This aspect is not as significant in comparative research as one might imagine, and it will therefore be examined here only briefly. At the same time, it is the most complex aspect, as the period of the Patriarchs and the beginning of Israelite existence are problematic. While the relevant Mari documents are of the Old Babylonian period (the first half of the 18th century B.C., according to the so-called Middle Chronology,

[8] W.F. Albright, *Yaweh and the Gods of Canaan*, London 1968, 71.

[9] Cf. Malul (above, n. 2), 52.

[10] For a more detailed account see Malamat, *op. cit.* (above, n. 5, English version), 29 f.

to which we adhere), the oldest portions of the biblical text date to the 12th–11th centuries B.C. A gap of 500 years or more thus separates the two sets of texts.

The prevailing assumption in modern biblical research is that the book of Genesis and the Former Prophets were edited during a later period, in the 7th century, or, as some would have it, in the 6th or 5th century. It has been recently proposed that their redaction is even of Hellenistic dating. On the other hand, it is possible that the Patriarchal stories and other parts of the Bible contain very ancient recollections from the 2nd millennium B.C. and perhaps even from the first half of that millennium, that is, within the very period of Mari or, in other words, during the Middle, rather than the Late Bronze Age (see below).

As an aside, I would surmise that while the existence of the Patriarchs should not be negated, the "Patriarchal Age" as such is not a well defined chronological period, nor can the Patriarchs be assigned to a specific timespan. Let us instead hypothesize an artificial scheme created by late historiographers consisting of a generational scheme, a kind of telescoping of extensive historical time periods in which centuries, perhaps, were collapsed into a narrow, reduced chronological framework. The impact of this approach raises the possibility that Israelite proto-history, which extended chronologically over a lengthy period, dovetails with the period of Mari documents. This possibility gains support from the other aspects here to be examined.

The implications of the second aspect, the geographical,[11] may be exposed on various levels: within the scope of the Mari documents one finds, among other regions, the one referred to in the Bible, and only there, by the name "Aram Naharaim", that is, the present day Jezireh stretching between the Habur and Euphrates rivers. The cities of Haran and Nahor, the ancestral habitats of the Patriarchs and their relatives, were, according to the Bible, located in this region. Great importance is therefore attributed to the fact that the Mari documents frequently mention these two cities as centers, even foci of tribal activity of nomads. Admittedly, these cities are also mentioned in later periods, however the earlier occurrence may be of relevance to us. The Mari documents shed light on the Patriarchal

[11] For an extended discussion see Malamat, *op. cit.* (above, n. 5, English version), 52–66.

movements between Mesopotamia and the West, including the Land of Canaan. We frequently hear of the mobility of emissaries and traders between the middle Euphrates and Syria, and even Palestine, and most significantly, also the wanderings of tribal groups. Contrary to the outmoded view of nomadic centrifugal movement out of the desert, a new model emerges of tribal wanderings, back and forth over the Fertile Crescent, rather like alternating electrical current. Such a model well suits a picture of Patriarchal wanderings, though, unlike the realistic documentation from Mari, these accounts were passed down as naive, legendary stories.

To this are to be added self-same toponyms known from Mari and the Bible. Above all, must be mentioned the term "Canaan" (*LÚ Kinaḫnum [meš]*) or more specifically, people from Canaan. In Mari this is the earliest recorded use of this toponym, which antedates the previously known first occurrence by some 300 years. Thus, the name Canaan is no longer in present-day language an anachronism as regards the first half of the 2nd millennium B.C. In Palestine proper an important, central city is frequently mentioned at Mari—Hazor. Recently, this identification has been unjustifiably rejected, locating the Hazor of the Mari texts at a small Syrian village called Hasur.[12] This village is about 300 km north of biblical Hazor, 18 km south of el-Hama and 50 km to the west of Qatna. But no tell has been discovered at this place, which also seems unsuitable for a major city so close to that of Qatna (which is of an area of 1,000 dunam). Though biblical Hazor does not occur in the Patriarchal tradition, it holds an important place in the tradition of the Israelite Conquest.

Since I have devoted a series of articles to the diplomatic and economic relations between Hazor and Mari (cf. below ch. 5B), a few words here will suffice concerning this issue. Hazor of the Mari period should be identified with its Middle Bronze Age IIB level (MB IIB), in which the extensive Lower City arose (see ch. 5c). Hazor covered an area of approximately 800–900 dunams (200–225 acres), making it by far the largest city in Palestine. The remains at Hazor reflect the northern, Syrian cultural sphere. Some twenty Mari references to Hazor in a variety of contexts are known today. Roughly half of these were added to the corpus during the past decade or so, and still more may exist.

[12] See M. Astour, "The Location of *Hasura* of the Mari Texts," *Maarav* 7 (1991), 51–65.

Thus, in the light of Mari, Hazor is found deserving the epithet "head of all those kingdoms" (Joshua 11:10), and its ruler, the title "King of Canaan" (Judges 4:2). I would like to refer here only to two unpublished references: one of these speaks of female musicians sent from Mari to the court of Hazor, thereby indicating the existence of a "school" of music at Hazor. The second reference apparently implies that one of the wives of Zimri-Lim, the last king of Mari (who reigned from c. 1775 to 1760 B.C.), called Atar-Aya, was a princess from Hazor. If this conjecture proves true, family bonds may well have existed between the Mari dynasty and that of Hazor—a surprise for the historian. For Hazor in the Mari documents see below chs. 5A, 5B and 5C.

In-Depth Comparisons

The two remaining comparisons are more than of technical significance to our problem, unlike the former comparisons.

As for the sociological aspects, Mari and the Bible are the primary sources in ancient Near Eastern literature for the reconstruction of semi-nomadic, tribal society.[13] In the other sources up to the time of Islam, tribal society is reflected as an archaic remnant or at most as a peripheral topic, while at Mari and in the Bible tribalism is manifested in full-bloom and vitality. We thus have ample opportunity for comparison, several examples of which we shall examine here.

A. Both at Mari and in the Bible, the tribal regime is patrilineal, while the basic social units are the Hebrew *mišpāḥā* (extended) family, the Hebrew *bēt āb*, and the Hebrew clan, in its biblical sense. Such units aggregated and formed sub-tribal entities and, eventually, whole tribes. The above phenomena are, in fact, universal, however their portrayal in our two sources is distinct: Mari presents a synchronic picture—varying degrees of settlement of the tribes, coexisting side-by-side simultaneously, ranging from nomadic tribal units to those which had already become sedentary. The Bible, on the other hand, reflects the degree of settlement diachronically, i.e., the various stages are presented as if they occur in sequence: first, the Patriarchs and

[13] For a more profound discussion see Malamat, *op. cit.* (above, n. 5, English version), 34–52.

the Israelites entering the Land of Canaan are semi-nomadic, but subsequently inherit the Land and settle it.

As stated by us elsewhere, the synoptical examination of the synchronic and diachronic aspects provide us with a virtual stereoscopic picture. Mari presents the events realistically, thereby making possible "fieldwork" of the sort carried out by present-day anthropologists. Yet, the Bible, with its clearly historical viewpoint, divides the process of settlement into different chronological stages. As one might expect, both sources refer to encounters between tribal society and the established urban culture and society, an ambivalent relationship of friction on the one hand and coexistence on the other. It would appear that despite the overt conflict between the nomadic Israelites with the Canaanites' urban population, at least as portrayed in the Bible, the experience in Mesopotamia was more moderate and involved a process of assimilation between the Akkadian-Old Babylonian society and the western Semitic nomadic tribes newly arrived upon the stage of history.

B. Institutions and rituals. I will here refer to only one example—treaty making by means of ritual. In Mari one of the possibilities was to slaughter the foal of an ass (*qatālum ḫayaram*), a relatively widespread ritual, perhaps originating in the West.[14] Now, recently a letter has been published from the northern periphery of the Mari kingdom which was sent to King Zimri-Lim. It is largely identical to a long-known document (*ARM* II 37), which reports the making of a treaty between a nomadic tribe and the local representative of Mari (see ch. 17 and there the biblical correspondences).

The last of the aspects to be examined—the ethnic-linguistic one—seems to be the most solid in the comparative analysis of Mari and the Bible. This aspect is primarily based upon the onomasticon and linguistic idiosyncrasies of the Mari texts—single words and terms, entire expressions, and even a complete sentence, which are common to both sources (not to mention sometimes peculiar morphology and syntax of the Mari idiom). Considerable portions of the population of the city of Mari and an even larger percentage of the population of the settlements and tribes within the realm of the Mari

---

[14] For this custom, peculiar to the Sim'alite tribes (*bᵉne Sim'al* = northern tribes) as against the Yaminites (southern tribes), see now B. Lafont in *Amurru* II (forthcoming).

kingdom were Western Semites or Amorites, just as were the Patriarchs of Israel. Thus the vernaculars of these population groups were Amorite dialects, in other words, a sort of archaic stratum of the Hebrew language. This also explains the similarity between personal names among the Patriarchal clan and the Mari onomasticon.

Let us limit ourselves to the name Yaʿaqob (Jacob), which, like most of the names of the Patriarchal family members, does not recur in the description of later periods of biblical Israel. The name does, however, frequently occur in a variety of forms (plus a theophoric element at Mari: Yahkub-Il, Haqbu-Il, Haqba-ahhu and Haqbu-Hammu). While the name Yaʿaqob indeed occurs in later Akkadian documents, the frequency and concentration of its appearance during the Old Babylonian, or the Amorite period, is unparalleled. Moreover, slightly later we know from Egyptian sources of a Hyksos ruler named Yaqob-El or Yaqob-Har, attested only on Egyptian scarabs. Another name of a Hyksos ruler has been discovered recently in Northern Palestine, more precisely on two scarabs found in the excavations of Kabri (the name there is Yakubum).[15] In the Bible, the name is Jacob, per se, and is thus sufficient indication of the existence of a solid and ancient core within biblical tradition.

I presented a variety of examples of West Semitic vocables at Mari, arranged by subject, in the book *Mari and the Early Israelite Experience.*[16] This list includes 40 items and there are undoubtedly more examples. These words do not serve exclusively as a parallel for linguistic analysis, but also provide a reflection of the conceptual framework and life-style of the West Semites. I do not wish to analyze here parallels which have already been included in my book, such as the geographical concepts of valley (*ḫamqum*, Hebrew *ʿēmeq*) or the four points of the compass; terms dealing with the plant or animal kingdom; terms referring to tribal units: *gāʾum*, Hebrew *gōy* and *ḫibrum*, Hebrew *ḥeber*; terms relating to settlement such as *niḫlatum*, patrimony, Hebrew *naḥalāh*, or *nāwûm*, Hebrew *nāweh*, pasturage, migratory group; or terms related to tribal leadership—*šāpiṭum*, Hebrew *šōfēṭ*, conventionally translated as "judge" in the Bible, but sometimes intended there in a broader sense of "ruler" as at Mari.

---

[15] On the Yakob-Har scarabs, see now D. Ben-Tor and R. Bonfil, in eds. S. Ahituv and E. Oren, *A. Kempinski Memorial Volume* (Beer-Sheba, forthcoming). On the Yakubum scarabs see A. Kempinski in S. Groll, ed., *Studies in Egyptology* (*FS M. Lichtheim*), Jerusalem 1990, 632–634.

[16] See Malamat, *op. cit.* (above, n. 5), 33.

I would like to conclude with some of the discoveries of the past few years. The word *lim* = Hebrew *lᵉōm*, originally clan, tribal unit,[17] is mentioned in relation to nomadic life-style. Since the first publications of the Mari documents, the names of the kings Yahdun-Lim and his son Zimri-Lim have been known, as well as that of the king of Aleppo, Yarim-Lim. *Lim* was generally explained in these names as a theophoric element, despite the fact that no deity with this name has ever been encountered. As long expected, *lim*, clan, has now been discovered as a word in its own right. It resembles the Hebrew word *ʿam*, at first a restricted tribal unit, but later, referring to entire peoples, which has not yet been found in cuneiform sources as an independent term (for this subject see ch. 16).

Surprisingly, even a complete sentence in Amorite has been preserved at Mari, in an unpublished document. This document opens with the sentence *mišpāṭum birit* = a judgement between (country X and country Y).[18] Indeed, it would appear that Amorite was not employed for writing, and no document in this language has yet been published. An illustrative piece of evidence is the request by the Mari viceroy Yasmah-Addu to his father, King Samsi-Addu: "Fetch for me a man who reads Sumerian and who speaks Amorite (*amurrim dabābim*)."[19]

In this context we may refer to a saying in post-biblical literature of the Jewish Sages, concerning the use of four distinct languages: "*laʿaz* (= Greek) for poetry, *rōmī* (= Latin) for war-making, *sursī* (= Aramaic) for lamentation, and *ʿibrī* (Hebrew) for speech. There are those who say: Even *ʾăššurī* for script; *ʾăššurī* has a script, but no language, *ʿibrī* has a language, but no script (R. Yonatan of Bet Guvrin, T. Yerushalmi, Meg. 1:11; Esther Rabba ch. 4). This Rabbinic saying may now be paraphrased regarding the linguistic situation in the Old Babylonian period: "Sumerian for writing and Amorite for speech;" "(Neo-)Sumerian has a script, but no (spoken) language and Amorite has a (spoken) language, but no script."

---

[17] See my contribution "A Recently Discovered Word for 'Clan' in Mari and its Hebrew Cognate," in eds. Z. Zevit *et alii*, *Solving Riddles and Untying Knots* (*FS J.H. Greenfield*), Winona Lake 1995, 177–179 and ch. 16.

[18] See J.-M. Durand, "Unité et diversités au Proche-Orient à l'époque amorrite," *La circulation des biens . . ., Actes 38ᵉ-RAI*, Paris 1992, 125.

[19] See previous note, 124 (document M. 7930⁺).

I have presented here only a sample of comparisons, mostly parallels, but contrasts too, between Mari and the Bible. Many areas may be added, such as comparative religion,[20] particularly in relation to prophecy or rather, intuitive prophecy, which apparently starts at Mari and reaches its apex in the Bible. This question however, over which I have long toiled,[21] is beyond the scope of the present essay.

---

[20] See recently N. Smart, "Comparative-Historical Method," *The Encyclopedia of Religion*, III, New York 1987, 571–574 and the brief paper of K. van der Toorn, "Parallels in Biblical Research . . ." *Proceedings Eleventh World Congress of Jewish Studies, Division A*, Jerusalem 1994, 1–8.

[21] Until the end of the 80s see the summary in my book *Mari and the Early Israelite Experience* (above, n. 5), 70–96 (see in the present volume ch. 6). Since then I have written several articles on newly published prophecies (see the various chapters in Part Two).

PART ONE

MARI AND THE WEST

THE CULTURAL IMPACT OF THE WEST (SYRIA-PALESTINE) ON MESOPOTAMIA IN THE OLD BABYLONIAN PERIOD*

The political and economic ties between the East and the West in the ancient Near East during the first third of the second millennium B.C. have been thoroughly examined and researched. However, it appears that such is not the case with regard to the various cultural facets of the region, for instance, religion and ritual, perhaps because these phenomena are not readily seen and cannot easily be grasped. This paper will discuss some of the material and especially spiritual aspects of the civilization of the area. One well-known source concerning the Old Babylonian period—possibly the main source—serving to throw light on the subject, may be found in the texts from the royal archives at Mari, in particular, texts published in recent years. The volume of texts from Mari concerning the West (J.-M. Durand, *Archives Royales de Mari* [= *ARM*] 26/3) is not yet available.[1] However, some of the texts to be included in this volume have been published over the last ten years or so, and we shall take them into consideration below.

A

Let us start with a subject which is tangible, such as the diplomatic marriages contracted between the rulers of Mari and princesses from the metropolitan cities of the north and center of (Western) Syria.[2] The Mari texts record a series of marriages of this sort, which most

* This article was originally published in: Festschrift H. Klengel, *Alt-Orientalische Forschungen*, 24 (1997), pp. 312–319.

[1] See J.-M. Durand, *Archive épistolaire de Mari* 1/3 (= *ARM* 26/3) (forthcoming).

[2] See compilation entitled *La femme dans le proche orient antique*, ed. J.-M. Durand, Paris 1987. On the princess from Aleppo see there F. Abdallah; cf. in particular J.-M. Durand, *ARM* 26/1, pp. 95–117; on Mari in general see B.F. Batto, *Studies on Women at Mari*, Baltimore 1974.

likely involved various cultural contacts. The first true king of Mari in the Old Babylonian period, Yahdun-Lim, an outstanding ruler in whose reign Mari (both city and kingdom) rose to become a leading state on the central Euphrates, married, among others, a princess from Aleppo, whose name remains unknown.[3] After his reign, Mari was conquered by Samsi-Addu (whose capital was Ashur) who, as is well known, appointed his younger son, Yasmah-Addu, to be viceroy of Mari. We already know that Samsi-Addu had in fact compelled his son to marry a princess from the city of Qatna in central Syria. The princess was known in Mari by the epithet "Beltum", i.e. Mistress, the first Lady of Mari.[4]

Again, with the return to power of the local royal family in Mari, Zimri-Lim, the last king of Mari, took a wife from each of the two places in the West mentioned above. The first, we now know, whom he wedded close to his ascension to the throne, was from Qatna and was named Dam-hurāṣi;[5] in the third or fourth year of his reign he also married the much praised princess Šibtu (another reading of her name is Šiptu/Šipṭu) from the royal court of Aleppo. This worthy woman was the daughter of Yarim-Lim, the powerful king of Yamhad, the capital of which was Aleppo in northern Syria.[6] It is possible that Zimri-Lim married a third princess from the West, Atar-Aya, who accompanied him on his great journey to Syria as far as the Mediterranean coast in the "ninth" year of his reign. In the relevant text, the editor takes this woman as originating in the city of Ugarit, but in J.-M. Durand's opinion, based on texts not yet published, she may even have come from the city of Hazor.[7]

Marrying wives from the aristocracy of the West strengthened the relations between the central Euphrates and the West and, no doubt, brought into the court at Mari customs and etiquette, ceremonies and a life-style widespread in the West (cf. the pagan cults intro-

---

[3] See J.-M. Durand, *MARI* 6 (1990), 291; *idem, La circulation . . . Actes 38ᵉ RAI*, Paris 1992, p. 108.

[4] The princess was accompanied to Mari by her maidservant; see D. Charpin, *ARM* 26/2, p. 11, No. 298: 29–30. She was the daughter of the king of Qatna, Išhi-Addu, and the text containing the list of gifts to be sent by the princess to Mari is *ARMT* 1, No. 77.

[5] See, recently, B. Gronenberg, Dam-hurāṣim, Prinzessin aus Qatna und ihr *nūbalum*, *Mém. de NABU* 3 (*Mém. M. Birot*), Paris 1994, pp. 132 ff.

[6] See one of the early discussions on this princess by P. Artzi – A. Malamat, The Correspondence of Shibtu, Queen of Mari, *Orientalia* 40 (1971), 75–87 (= below ch. 19); and see now P. Villard, *MARI* 7 (1993), 318 f.

[7] Cf. J.-M. Durand, *ARMT* 23, p. 475, n. 52.

duced into Jerusalem by the foreign wives of King Solomon; 1 Kings 11:1–8). By the way, a kind of mirror image of these marriages may be found in the stories of the Patriarchs, as told in Genesis. There, the "direction" of the marriages is reversed: wives coming from Eastern Syria to the far West, like the noble women Rebekkah, Lea and Rachel from the city of Nahor (on the north-western branch of the Habur river) who were married by Isaac and Jacob.

As in the Bible, it may be assumed that there was also some form of clan or tribal relationship between Mari and the West. All the above places were already inhabited by West Semitic tribes or, in other words, Amorite tribes, at the beginning of the second millennium B.C.,[8] and these tribes cultivated *inter alia* ties through marriage. The royal custom of marrying wives from the West was current even in the neo-Assyrian period; one of King Sennacherib's wives, for instance, was Naqia-Zakutu, who came from Syria, or may even have been from Palestine. Moreover, it is possible that one of the wives of Ashurnasirpal II (in our reading Yapha), who was apparently the mother of King Shalmaneser III and whose royal tomb has recently been discovered, also came from the West.[9] The same holds true for the newly discovered name of Atal(ya), presumably one of the wives of King Sargon II.

Let us now discuss another feature in which the links between East and West are more or less evident: visits by the sons of the aristocracy of southern Mesopotamia to Mari and, apparently, subsequently to Western cities. There they were undoubtedly influenced by the local culture which they then brought back to their place of origin in the East. Relevant to this subject is document *ARM* 26/2, No. 375,[10] which consists of a letter from Yarim-Addu, delegate of Mari in Babylon, addressed to King Zimri-Lim. The writer reports to his sovereign that Hammurabi, king of Babylon, has sent his son, Mutu-Numaha, to Mari, after having first sent his elder son there. Hammurabi then commands: "Send this boy (i.e. the younger son)

[8] On the Amorite tribes during the Mari period, see, e.g., M. Anbar, *Les tribus amurrites de Mari*, Freiburg-Göttingen 1991, and *ibid.* for earlier literature.

[9] Supporting evidence is apparently to be found in her name which may be read *Ia-pa-a*, possibly meaning "beautiful" (cf. Hebrew *yapha*), although the author considers possible, *inter alia*, a West Semitic etymology from the root *nby*, reading the name *Ia-ba-a*; see A. Fadhil, *BaM* 21 (1990), 461–470, esp. p. 466. With regard to the discovery of the royal name Atal(ya), I have not been able to acquire any accurate details.

[10] D. Charpin, *ARM* 26/2, No. 375.

either to Yamhad or to Qatna, as you see fit!" Mention is also made of the Babylonian companion who travelled with the boy on his journey abroad. In addition, in this document, emissaries from various cities are mentioned, including Qatna and Hazor, who gathered around Yarim-Addu to listen to his instructions. One may ask, was there some connection between the summoning of the emissaries and the proposed visit to the West by Hammurabi's son, that is to say, should he have visited only Yamhad or Qatna, or also Hazor? Other texts concerning the journey of two of Hammurabi's sons (the eldest and a younger brother) to Mari, and their stay there, have recently been published; some of them relate indirectly to the text discussed above.[11]

As in the case of the marriages mentioned above, a mirror image of this subject may be found in a planned royal departure from the West to the central Euphrates. We refer to the famous intended visit, in the reign of Zimri-Lim, to be undertaken by the son or the envoy of the king of Ugarit to the palace in Mari in order to see its splendour; the planned visit is documented in a text published approximately fifty-five years ago.[12] Other Westerners are escorts from Qatna and Hazor travelling to Mari and as far as Babylon, accompanying missions returning to these cities (*ARMT* VI 78). In this connection, it is of interest that several Syrians from an earlier period are mentioned in the Ur III archival sources.[13]

B

Now we turn to cultural matters—literature, prophecy and law—but first, let us mention the intriguing short paper on this subject by Th. Jacobsen, which has not received the attention it merits.[14] Jacobsen put forward an unusual hypothesis with regard to the well-known Babylonian legend of the Creation, *Enuma Elis*, especially with re-

---

[11] B. Lion, Des princes de Babylon à Mari, *Mém. de NABU* 3, pp. 221–234.

[12] See A. Malamat, *MEIE* 1989, repr. 1992, pp. 25 f. and n. 71; cf. there references to publishing of text.

[13] See lately D.I. Owen, Syrians in Sumerian Sources from the Ur III Period, in *New Horizons in the Study of Ancient Syria*, eds. M.W. Chavalas, J.L. Hayes (*Bibliotheca Mesopotamica* 25), Malibu 1992, pp. 107–176, esp. 114–5.

[14] Th. Jacobsen, The Battle between Marduk and Tiamat, *JAOS* 88 (1968), 104–108. His hypothesis is especially relevant concerning the battle against the sea god; see ch. 2.

gard to the passage describing the struggle between the storm god Marduk and the primeval sea Tiamat (cf. Hebrew *t^{e}hom* = "abyss"). According to Jacobsen, this episode and the story in general did not originate in the East (south-eastern Mesopotamia), as is generally accepted, but originated in the West, along the Syrian coast, during the Amorite period. The story was subsequently brought east by the Amorite tribes. Since Jacobsen did not submit solid evidence to prove his hypothesis, his approach must remain purely speculative. On the other hand, W.G. Lambert recently assumed that both the Western version of the battle with the Sea, as well as the Eastern *Enuma Elis*, go back to an early common origin spreading from the Indus Valley to the Aegean.[15]

Nevertheless, one of the arguments in support of Jacobsen's thesis may actually be found in the Babylonian story of the Creation, in one of the fifty theophoric names given to the god Marduk recorded on Tablet VII of the composition (although it is possible that this last part was added at a later date). The name in question is that of the god Addu, written in the story according to the Western fashion: AD. DU (ADAD is the form of the Eastern Akkadian). This god, without any doubt, is identical with the Great God of Aleppo called by the same name.[16]

Real evidence for the battle between the storm god Addu from Aleppo and the sea god (apparently, originally, the Mediterranean sea, as claimed by Jacobsen) appears unexpectedly in one of the Mari letters published recently and to be included in the Mari volume *ARM* 26/3.[17] This letter contains a "prophetic text", that is to say, a letter sent to Zimri-Lim by Nur-Sin, ambassador of Mari at the court of Aleppo, and which includes prophetic words uttered by the god Addu intended for the king of Mari. The prophet or diviner, by the name of Abiya, bears the title *āpilum*, i.e. respondent,[18] a particular

[15] Most recently W.G. Lambert in *I Studied Inscriptions From Before the Flood*, eds. R.S. Hess and D.T. Tsumura, Winona Lake, IN., 1994, Second Postscript (Sept. 1994), p. 111.

[16] See S. Dalley, *Myths from Mesopotamia*, Oxford 1989 (1991), pp. 230, 272.

[17] Text published by J.-M. Durand, Le mythologème du combat entre le dieu de l'orage et la mer en Mésopotamie, *MARI* 7 (1993), 41 ff. On this text and its comparison with the biblical material, see A. Malamat, A New Prophetic Message from Aleppo and its Biblical Counterparts, *Understanding Poets and Prophets. Essays in Honour of G.W. Anderson*, ed. A.G. Auld, Sheffield 1993, pp. 236–241 (Hebrew version in *Qadmoniot* 105–106, (1994), 44–46). See below ch. 14.

[18] The meaning of this title and the nature of the diviner have been debated; see,

kind of seer who often appears in the Mari texts. After reciting the history of the kingdom of Mari and the changes in its ruling dynasties, the god declares: "I have restored you (Zimri-Lim) to the throne of your father and I have given you the weapons with which I vanquished the sea. I have anointed you with the oil of my luminosity." Anointment in the coronation rite is peculiar to the West, although occasionally it does occur in the East.[19] "Sea" (*tâmtum/temtum*) here means the mythical sea, the ocean. Various demands of Zimri-Lim are then made by the god Addu.

The above text is at present the oldest example in the West of the motif widespread throughout the ancient Near East concerning the struggle between the storm god and the sea god. Several seals, possibly, bear more or less contemporaneous depictions of this battle.[20] Familiarity with this motif is found in the West, especially in Ugarit, some 400 years after the Mari period, and echoes of it may be heard beyond Ugarit in the Bible and even in post-biblical literature.[21] Moreover, the tales from Ugarit mention the weapons with which the storm god vanquished the sea god. (In Ugarit, the storm god is Baal, not Addu, the latter known widely as Hadad.) These weapons were a club and a spear. As stated in the above-mentioned text from Mari, the weapons (no doubt manufactured in Aleppo in accordance with the mythical description in the story) were given by the king of Aleppo to Zimri-Lim. One wonders if a number of samples of the weapons were produced and also given to other vassals of the king of Aleppo.

In his article, Durand mentions a short new instructive text which is apparently connected to the above-mentioned prophetic text; according to this new text, Zimri-Lim placed weapons of the god Addu of Aleppo in the temple of Dagan, in the city of Terqa, situated some 70 km north-west of Mari.[22] It may be assumed that when the

e.g., A. Malamat, *MEIE*, pp. 86–87. Note that there is also one reference to a diviner of this type in the city of Babylon.

[19] On anointing kings as a western custom, see now A. Malamat, ch. 14, p. 152; cf. Durand, *MARI* 7, p. 53 (there also reference to Ebla). On anointing as a distinct royal Mesopotamian institution, see recently S. Dalley, Anointing in Ancient Mesopotamia, in *The Oil of Gladness. Anointing in the Christian Traditions*, eds. M. Dudley and G. Rowell, London 1993, pp. 19–25.

[20] See P. Matthiae, Some Notes on the Old Syrian Iconography of the God Jam, in D.J.W. Meijer (ed.), *Natural Phenomena*, Amsterdam etc., 1992, pp. 169–192.

[21] Cf. now A. Malamat, Das heilige Meer, in *Wer ist wie du, Herr, unter den Göttern?*, (FS O. Kaiser), ed. I. Kottsieper *et alii*, Göttingen 1994, pp. 65–74.

[22] See Durand, *op. cit.* (n. 17), p. 53 (A. 1858).

weapons were brought from Aleppo in the West to the region of the central Euphrates, the mythical story itself moved east together with them, but so far no mention of it has been found in Mari proper.

C

The "prophetic" text discussed above brings us to another cultural phenomenon of the ancient Near East, which probably developed in its western regions and in time moved east, that is to say, the revelation of the prophecy itself and the proclamation of prophetic words. In the eastern regions, such as Babylonia, and to a lesser degree in the West, divination was of a mantic nature, that is to say, entreating the will of the deity involved special skills and techniques, the chief diviner bearing the title *bārû* ("seer"). He foretold the future by inspecting the entrails of an animal, in particular the liver of a sheep. Now this type of divination was also widespread in Mari, but there, and in the regions of the West, there developed another type of divination which in time gained prominence.[23] This kind of divination may be called "intuitive prophecy" (other terms defining this phenomenon are also used) because no mantic or magic technique was used; instead, it resulted from divine inspiration. (In the ancient world the phenomenon of such inspiration was considered to come from the "outside", while today, especially in psychology, it is said to come from the "inside".) (See ch. 6, p. 61 and ch. 13, pp. 140 f.)

Prophecy in Mari, in comparison with prophecy in the Bible, has been discussed in detail elsewhere.[24] (See Part Two below.) In this paper we shall concentrate on the possibility that intuitive prophecy was by and large a western phenomenon[25] and not an eastern one,

---

[23] See Durand, *ARMT* 26/1, pp. 377–453, in which most of the Mari prophecies have been collected, with the exception of a few which will appear in *ARMT* 26/3. Texts containing "prophecies" in dreams also appear in vol. 26/I, pp. 455–483.

[24] See A. Malamat, *Mari and Israel*, Jerusalem 1992 (Hebrew), pp. 123–145. The English version (above, n. 12) was published earlier in 1989 (1992) and does not discuss, in contrast to the Hebrew version, the Mari prophecies that first appeared in *ARMT* 26/1. It is appropriate to mention here two recent additional discussions of Mari prophecies; see D. Charpin, Le contexte historique . . . des prophéties . . . à Mari, *SCMS*, Bulletin 23, May 1992; J.M. Sasson, The Posting of Letters with Divine Messages, *Mém. de NABU* 3, pp. 299–317.

[25] Cf. also Durand, *op. cit.* (above, n. 23), esp. pp. 408, 412, but in *MARI* 7, pp. 49 f. he conceives of prophecy as a phenomenon encompassing both the East and West.

as some scholars think.[26] Since this kind of prophecy or divination sometimes involved entering into a state of ecstasy, as described both in Mari texts and in the Bible, it is actually possible to find in the expanse of time extending between these two corpora ecstatic prophets in the West. One example is the diviner from Byblos, described in the Wen-Amon tale from Egypt, dating from the 11th century B.C.

Admittedly, "intuitive prophets" from the Mari period are also to be found in Babylonia (the diviner mentioned there in the Mari texts is also called *āpilum: ARMT* 26/2, No. 371), and even texts from outside Mari speak of this form of prophecy in the east and the south. Above all, mention must be made of the texts from Ishchali to the east of the Diyala and Tigris. There, the goddess Kittitum sends prophetic messages to Ibal-pi-Il, King of Ešnunna.[27] However, this example does not prove that this type of prophecy originated in the above-mentioned region; a more acceptable explanation is that it came from the West following the massive Amorite migration eastwards to southern Mesopotamia. In particular, with regard to Babylonia as well as to Ešnunna, assumptions have been made that some kind of Amorite enclaves existed there or, at least, that the Amorite elements living there were considerable.[28]

Thus may be explained the astonishing similarity of the Codex Hammurabi and, to an even greater extent, the more or less contemporaneous Law of Ešnunna, with certain legal portions of the Bible, especially those found in the Book of Exodus. Thus we come to the realm of ancient Near Eastern law in Mesopotamia. Most of the legal codes do not bear any resemblance to the Bible, with the exception of the two codices mentioned above. (So far no remains of possible Amorite legal codes have been discovered.) Much has been written on this subject, but we shall confine ourselves to mentioning here a recent opinion (also voiced by others), that of W.G. Lambert,[29] who considers, that the laws of "an eye for an eye, a

---

[26] This latter opinion is held, e.g., by A.R. Millard, La Prophétie et l'écriture . . ., *RHR* 202 (1985), 125–145; for reservations on this opinion, see Charpin (above, n. 24), p. 30, n. 36; and see further Durand, *op. cit.* (above, n. 17), p. 50.

[27] See M. de Jong Ellis, *JCS* 37 (1985), 61–85; *idem, MARI* 5 (1987), 235–266. The author concludes here (as we also do) with the assumption that this type of prophecy was brought to Ishchali by West Semitic or Amorite elements.

[28] With regard to Babylonia, see Albright's daring supposition claiming that the early Hebrews founded the First Old Babylonian dynasty at Babylon; W.F. Albright, *Yahweh and the Gods of Canaan*, London 1968, p. 71.

[29] W.G. Lambert, Interchange of Ideas between Southern Mesopotamia and Syria-

tooth for a tooth" etc. (the *lex talionis*), included both in the Bible (Ex. 21:23–24) and in the Codex Hammurabi (##196–200), constitute an innovation. Such laws, also attested outside the legal corpora in practice both in Amorite circles as well as in biblical narrative,[30] are not found elsewhere in the ancient Near East. They must, without doubt, be considered as belonging to the Amorite cultural heritage, that is to say, they came ultimately to Babylonia from the West.

As for the laws of Ešnunna,[31] there is an amazing similarity between the Bible (Ex. 21:28–32), and the law of the "Goring Ox" (Ešnunna, ##53–55), as well as the different forms of punishment meted out to a thief who steals by day, who must pay only a monetary fine, while a thief who steals at night must be put to death (clauses 12–13); compare the biblical text which speaks of a thief on whom the sun shines and of a thief who "breaks in", i.e. steals during the darkness of night (Ex. 22:1–2). There is no doubt that in the legal field there existed a strong connection between East and West, and it may be assumed that these "primitive laws" were first conceived by the Amorites and were then brought to the East and South-East from the West.

D

More problematic are the following issues which bring us back to the realm of religion and to the epic tale, this time to the Epic of Gilgamesh. As is well-known, a portion of one of the versions of the

---

Palestine . . ., *Mesopotamien und seine Nachbarn* (*Berliner Beiträge zum Vord. Orient*, 1), eds. H.J. Nissen und J. Renger, Berlin 1982, pp. 312 f.; and most recently *idem, I Studied Inscriptions* . . . (above, n. 15), pp. 111–113. This paper (without the Postscripts) is reprinted from his original article in 1965 (for it see *ibid.*, p. 96). See also T. Frymer-Kenski, Tit for Tat: The Principle of Equal retribution in Near Eastern and Biblical Law, *BA* 43 (1980), 230–234, who adduces further talionic laws in CH and the Bible; and recently E. Otto in D.R. Daniels *et alii* (eds.), *Ernten was man säht* (*FS K. Koch*), Neukirchen 1991, pp. 101–130, esp. pp. 107 ff.

[30] As for Mesopotamia, see the letter of Rim-Sin, the Amorite ruler of Larsa, ordering a slave to be thrown into a furnace as revenge for the latter's casting a young slave into the oven; *BIN* VII (1945), No. 10. Cf. J.B. Alexander, *JBL* 69 (1950), 375 ff.; G.R. Driver, *AfO* 18 (1957), 129 (courtesy Prof. A. Shaffer). As to the narratives in the Bible, see now Ph.J. Nel, The Talion Principle in Old Testament Narratives, *JNSL* 20 (1994), 21–29.

[31] Cf. the laws of Ešnunna as edited by R. Yaron, *The Laws of Eshnunna*, Jerusalem-Leiden 1988, 51–77.

Epic, dating from the Old Babylonian period, the so-called Bauer Fragment, describes the journey undertaken by Gilgamesh and his companion Enkidu to the cedar forest protected by the monster Huwawa.[32] In contrast with the other versions of the Gilgamesh Epic, the actual location of the cedar forest is specifically mentioned here, for during the life and death struggle between the heroes and the monster, the mountains of Sirion (Saria) and Lebanon trembled. In other words, the site of the battle was the great cedar forest growing on these mountains and in the Lebanon Valley, right in the midst of the lands inhabited by the Amorites.

However, this does not provide sufficient evidence in itself that the Epic of Gilgamesh, or parts thereof, were composed under Amorite influence and were transported to southern Mesopotamia. Lambert himself thinks that there is clearly another western motif contained in the Epic of Gilgamesh. He refers to Tablet V, col. 1:6 of the later official version, in which it is mentioned that the cedar forest (which remains nameless) was the seat of the gods (*mūšab ilāni*), that is to say, the mountain forest served as a place of assembly or a pantheon of the gods, in other words a sort of Olympus. Lambert sees this clearly as the expression of an Amorite theme, since such mountains serving as the seats of the gods are found in Ugarit, and are reflected in the Bible and in Greek mythology, but do not exist in Sumer and Babylonia.[33]

We have restricted ourselves to a few points which may possibly prove that the Amorites and the West had a certain influence in eastern and southern Mesopotamia; certainly, further evidence can be and must be presented,[34] such as various customs, e.g., the ritual

---

[32] Cf. publication T. Bauer, Ein viertes altababylonisches Fragment des Gilgameš Epos, *JNES* 16 (1957), 254–262. On its importance for the study of the Mari texts (esp. the inscription of Yahdun-Lim) and the Bible, see A. Malamat (above, n. 12): "The Lebanon, Gilgameš and a Hebrew Psalm," pp. 116 ff. For a new translation and collation, see K. Hecker, *Mythen und Epen* II, *TUAT* III, 4 (1994), pp. 612–613; and see a new edition of the Gilgamesh Epic in R.J. Tournay – A. Shaffer, *L'épopée de Gilgamesh*, Paris 1994, pp. 124 ff. The mountain of Lebanon is also mentioned in a later version of the Gilgamesh Epic from the city of Uruk. The location of the forest in the Lebanon had already been assumed by scholars in the early 20th century, e.g., by A.T. Clay, *The Empire of the Amorites*, New Haven 1919, pp. 87 f.

[33] Lambert, *op. cit.* (n. 29), pp. 313–314; *idem*, in *Babylonien und Israel*, ed. H.P. Müller, Darmstadt 1991, p. 112. However, it is precisely this point as evidence of Amorite influence which is doubtful, since the temples in Sumerian literature were also described as mountains in which the gods assembled. Cf., e.g., the name of the Nippur temple of Enlil Ekur (My thanks to Prof. A. Shaffer on this point).

[34] See the instructive article by Durand, in *La circulation*... (above, n. 3), on the

of treaty making by means of killing the foal of an ass.[35] One of the main points to be put forward is linguistic, since both at Mari and in other Mesopotamian cities discoveries have been made of the abundant use of the Amorite language, or to be more precise, of Amorite dialects, which also penetrated Canaanite and biblical Hebrew.[36] But this point needs to be discussed separately. In any case, it appears that the common view of Babylonia as the "vision of all" must nowadays be modified in favour of its western periphery.[37]

---

dual descriptive titles, e.g., a man belonging to Akkad who belonged at the same time to the Amorites (p. 113). In addition, the Akkadian (or Sumerian) language coexisted with the spoken Amorite vernacular (pp. 124–125). Durand also mentions professions and occupations typical among the Amorites in the kingdom of Mari (pp. 126 ff.). Elsewhere, he expresses his opinion that the Cult of the Dead (such as the existence of *betyls*) was also a Western affair; cf. Durand, *Miscellanea Babyloniaca* (*Mélanges Birot*), Paris 1985, pp. 79–84. Customs typical of the West, on the one hand, and of the East, on the other, have also been examined by Charpin, in Mari entre l'est et l'ouest..., *Akkadica* 78 (1992), 1–10, but the author diminishes the significance of these differences within the two regions of the ancient Near East.

[35] See Durand, *ARMT* 26/1, pp. 121 f. and most recently Malamat, *IEJ* 45 (1995), 226–229. For a list of references to this ritual in the Mari texts up to 1990, see Charpin, *Mélanges J. Perrot*, Paris 1990, pp. 116/7, n. 35 and cf. below ch. 17.

[36] See, e.g., list of Amorite linguistic terms from Mari, in Malamat (above, n. 12), p. 33.

[37] See, e.g., Durand, in *La circulation*... (above, n. 3), p. 128.

3

THE SACRED SEA*

In a discussion of sacred space, we ought not to overlook bodies of water such as rivers (with their river ordeals), wells and springs (note the theophanies at such localities), lakes and seas. Moreover, when such a discussion focuses on the Levant—and more specifically Syria-Palestine—then the Mediterranean Sea is of immediate concern. We shall thus deal mainly with this sea, over a time span from approximately 1800 B.C.E. to the Byzantine period. Such a *longue durée* of some 2,500 years should enable us to expose elements of the divine nature of the Mediterranean, to the extent that they are to be found—a matter that has scarcely received its due scholarly consideration.[1]

My starting point will be the documents from the ancient city of Mari,[2] situated on the Euphrates, some 25 km to the north of the present-day Iraqi-Syrian border, within Syria. King Yahdun-Lim, the first true ruler of Mari in the Old Babylonian period, who brought prosperity to his kingdom, left one highly intriguing document of great importance to our subject, known as the Foundation Inscription from the temple of the god Šamaš.[3] Here Yahdun-Lim vividly

* This article has originally been published in: Kedar, B.Z., Werblowsky, R.J.Z. (eds.), *Sacred Space: Shrine, City, Land*, Macmillan Basingstoke, UK and the Israel Academy of Sciences and Humanities, Jerusalem 1998 (forthcoming).

[1] This study, prepared with the assistance of a grant from the Basic Research Foundation administered by the Israel Academy of Sciences and Humanities, is based on an extensive revision and expansion of material appearing in my chapter "Kingly Deeds and Divine Exploits," in A. Malamat, *MEIE*, pp. 107 ff.

On the mythological nature of the sea, see the comprehensive work by O. Kaiser, *Die mythische Bedeutung des Meeres in Ägypten, Ugarit und Israel* (*BZAW* 78), Berlin 1962. Kaiser's horizon is limited to the three places mentioned in the book's title, thus excluding Mari and the talmudic and Greek sources.

[2] On the city of Mari and the documents unearthed there see Malamat, *Mari* (above, n. 1).

[3] The document was published by G. Dossin, "L'inscription de fondation de Iahdun-Lim, roi de Mari," *Syria* XXXII (1955), pp. 1–28; and see D. Frayne's newer study, "Iahdun-Lim, Text 2," in *The Royal Inscriptions of Mesopotamia*, IV: *Old Babylonian Period* (*2003–1595 B.C.*), Toronto-London 1990, pp. 604–608. For an early interpretation of the passage given below, see A. Malamat, "Campaigns to the Mediterranean by Iahdun-Lim and Other Early Mesopotamian Rulers," in H. Güterbock & T. Jacobsen (eds.), *Studies in Honor of B. Landsberger* (*AS* 16), Chicago 1965, pp. 367 ff.

describes a bold campaign to the West through Syria, finally reaching the Mediterranean coast, the crowning achievement of his military operations. The relevant passage in this document implies that the Mediterranean Sea was regarded, at least at Mari, as a divine-mythological entity hundreds of years earlier than scholars previously realized. The passage in question reads:

> Since days of old, when god built Mari, no king residing in Mari had reached the sea (*tāmtum*). To the Cedar Mountain and the Boxwood (Mountain) . . . they had not reached. . . . But Yahdun-Lim . . . marched to the shore of the sea (*tāmtum*) in irresistible strength. To the Ocean (*ayabba*, "Vast Sea") he offered his great royal sacrifices, and his troops cleansed themselves with water in the Ocean (*ayabba*). To the Cedar and Boxwood Mountain, the great mountains, he penetrated, and boxwood, cedar, cypress (or juniper?) and *elamakkum* trees, these trees he felled. He stripped (the forest) bare(?), established his name, and made known his might. He subjugated that land on the shore of the Ocean (*ayabba*). He made it obedient to his command; he caused it to follow him. He imposed a permanent tax upon them that they should bring their taxes to him regularly. (Yahdun-Lim Foundation Inscription col. i 34–iii 2)

The king of Mari praises himself for his unprecedented campaign to the Mediterranean shore. The extraordinary encounter with the Mediterranean was accompanied by cultic ceremonies—the offering of sacrifices to the sea, which is most likely a West Semitic or Amorite notion, later adopted by the Mesopotamians. Furthermore, the king's troops bathed in its waters in what was surely a cultic ritual, a sort of baptism. The significance of such an act is probably indicated, in addition, by the use of the Akkadian verb *ramākum*, which refers to cleansing the entire body in water in a ritualistic context.[4] Thus, we may liken the function of the Mediterranean here to that of a *miqweh* in Judaism, a ritual bath for purifying the body; metaphorically, the Mediterranean would be a sort of macro-*miqweh*.

In the first millennium B.C.E., the neo-Assyrian monarchs also recorded their arrival on the Mediterranean coast. They offered sacrifices at the seashore to their gods, but not explicitly to the god of the Sea. Their troops dipped their weapons in the water, symbolically purifying them, with no further ceremony. They thus were following the example of Sargon the Great of Akkad, who, in the

[4] The verb *ramākum* means simply "to wash"; its ritualistic sense in certain contexts, however, is indicated by the noun *rimkum*, particularly in the ritual series *bīt rimki*; and cf. *AHw* II, p. 985: "Bad[ekult], Ganzwaschung."

twenty-fourth century B.C.E., washed his weapon in the sea.[5] However, it should be noted that he did so in the Lower Sea, that is, the Persian Gulf. Here, too, the dipping of weapons in the sea doubtless indicates the sacred and purifying aspect of such a great body of water, but Yahdun-Lim's inscription differs with regard to the deity involved and to the actual ritual use of the sea's waters.

In dealing with Yahdun-Lim's inscription many years ago, I touched on the illuminating distinction between the two Akkadian terms used here to designate the sea.[6] We see the ordinary word for sea, *tāmtum* (*tiamtum*), used twice in a secular, empirical sense. In contrast, the solemn term *ayabba*, recorded three times, has a mythological aura to it. In its Sumerian form, A.AB.BA, it already appears in Ebla[7] and in Old Akkadian (spelled AB.A in a lexical text from the second half of the third millennium B.C.E.), in connection with Sargon the Great and the West Semitic king Shamshi-Adad I (early eighteenth century B.C.E., slightly after Yahdun-Lim), who both fought campaigns in the West.[8] In all of these texts, the word A.AB.BA undoubtedly refers to the Mediterranean, while in other texts it designates the Persian Gulf. The word seems to be reminiscent of the Greek concept of *Okeanos*, in both its mythological and its factual, marine sense.[9]

In the El-Amarna letters[10] of the fourteenth century B.C.E., and particularly in the letters of the king of Byblos on the Syrian coast and those of the king of Tyre and the king of Jerusalem, *ayabba* appears several times with reference to the Mediterranean Sea, or perhaps only part of it. It is also used at El-Amarna in a literary-epic composition, where the word escaped scholarly attention until recently (*EA* 340).[11] There, A.AB.BA (not to be read *tāmtum*, as by the

---

[5] See the text on Sargon the Great in *ANET*³, p. 467b.

[6] See Malamat, "Campaigns" (above, n. 3), p. 367.

[7] See G. Pettinato, *MEE*, nos. 1343, 016; cf. M. Krebernik, *ZA* LXXII (1982), p. 43; von Soden, *AHw* III, p. 1353, s.v. *tiamtu(m), tāmtu(m)*, and see there the unusual form *ab*). For Eblaite notions on Adad's battle against the sea note now P. Fronzaroli, *MARI* 8 (1997), pp. 283–290.

[8] Cf. Malamat, "Campaigns" (above, n. 3), pp. 367–368.

[9] Cf. G.M.A. Hanfmann, in the *Oxford Classical Dictionary*, Oxford 1949 (reprinted 1953), p. 616, s.v. *Oceanus* (*mythological*); F. Lasserre, in *Der kleine Pauly*, IV, Munich 1979, pp. 267 f., s.v. *Okeanos*, I: Mythologie; M. Eliade (ed.), *The Encyclopedia of Religion*, New York 1987, XI, pp. 53–54, s.v. *Oceans*.

[10] See Amarna letters nos. 74, 105, 114 (Byblos); 151 (Tyre); 288 (Jerusalem). For a translation (and most recent edition) of the documents, see W.L. Moran, *Les Lettres d'El-Amarna*, Paris 1987.

[11] See now P. Artzi, "A Further Royal Campaign to the Mediterranean Sea?" in

editor) most likely signifies the Mediterranean or Great Sea and not simply any sea. Although the text is very fragmentary, it seems that a royal military campaign, like the expeditions of Yahdun-Lim and of other Mesopotamian rulers, was conducted as far as this sea.

The precise meaning and etymology of the Sumerogram A.AB.BA, rendered *a(y)yabba* in Semitic, is still obscure, despite its relatively frequent use in Sumero-Akkadian literature.[12] A recently published Old Babylonian bilingual hymn from South Babylonia gives us the earliest equation of the two terms. To be sure, the editors of the hymn suggest reading *a-ia-a-ma* instead of *a-ia-a-ba*[13]—thus tempting us to interpret the spelling *ayyama* as Canaanite-Hebrew *yam*, the sea proper—but this assumption is far-fetched.

Several years ago, reference was made to an unpublished document from Mari which is of great significance for the concept of a sacred sea, notably the Mediterranean.[14] Now that this document, a letter from Zimri-Lim's ambassador at Aleppo to the king of Mari, has been published, we may consider more fully its impact on our issue.[15] Adad, the great god of Aleppo, was engaged in a battle with the sea, wielding weapons against the rebellious Mediterranean.

After the sea's defeat, the weapons were presented as a coronation gift to Zimri-Lim, king of Mari and son of Yahdun-Lim, when he made a pilgrimage to Aleppo. It is likely that these weapons were similar to those illustrated on Syrian seals of the Old Babylonian period rather than the club and spear (*ṣmd* and *ktp*) in the Ugaritic myth that were depicted four or five hundred years later on the stele of "Baal and the thunderbolt!" This stele ("Baal au foudre") at Ugarit, depicts the battle of Baal with Yamm, the sea deity.[16]

Festschrift A. Malamat (*EI* 24), 1993, pp. 23–30 (in Hebrew), and see there for the other references in *EA*.

[12] For this term see the dictionaries: *CAD* A/1, p. 221, s.v. *ajabba; AHw*, p. 23, s.v. *a(j)jabba*, and above, n. 7; and see the important remark by A. Goetze in *JCS* IX (1955), p. 16, n. 58.

[13] Published by B. Alster & U. Yeyes, *ASJ* XIV (1990), p. 8; and see the comments concerning a.ab.ba by D. Charpin (*NABU*, 1990, no. 122, p. 101), who rejects the reading *a-ia-a-ma*, as well as A.R. George (*ibid.*, 1991, no. 19, p. 16).

[14] D. Charpin & J.-M. Durand, "Fils de Sim'al': Les origines tribales des rois de Mari," *RA* LXXX (1986), p. 174.

[15] See J.-M. Durand, "La mytholegème du combat entre le dieu de l'orage et la mer en Mésopotamie," *MARI* VII (1993), pp. 41 ff. In the text, which bears the number A. 1968, the sea is represented by the word *temtum*. On this document see my paper "A New Prophetic Message from Aleppo and Its Biblical Counterparts," below ch. 14.

[16] Cf. now P. Bordreuil, "Recherches Ougaritiques," *Semitica* XL (1991), pp. 17–27,

This leads us straight to Ugarit of the fourteenth and thirteenth centuries B.C.E., perhaps the major source for the divinity of the sea. The Ugaritic texts recount several epic tales of the war between the god of the sea (*Yamm*) and other deities.[17] These myths may have originated centuries earlier, presumably in the Old Babylonian period—that is, in the age of Mari. Yamm, the god of the sea, is most prominent in the Ugaritic pantheon and is equated there, *inter alia*, with the term A.AB.BA. Moreover, the element *yamm*, sea, appears in personal names both at Mari and at Ugarit, as a theophoric name-element. At Ugarit, Yamm is known by the epithets "Prince Yamm" (*zbl ym*) and "Judge Nahar" (*ṯpt nhr*), the ruler of the river. Yamm represents the cosmic force of raging waters, a personification most likely derived from the character of the Mediterranean Sea, whose waters threatened the coast and occasionally inundated it.

Many Ugaritic myths, echoed faintly in the poetic parts of the Bible, derive from this conception of the Mediterranean. The classic myth of Ugarit concerns the struggle between Yamm, the sea deity, and Baal, Lord of the Earth and of fertility,[18] which may go back to Old Babylonian times, an assumption now supported by the material from Mari. The Ugaritic text is too fragmentary to provide a continuous narrative, but it may be outlined as follows. The god Yamm, beloved son of El, the head of the Ugaritic pantheon, seeks majestic status. El proclaims that status for him and promotes the construction of Yamm's palace, but Baal, another son of El, is jealous and battles Yamm for hegemony. Eventually it is Baal, with the help of his sister, the goddess Anat, who strikes the fateful blow for power. It is then that Baal rises to kingship and erects his palace, similar to the event in Mari.

On the other hand, the myths of Yamm's contest with the goddess Anat and his struggle against the goddess Aṯatar are poorly preserved. It is significant that Yamm is included in the sacrificial lists of the gods at Ugarit, indicating his integral position in the canonical pan-

---

and the more recent article by P. Bordreuil & D. Pardee in *MARI* VII (1993), pp. 63–70. For the Syrian OB seals see, e.g., D. Collon, "The Aleppo Workshop," *UF* 13 (1981), pp. 33–44 (courtesy M. Popko).

[17] See Kaiser, *Die mythische Bedeutung* (above, n. 1), pp. 40 ff.; S. Loewenstamm, *Comparative Studies in Biblical and Ancient Oriental Literatures* (*AOAT* 204), Neukirchen-Vluyn 1980, pp. 346–361; S.L. Gibson, *Canaanite Myths and Legends*, Edinburgh 1978, pp. 37–45.

[18] Cf. Kaiser, *Die mythische Bedeutung* (above, n. 1), p. 58; and M. Dietrich *et al.*, *Die keilschriftalphabetischen Texte aus Ugarit*, Neukirchen-Vluyn 1976, I, 39:19, 46:6.

theon of Ugarit. A further list of deities includes ^{d}A.AB.BA (= Yamm), and here it expressly carries the theophoric determinative DINGIR = god. Most significantly, in parallel lists of the gods in the Ugaritic language proper, the counterpart of A.AB.BA is Yamm, the West Semitic god of the sea.[19] In other words, several hundred years after Yahdun-Lim, the god bearing the name of the West Semitic word for sea, *yamm*, was identified in Ugarit with the Sumerogram A.AB.BA—the very form that appears in Yahdun-Lim's inscription.

Close in time to Ugarit are the documents from Emar, which also speak of the god Yamm. The editor of these texts, followed by several scholars, interprets the deity named Ashtar (*ša*) *abi*, mentioned several times, as "Ashtar (Ishtar) of the Sea" (taking the word *abu* as identical with A.AB.BA).[20] However, this interpretation of *abu* has been contested by other scholars, who assume that the word refers to *abū*, "father, ancestor," or that it is equivalent to Hurrian or Akkadian *apu/abu* ("pit") and Hebrew *ōb*, "spirit of the dead."[21]

Before we approach the Hebrew Bible and the Egyptian sources, which display the closest affinity in this regard to Ugarit, let us mention in passing the Hittite sources from Anatolia, where, like in Akkadian and in the Bible (which refers to *hayyam haggādōl*), the Mediterranean is frequently called the "Great Sea." In these texts the sea is conceived, at times, even as a deity—for example, in the fourteenth-century B.C.E. treaty lists of Suppiluliuma I—and sacrifices are brought to it.[22]

Three Egyptian tales are also relevant to our subject, two of them dating from the period of the New Kingdom. Here the sea deity bears the Canaanite appellation "Yam," a loan word appearing in Late Egyptian, from the eighteenth dynasty (fifteenth century B.C.E.) on, as an alternative to the indigenous term *w3ḏ-wr* (literally, "the

---

[19] See Nougayrol, *Le palais royal d'Ugarit*, IV, Paris 1955/6, pp. 45 (l. 29) and 58. The deity Yamm yielded a theophoric element in the onomasticon of Ugarit, but more surprisingly already at Mari and, later, in biblical Hebrew.

[20] See D. Arnaud, *Emar* VI:3, Paris 1986. Nos. 153:2, 274:9, 373:92, etc. And see more recently the remarks of J. Oliva (*NABU*, 1993, no. 94), who, however, casts doubt on this interpretation.

[21] Oliva (above, n. 20). But for an association of Ashtarte with a river god (^{d}ID) already in Old Akkadian or even in the late Early Dynastic period, and in connection with Mari, see W.G. Lambert, "The Pantheon of Mari," *MARI* 4 (1985), pp. 535–537. It should be borne in mind that the deity Yamm at Ugarit bears the epithet "Judge/Ruler of the River" (see above).

[22] Cf., e.g., M. Popko, "Hethitische Rituale," *AOF* 14 (1987), p. 262; G. Wilhelm, "Meer: bei den Hethitern" (3: Meer in der Religion), *RLA* VIII:1, pp. 4–5.

great green"), not only in myths but also in factual texts.[23] In a legend known as the "Tale of Two Brothers,"[24] Yam snatches a lock of hair from the head of his younger brother's wife. This part of the story takes place in the "Valley of the Cedar (or Pine)," apparently in Lebanon, and more specifically in the Beqa valley. Thus, it may be assumed that this Egyptian tale was influenced by Canaanite mythology. The second legend,[25] related in a small fragment of the so-called Astarte Papyrus from about 1300 B.C.E., consists of an actual Canaanite myth. Yam, who holds dominion over the earth and its deities, is entrapped by the beauty of Astarte, the Canaanite goddess, as she sits naked on the sea-shore, thus bringing him into conflict with her consort. The myth reflects the violent power of the sea, which threatens mariners and inhabitants of the coast alike. Finally, in the tale of the Swallow and the Sea (Yam),[26] written in Demotic and dating very late, from the Roman period, Yam is portrayed as a robber. Asked by the swallow to guard her young, he eventually carries them away. The swallow, in revenge, empties the sea with her beak and fills it with sand.

Coming now to the Bible, it displays faint echoes of the rebellion of a mythic sea deity and its accompanying monsters against Yahwe, the God of Israel, as noted in particular by the late Professor Cassuto.[27] In fact, one of the central themes in the comparative study of biblical literature and Ugaritic poetry relates to this conflict. Numerous

---

[23] Cf. A. Erman & H. Grapow, *Wörterbuch der ägyptischen Sprache*, I, Berlin 1926, p. 78; R. Giveon, *LÄ*, III, Wiesbaden 1980, cols. 242–243, s.v. *Jam* (Meer). R.O. Faulkner, in *A Concise Dictionary of Middle Egyptian*, Oxford 1962, s.v. *w3ḏ-wr*, p. 56, cites one form that should be read *w3ḏ-wr-ʾim*(!), that is, the unusual idiom "Great Green *Yam*."

[24] M. Lichtheim, *Ancient Egyptian Literature*, II, Berkeley, Calif., 1976, pp. 203 ff.

[25] Cf. Kaiser, *Die mythische Bedeutung* (above, n. 1), pp. 81 ff.; R. Stadelmann, *Syrisch-Palästinensische Gottheiten in Ägypten*, Leiden 1967, pp. 125 ff.; and E. Brunner-Traut, *Altägyptische Märchen*, Munich 1989, pp. 107–110 and 301–302.

[26] Cf. Kaiser, *Die mythische Bedeutung* (above, n. 1), pp. 80 f.; Brunner-Traut, *Altägyptische Märchen* (above, n. 25), pp. 161–162, 317 f.

[27] See U. Cassuto, *Biblical and Oriental Studies*, II, Jerusalem 1975, pp. 70 ff. On *yam* in the Bible see also R. Ringren, ים, *ThWAT*, III, Stuttgart 1982, cols. 649 ff.; as well as O. Eissfeldt, "Gott und das Meer in der Bibel," *KS* III (1966), pp. 256–264. On the dragon monster see M.K. Wakeman, *God's Battle with the Monster*, Leiden 1973. And see most recently T. Binger, "Fighting the Dragon," *SJOT* VI (1992), pp. 139 ff.; and J. Day, "Dragon and Sea," *Anchor Bible Dictionary*, II, New York 1992, pp. 228–231. See now N. Wyatt, *Myths of Power*, Münster 1996, pp. 127 ff.; he claims (p. 134) that the Mari passages are closer to the Bible than to the Ugaritic sources.

allusions to this theme, including the demonic creatures associated with the sea god Yam, are found in the poetic passages of the Bible. Examples include Psalms 74:13 ("Thou didst divide the sea [*yam*] by thy might; thou didst break the heads of the dragons on the waters"); Job 7:12 ("Am I the sea [*yam*], or a sea monster, that thou settest a guard over me?"); and, in the prophetic literature, passages like Isaiah 51:9–10 ("... was it not thou that didst cut Rahab in pieces, that didst pierce the dragon? Was it not thou that didst dry up the sea [*yam*], the waters of the great deep ...?") and Jeremiah 5:22 ("Do you not fear me? says the Lord ... I placed the sand as the bound for the sea [*yam*], a perpetual barrier which it cannot pass; though the waves toss, they cannot prevail, though they roar they cannot pass over it").[28]

It is possible, and even likely, that at the late stage of the composition of the biblical passages these metaphors of raging waters were already viewed as referring to cosmic forces, but it is logical that they ultimately reflect what was seen as the divine nature of the Mediterranean Sea. In talmudic literature this concept, surprisingly, occurs more overtly than in the Bible. The Sages hinted at it in midrashim like this one: "When the Holy One, blessed be He, created the sea (*yam*), it went on expanding, until the Holy One, blessed be He, rebuked it and caused it to dry up" (BT *Hagiga* 12a). Above all, this theme is to be seen in the talmudic appellation *śar šel yam*, "prince of the sea," so reminiscent of "Prince Yamm" at Ugarit.[29]

Let us finish with two sources from Greek authors of the classical and post-classical period, both alluding to notions and practices originating in the East. First, in a well-known episode related by Herodotus (VII, 34 ff. and 54), the bridges of ships crossing the Hellespont during the Persian-Greek war in 480 B.C.E. were broken and scattered. Xerxes subsequently "punished" the rebellious sea, proclaiming that "no man is to offer thee sacrifice, for thou art a turbid and briny river." When the Persians were finally about to cross the straits, Xerxes brought incense and "at sunrise poured a libation from a golden phial into the sea, praying to the sun that no accident should befall him" in his attempt to subdue Europe—thus echoing the belief that

---

[28] For the Bible in general see F.M. Cross, *Canaanite Myth and Hebrew Epic*, Cambridge, Mass., 1973, pp. 121 ff. On Psalm 74:13 see J.C. Greenfield, in S.E. Balentine & J. Barton (eds.), *Language, Theology and the Bible* (*Essays in Honour of James Barr*), Oxford 1994, pp. 113–119.

[29] Cassuto, *Biblical Studies* (above, n. 27), p. 71.

the Mediterranean Sea and the Pontus were a deity, or at least that the Persians conceived of them as having a sacred nature.

Another seldom-noted but intriguing passage, this one from late antiquity, reveals the tenacity of this cultic and sacred tradition. The Byzantine historian Procopius of Caesarea (sixth century C.E.), in his *De bello persico* (II:XI, 1), describes how Chosroes, the Sassanian king, having taken Antioch from Justinian, went down to the Mediterranean shore and "bathed himself alone in the sea water, and after sacrificing to the sun and other such divinities . . . he went back." This ritual bathing of royalty in the Mediterranean in the sixth century C.E. closes the circle which opened with King Yahdun-Lim of Mari and his troops around 1800 B.C.E. It was based, as we saw, on early West Semitic—Amorite/Canaanite—concepts of the sacred sea, which find clear expression centuries later at Ugarit and in the Egyptian tales, and occur still later in the biblical and talmudic traditions.

MARI AND ITS RELATIONS WITH THE EASTERN MEDITERRANEAN*

Professor Cyrus H. Gordon spent much of his academic life investigating the relations between the Mediterranean region and the Levant. It is most apt to dedicate this study in his honour.

Mari of the Old Babylonian period is to be dated within the 18th century B.C.E., according to the so-called Middle Chronology, the first part of this century and according to the Low Chronology, its second part and slightly beyond. In either case, it falls within the Middle Bronze Age.

I shall deal with Mari's contacts with the Mediterranean on two distinct planes: starting with the religious-mythological plane, we shall pass later on to more earthly issues: the exchange of goods between Mari and the Mediterranean or, more specifically, the Aegean. We shall thus investigate, albeit on a narrow scale, import and export between East and West in the 18th century B.C.E. or the Middle Bronze Age.

As for our first theme, with which I have dealt already on previous occasions,[1] we now have from Mari two overt witnesses attesting to the conceptualization of the Mediterranean as a religious—mythological entity, one item known already long ago, the other published only recently.

Over forty years ago, in 1955, the Mari epigrapher George Dossin published a royal inscription of King Yahdun-Lim,[2] the first true ruler of Mari in the Old Babylonian period. The inscription, written on the foundation bricks of the temple of Shamash at Mari, is known as the Great Yahdun-Lim Inscription. In poetic style, Yahdun-Lim describes his bold campaign to the Mediterranean shore and the subjugation of its inhabitants. Above in ch. 3, p. 25 we cite a few

* This article will also be published in Festschrift C.H. Gordon *Boundaries of the Ancient Near Eastern World*, eds. M. Lubetski *et al.*, *JSOT Supplements* (forthcoming).

[1] Cf. A. Malamat, *MEIE*, pp. 107–112; *idem*: in eds. I. Kottsieper *et alii*, "*Wer ist wie du, Herr, unter den Göttern?*" (FS O. Kaiser), Göttingen: Vandenhoek & Ruprecht, 1994, pp. 65–74 and ch. 3 above.

[2] G. Dossin, *Syria* 32 (1955), pp. 1–28.

relevant lines of this inscription, describing the dramatic encounter of King Yahdun-Lim and his army with the Mediterranean, a high point of Yahdun-Lim's feats.[3]

The other, recent evidence from Mari, touching on the mythological character of the Mediterranean, is to be found in a letter sent to King Zimri-Lim at Mari (the son of the aforementioned Yahdun-Lim and last king of Old Babylonian Mari) by his ambassador to Aleppo in the days of its King Yarim-Lim.[4] The ambassador informs the king of Mari of a prophecy proclaimed by a prophet of the god Addu (alias Hadad), the Great god of Aleppo. Relevant here is only a short passage of the prophecy relating to a battle between the god Addu and the god of the sea (obviously hinting at the Mediterranean). The weapons with which Addu defeated his opponent are said to have been handed over to Zimri-Lim, when he made pilgrimage to Aleppo. The myth of the battle between the two deities, which no doubt originally reflected the furious character of the raging waters of the Mediterranean, is mentioned, as far as I know, for the first time in the Mari period. Centuries later it is prominent above all in the myths and epics of Ugarit.[5]

Now we shall pass over to the other plane—to Mari documents referring to deliveries of goods from the Mediterranean to Mari and vice versa. We have only a few references so far about Alashia, the ancient name of Cyprus or of a specific city on this island. From there were delivered to Mari consignments of considerable quantities of copper (up to 20 kg and more).[6] But above all, there are Mari references to Kaptara, Biblical Caphtor, the erstwhile name of the island of Crete or of the Aegean region as a whole.

The most illustrative and significant Mari document in this context is A. 1270, published by G. Dossin in 1970 and analyzed by me soon after its publication.[7] The relevant passage in this commercial

---

[3] The Mediterranean is termed in this instance unusually *ayyabba* (A.AB.BA), the king offering to the sea "great royal sacrifices"; see above ch. 3, pp. 26 ff.

[4] Published by J.-M. Durand, *MARI* 7 (1993), pp. 41 ff. and see below ch. 14.

[5] See the recent treatment by P. Bordreuil and D. Pardee, *MARI* 7 (1993), pp. 63–70.

[6] On the trade relations between Mari (and Babylon) and Cyprus, as well as Crete, see M. Heltzer, *Minos* 24 (1989), pp. 7–15, and for a new occurrence of Alashia in Mari texts see D. Charpin, *RA* 84 (1990), pp. 125–127. For the extensive commercial activities of Mari in the West as far as the Mediterranean coast, see most recently A. Altman, *Michmanim* 9 (1996; University of Haifa), pp. 39–56.

[7] Dossin, *RA* 64 (1970), pp. 97 ff. and Malamat, *IEJ* 21 (1971), pp. 31–38; cf. Heltzer, *op. cit.* (above, n. 6), pp. 10–12.

text for us is that concerning the tin (*annakum*) consignments, so vital for the manufacture of bronze, dispatched from Mari to the West. Tin came to Mari from the East, perhaps from Baluchistan and Afghanistan,[7a] and was shipped in the West to destinations such as Aleppo, Qatna and as far south as Hazor. To the latter were sent three separate consignments of tin, totalling some 35 kg (which meant the manufacture of 7 to 10 times as much bronze). Let us cite the final part of this document which concerns Crete, on the basis of a new collation of the tablet by P. Villard (*ARMT* XXIII 556:28 ff.):[8]

> 1^{+} $1/3$ minas of tin for the Caphtorite (*Kap-ta-ra-i-im*)
> $1/3$ mina tin for the dragoman (*targamannum*) (of the) Chief [merch]ant of the Caphtorite(s) at Ugarit

This passage testifies to the commercial activities between Mari and Crete carried out at Ugarit, the most significant trade emporium on the Syrian coast. Three persons are mentioned in the passage: one is called simply the Caphtorite, the second is an interpreter, most likely of Cretan origin as is evident from the context. His presence implies a more than casual contact between Crete and the Levant.[9] The third is the Chief (ugula) of the Caphtorite merchants (*tamkaru*), perhaps the head of the commercial delegation. The interpreter (a word mentioned in Akkadian only rarely) was a vital functionary in the transaction, since the Mari emissaries spoke an Amorite dialect, whereas the Cretans of this period—Middle Minoan II—utilized a language, called in scholarly parlance, "Linear A". Durand even assumes that on this occasion at Ugarit the kings of Mari (i.e. Zimri-Lim) and Crete met personally,[10] an assumption which must remain doubtful

---

[7a] Cf. J.-L. Montero Fenollós, "L'activité métallurgique . . .", espec. 9, *Akkadica* 103 (1997), pp. 6–28.

[8] See P. Villard, *ARMT* XXIII 556:28–31. The restoration *[dam-ga]r k[a]p-ta-ra-a*, "Caphtorite merchant" was suggested by Durand instead of the reading of Dossin, *ka-ra-i-[i]m*, "Carian?", which we still accepted in *IEJ* 21 (1971), p. 38. For the tin ratio in bronze manufacture see W.W. Hallo, *Origins*, Leiden: Brill, 1997, p. 45 and there p. 158 on *targamannum*.

[9] See most recently E.H. Cline, *Aegaeum* 12 (1995), esp. pp. 267, 273, and cf. M.H. Wiener in *The Function of the Minoan Palace* (below, n. 19), pp. 262–264. For a decipherment of Linear A as a Northwest Semitic language (i.e., a language similar to the Mari idiom), see the treatments of C.H. Gordon, *Evidence for the Minoan Language*, Ventnor, N.J.: Ventnor Publishers, 1966; *Ugarit and Minoan Crete*, New York: Norton & Company, 1966, pp. 29–39. If his conclusions are feasible, there remains the query why in the above transaction an interpreter was needed at all.

[10] See *MARI* 6 (1990), p. 40, n. 3.

since the word "Caphtorite" is not preceded by the determinative LÚ, which in Mari may indicate a person as well as a ruler. On the other hand our text relates to the grand journey of King Zimri-Lim to the West and most likely also to Ugarit in his "9th" regnal year.

Crete of the Middle Minoan II period was flourishing and *inter alia* trading goods, not only among various cities within the island itself, but exporting them also to Egypt and the Levant.[11] The trade relations seem to have taken place on the level of the palaces and their ruling circles, which had the means to maintain long-distance trade routes. The commerce most likely brought cultural influences in its wake. First and foremost come to mind the palace frescoes of Mari and those of Knossos and other sites in Crete.[12] There is an ongoing debate among scholars about the issue of who influenced whom. In the early stages of research it was assumed that Knossos influenced Mari. But this is not likely from a chronological point of view. Thus, the opposite opinion has subsequently been put forward. If one may consider a mutual influence at all, which remains uncertain, it would be rather Mari (and perhaps later Alalakh VII, early 17th century B.C.E.) which influenced Knossos or the Cretan frescoes at large.[13] In this connection a letter sent to Mari may be of interest, indicating the wish of the ruler of Ugarit to dispatch his son or his emissary to visit and inspect (*amārum*) the Mari palace (in order to imitate its splendor?).[14]

---

[11] See E. Schachermeyr, *Agäis und Orient*, Wien: Österreichische Akademie der Wissenschaften, 1967, pp. 30 ff.; W. Helck, *Die Beziehungen Agyptens und Vorderasiens zur Agäis bis ins 7. Jahrhundert v. Chr.*, Darmstadt: Wissenschaftliche Buchgesellschaft, 1979, pp. 106 ff.; A.B. Knapp, *BA* 55 (1992), pp. 52–72. From the Aegean end see, e.g., M.H. Wiener in ed. N.H. Gale, *Bronze Age Trade in the Mediterranean*, Jonsered: Paul Aströms Förlag, 1991, pp. 325–350; and for a general statement concerning the Levant most recently O. Dickinson, *The Aegean Bronze Age*, Cambridge (Eng.): Cambridge University Press, 1994, pp. 244 f.

[12] For more recent comparative remarks between these wall-paintings see B. Pierre (-Müller), *MARI* 3 (1984), pp. 222–254, esp. pp. 226, 232; *MARI* 5 (1987), pp. 551–576 (and the comparative chronological table on p. 573); *MARI* 6 (1990), pp. 463–558 (e.g., p. 498). On the relationship between the frescoes, dating to a somewhat later period, from Tel Kabri and Alalakh VII, as well as those from Crete and Thera see the remarks of W.D. Niemeier, *Aegaeum* 7 (1991), pp. 189–200 and 12 (1995), p. 284. For the latter sites, as well as the frescoes at Tell el-Dabʿa see now the remarks in the Symposium on "Trade, Power and Cultural Exchange: Hyksos Egypt and the Eastern Mediterranean World 1800–1500 B.C.", The Metropolitan Museum of Art, published in *Ägypten und Levante* 5 (1995).

[13] E.g., R.W. Hutchinson, *Prehistoric Crete*, Harmondsworth: Penguin Books, 1963, pp. 178 f.

[14] For the document published by Dossin, see C.F.A. Schaeffer, *Ugaritica* 1, Paris: Geuthner, 1939, p. 16.

The tin-text from Mari, mentioned above, refers to export from that kingdom to Crete, while all the subsequent references in the inventories from Mari indicate objects brought to the Mari palace or distributed by it. There was a notable exchange of commodities between Mari and Mediterranean coastal cities, foremost among these, Ugarit and Byblos.[15] The Cretan objects mentioned in these inventories seem, in particular, to have been mostly luxury items sent to Mari. It is, however possible that the gentilic or adjective *kaptarum*, *kaptaritum*, "Caphtorite, Cretan",[16] does not refer to Crete as such, but designates only Cretan craftsmanship or technique rather than a distinct country. In other words, it may refer to objects made "after the technique of the land of Crete". But even so, there was direct contact between Mari and Crete (or Cretan artisans). Compare, e.g., the robes of Aleppo (*yamhādu*) or Byblos (*gublāyu*), which refer to a specific style of dress common in the West rather than to the cities in the West themselves.

Let us start with the so-called Cretan weapons,[17] especially with one described in document A. 675, an excerpt of which was published by G. Dossin in 1939 (now fully edited in *ARMT* XXV 106:10–13), and dealt with by Mrs. Maxwell Hyslop.[18] The text reads "A weapon of Caphtor with pommel and base overlaid with gold and pommel inlaid with lapis lazuli". The nature of the weapon (perhaps dedicated to a deity) is not indicated, but it seems to have been a ceremonial dagger, since it was guilded and inlaid with lapis. The question remains if it was an export from Crete, or made on Syrian soil in the mode of Cretan craftsmanship. Other guilded weapons inlaid with lapis are designated as Cretan in *ARMT* XXI 231:1–4. The text mentions later on (ll. 15–16) a guilded lance (*imittum*) and other weapons. A Cretan weapon is also mentioned in *ARMT* XXIII 104:30' and perhaps in *ARMT* XXIV 98:10' (its top incrusted with lapis). In *ARMT* XXV 601:10–13 a Caphtorian weapon is recorded, its top and base covered with gold and furthermore, the top incrusted

[15] Cf. H. Limet in eds. E. Gubel and E. Lipiński, *Phoenicia and its Neighbours, Studia Phoenicia* III, Leuven: Peeters, 1985, pp. 13–20.

[16] Cf. W. von Soden, *Orientalia* 58 (1989), p. 428 on *ARMT* XXV 39:10 and p. 430 on 499:8'.

[17] On Minoan metalwork and weapons see, e.g., J.D.S. Pendlebury, *The Archaeology of Crete*, New York: Norton, 1965, pp. 118 ff.; H. Buchholz und V. Karageorghis, *Altägäis und Altkypros*, Tübingen: Wasmuth, 1971, pp. 51 ff., 170 ff. and Pls. on pp. 267 ff. and the listing of weapons by Wiener, *op. cit.* (above, n. 11), pp. 337 f.

[18] Iraq 32 (1970), pp. 165 f. and Pl. XXXII.

with lapis. In a fragmentary text of various metal weapons, "Caphtor" has to be restored, *ARMT* XXV 39:10; see also *ib.* 610:8 (see above, n. 16).

Likewise prominent in the economic texts from Mari are Cretan ceramics, especially luxury ware, well known among the pottery from Middle Minoan Crete. A place of pride is held by the so-called Kamares ware,[19] found also at Ugarit, at Byblos, at Qatna and at the lower city of Hazor.[20] Pottery vases and vases of precious metal from Crete are mentioned in the following Mari inventories: *ARMT* XXV 8:3; 10:6; 45:2,4 (an engraved jar); 499:21 (4 vases); 511:8; 515:8 (a vase made of gold); 523:12; 526:4 (4 vases); 530:2. There is also an occurrence of a goblet or cup (*sappum*).

In addition to ceramics from Crete, textiles are mentioned in Mari texts (*ARMT* XXII 324, col. II:8–9) as well as a pair of shoes (*ARMT* XXI 342:5–6), which was forwarded by the king of Mari to King Hammurabi of Babylon.[21] About other prestige products from Crete we have no certain knowledge since the Akkadian term designating the object eludes us. See *ARMT* XXIII 104:30' (one leather box for a weapon?); XXV 393:13 (*bur-zi*);[22] 507:3 (^{giš} *kur-sa-lu*, cf. *ARMT* VII 237:3); 610:8 (*marhašu* UD.KA.BAR), a bronze object.

Let us end by citing a small administrative document, published recently,[23] which mentions the manufacture at Mari of a "Cretan"

---

[19] For MM II pottery in general see Buchholz-Karageorghis, *op. cit.* (above, n. 17), Pls. on pp. 298 ff.; for the Kamares ware see in particular Ph.P. Betancourt, *The History of Minoan Pottery*, Princeton: Princeton University Press, 1985, pp. 95 f. and cf. more recently G. Walberg, "Political and Provincial Workshops in the Middle Minoan Period", in eds. R. Hägg and N. Marinatos, *The Function of the Minoan Palace*, Symposium, Stockholm: Paul Aström Förlag, 1987, pp. 281–285.

[20] For Ugarit see Schaeffer, *Ugaritica* I (above, n. 14), pp. 22 ff., 53 ff. and *Ugaritica* II, Paris: Geuthner, 1949, pp. 51, 256; Fig. 109 A and Pl. 38; for Byblos see Schaeffer, *Stratigraphie* comparée . . ., London: Oxford University Press, 1948, p. 66 and Fig. 72; for Qatna see *ibidem*, p. 117 and Fig. 102; Du Mesnil du Buisson, *Le site archéologique de Mishrifé-Qatna*, Paris: De Boccard, 1935, p. 66, Figs. 15–16. For Hazor see T. Dothan in Y. Yadin *et alii*, *Hazor* II, Jerusalem: Magnes Press, The Hebrew University, 1960, p. 91 and Pl. CXV, nos. 12–13 (area C). I thank Prof. Trude Dothan for illuminating discussions on the Kamares ware in the Levant.

[21] Cf. E.H. Cline, *Sailing the Wine-Dark Sea, International Trade and the Late Bronze Age Aegean*, Oxford: BAR International Series 591, 1994, p. 127 and pp. 126–128, for a listing of the various Mari references on Crete, Cretan.

[22] Perhaps to be read in Akkadian *pursitum*, as suggested by M. Anbar, *MARI* 6 (1990), p. 656, referring to a cultic vessel.

[23] See P. Villard, *UF* 18 (1986), p. 402 n. 107, who referred to the tablet; it was published in full by M. Guichard, *NABU* 1993/2, pp. 44–45; cf. E. Porada in *Ägypten und Levante* 5 (above, n. 12), pp. 126–127.

barque (^{giš} má tur *kaptaritum* ^{ki}). Again, the intention is most likely in reference to a miniature ship made in the Cretan style. M. Guichard, who published the text, compares in this context the depictions of ships hundreds of years later on the sarcophagus at Haghia Triada and on the frescoes excavated at Thera.

In conclusion, it is clear that there were extensive contacts between the eastern Mediterranean and Mari in the early 2nd millennium B.C.E. In the commercial activities of the Middle Bronze age, tin was the major commodity sent from Mari to Crete (for bronze manufacture), while the Aegean region exported mainly Minoan luxury goods to the palace of Mari. As is known, in later times Cretan exports to Syria increased, but Mari was no longer on the scene.

Bibliography

Altman, A., "Reconsideration of the Trade Relations between Mesopotamia and Canaan during the Middle Bronze Age", *Michmanim* 9 (1996), pp. 39–56.

Bordreuil, P. and Pardee, D., "Le combat de Ba'lu avec Yammu d'après les textes Ougaritiques", *MARI* 7 (1993), pp. 63–70.

Buchholz, H. und Karageorghis, V., *Altägäis und Altkypros*, Tübingen: Wasmuth, 1971.

Charpin, D., "Une mention d'Alasya dans une lettre de Mari", *RA* 84 (1990), pp. 125–126.

Cline, E.H., *Sailing in the Wine-Dark Sea, International Trade and the Late Bronze Age Aegean*, Oxford: BAR International Series 591, 1994.

——, "Tinker, Tailor, Soldier, Sailor: Minoans and Myceneans Abroad", *Aegaeum* 12 (1995), 265–287.

Dickinson, O., *The Aegean Bronze Age*, Cambridge: Cambridge University Press, 1994.

Dossin, G., "L'inscription de fondation de Iahdun-Lim, roi de Mari", *Syria* 32 (1955), pp. 1–28.

——, "La route de l'étain en Mésopotamie au temps de Zimri-Lim", *RA* 64 (1970), pp. 97–106.

Dothan, T. in Yadin, Y., *et alii*, *Hazor* II, Jerusalem: Magnes Press, 1960.

Du Mesnil Du Buisson, *Le site archéologique de Mishrifê-Qatna*, Paris: de Boccard, 1935.

Durand, J.-M., "Le mythologème du combat entre le dieu de l'orage et la mer en Mésopotamie", *MARI* 7 (1993), pp. 41–61.

Gordon, C.H., *Evidence for the Minoan Language*, Ventnor, N.J.: Ventnor Publishers, 1966.

——, *Ugarit and Minoan Crete*, New York: Norton & Company, 1966.

Guichard, M., "Flotte crétoise sur l'Euphrates?" *NABU* 1993/2, pp. 44/5.

Helck, W., *Die Beziehungen Ägyptens und Vorderasiens zur Agäis bis ins 7. Jahrhundert v. Chr.*, Darmstadt: Wissensch. Buchgesellschaft, 1979.

Heltzer, M., "The Trade of Crete and Cyprus with the East", *Minos* 24 (1989), pp. 7–28.

Hutchinson, R.W., *Prehistoric Crete*, Harmondsworth: Penguin Books, 1963.

Limet, H., "Les relation entre Mari et la cote Méditerranéenne sous la règne de Zimri-Lim", in eds. E. Gubel and E. Lipinski, *Phoenicia and Its Neighbours, Studia Phoenicia* III, Leuven: Peeters, 1985, pp. 13–20.

Malamat, A., "Syro-Palestinian Destinations in a Mari Tin Inventory", *IEJ* 21 (1971), pp. 31–38.
——, *Mari and the Early Israelite Experience* (the Schweich Lectures 1984), Oxford: Oxford University Press, 1989 (1992).
——, "A New Prophetic Message from Aleppo and Its Biblical Counterparts", in ed. A.G. Auld, *Understanding Poets and Prophets* (*FS G.W. Anderson*), Sheffield: Almond Press, 1993, pp. 236–241.
——, "Das heilige Meer" in eds. I. Kottsieper *et alii*, *"Wer ist wie du, Herr, unter den Göttern?"* (*FS O. Kaiser*), Göttingen: Vandenhoek & Ruprecht, 1994, pp. 65–74.
Montero Fellós, J.-L., "L'activité métallurgique dans le Haut-Euphrate syrien. IIIe et IIe millénaires av. J.C., *Akkadica* 103 (1997), pp. 6–28.
Niemeier, W.D., "Minoan Artisans Travelling Overseas: The Alalakh Frescoes and the Painted Plaster Floor at Tel Kabri" *Aegaeum* 7 (1991), pp. 189–201.
Pendlebury, J.D.S., *The Archaeology of Crete*, New York: Norton, 1965.
Pierre, B., "Décor peint de Mari et au Proche-Orient", *MARI* 3 (1984), pp. 223–254; and B. Pierre-Müller, *MARI* 5 (1987), pp. 551–576; *MARI* 6 (1990), pp. 463–558.
Porada, E., in Symposium of Metropolitan Museum of Art: Trade, Power and Cultural Exchange—Hyksos Egypt and the Eastern Mediterranean World 1800–1500 B.C., *Ägypten und Levante* 5 (1995).
Schachermeyr, E., *Ägäis und Orient*, Wien: Österr. Akademie der Wissenschaften, 1967.
Schaeffer, C.F.A., *Ugaritica* I, 1939; *Ugaritica* II, 1949, both Paris: Geuthner.
——, *Stratigraphie comparée* . . . London: Oxford University Press, 1948.
Villard, P., "Textes sur les metaux" in *ARM* XXIII, Paris: Editions Recherche Civilisations, 1984, pp. 453–585.
——, "Un roi de Mari à Ugarit", *UF* 18 (1986), pp. 387–412.
Wiener, M.H., "Trade and Rule in Palatial Crete", in eds. R. Hägg and N. Marinatos, *The Function of the Minoan Palace*, Princeton: Princeton University Press, 1985, pp. 261–267.
——, "The Nature and Control of Minoan Foreign Trade", in ed. N.H. Gale, *Bronze Age Trade in the Mediterranean*, Jonsered: Aströms Förlag, 1991, pp. 325–350.

5A

HAZOR ONCE AGAIN IN NEW MARI DOCUMENTS*

In continuing our studies on the city of Hazor in the Mari documents,[1] we avail ourselves now of the latest three volumes of Mari texts, *ARMT* 23, 24 and 25, in which seven occurrences of Hazor are attested. (In the meantime appeared vol. 26/1–2, in which Hazor is mentioned only once [*ARMT* 26/2 375]. In vol. 27 the toponym is not attested.) This number equals the seven references to Hazor in earlier Mari volumes, to be added to a few other instances, giving a new total of nineteen occurrences. This is a considerable number if we take into account the distance between Mari and Hazor, the latter perhaps being the only city in Palestine mentioned in the Mari archives.[2]

While the earlier references were contained to a great extent in Mari letters, and were thus of a more lively and even piquant nature, the new material is entirely of an economic and administrative context—somewhat dry in character. Nevertheless, it is still of considerable interest, in addition to the very mention of Hazor and its king Ibni-Adad.

ARMT 23 contains three new references to Hazor, as well as one earlier instance in a newly collated document with significantly improved readings (text 556).[3] In two of the new documents the name

* This article was originally published in: M. Lébeau et Ph. Talon (eds.), *Reflets des deux fleuves* (FS A. Finet), Akkadica Suppl. 6, Leuven (1989), 117–118.

[1] Festschrift A. Finet, see the series of papers by the present author: *JBL* 79 (1960), pp. 12–19; in J.A. Sanders (ed.), *Near Eastern Archaeology in the Twentieth Century* (*Essays in Honor of N. Glueck*), Garden City, N.Y., pp. 164–177; *IEJ* 21 (1971), pp. 31–38; *JJS* 33 (1982) (Essays in Honor of Y. Yadin), pp. 71–79; *BA* 46 (1983), pp. 169–174, and below chs. 5B, 5C. For on up-to-date survey, listing 19 occurrences of Hazor (of the West) in Mari, see M. Bonechi, "Relations amicales Syro-Palestiniennes: Mari et Hazor," Mém, *NABU* 1, Paris 1992, pp. 9–22.

[2] Previously we had surmised that the city of Laish (later Dan), some 30 kilometers to the north of Hazor, was mentioned in A. 1270, l. 21. Yet in a recent document, *ARMT* 23 535, the very same toponym (read by the editor as Layaš) appears in the north of Syria on the route between Aleppo and Ugarit. If both references are to one and the same place, a location near Hazor would be ruled out. But it is still possible—thanks to the close association of Layiš with Hazor in the first mentioned document—that there were two cities of similar name, one in northern Palestine, the other far to the north in Syria.

[3] Cf. P. Villard in *ARMT* 23, pp. 528 f.

of Hazor or its king is badly damaged but the restoration is without doubt. Text 243 notes a messenger from Hazor to Mari in the arrival of messengers from Babylon and other sites who received choice cuts of mutton during their stay at the Mari palace. This text thus resembles *ARMT* 12 747, listing eighteen persons from various localities, messengers, artisans, a singer, etc., to be provided by the palace.[4] Text 541 is part of a group of documents which indicate a "grand tour" of Zimri-Lim to the West (texts 535–548). It concerns the visit of the Mari king (in his "9th" year) to his father-in-law, Yarim-Lim, of Aleppo, most likely continuing with his entourage to Ugarit on the Mediterranean shore.[5] According to this text, a consignment of clothing was sent by Zimri-Lim to the king of Hazor, most significantly in year 9' of Zimri-Lim's reign—the very same year of the king's journey to the West.

The last text, 505, refers to a shipment of 84 head of cattle received at Hazor along with (?) six mules or onagers (*parû*). The editor of this text[6] has noted an interesting feature of the script, which is somewhat peculiar and "provincial", particularly in the writing of the numeral "84".[7] The question arises whether the scribe himself could have been a Hazorite who had been trained locally in Canaan in the cuneiform scribal craft. There is considerable evidence of a scribal school at Hazor in Old Babylonian times. Several cuneiform documents: clay liver models, a law suit and a fragment of a ḪAR.ra-*ḫubullu*-like lexical list—have been unearthed, in addition to a personal name incised on a jar.[8] Thus it seems likely that the huge city of Hazor, covering some 800 dunams (80 hectares) in the MB II period, contained a scribal school as well as an archive.[9]

---

[4] Cf. J.M. Sasson, *BASOR* 190 (1968), p. 53 and A. Malamat, *Near Eastern Archaeology* (above, n. 1), p. 165.

[5] On Zimri-Lim's grand tour, see J.M. Sasson, *BA* 47 (1984), pp. 246–251; and now the detailed analysis by P. Villard, "Un roi de Mari à Ugarit", *UF* 18 (1986), pp. 387–412.

[6] D. Soubeyran, *ARMT* 23, p. 435.

[7] Numeral 84 was written in a non-Akkadian ("Western", A.M.) manner, according to the editor (See Addendum).

[8] For fragments of clay liver models see B. Landsberger – H. Tadmor, *IEJ* 14 (1964), pp. 201–218; for a lexical text, see H. Tadmor, *IEJ* 27 (1977), pp. 1–11; for a legal document see W.W. Hallo and H. Tadmor, *IEJ* 27 (1977), pp. 98–102; for the PN see P. Artzi – A. Malamat, apud Y. Yadin, *Hazor* II, Jerusalem 1960, pp. 115 f.

[9] On the excavations of Hazor see the comprehensive summary by Y. Yadin, *Hazor* (*The Schweich Lectures 1970*), Oxford 1972. Recently, before his death, Yadin announced that he possibly had found the whereabouts of the postulated archive on the excavation plans, and he considered excavating there.

In *ARMT* 24[10] Hazor is mentioned once in text 75, again badly damaged. A messenger from Hazor together with emissaries from Babylon and Yamḫad, is mentioned in connection with a special event at the Mari palace: a three-jar shipment of wine to the royal cellar of the palace. It is of interest that the simultaneous visit at Mari of envoys from Hazor, Yamḫad and Babylon is attested on various occasions (cf. above, *ARMT* 12 747).

The three references in the latest volume from Mari, *ARMT* 25,[11] mention dispatches from the king of Hazor to Zimri-Lim of precious objects—gold and silver vessels, as well as gold jewellery.[12] Yet the intriguing point is that all the valuables circulated to places other than Mari proper. Text 43 divulges that a gold ring, or rather necklace (note its heavy weight) and three silver jars or vases were deposited at Ugarit (lit., *ina Ugarit*), most likely on the occasion of Zimri-Lim's journey through Syria.[13] Ugarit is now frequently mentioned as a depot (*pisannu*) for the king of Mari, and a site where his officials, especially Dariš-libūr, the "ambassador" to Aleppo, were to be found.[14] Text 103 reveals that a golden jar was dispatched to a depot of the king of Mari at a site the name of which is unfortunately damaged. Finally, text 119 details the transfer of a silver ring (or necklace) to the king of Karana (a site north of Mari) at a place called Šunā. The private purse of Zimri-Lim at this locale is also attested in other documents (*ARMT* 22 138:7–8; 25 104:6). This place has recently been identified with Tall al-Ḥamidiya in the Habur triangle north of Tell Brak.[15] The text begins: *1 ḫu-ul-lu Ḫa-ṣu-ri*^{ki}, that is, a Hazorite ring, or even a ring made after the fashion of Hazor. The king of Hazor

---

[10] Published by P. Talon, *Textes administratifs des salles "Y et Z" du Palais de Mari*, Paris 1985.

[11] Published by H. Limet, *Textes administratifs relatifs aux métaux*, Paris 1986. For the following texts see also H. Limet's summary in *Studia Phoenicia* III, Leuven 1985, pp. 13 ff.

[12] On precious metals and stones obtained at Hazor, see a new Mari document referred to by M. Birot in *Syria* 50 (1973), pp. 10 f., who kindly granted me the publication of his transliteration. See my two papers mentioned above, n. 1: *JJS* 1982 and *BA* 1983. While in the above document there is only talk about receiving gold and silver at Hazor (which allegedly had been robbed at Emar), in our present documents there is actual proof of such objects present at Hazor.

[13] Cf. now P. Villard, *op. cit.* (above, n. 5), p. 391.

[14] For two of his letters from Syria to Zimri-Lim (to be published in full in *ARMT* 26) see preliminarily J.M. Sasson in J.R. Kupper and J.M. Durand (editors), *Miscellanea Babyloniaca* (*Mélanges M. Birot*), Paris 1985, pp. 253–255. For Dariš-libūr's stay at Ugarit, see, e.g., *ARMT* 23, pp. 463 ff.

[15] For the identification of Šunā see now S. Eichler *et alii*, *Tall al Ḥamīdiya* 1 (*Vorbericht* 1984), Freiburg-Göttingen 1985, p. 63.

is not mentioned in this context. One may wonder whether the ring had not originally been sent to Mari and deposited there with the reserves(?) of Dariš-libūr.

In sum, the customary gifts[16] of various rulers to the king of Mari were sometimes allocated to cash-lots that the king maintained outside his capital, even in distant lands, as we now learn with regard to Hazor and other places as well.[17] The movement of such precious objects[18] from Hazor to Mari also allows us to visualize the "mobility" of Zimri-Lim through large areas in times of war and peace as well as the goods given by Hazor in exchange for the considerable tin shipments received from Mari.

Addendum par Emile PUECH

A la demande de M. le Prof. Malamat et dans l'attente de la publication de la copie ou d'une reproduction, il est possible de suggérer une explication "provinciale" au sujet de "la forme inhabituelle des chiffres d'une tablette" concernant Ḫaṣor (*ARM* XXIII 505, pp. 434s). L'auteur note: "84 écrit avec huit clous obliques et deux verticaux". Sachant que les scribes cananéens transposent un cercle de l'écriture linéaire par un clou oblique, *e.g. 'aïn* (E. Puech, *Quelques remarques sur l'alphabet au deuxième millénaire*, dans *Atti del 1 congresso internazionale di studi fenici e punici*, Rome 1983, 579s), les 8 clous obliques pour 80 semblent bien s'insérer dans la tradition provinciale (école cananéenne?) de l'écriture, voir les 8 points de l'ostracon de Bet Shemesh (E. Puech, *Origine de l'alphabet, RB* 93, 1986, 176s) où la lecture 80, de préférence à 8, semble aussi s'imposer. Les deux clous verticaux pourraient valoir 2, ou 4 si on compte les deux traits de la forme "*gimel*" rendue par un seul clou dans l'alphabet cunéiforme alphabétique. Cela appuierait l'origine ou la formation provinciale du scribe de la tablette.

---

[16] For this subject in a broader scope see C. Zaccagnini, "On Gift Exchange in the Old Babylonian Period", *Studi Orientalistici in Ricordo di F. Pintore* (*Studia Mediterranea* 4), 1983, pp. 189–253.

[17] For a list of places where cash-lots of the king of Mari were mentioned see *ARMT* 25, p. 27.

[18] For the issue in general see A. Archi (ed.), *Circulation of Goods in non-Palatial Context in the Ancient Near East*, Rome 1984.

5B

MARI AND HAZOR: TRADE RELATIONS IN THE OLD BABYLONIAN PERIOD*

The excavations at Mari, located on the Euphrates to the north of the Syrian-Iraqi border, have yielded some 20,000–25,000 tablets in Akkadian cuneiform from the Old Babylonian Period (the 18th century B.C.E.). By now, some 7,000—odd tablets seem to have been published in over 25 volumes (*ARMT*; the latest are vol. 26/1–2 and vol. 27).[1] So far 19 letters and administrative/economic documents mentioning Hazor in northern Palestine have been found at Mari.[2] This is a considerable number, taking into account the vast distance between the two sites. Hazor is the southernmost western locality documented at Mari. True, there may be a reference to a site further south, in central or southern Palestine, but the document is damaged where the toponym in question appears.[3] Thus, Hazor remains at the edge of Mari's economic sphere of influence, but seems to have been politically independent, unlike its northern neighbor Qatna in middle Syria. Aleppo, still further north, held a measure of supremacy over Mari. We can view the relationship between Mari and Hazor as both central and peripheral and as having all the sociological ramifications inherent in such a constellation.[4]

Of the 19 documents attesting to ties between Mari and Hazor, seven are letters sent by Zimri-Lim, the last king of Mari, or by his royal officials. These documents testify to the exchange of messengers, some of them having no doubt acted also as merchants. Once or

* This article was originally published in: *Biblical Archaeology Today, 1990*, Jerusalem 1993, Pre-Congress Symposium, Suppl., pp. 66–70.

[1] For an up-to-date list of the Mari volumes, see at the end of this volume "A List of *Archives royales de Mari.*"

[2] For a summary of the texts mentioning Hazor, see the literature in ch. 5A, n. 1.

[3] *ARMT* 6, 23:23. For the various suggestions proposed for the illegible place-name, see Malamat, MEIE, pp. 61–2. But N. Na'aman *RA* 75 (1981), opts for the northern toponym Carchemish.

[4] Cf., for example, M. Rowlands, M. Larsen, K. Kristiansen (eds.), *Centre and Periphery in the Ancient World* (Cambridge 1987) and the introduction there by M. Rowlands, "Theoretical Perspectives." For the ancient Near East, see the chapters by L. Marfoe, M.T. Larsen and C. Zaccagnini.

twice a messenger from Hazor was entertained at the palace of Mari together with emissaries from other important cities, but unfortunately we do not know if the person's mission was diplomatic or economic or both.

The special significance of these documents is their revelation of all the major goods exported dispatched from Mari to the West and vice-versa contained in the economic texts. As is well known, the major export to the West was tin, vital for the manufacture of bronze. Bronze is produced by alloying copper with tin at a ratio of 1:7–10. Bronze is much stronger and more practical than pure copper, particularly for the manufacture of tools and weapons. There was a great increase in the use of bronze during the corresponding MB II period in Palestine. Thus, Mari's tin trade with the West flourished. Mari received the tin from the East via Iran, perhaps from Afghanistan and Pakistan. (The recent theory that the Taurus Range in southern Anatolia[5] was the ancient Near East's source of tin remains without decisive proof.) In Syria-Palestine, copper was readily available, but tin—like crude oil in recent times—had to be brought from afar. Two economic texts from Mari relate to shipment of this strategic commodity to Hazor. In one of these documents (*ARMT* 7, 236), Hazor is mentioned together with the land of Yamḫad, whose capital was Aleppo, as the destination of a shipment of about 5 kg of tin—sufficient to yield 35 to 45 kg of bronze. The other text, the "tin document,"[6] is of considerable significance in several respects. After stating the amount of tin reserves at Mari at the time, it specifies the consignments of the metal to be sent from Mari to various destinations in the West. Certain points of the original reading by Dossin have recently been collated anew, and we base our interpretation on the latter study (*ARMT* 23, 556:18–32). After recording the largest consignment, which was sent to Aleppo, we read of "8⅓ minas" or approximately 5 kg for Ewri-Talma, ruler of Layašim (or Layišim). It is mentioned just before Hazor in our tablet and was first identified with the biblical city of Laish (later Dan),[7] some 30 km north of Hazor. Indeed, Laish was an important city during the Mari period.

[5] See K.A. Yenner and H. Ozbal, "Tin in the Turkish Taurus Mountains," *Antiquity* 61 (1987), 220–226, and similar articles by them. But see now the response by J.D. Muhly, *AJA* 97 (1993), pp. 234 ff.

[6] Published by G. Dossin, *RA* 64 (1970), 97–106, and cf. A. Malamat, *IEJ* 21 (1971), 31–38 and P. Villard, *ARMT* 23, 528 ff.

[7] Cf. Malamat (see n. 6).

However, in a new text, a similar toponym appears in a context in the far north, between Aleppo and Ugarit (*ARMT* 23, 535: iv, 27). The close association of Laish with Hazor in our document may suggest the existence of two cities with the same name, one in northern Palestine and the other far to the north in Syria—a phenomenon of homonyms well known in the Amorite sphere.

The most important city mentioned in the "tin document" is undoubtedly Hazor, which was to receive three tin consignments totalling over 50 minas, that is a quantity sufficient for some 400 kg of bronze. Although to date excavations at Hazor over an area of 16 acres have yielded very few bronze utensils,[8] we must assume that intensive bronze production took place there in the MB II period. From the "tin document" we learn for the first time the name of Hazor's king: Ibni-Adad, which is an Akkadian form of the local West Semitic name Yabni-Addu. Perhaps another person of Mari's royal dynasty is mentioned, namely Atar-Aya, one of Zimri-Lim's wives. On the basis of as yet unpublished material from Mari, it has been surmised that Atar-Aya was a princess from Hazor—revealing dynastic ties between Mari and northern Palestine, an unanticipated windfall for the historian. The next entry in our document deals with a tin consignment to Qaṭna in middle Syria. A Caphtorite (a merchant from Crete) is there mentioned and after him a dragoman, who served as the spokesman or chief merchant in the Cretan commercial colony at Ugarit. The seaport of Ugarit cultivated close ties with the Aegean throughout its history, and there is clear archaeological evidence at that site of commerce with the Aegean during the Mari period (i.e. Middle Minoan II pottery), such as Kamares ware (see above ch. 4, pp. 38 f.), a degenerate piece of which was also discovered at Hazor. In short, it seems likely that Mari, especially in the days of Zimri-Lim, was responsible for the intensification of bronze manufacture, or in modern parlance, industrialization—encountered in the Canaanite sphere.

Now let us consider products shipped from Hazor to Mari. In this connection, the economic tablets at Mari are quite laconic and at times vague. There is mention of a three-jar shipment of wine at the Mari palace witnessed by a messenger from Hazor (*ARMT* 24, 75). There is no express statement that the wine jars came from Hazor,

---

[8] The absence of any bronze artifacts at Hazor in MB II is noteworthy; see the excavation reports, recently A. Ben-Tor (ed.), *Hazor III–IV. Text* (Jerusalem 1989).

but this was most likely the case, as Syria-Palestine was well known for its wine exports and, moreover, wine of the best quality. There are many references to caravans from various places in the West, such as Aleppo or Carchemish, shipping scores of wine and olive oil jars to the palace of Mari.[9] Another export from Hazor were precious objects, sent as gifts to the king of Mari, a diplomatic gesture commonly made by the rulers of this and later periods. Among the precious items from Hazor[10] were gold and silver vessels and gold jewelry (*ARMT* 25, 43, 103, 129), including a ring or, perhaps, a necklace, judging by its weight. Interestingly enough, most of these gifts were sent to Zimri-Lim during his grand journey to Aleppo and further on to Ugarit. The items from Hazor were stored in various depots in distant regions, such as that in Ugarit, which were maintained by the king of Mari.

Relevant to these precious objects is a most intriguing Mari letter which I had the privilege to transliterate and translate.[11] The letter, written by Zimri-Lim, was addressed to his father-in-law Yarim-Lim, king of Aleppo, and pertains to relations between Mari and Hazor. A Mari official or craftsman was dispatched all the way to Hazor to obtain "silver, gold, and precious stone(s)," either as raw materials or as finished products. The Hazorites claimed that the emissary made off without paying for the goods, and thus they detained a merchant caravan from Mari. This document proves that precious metals were commodities *per se* in Canaanite cities in MB II. They are otherwise attested only rarely by such evidence as in an Akkadian legal document from Hazor ("200 pieces of silver") and by sporadic finds of gold and silver objects in contexts of this period, mainly in tombs at such sites as Gezer and Megiddo and from a little later at Tell el-ʿAjjul. A few centuries later, large quantities of gold and silver were listed among the booty seized by Thutmose III in northern Palestine, but surely neither Hazor nor any other site within Canaan was the ulti-

---

[9] Cf., for example, *ARMT* 7, 238. For recent references to these foodstuffs dispatched from the West, channeled here through the city of Emar, see J.-M. Durand, *MARI* 6 (1990), 72 ff. For earlier documentation, see, for example, H. Limet, "Les relations entre Mari et la côte Mediterranéene sous le règne de Zimri-Lim," in *Studia Phoenicia* 3 (Leuven 1989), pp. 13–20, and for previous literature, see n. 1.

[10] See Limet, "Les relations" (see n. 9), pp. 13 ff.; A. Malamat in *Reflets des deux fleuves* (*Mélanges A. Finet*) (*Leuven* 1989), pp. 117 ff.

[11] A. Malamat, *JJS* 53 (1982), 71–79; and adjustments as well as additional insights, *idem*, *BA* 46 (1983), 169–174. See now Durand, *MARI* 6 (1990), pp. 63 f.

mate source of these materials: We must assume that at least the gold was brought from Egypt, the major supplier of this material in antiquity.[11a]

Another important aspect reflected in the document under discussion relates to trade customs. The messenger who allegedly stole the precious objects testified that he had received a "bill of sale"[12] but was robbed of it together with the goods at Emar on the Great Euphrates Bend, thus being left without proof of his innocence. In this letter, Zimri-Lim was clearly seeking to prod his father-in-law, the king of Aleppo, into recovering the stolen property, hence, Yarim-Lim was sovereign of northern Syria, including Emar.[13] The major theme underlying the whole episode pertains to international law regarding merchants or agents in trouble on foreign soil. No doubt, this sort of incident led to interstate agreements guaranteeing the protection of merchants abroad, as exemplified at Ugarit, at Babylon and in Egypt.

Finally, we will relate to another item from Syria-Palestine exported to Mari and Mesopotamia. The Mari documents frequently mention products characteristic of Syria-Palestine from places like Aleppo, Qatna, or the seaport of Byblos or Gebal (Gubla).[14] Among the more important items were different kinds of precious trees and timber, most significantly, cedar. Likewise, horses from Amurru,[15] which had the prestige of modern-day Arabian horses, were exported. Of the greatest significance, however, were the foodstuffs, especially wheat, olive oil, and wine, as well as honey (we are not certain if the

---

[11a] Cf. most recently P. Artzi 21, *AoF* 24 (1997), who analyzes *EA* 16, which attests to the vast amount of Egyptian gold expected by the king of Assyria (espec. p. 323, lines 14–18 and p. 330). For Hazor in Egyptian sources see S. Aḥituv, *Canaanite Toponyms in Ancient Egyptian Documents* (Jerusalem and Leiden 1984), pp. 116 f.

[12] Thus, our translation for *kunukku* in line 22 of the document, which means not only "seal," but also "sealed document," referring here, most likely, to a "bill of sale."

[13] On the reverse of the letter is a damaged part of about twelve lines. In Malamat, *Mari* (see n. 1), p. 66, we suggest that Zimri-Lim demanded help from Yarim-Lim in obtaining the release of a Mari caravan detained by Hazor. A collation of the original tablet (T-H 72–16, to which we had no access) yielded a different but satisfactory reading of the lacuna; see Durand, *MARI* (see n. 9), pp. 63 ff., who believes that the lacuna relates to the Mari messenger of whom the king of Aleppo wishes to get hold.

[14] On Byblos, see G. Dossin (1939), 111 and *idem, RA* 64 (see n. 6). On Qatna and the trade routes between it and Mari, see now F. Joannès, *MARI* 8 (1997), pp. 397 ff.

[15] Regarding *Amurru* horses, cf. the Alalaḫ texts, which are slightly later than Mari. See D.J. Wiseman, *The Alalah Tablets* (London 1953), no. 269, 1.2 49, and cf. B. Landsberger, *JCS* 8 (1954), 56a (n. 103).

latter refers to figs and dates or to honey produced by bees). The above indicate stability in settlement over a long period. The Syro-Palestinian species of the above foodstuffs were considered to be of excellent quality and were highly esteemed in Mari and Mesopotamia in general. Large quantities were shipped to the East. It is noteworthy that the main exports from the West conform to the so-called "seven varieties" of plants in which, according to Deuteronomy 8:8, Canaan excelled: "A land of wheat and barley [grown also in Mesopotamia], of vines, figs and pomegranates [absent in the Mari sources], a land of olive trees and honey." The "Tale of Sinuhe," an Egyptian story from the 20th century B.C.E., that is, some 200 years prior to the Mari documents,[16] also depicts Canaan as such a fertile land.[17]

Addendum: In the renewed excavations of Hazor were unearthed in 1991 two cuneiform tablets (a letter and an administrative text), both fragmentary, listing PNs characteristic of the Mari documents. Surprisingly, in the summer of 1996 two Middle Bronze age documents were discovered, a mathematical fragmentary prism of the type known at Mari, and a partially preserved letter. The letter records deliveries of sacrificial animals to Mari and of vast amounts of textiles and metals (amongst them gold). Thus, the letter confirms interestingly, from the other end, the close commercial and cultural ties between Mari and Hazor (W. Horowitz, *IEJ* 46 [1996], 268 f. and *IEJ* forthcoming).

[16] For a translation of the story of Sinuhe and the relevant passage there, see M. Lichtheim, *Ancient Egyptian Literature* I (Berkeley 1973), pp. 226 ff.

[17] For a general survey of the Mari trade, emphasizing the trade with the West, see now C. Michel, "Le commerce dans les textes de Mari," *Amurru* 1 (1996), 385–426.

5c

MARI AND HAZOR: THE IMPLICATION FOR THE MIDDLE BRONZE AGE CHRONOLOGY*

Where textual evidence goes hand in hand with archaeological data, the chronological issues gain in significance and reliability. Such is the case with Mari, on the mid-Euphrates, and Hazor in Northern Palestine. So far 19 documents in Mari make mention of the city of Hazor, its king or inhabitants.[1] This number is considerable when we take into account the vast distance of over 600 km separating the two sites.[2]

Almost the entire Mari corpus concerning Hazor—consisting of both letters from Mari as well as administrative/economic documents—relates to Zimri-Lim, the last king of Mari who ruled some 15 years until his defeat by Hammurabi of Babylon. Only one Mari document is earlier by several years, a letter of king Šamši-Adad, who seized Mari for some 2 decades and installed there his son Yasmaḫ-Adad as viceroy who outlived his father (the so-called Assyrian Interregnum).[3]

This time-span then encompasses the intense relations between Mari and Hazor, a period of some 20 years at least. The problem facing us is how to determine this period in absolute terms and to accomodate it within the overall chronological system.

---

* This article was originally published in *Ägypten und Levante* 3 (1992), pp. 121–123.

[1] See the series of studies by the present author on Hazor in the Mari documents, dealing *inter alia* with chronological problems: *JBL* 79 (1960), pp. 12–19; in J.A. Sanders (ed.), *Near Eastern Archaeology in the Twentieth Century* (*Essays in Honor of* N. Glueck), Garden City, N.Y., pp. 164–177; *IEJ* 21 (1971), pp. 31–38; *JJS* 33 (1982) (*Essays in honour of* Yigael Yadin), pp. 71–79; in M. Lebeau et Ph. Talon (eds.), *Reflets des Deux Fleuves* (*Mélanges* A. Finet), Leuven 1989, pp. 117–118; A. Malamat, *MEIE*, pp. 55–69.

[2] In *ARM* VI 23:23 most likely another place in Palestine is mentioned. According to the sequence of Syro-Palestinian cities there, listed from north to south, the location seems to have been in central or southern Palestine. Yet the toponym is damaged beyond any repair. For various restorations, A. Malamat, *op. cit.* (n. 1), pp. 61 f.

[3] The document in question is A. 2760, a few lines were published by G. Dossin, *RSO* 32 (1957), pp. 37–38; for the final publication see Bonechi, *Mém. NABU* 1, p. 10.

We shall delineate here the various chronological possibilities taking into account the archaeological evidence from the excavations of Hazor. Hazor was excavated under the direction of Y. Yadin during four principal seasons starting in 1955.[4] Prior to the MB Age II, Hazor was a stately medium size city of some 100 dunams (10 hectares) at its base, comparable to several other sites in Palestine. In the MBA II B, however, Hazor grew to greatness and rose to international significance, thanks to the erection of a fortified lower city, stretching out to the north of the early mound over an area of some 600 to 700 dunams (70 hectares). The ramparts surrounding the lower city were over 3 km long. Hazor became by far the largest city in Palestine and took on the size and form of some places of this period in Syria, such as Qatna, 300 km to the north of Hazor covering an area of some 1000 dunams (100 hectares), and further north Tell Mardikh–Ebla (56 hectares), Aleppo (beneath the present-day city) and Carchemish (100 hectares), while Mari proper occupied an area of only 54 hectares. By virtue of this resemblance Hazor can be conceived of as a Syrian-like rather than Palestinian site.

Yadin hardly touched the possibility that the lower city of Hazor may have come into existence, at least in part, already in an earlier phase, that is in MB II A,[5] as actually was the case concerning the acropolis at the site. The latest excavation reports of Hazor, published years after Yadin's death[6] are virtually silent on this issue, referring only to some pottery types characteristic of the late MB II A and continuing into early MB II B.

However in a paper published recently, A. Kempinski and the late I. Dunayevsky[7] report on their trial dig in 1965 of the eastern rampart in the south of the lower city, revealing an abundance of MB II A pottery. Hence, according to these scholars, the lower city or at least a part thereof, was founded and fortified already in this

---

[4] On the excavations see the summary by Y. Yadin, *Hazor* (*The Schweich Lectures 1970*), Oxford 1972; *idem*, "Hazor" in M. Avi-Yonah (ed.), *EAEHL* II, Jerusalem 1976, pp. 474–495.

[5] Cf. Y. Yadin, *ZDPV* 94 (1978), p. 21 and there the differing views of R. Amiran and A. Kempinski.

[6] A. Ben-Tor (ed.), Y. Yadin *et al., Hazor III–IV, Text,* Jerusalem 1989. For the sparse MB II A pottery which originates late in this period, see p. 7, and *Hazor V*, 1997, for a chronological debate on MB Hazor (pp. 6 ff. by A. Ben-Tor and pp. 321 ff. by A. Maeir).

[7] The Eastern Rampart of Hazor, *Atiqot* 10 (1990), pp. 23–28 (Hebrew; English summary p. 13*).

earlier phase, like other sites, especially in the coastal region of Palestine.[8] Kempinski synchronizes this level with the references of Hazor in Mari and in the later series of the Execration texts (E 15). But only after several decades, in the MB II B age, was the lower city fortified and assumed its maximal extension; it was just then that the city was referred to in the Mari documents (as mentioned, according to the above authors, this occurred still in the MBA II A, while in contrast, we are inclined to vouch already for a MB II B age).

After this background material, let us approach the chronological issues involved.[9] It is reasonable and safe to assume that it was the city of Hazor stretching over the huge lower area which attracted Mari, similarly to the huge mound of Qatna. Indeed, the pre-eminence accorded Hazor during the MB II B age led to its Mesopotamian connection—both to Mari as well as to Babylon. According to one Mari document messengers from Babylon, who stayed for some time at Hazor returned to their homeland escorted by officials from Hazor (*ARM* VI 78).

Having postulated the equation of the MB II B level at Hazor (Upper City level XVII, lower city level 4) with Old Babylonian Mari, a further step is to try to establish an absolute dating for both entities involved. The still controversial dates of the MBA II in Palestine[10] as well as the speculative chronological system concerning the Old Babylonian Period in Mesopotamia, could yield various possibilities in determining absolute dating, with no decisive solution at this point. We shall hereafter delineate four main solutions which have in our opinion the optimal chances for acceptability:

[8] See recently A. Mazar, *Archaeology of the Land of the Bible*, New York etc. 1990, pp. 176 ff.

[9] References to several specific studies: W.F. Albright, Palestine before about 1500 B.C., *Chronologies in Old World Archaeology*², Chicago 1965, pp. 54–57. For other references to Albright's intensive occupation with the MB II chronology see Mazar, *op. cit.*, p. 228 n. 23 and for Mazar's own treatment, there, pp. 193 ff.; P. Gerstenblith, *The Levant at the Beginning of the Middle Bronze Age*, Winona Lake, IN, 1983, pp. 101–108; W.G. Dever, Palestine in the Middle Bronze Age, *BA* 50 (1987), pp. 148–177.

[10] See the widely differing views between B. Mazar, The Middle Bronze Age in Canaan, *The Early Biblical Period*, Jerusalem 1986, pp. 1–34; W.G. Dever, Relations Between Syria-Palestine and Egypt in the "Hyksos" Period, in *Palestine in the Bronze and Iron Ages* (*FS O. Tufnell*), ed. J.N. Tubb, London 1985, pp. 69–87, and the much lower chronology by W.F. Albright, *BASOR* 209 (1973) and by M. Bietak, based on the results of his excavation at the Delta site of Tell el-Dabʿa; cf. his latest statement: The Middle Bronze Age of the Levant—A New Approach to Relative and Absolute Chronology, in P. Åstrom (ed.), *High, Middle or Low?* Part 3 (Gothenburg), 1989, pp. 78–107. The gap in chronology between these two systems amounts to over 100 years.

(1) High dating for MBA II B in Palestine: 1800 to 1650 B.C. (Mazar, Kenyon-concerning beginning of phase B); alternatively:

(2) Lower dating for MB II B: 1750–1650 B.C. (Albright—further lowering its start to 1700 B.C., Yadin and many other archaeologists).

(3) Old Babylonian Mari according to Middle Chronology: first half of the 18th centrury B.C.—reign of Hammurabi 1792–1750 B.C., destroying Mari about 1760 B.C. (majority of Assyriologists and preferred by most historians).

alternatively:

(4) Mari according to Low Chronology: second half of 18th—beginning of 17th centuries B.C.—reign of Hammurabi 1728–1686 B.C., destroying Mari about 1696 B.C. (preferred by certain Assyriologists and majority of Egyptologists).

The interplay between these four suppositions leads to the following conclusions: (a) Adopting the Middle Chronology for Mesopotamia necessitates accepting the higher date for MB II B, placing Hazor's initial greatness into the first half of the 18th century. Unless, of course, the Mari documents would refer to a postulated MB II A city at Hazor, the remains of which have not been unearthed in the lower city, except for the above mentioned potsherds. (b) Adopting the Mesopotamian Low Chronology, lowering the dates of Mari by more than half a century, one is compelled to lower in a like manner also the dates of Greater Hazor and the beginning of the MBA II B. (c) Vice versa, by raising the beginning of the MB II B to *ca.* 1800 B.C., we must adopt the Middle Chronology for Mari. (d) By lowering the archaeological date for the beginning of MB II B to *ca.* 1750 we better accept the Mesopotamian Low Chronology.

Perhaps a point in favor for this latter dating is the conspicious fact that Egypt is entirely absent from Mari, both in objects or documentary evidence, a fact presumably referring to a weak and feeble country after the mighty Middle Kingdom. In the initial 18th century, that is during the end of the 12th and beginning of the 13th dynasties, Egypt was still strong and expanding and one would expect it to have been mentioned at Mari, with the latter spreading its influence over Syria and northern Palestine.[11] On the other hand, in the outgoing 18th and beginning of the 17th centuries B.C., Egypt in its 2nd Intermediate Period was in a rapid process of decline, hardly being able to interfere or maintain contacts in Asia. Yet this fact in

[11] A. Malamat, *MEIE*, especially pp. 1 ff.

itself cannot lead to a decisive solution, as claimed by von Soden and Albright in the early years of the Mari research.[12]

Conversely, the similarity between the pottery of MB II A Palestine and the pottery of the Old Assyrian colonies in Cappadocia has been pointed out.[13] But the Cappadocian finds (Karum Kanish I b) precede Mari at least in the main, by half a century or even more. Thus Mari would well synchronize with a later period, i.e. the MB II B.[14]

---

[12] Cf. W.F Albright, Remarks on the Chronology . . . *BASOR* 184 (1966), pp. 29 f.

[13] Cf. R. Amiran, Similarities Between the Pottery of the MB II A Period and the Pottery of the Assyrian Colonies, *Anadolu* 12 (1970), 59–62.

[14] C.W. Whittaker, The Absolute Chronology of Mesopotamian Chronology, *ca.* 2000–1600 B.C., *Mesopotamia* 24 (1989), pp. 73–100, excludes Mari from his survey and is thus of little value in our context.

PART TWO

PROPHECY

6

INTUITIVE PROPHECY – A GENERAL SURVEY*

A phenomenon attested in the ancient Near East only at Mari and in the Bible is intuitive prophecy—that is, prophetic revelation without resort to mantic or oracular devices and techniques. This is not "run-of-the-mill" haruspicy, or any similar variation of examining the entrails of sacrifices, which was in the province of the formal cult priests and sorcerers and which generally served the royal courts throughout most of the ancient Near East. Indeed, one of the most remarkable disclosures at Mari is this informal type of divination, which existed alongside the more "academic" mantic practices. These Mariote diviner-prophets were spontaneously imbued with a certain consciousness of mission, and with a divine initiative.

In the religion of Israel, of course, prophecy held—and holds—a far greater significance than the somewhat ephemeral role evident at Mari. The prophetic utterances at Mari have almost nothing comparable to the socio-ethical or religious ideology of biblical prophecy (but see below, p. 63). Generally, the Mari oracles are limited to a very mundane plane, placing before the king or his delegates divine demands of a most material nature and reflecting a clear *Lokalpatriotism*, concerned solely with the king's personal well-being.

The corpus of known prophetic texts from Mari—that is, documents conveying prophecies (including prophetic dreams)—presently numbers about fifty-five.[1] Several works have appeared which discuss this material (save one document, published in 1975; and see below),[2] and we can now summarise our under-standing of this topic as follows.

---

* This chapter was originally published in: A. Malamat, *Mari and the Early Israelite Experience*, 1989 (1992), pp. 79–96.

[1] See Malamat 1956, 1958, 1966, 1980, 1987 (the latter including all the material published to about 1986). Almost all the "prophetic" texts have been newly collated and collected in J.-M. Durand, *ARMT* XXVI/1, Paris 1988, which remains the basic source of this material.

[2] We cite here only general works on the entire corpus of "prophetic" materials and not studies of individual Mari documents: Ellermeier 1968; Moran 1969a; Moran, in *ANET*, pp. 623–625, 629–632; Huffmon 1970; Craghan 1974; Noort 1977; Wilson 1980; Schmitt 1982, Nakata 1982a; Dietrich 1986; van der Toorn 1987; Parker 1993; Cagni 1995, recently Lemaire 1996 and Huffmon 1997. For full references see *Bibliography* at the end of the chapter.

Two Types of Diviners at Mari

A Mari letter not directly related to our subject can serve as a key for understanding the reality behind prophecy at Mari. Baḫdi-Lim, the palace prefect, advised Zimri-Lim: "[Verily] you are the king of the Ḫaneans (i.e. the nomads), [but s]econdly you are the king of the Akkadians! [My lord] should not ride a horse. Let my [lord] ride in a chariot or on a mule and he will thereby honour his royal head!" (*ARMT* VI 76: 20–25). This is a clear reflection of the two strata comprising the population of Mari: West Semites (Ḫaneans, the dominant tribal federation of the kingdom), on the one hand, and a veteran Akkadian component, on the other.[3] The symbiosis between these two elements left a general imprint on every walk of life at Mari, including religion and cult.

It is in this context that we can understand at Mari (and for the present, with one late exception,[4] only at Mari) the coexistence of the two patterns noted above of predicting the future and revealing the divine word. As at every other Mesopotamian centre, we find here the typical Akkadian divination as practised by specially trained experts, above all the *bārûm* or haruspex. We are familiar with several such experts at Mari, the best known of whom was Asqudum, whose spacious mansion has recently been uncovered not far from Zimri-Lim's palace.[5] The activities of these "professionals" was usually confined to such crucial matters as omens for the security of the city.[6] Alongside this academic, supposedly "rational" system, we are confronted at Mari with an atypical phenomenon in Mesopotamia—intuitive divination or prophecy, the informal acquiring of the word of god. Indeed, this is the earliest such manifestation known to us anywhere in the ancient Near East. This type of prophecy should properly be regarded as one of a chain of social and religious prac-

[3] Charpin & Durand 1986 now suggest that the duality in the above text refers to two geographical components of Zimri-Lim's kingdom: Terqa and the Land of the Ḫaneans, and the land of Akkad.

[4] I.e. neo-Assyrian prophecy; see Weippert 1981, 1985; Hecker 1986; Parpola forthcoming (but in these prophecies the element of prophetic mission is entirely absent) and see below, n. 8.

[5] See Margueron 1982, 1983, 1984. On the archive of Asqudum discovered on the site, see Charpin 1985. Asqudum's wife, Yamama, was either the daughter or the sister of Yaḫdun-Lim.

[6] The texts have recently been collected in Parpola 1983. For extispicy in Mesopotamia in general, and at Mari in particular, see Starr 1983, pp. 107 f. and Index, s.v. *Mari* (p. 141); and cf. the comprehensive Bottéro 1974.

tices exclusive to Mari and, in part, similar to those found in the Bible.

This informal type of divination at Mari places biblical prophecy in a new perspective. Both phenomena bypass mantic or magic mechanisms, which require professional expertise; rather, they are the product of psychic, non-rational experience. The essential nature of prophecy of this type entails certain dominant characteristics, the three most significant of which, in my opinion, are delineated as follows:[7]

(a) Spontaneous prophetic manifestations resulting from inspiration or divine initiative (in contrast to mechanical, inductive divination, which was usually initiated by the king's request for signs from the deity). In this connection we may compare the utterance of Isaiah, communicating the word of God: "I was ready to be sought by those who didn't ask for me; I was ready to be found by those who didn't seek me. I said, 'Here am I, here am I . . .'" (Isaiah 65:1).

(b) A consciousness of mission, the prophets taking a stand before the authorities to present divinely inspired messages (cf. ch. 7).

(c) An ecstatic component in prophecy, a somewhat problematic and complex characteristic. This concept should be allowed a broad, liberal definition, enabling it to apply to a wide range of phenomena from autosuggestion to the divinely infused dream. Only in rare instances did this quality appear as extreme frenzy, and even then it is not clear whether it was accompanied by loss of senses—for the prophets always appear sober and purposeful in thought, and far from spouting mere gibberish.

These particular characteristics—not necessarily found in conjunction—link the diviner-prophet at Mari with the Israelite prophet more than with any other divinatory type known in the ancient Near East.[8] Nevertheless, in comparing Mari and the Bible, one cannot ignore the great differences between the two types of source-material: respectively first-hand documents, as against compositions which had undergone lengthy, complex literary processes. Furthermore, the

[7] Noort 1977, pp. 24 ff., rejects the characteristics mentioned below as typical of prophesying at Mari and accordingly denies any relationship to biblical prophecy. But his approach is too extreme in requiring every single characteristic to appear in each and every "prophetic" text. He has justifiably been criticized, for example, by Nakata 1982b, pp. 166–168.

[8] Perhaps except for the *rāgimu* (fem. *rāgintu*), "the pronouncer", "speaker" of the neo-Assyrian period, addressing Esarhaddon and Ashurbanipal. See Weippert 1981, Parpola forthcoming. And see below, n. 25.

documentation concerning prophecy at Mari is mostly restricted to a very short span of time, perhaps only to the final decade (or less) of Zimri-Lim's reign. In comparison, the activity of the Israelite prophets extended over a period of centuries.[9] In other words, here too, Mari represents a synchronous picture, a cross-section at one particular point in time, while the Bible gives a diachronous view, tracing the development of the prophetic phenomenon over a period of time.

Prophecy at Mari and in the Bible—Similarities and Differences

Despite the external, formal similarity between the diviner-prophets at Mari and the Israelite prophets, there is an obvious discrepancy in content between the divine messages and in the function they assumed, as well as, apparently, in the status of the prophets within the respective societies and kingdoms. In Israelite society, the prophet seems usually to have enjoyed a more or less central position, though certain types of prophet were peripheral. At Mari, however, the prophets apparently played only a marginal role.[10] Admittedly, this distinction might merely be illusory, deriving from the nature of the respective source materials. In both societies many of the prophets, basing on their place of origin and locale of activity, came from rural communities: in Mari, from such towns as Terqa and Tuttul, and in Judah, from Tekoa (Amos), Moreshet (Micah), Anathot (Jeremiah) and Gibeon (Hananiah); but others resided in the respective capitals.

As for contents, the prophecies at Mari are limited to material demands on the king, such as the construction of a building or a city

[9] The lengthy span of prophecy in Israel is especially evident if we include, for our present purposes, both the early, "primitive" prophets as well as the late, "classical" ones, who were not so decidedly distinct from one another. This distinction has gained currency ever since the over-emphasis of the Canaanite origin of early Israelite prophecy; cf. Hölscher 1914, and Lindblom 1962, pp. 47 and 105 ff. In contrast, subsequent scholars occasionally pointed out the continuity of certain early elements through the period of classical prophecy; see e.g. Haran 1977 (with earlier literature).

[10] The question of centre and periphery in the status of the prophets has been raised only in recent years, under the influence of sociology. See Wilson 1980, where the peripheral role of all Mari prophets is emphasised, when compared with the central role of the *bārûm*; and see Petersen 1981. The authors consider the *nāḇīʾ* and the *ḥōzeh* to be "central" in both Israel and Judah, while the *rōʾeh* and the *ʾīš hāʾᵉlōhīm*, as well as the *bᵉnē nᵉḇīʾīm* ('sons' of the prophets) are regarded as peripheral.

gate in some provincial town (*ARMT* III 78; XIII 112), the offering of funerary sacrifices (*ARMT* II 90; III 40), the despatch of valuable objects to various temples (A. 4260), or the request of property (*niḫlatum*) for a god (A. 1121; the reference is surely to a landed estate sought by a sanctuary and its priestly staff).[11] Many of the more recently published Mari prophecies refer to military and political affairs, above all the welfare of the king and his personal safety. He is warned against conspirators at home and enemies abroad (*ARMT* X 7, 8, 50, 80), especially Ḫammurabi, king of Babylon (see below), who was soon to conquer Mari. This sort of message is very distinct from biblical prophecy, expressing a full-fledged religious ideology, a socio-ethical manifesto and a national purpose. But this glaring contrast might actually be something of a distortion. At Mari nearly all the "prophetic" texts were discovered in the royal-diplomatic archives of the palace (Room 115), which would serve to explain their tendency to concentrate on the king. Prophecies directed at other persons presumably did exist but, on account of their nature, have not been preserved. In comparison, had the historiographic books of the Bible (Samuel, Kings and Chronicles) alone survived, we would be faced with a picture closely resembling that at Mari, in which Israelite prophecy, too, was oriented primarily toward the king and his politico-military enterprises.

A glimmer of social-moral concern can, however, be seen at Mari in a prophetic message which is contained in two recently joined fragments (A. 1121 + A. 2731):[12] A diviner-prophet urges Zimri-Lim, in the name of the god Adad of Aleppo: "When a wronged man or woman cries out to you, stand and let his/her case be judged." This command has an exact parallel in Jeremiah's sermon to kings: "Execute justice in the morning, and deliver from the hand of the oppressor him who has been robbed" (Jeremiah 21:12; and cf. 22:3).

A tangible example of the imposition of obligations on the king at Mari is found in one letter (*ARMT* X 100), in which a divinely imbued

---

[11] Interestingly, the divine threat of Adad hanging over Zimri-Lim should he refuse to donate the estate—"What I have given, I shall take away . . ." (A. 1121, l. 18)—closely mirrors Job's words: "The lord gave and the Lord has taken away . . ." (Job 1:27).

[12] For the join (initially proposed by J.-M. Durand) of A. 1121, published long ago, and a fragment previously published only in translation, see Lafont 1984. For earlier treatments of the following passage, see, *inter alia*, Anbar 1975, and Malamat 1980, p. 73 and n. 6. On a translation and an analysis of this document see below ch. 9.

woman writes to the king directly, with no intervention of a third party (although a scribe may have been employed). The woman (whose name is apparently to be read Yanana) addressed Zimri-Lim in the name of Dagan concerning a young lady (her own daughter, or perhaps a companion) who had been abducted when the two of them were on a journey. Dagan appeared to the woman in a dream and decreed that only Zimri-Lim could save and return the girl. Thus, a woman who was wronged turned to the king in seeking redress, in the spirit of the prophetic commands adduced above.

All told, the analogy between prophecy at Mari and that in Israel is presently still vague, the two being set apart by a gap of more than six centuries. Furthermore, many of the intervening links are "missing". It would thus be premature to regard Mari as the prototype of prophecy in Israel.[13] But the earliest manifestation of intuitive prophecy among West Semitic tribes at Mari should not be belittled, notwithstanding its still enigmatic aspects. In this regard we can put forward two assumptions (which are not mutually exclusive):

(a) Intuitive prophecy was basically the outcome of a specific social situation—an erstwhile non-urban, semi-nomadic, tribal society. Urban sophistication, no matter how primitive, naturally engenders institutionalized cult specialists, such as the *bārû* (haruspex), the foremost of the diviner types in Mesopotamia and part and parcel of the cult personnel of any self-respecting town or ruler.

(b) The phenomenon of intuitive prophecy was a characteristic of a particular *Kulturkreis* which extended across the West, from Palestine and Syria to Anatolia, and as far as Mari in the east. This assumption is based mainly on the ecstatic element in prophecy, attested throughout this region (albeit rather sporadically). It is found outside the Bible in such cases as the prophets of the Hittite sources, at Byblos (as mentioned in the Egyptian Tale of Wen-Amon), in Syria (in the Aramaic inscription of Zakkur, king of Hamath), and in notations in classical literature (cf. ch. 7, p. 85).[14]

---

[13] Here I fully agree with Noort 1977; see his summary on p. 109; I do reject, however, the remarks such as those of Schmitt 1982, p. 13.

[14] For Ešnunna see below n. 25. The West as a separate *Kulturkreis* from the East (Southern Mesopotamia) with regard to certain basic religious elements has been appreciated by Oppenheim 1964, pp. 221 ff. Several scholars assume that prophecy in both Mari and Israel originated in the Arabian-Syrian desert; see, e.g., Rendtorff 1962, p. 146. For the ecstatic prophet in Hittite sources, see *ANET*, p. 395a; for the prophet from Byblos, see Cody 1979, pp. 99–106. The author derives the Egyptian word *ʿḏd* from the West Semitic *ʿdd*, which in the Aramaic inscription of Zakkur (see below) designates a type of diviner-prophet; and see Malamat 1966, p. 209 and n. 2.

Let us now delve deeper into the data at hand concerning prophecy at Mari. Since 1948, some fifty letters addressed to the king (almost all of them to Zimri-Lim) and containing reports on prophecies and divine revelations have been published. The senders were high ranking officials and bureaucrats from all over the kingdom. About half were women, mostly ladies of the palace, headed by Šibtu, Zimri-Lim's principal queen. Several of the letters contain two individual visions and thus the total number of prophecies is some sixty. In several cases the correspondent was the prophet himself (though the letters *per se* may well have been written by scribes; one is reminded of Baruch son of Neriah, Jeremiah's anamuensis; see below ch. 11). Thus, a prophet acting in the name of Šamaš of Sippar (A. 4260); the court lady Addu-Duri (*ARMT* X 50); and a woman named Yanana (mentioned above; *ARMT* X 100). As already noted, the words of the diviner-prophets, whether transmitted through intermediaries or dispatched directly to the king, were generally formulated with utmost lucidity. This was perhaps due to the slight interval between the actual prophetic experience and the committing of the vision to writing. How much more is this so in connection with biblical prophecy, which generally has undergone repeated editing (though certain prophecies may well have been preserved in their pristine form).

This raises the possible conclusion (not usually considered), that the messages of the diviner-prophets at Mari may originally have been pronounced in the West Semitic dialect conventionally designated "Amorite". Should this be the case in the documents before us, the original words of the prophecies (or at least some of them) would have already been rendered into the language of the chancery, Akkadian—either by the officials writing or by their scribes. Such an assumption could also serve to explain why the "prophetic" texts at Mari display a relatively greater number of West Semitic idioms and linguistic forms than do the other Mari documents. If these assumptions are correct, the transmission of the prophetic word, *ipsissima verba*, to the king's ear, was considerably more complex than outwardly appears.

The diviner-prophets at Mari were of two types: professional or "accredited"—recognisable by distinctive titles (as were the biblical *rō'eh*, *ḥōzeh*, *nāḇī'* and *'īš 'elōhīm*); and casual—lay persons who held no formal title (see below). Thus far, five different titles are known at Mari designating "cult" prophets (if we may use a term current in Bible studies):

(1) The title *nabûm*, pl. *nabî*, cognate of Hebrew *nāḇîʾ*, "prophet", occurs in Mari only once (*ARMT* XXVI/1 216:7), referring to prophets of the Ḫaneans, i.e. of the nomadic population.[15]

(2) A priest (*šangûm*) is mentioned once as a prophet (*ARMT* X 51), imbued with a prophetic dream containing a warning; in the Bible, too, Ezekiel was originally a priest, and so was Pashhur, son of Immer, who inter alia prophesized (Jeremiah 20:1, 6).

(3) There are several references to the prophetic *assinnum* (*ARMT* X 6, 7, 80),[16] though this term is not entirely clear in meaning. Based on later sources, it might refer to a eunuch, a male prostitute or a cult musician. One such functionary served in a temple at Mari and prophesied in the name of Annunītum (a goddess normally associated with women), apparently while disguised as a woman (perhaps in the manner of present-day transvestites).

(4) In a few instances (*ARMT* X 8; XXVI/1 199, 203), a prophetess bears the title *qammātum* (or possibly *qabbātum*, to be derived from Akkadian *qabûm*, "speak, pronounce"?).[17]

(5) One of the best known of the "accredited" prophets at Mari is the *muḫḫûm* (fem. *muḫḫūtum*)[18] who, as etymology would indicate, was some sort of ecstatic or frenetic.[19] The peculiar behaviour of this type of prophet led him to be perceived as a madman, similar to the biblical *mᵉšuggaʿ*, a term occasionally used as a synonym for *nāḇîʾ* (2 Kings 9:11; Jeremiah 29:26; Hosea 9:7).[20] We may also mention instances of the Akkadian verb *immaḫu* (3rd person preterite), derived from the same root as *muḫḫûm*, and used in the N-stem, resembling Biblical Hebrew *nibbāʾ* (cf. also *hitnabbēʾ*). This word, *immaḫu*, means "became insane", "went into a trance" (*ARMT* X 7:5–7; 8:5–8). Besides the five unnamed *muḫḫûms* mentioned in the "prophetic" docu-

---

[15] In the 13th/12th centuries B.C. this term also occurs at Emar, see Fleming 1993, pp. 179 ff.; Lemaire 1996, pp. 427 f.

[16] For this prophet see, e.g., Wilson 1980, pp. 106–107, with bibliography and Parpola forthcoming.

[17] For this term, see Durand 1988, pp. 379 ff.

[18] See Durand 1988, pp. 386 ff.

[19] The *purrusum* form of the noun is peculiar to Mari (in other Akkadian sources we find the form *maḫḫûm* from Middle Babylonian onwards). This nominal form designates bodily defects and functionally resembles the Hebrew *qittēl* form used in such words as *ʿiwwēr*, "blind", *pissēaḥ*, "lame", and *gibbēn*, "hunchback". See Holma 1914 and Landsberger 1915, pp. 363–366 for the Akkadian.

[20] Malamat 1966, pp. 210–211 and n. 4, for additional references and earlier bibliography on *muḫḫûm*.

ments, the recently published volumes of Mari documents[21] include new administrative material naming five *muḫḫûms*, along with the deities they served. These documents are lists of personnel receiving clothes from the palace. In a previously published list, there is a reference to an *āpilum* (*ARMT* IX 22:14; and see below). This would imply that the *muḫḫûm* (as well as the *āpilum*) received material support from the royal court. A surprising feature here is that four of the named *muḫḫûms* have strictly Akkadian (rather than West Semitic) names: Irra-gamil, *muḫḫûm* of Nergal; Ea-maṣi, *muḫḫûm* of Itur-Mer (*ARMT* XXI 333:33'/34'; XXIII 446:9', 19'); Ea-mudammiq, *muḫḫûm* of Ninhursag; and Anu-tabni, *muḫḫūtum* of the goddess Annunītum (*ARMT* XXII 167: 8' and 326:8–10); the fifth was a *muḫḫûm* of Adad, mentioned with the intriguing notation that he received a silver ring "when (he) delivered an oracle for the king" (*ARMT* XXV 142:3'). Another *muḫḫūtum* with court connections was named Ribatum; she sent an oracle to Zimri-Lim concerning the two tribal groups, the Simalites and the Yaminites.[22]

It is possible that on the whole these prophets, who were dependent on the royal court of Mari, had already been assimilated into Akkadian culture to a great extent, hence their Akkadian names. In any case, the direct contact with the royal court calls to mind the court prophets in Israel, such as Nathan the *nāḇīʾ* and Gad the *ḥōzeh*, who served David and Solomon, or the Baal and Ashera prophets functioning at the court of Ahab and Jezebel.

(6) Finally, there was the *āpilum* (fem. *āpiltum*), a prophetic title exclusive to Mari and meaning "answerer, respondent" (derived from the verb *apālum*, "to answer").[23] Unlike the other types of prophets, *āpilums* on occasion acted in consort, in groups similar to the bands of prophets in the Bible (*ḥeḇel* or *lahᵃqat nᵉḇîʾîm*). The *āpilum* is attested in documents covering a broad geographical expanse, with a wider distribution than any other type of prophet—from Aleppo in northern Syria to Sippar near Babylon. Thus, an *āpilum* of Šamaš of Sippar, addressing the king of Mari directly, demanded a throne for Šamaš, as well as one of the king's daughters(?) for service in his

[21] *ARMT* XXI; *ARMT* XXII; *ARMT* XXIII; *ARMT* XXV; *ARMT* XXVI/1.
[22] Charpin & Durand 1986, p. 151 and n. 7.
[23] Malamat 1966a, pp. 212–213 and n. 2, for the various spellings *apillû, aplûm, āpilum*; and see *CAD* A/2, p. 170a; Malamat 1980, pp. 68 ff.; Anbar 1981, p. 91.

temple.[24] He also demanded objects for other deities (including an *asakku* or consecrated object): Adad of Aleppo, Dagan of Terqa and Nergal of Ḫubšalum (A. 4260). Another *āpilum* was in the Dagan temple at Tuttul (near the confluence of the Baliḫ and the Euphrates rivers) and there was an *āpiltum* in the Annunitum temple in the city of Mari itself. And an *āpilum* of Dagan, bearing the strictly Akkadian name Qišatum, received bronze objects from the palace, like the "gifts" from the king noted above.[25] It is noteworthy that the *muḫḫûm* and the *muḫḫūtum* functioned in these very same sanctuaries as well, indicating that two different types of diviner-prophets could be found side by side. Indeed, in the Dagan temple at Terqa, three types of prophet were at work simultaneously: a *muḫḫûm*, a *qammātum* and a dreamer of dreams.

Affinities in Terminology and Contents—Mari and Israel

The terms *āpilum* and *muḫḫûm* would appear to have counterparts in biblical Hebrew. The terms *ʿānāh* and *ʿōneh*, "answer" and "answerer", respectively, can refer to divine revelation.[26] Most significantly, the very verb *ʿānāh* is used at times to describe the prophet's function as God's mouthpiece, whether actually responding to a query put to the deity or not. This is clearly seen, for instance, in 1 Samuel 9:17: "When Samuel saw Saul, the Lord answered him; 'Here is the man of whom I spoke to you! He is it who shall rule over my people.'" This is also indicated by Jeremiah's condemnation (23:33 ff.) of one Hebrew term for prophetic utterance, *maśśāʾ* (cf., e.g., Lamentations 2:14 and 2 Kings 9:25), and his commendation of the more "legiti-

---

[24] Interestingly, compliance with this prophetic demand seems to be alluded to in the female correspondence. Further on in our document the name of Zimri-Lim's daughter is given as Erišti-Aya. A woman by this name sent several doleful letters to her parents from the temple at Sippar; see *ARMT* X 37:15; 43:16, etc. Cf. Kraus 1984, p. 98 and n. 224; and Charpin & Durand 1985, pp. 332, 340.

[25] Another *āpilum*, of Marduk(!), is mentioned in a Mari letter from Babylon concerning Išme-Dagan, king of Assyria, denouncing him for delivering treasures to the king of Elam (A. 428:21–28); see Charpin, *ARMT* XXVI/2 371. "Prophetic" documents of this same period have been discovered also at Ishchali, on the Lower Diyala river, seat of the goddess Kititum; her oracles, addressed to Ibal-pi-El, king of Ešnunna, a contemporary of the Mari kings, are similar in tone and message to those from Mari, but they are quite different in their mode of transmission, for they appear in the form of letters from the deity herself, with no prophetic intermediary involved. See Ellis 1987, pp. 251–257.

[26] Malamat 1958, pp. 72–73.

mate" *ʿānāh* in its stead: "What has the Lord answered and what has the Lord said?" (Jeremiah 23:37). The term *maʿanēh ʾĕlōhīm* (lit. "God's answer"), meaning the word of the Lord, occurs once in the Bible, in Micah 3:7, which also elucidates the use of *ʿnh* in connection with the oracles of Balaam: "Remember now, O my people, remember what Balak king of Moab devised and what Balaam the son of Beor *answered* him" (Micah 6:5). The verb *ʿānāh* here does not indicate response to a specific question put forth to Balaam but, rather, the prophetic oracle which Balaam was compelled to deliver in Israel's favour. It is possible that this non-Israelite diviner, who is never designated *nābīʾ*, was a prophet of the *āpilum* ("answerer") type. The analogy might be strengthened by the cultic acts performed by Balaam, on the one hand (Numbers 23:3, 14–15, 29), and by the band of *āpilums*, on the other hand (A. 1121, esp. ll. 24–25)—both soliciting the divine word.[27]

It is of interest that the recently discovered "Balaam Inscription" from Tell Deir ʿAlla in Transjordan, from the late 8th or early 7th century B.C. and written in either an Ammonite or "Israelite-Gileadite" dialect, enumerates various types of sorcerers, including a woman designated *ʿnyh*. The latter term most likely means "(female) respondent", that is, a semantic equivalent of the Mari term *āpiltum*.[28] This interpretation gains cogency through the phrase following the reference to the woman: *rqḥt mr wkhnh*, "a perfumer of myrrh and priestess". Even more significant is the Aramaic inscription of Zakkur, king of Hamath, from about 800 B.C. In his hour of peril, Zakkur turned

[27] Balaam was certainly not a prophet of the *bārûm* type, as was long ago suggested in Daiches 1909, pp. 60–70. This claim has often been refuted, correctly; see Rofé 1979, p. 32, n. 53. Offering sacrifices in preparation for deriving the word of the deity as is found in the Balaam pericope are similarly alluded to at the beginning of Mari texts *ARMT* XIII 23 and A. 1221; they are explicitly mentioned in a "prophetic" document (cf. Dossin 1966) which was published in full in Durand 1988, pp. 215 (A. 455): "... One head of cattle and six sheep I will sacrifice ...", that is, seven sacrificial animals. In what follows, a *muḫḫûm* "arises" and prophesies in the name of Dagan. Compare the seven altars, seven bulls and seven rams which Balaam had Balak prepare before delivering his oracle (Numbers 23:29–30).

[28] See the Deir ʿAlla inscription, first combination, l. 11; Hoftijzer & van der Kooij 1976, pp. 180, 212. The editors interpreted *ʿnyh* as a female answerer, indicating a prophetess, following our conclusion concerning the title *āpilum* at Mari and its relationship to biblical terminology. This opinion has been accepted by Rofé 1979, p. 67 and n. 33, among others. Indeed, in the dialect of this inscription verbs with a third weak radical are spelled preserving the *yod* before the final *he*, like Hebrew *bōḵiyāh* (I must thank B. Levine for this information). This term has nothing to do with "poor woman", despite the Hebrew homograph *ʿnyh*, as various scholars contend; see, e.g., Caquot & Lemaire 1977, p. 200; McCarter 1980b, p. 58; Weippert 1982, p. 98; and Hackett 1984, p. 133, s.v. *ʿnyh*.

to his gods, "and Baalšamayn responded to me (*wyʿnny*) and Baalšamayn [spoke to me] through seers and diviners" (*ʿddn*; ll. 11–12).[29]

A probable overlap of the prophetic activity of the *āpilum* and that of the *muḫḫûm* is indicated in a letter containing the message of a *muḫḫūtum*, imploring the king of Mari not to leave the capital to wage war at that time; it declares: "I will *answer* you constantly" (*attanapal; ARMT* X 50: 22–26). In other words, there are cases where a *muḫḫûm* would be involved in the act of "answering" (*apālum*).

Before turning to the matter of lay prophets at Mari, let us examine two prophecies of similar content, reminiscent of the biblical oracles "against the nations": one of an *āpilum* (curiously spelled here *aplûm*); and the other of "the wife of a man", that is, a lay woman. Both reports were transmitted through Kibri-Dagan, Zimri-Lim's governor at Terqa. The *āpilum/aplûm* "arose" in the name of Dagan of Tuttul, "and so he said as follows: 'O Babylon! Why doest thou ever (evil)? I will gather thee into a net! . . . The houses of the seven confederates and all their possessions I shall deliver into Zimri-Lim's hand!'" (*ARMT* XIII 23:6–15). This prophecy, which contains several motifs well known in the biblical prophecies of doom,[30] reflects the deteriorating relations between Mari and Babylon, brought about by Ḫammurabi's expansionist aspirations. The other prophecy explicitly mentions Ḫammurabi as an enemy of Mari (*ARMT* XIII 114). A divinely inspired woman approached Kibri-Dagan late one afternoon with the following words of consolation: "The god Dagan sent me. Send your lord; he shall not worry [. . .], he shall not worry. Ḫammurabi [king] of Babylon . . . [continuation broken]." The urgency of the matter is indicated by the fact that the letter bearing this encouraging message was dispatched the very day it was uttered.

From these two prophecies—and possibly from most of the visions concerning the king's safety—it is apparent that they were recorded at a time of political and military distress at Mari. This, too, would

[29] See Gibson 1975, pp. 8 ff. The author there translates the word *ʿddn* as "(prophetic?) messengers" on the basis of *ʿdd* in Ugaritic (p. 15), and cf. above, n. 14. For a possible connection between prophecy at Mari and that at Hamath, see Ross 1970.

[30] Especially the motifs of gathering into a net and delivering into the hand, which are found frequently in both ancient Near Eastern and biblical literature in connection with vanquishing an enemy; Malamat 1980, pp. 217 f. and cf. Heintz 1969, who relates these motifs to the "Holy War" in the ancient Near East and the Bible.

be analogous to Israelite prophecy, which thrived particularly in times of national emergency—such as during the Philistine threat in the days of Samuel and Saul, during Sennacherib's campaign against Jerusalem, and especially at the time of Nebuchadnezzar's moves against Judah. The crisis factor was certainly one of the principal forces engendering prophetic manifestations in both Mari and Israel.[31] However, in contrast to the Bible with its prophecies of doom and words of admonition against king and people, the messages at Mari were usually optimistic and sought to placate the king rather than rebuke or alert him. Such prophecies of success and salvation (see *ARMT* X 4, 9, 10, 51, 80), coloured by a touch of nationalism, liken the Mari prophets to the "false prophets" of the Bible. Surely, the corresponding prophecies are quite similar. Indeed, one of the prominent "false prophets" in the Bible, Hananiah of Gibeon, Jeremiah's rival, rashly proclaimed in the name of the Lord (and not in the name of a foreign god) the impending return of the Judean exiles from Babylonia: "for I will break the yoke of the king of Babylon" (Jeremiah 28:4). How reminiscent is this of the *āpilum*'s prediction against Babylon (see above, *ARMT* XIII 23). In both instances the message is a whitewashing of the critical situation, for such prophets of peace served the "establishment" and expressed its interests (compare the four hundred prophets at Ahab's court, who prophesy "with one accord"; 1 Kings 22:13).[32]

In contrast to Mari, the Bible is replete with prophecies unfavourable to king and country; their heralds, the so-called prophets of doom (or "true" prophets), were constantly harrassed by the authorities. One well-known case is that of Amos who, at the royal sanctuary at Bethel, foretold of King Jeroboam's death and the exile of the people (Amos 7:10–13). In reaction, the priest Amaziah, by order of the king, expelled the prophet to Judah in disgrace. Jeremiah provoked an even more violent response, in the days of both Jehoiakim and Zedekiah. Pashhur (the priest in charge of the temple in Jerusalem), when confronted by the prophet's words of wrath, "beat Jeremiah

---

[31] This has been indicated by, among others, Uffenheimer 1973, pp. 27, 37; Noort 1977, pp. 93, 109; and Blenkinsopp 1983, p. 45. Remarkably, just prior to Ḫammurabi's conquest of Mari there is a noticeable rise in future-telling activities of the *bārûm*; see Starr 1983, p. 107.

[32] For the "false" prophets and their dependence on the Israelite establishment, see, among others, Buber 1950, pp. 253 ff.; Hossfeld & Meyer 1973; de Vries 1978.

the prophet, and put him in the stocks that were in the house of the Lord" (Jeremiah 20:2).

At certain times, however, we do find close cooperation between king, priest and prophet. A priest occasionally officiated as an intermediary between the king and the prophet, as when Hezekiah sent emissaries to Isaiah (2 Kings 19:20 ff. = Isaiah 37:2 ff.) and Zekediah to Jeremiah (Jeremiah 21:1 ff.; 37:3 ff.). Similarly, Hilkiahu, the high-priest, headed the royal delegation which Josiah sent to Huldah the prophetess (2 Kings 22:12 ff.). The roles are inverted at Mari, where a prophet's report could be conveyed to the king via a priest. According to two documents (*ARMT* VI 45 and X 8), prophetesses appeared before Aḫum the priest, who served in the temple of Annunītum in Mari proper. Once Aḫum reported the message to Baḫdi-Lim, palace prefect, who passed it on to the king; at another time he transmitted the prophetic words to the queen, Šibtu.[33] In the latter case, a new element appears, to which we have alluded only briefly above—the frenetic here was a mere maidservant named Aḫatum and had no prophetic title—that is, she was a simple lay-person.

Lay Prophets and Message Dreams

More than half the "prophetic" documents from Mari deal with lay-persons, "prophets" not "accredited" to any sanctuary. Among these we find such designations as "a man", "a woman", "a man's wife", "a youth" and "a young woman (or 'maidservant')", as well as several instances of persons who are merely mentioned by name. In one case a prophetic message was elicited from "a man and a woman" (lit. "male and female"), who prophesied jointly (*ARMT* X 4). Because this manner of prophecy was uncommon and surprising at Mari, it should be examined briefly.

Queen Šibtu wrote to her husband that she had asked a man and a woman to foretell the fortunes of Zimri-Lim's forthcoming military

---

[33] Moran 1969a, p. 20, holds that *ARMT* VI 45 deals with the same event as *ARMT* X 50, while Sasson 1980, p. 131b, associates it with *ARMT* X 8. Neither suggestion is compelling. *ARMT* X 50 does not mention a priest by the name of Aḫum, but someone else, while *ARMT* X 8 mentions a prophetess by name but without title, and *ARMT* VI 45 speaks of an anonymous *muḫḫūtum*. It may be assumed, therefore, that both professional and lay prophets would occasionally appear before Aḫum, a priest in Mari.

venture against Išme-Dagan, king of Ashur. As noted, the mode of divination here is exceptional, and has led to various scholarly interpretations.[34] The key sentence at the opening of Šibtu's letter reads (according to a recent collation): "Concerning the report on the military campaign which my lord undertakes, I have asked a man and a woman about the signs (*ittātim*) when I plied (them with drink) and the oracle (*egerrûm*) for my lord is very favourable" (*ARMT* X 4:3–37). Šibtu immediately inquired of the fate of Išme-Dagan, and the oracle "was unfavourable". This query concerning the fate of the enemy recalls how king Ahab consulted the four-hundred prophets, prior to his battle against the Arameans (1 Kings 22:6 ff.). Further on, Šibtu cited the full prophecy proclaimed by the two persons, which contains several motifs found in biblical prophecies.[35] How are we to perceive this kind of divination? It has been suggested that the man and woman themselves served as a sign and portent, partly on the basis of the words of Isaiah (8:18): "Behold, I and the children the Lord has given me are signs and portents in Israel"—but such an interpretation seems forced. Rather, the queen seems to have selected a couple at random, offering them drink (perhaps wine) to loosen their tongues and thus obtained an *egerrûm*-oracle, based on "chance utterances". This type of divining, known as cledomancy, has been likened to the divinatory method known in Hebrew as *bat qōl* (literally "a trace of a voice", usually translated "echo"). The same Hebrew term is found in talmudic sources, where it serves as an *ersatz* for prophecy *per se*.[36]

Among lay prophets as well as transmitters of prophetic reports, there was an unusually large proportion of women, mostly from Zimri-Lim's court. Indeed, one of the king's daughters explicitly stated to her father: "Now, though I am a (mere) woman, may my father the

[34] On *ARMT* X 4, and the mode of prophesying, see the recent studies: Finet 1982, Durand 1982; Durand 1984a, pp. 150 ff.; and Wilcke 1983, p. 93.

[35] Note, above all, the motif of the gods marching alongside the king in time of war and saving him from his enemies, a motif resembling the intervention of the Lord in the wars of Israel. This involves also driving the enemy into flight; cf.: "Arise, O Lord, and let they enemies be scattered . . ." (Numbers 10:35; and see also Psalms 68:2) [in relation to the above-mentioned biblical parallel, note the utterance of the prophet Micaiah the son of Imlah concerning the dispersion of the Israelite army (1 Kings 22:17)], and eventually decapitating the foe who would be trampled under the foot of the king of Mari (see, e.g., Joshua 24:25). And see Weinfeld 1977.

[36] For this type of oracle, see *CAD* E, s.v. *egirrû*, p. 45: ". . . oracular utterances . . . which are either accidental in origin (comp. with Greek *kledon*) or hallucinatory in nature. . . ." For the parallel with Hebrew *bat qōl*, see Sperling 1972.

lord harken unto my words. I will constantly send the word of the gods to my father" (*ARMT* X 31:7'–10'). Some prophetesses and female dreamers of dreams sent their prophecies directly to the king, without a mediator (*ARMT* X 50, 100). Šibtu, more than anyone else, served as an intermediary for conveying prophetic messages to her husband. This would call to mind rather bizarre episodes throughout history, where a "prophet" or mystic used or exploited a queen so as to bring his visions and message to the attention of her husband, the king. Among the "accredited" prophets, too—as we have seen—there were many women, as there were in the Bible. The outstanding of these were Deborah, wife of Lapidoth (Judges 4:4) and Huldah, wife of Shallum (2 Kings 22:14). In both instances the Bible specifically notes that they were married women, probably to stress their stability and reliability—as in the case of the "wife of a man", one of the Mari prophetesses (*ARMT* XIII 114:8). (See ch. 7 below).

Are there any characteristics which distinguish the "accredited" prophets from the lay ones? Two prominent features have been noticed by scholars: (a) Only in the case of the "accredited" are the actual messages preceded by the verb *tebû*, "to arise" (e.g. "he/she arose and . . ."), somehow alluding to prophetic stimulation in the temple.[37] Synonymous expressions are used in connection with the biblical prophets, as well (Deuteronomy 13:2; 18:15, 18; 34:10; Jeremiah 1:17; etc.); note in particular Ezekiel: "And set me upon my feet" (Ezekiel 2:2; and cf. Ezekiel 3:22–24; Daniel 8:17–18; 10:10–11; 2 Chronicles 24:2). (b) Among the lay prophets, dreaming is prevalent as the prophetic means, while this medium is totally absent among the "accredited" prophets.

Almost half the published prophecies from Mari were revealed in dreams. Phenomenologically, we thus find two distinct categories of acquiring the divine word. "Accredited" prophets enjoyed direct revelation while fully conscious; whereas lay prophets often received revelations through dreams. The latter was a widespread phenomenon throughout the ancient Near East, including Israel.[38] At Mari, as in the Bible, we find a specific subcategory of "message dream"

---

[37] See, in particular, Moran 1969b, pp. 25–26; and Weinfeld 1977, pp. 181–182.

[38] Malamat 1966, pp. 221 f. and n. 1 on p. 222, for literature on the dream in the Bible; for the ancient Near East, see the basic study of Oppenheim 1956, and see now Gnuse 1996. Durand points out that dream prophecies of the 2nd millennium were common and typical of the West (Mari and Anatolia); see Durand, 1997b, p. 282 and 1997a, pp. 129 ff.; on the prophetic dream see also below ch. 7.

alongside ordinary revelatory dreams—that is, dreams in which the message was not intended for the dreamer himself, but rather for a third party (in the Bible, see Numbers 12:6; Jeremiah 23:25 ff.; 29:8; Zachariah 10:2; etc.).

The two above categories of prophecy now clarify a parallel distinction made in the Bible, especially in legal contexts: "If a prophet arises among you, or a dreamer of a dream, and gives you a sign or a wonder . . ." (Deuteronomy 13:1 ff.). In an incident involving Saul, the Bible is explicit in differentiating between three distinct divinatory methods: "The Lord did not answer him, either by dreams or by Urim or by prophets" (1 Samuel 28:6; and see v. 15).[39] Even Jeremiah regarded the dreamer as a distinct type of prophet (Jeremiah 27:9), though he belittled this medium, contrasting it with "the word of God" and associating it with false prophets: "Let the prophet who has a dream tell the dream, but let him who has my word speak my word faithfully. What has straw in common with wheat?" (Jeremiah 23:28). This deflated status of the dream as a source of prophetic inspiration also finds clear expression in the Rabbinic dictum comparing sleep to death, just as "a dream is a withered prophecy" (*nōḇelet nᵉḇūʾāh ḥᵃlōm*; Genesis Rabba 44:17).

The Mari letters reporting dream-revelations are usually structured on a regular scheme: (1) the male or female dreamer; (2) the opening formula of the dream—"(I saw) in my dream" (*ina šuttīya*—an obviously West Semitic form identical with Biblical Hebrew *baḥᵃlōmī*; cf. Genesis 40:9, 16; 41:17);[40] (3) the content of the dream, based on a visual or, more often, an auditory "experience"; and finally, (4) the communicator's comments, in many cases including a statement that a lock of the prophet/prophetess's hair and a piece of the hem of his/her garment are being sent to the king as well.

In one illuminating incident at Mari, where the same dream recurred on two successive nights, the dreamer was a mere youth (*ṣuḫārum*), to whom a god appeared in a nocturnal vision. The dream was eventually reported to the king by Kibri-Dagan: "Thus he saw

[39] An exact parallel to these three alternative means of inquiring of the deity may be found in the Plague Prayers of the Hittite king Muršili II; see *ANET*, pp. 394b–395a; and Herrmann 1965, pp. 54 f.

[40] The West Semitic form was pointed out by M. Held, apud Craghan 1974, p. 43, n. 32. The standard Akkadian form would be *ina šuttim ša āmuru/aṭṭulu*; compare a similar West Semitic usage in one of the first prophecies published: *ina pānīya*, lit. "in front of me", meaning "on my way"; see Malamat 1956, p. 81.

(a vision) as follows: 'Build not this house . . .; if that house will be built I will make it collapse into the river!' On the day he saw that dream he did not tell (it) to anyone. On the second day he saw again the dream as follows: 'It was a god (saying): "Build not this house; if you will build it, I will make it collapse into the river!"' Now, herewith the hem of his garment and a lock of hair of his head I have sent to my lord . . ." (*ARMT* XIII 112:1'–15'). The boy, who apparently had no previous prophetic experience, did not at first realize the source of his dream; only when it recurred the next night did he become aware of its divine origin and of the mission imposed upon him. This immediately calls to mind young Samuel's initial prophetic experience, while reposing in the temple at Shiloh (1 Samuel 3:3 ff.). The Lord informed him, in a nocturnal vision, of the impending demise of the Elide clan. In Samuel's case, it was only after the fourth beckoning (though on the same night) that he comprehended the divine nature of the vision (see below ch. 7, p. 99).[41]

In general, novice and inexperienced prophets were unable to identify divine revelations when first encountered (as in the case of Samuel; see 1 Samuel 3:7). Hence we find the repetition of the manifestation, both at Mari and in the Bible. Jeremiah's initial call is also most illuminating: he too was reluctant to accept his prophetic calling, pleading youthfulness (Jeremiah 1:6–7). After bolstering the youth's confidence, God tested him by a vision: "And the word of the Lord came to me saying: 'Jeremiah, what do you see?', and I said: 'I see a rod of almond (Hebrew: *šāqēd*).' Then the Lord said to me: 'You have seen well for I am watching (*šōqēd*) over my word to perform it'" (Jeremiah 1:11–12). God, in his response, expressly confirmed the reliability of the prophet's perception—a totally unique event in the realm of prophetic vision in the Bible—and thus proving Jeremiah's fitness to undertake his prophetic mission.[42]

---

[41] See Malamat 1980, pp. 223 ff.; and Gnuse 1984, esp. pp. 119 ff. The phenomenon of an identical dream recurring several times is known especially from the Classical world; see Hanson 1978, p. 1411, and the passages from Cicero, *De divinatione*, cited there.

[42] See Malamat 1954, esp. pp. 39–40.

Prophetic Credibility

In a relatively recently published "prophetic" text from Mari (A. 222),[43] the name of the writer has been lost, as has the name of the recipient (who was probably Zimri-Lim, recipient of the other letters). We read:

> The woman Ayala saw (*iṭṭul*) in her dream as follows:
>
> > A woman from Šeḫrum (and) a woman from Mari in the gate of (the temple of) Annunītum . . ./line missing/which is at the edge of the city—quarrelled among themselves. Thus (said) the woman from Šeḫrum to the woman from Mari: "Return to me my *position as high priestess* (the vocable *enūtum* may refer instead to 'equipment'); either you sit or I myself shall sit.
>
> By the *ḫurru*-bird I have examined this matter and she could see (*naṭlat*) (the dream). Now her hair and the hem of the garment I am sending along. May my lord investigate the matter!"

The nature of the dispute between these two women is not entirely clear although it may involve rivalry over the office of the high priestess. The penultimate passage relates that the writer confirmed the validity of the vision by means of augury. This divinatory device, well known in the classical world, appeared at a very early period in Hither Asia.[44] In this instance, the examination 'proved' that the woman actually did see (*naṭlat*), that is, she actually did see the vision she claimed to have seen. Inasmuch as the verb *amāru*, "to see (a dream)", is synonymous and interchangeable with *naṭālu*, the intention here seems to be that the woman was indeed competent and experienced in the art of dream oracles.[45] Thus, the meaning is precisely as the editor of the text translated: "Elle a bien eu ce songe!"—just like God's words to Jeremiah: "You have seen well" (*hēṭab̲tā lir'ōt*)!

---

[43] The document was published by Dossin 1975 (attributed by him to King Yaḫdun-Lim!); and see the comments in Sasson 1983, p. 291. The latter's interpretation of *enūtum* (see below) as "utensils" rather than "priesthood" is generally preferred.

[44] Divination by bird behaviour is a typically western practice; cf. Oppenheim 1964, pp. 209–210. This practice was especially widespread among the Hittites; see Kammenhuber 1976, who deals only briefly (p. 11) with the kind of bird mentioned in our text: *MUŠEN ḪURRI*; for this bird, see Salonen 1973, pp. 143–146; and cf. McEwan 1980 and now Durand 1997b, pp. 273 ff.

[45] See *CAD* A/2, s.v. *amāru* A 2, p. 13: to learn by experience (especially stative . . .). The stative form with the meaning "experienced, trained" is particularly prevalent in the Mari idiom, and we may therefore assume a similar nuance for the stative of *naṭālu: naṭlat* in our document.

The writer did not suffice with his own examination of the dream, and sent the woman's hair and the hem of her garment to the king—for his examination.

This unique and somewhat puzzling practice, attested only in connection with the Mari prophets, is mentioned on nine different occasions; that is, in a third of all the "prophetic" letters. Several scholarly interpretations have been offered, all of which remain in the realm of speculation. This procedure was clearly related in some manner to the reliability of the diviner and of his message. In most of the cases, the prophet's words were presented to the king only as recommendations, the final decision to act upon them remaining in his hands: "Let my lord do what pleases him"; "Let my lord do what, in accordance with his deliberation, pleases him." (In this matter, these prophecies decidedly differ from biblical prophecy, which is absolute and "non-negotiable".) Several points should be noted in this context.

The lock of hair and the hem of the garment are unequivocally personal objects,[46] specific to their individual owners, and seem to have served as a sort of "identity card". In the Bible, we read how David took the fringe of Saul's robe in the cave near En-Gedi (1 Samuel 24, espec. v. 4), in order to show him that Saul had been entirely at his mercy. In other words, the Mari procedure may primarily have had a legal significance, more than a religio-magic meaning, as often suggested. These personal items may also have been sent to the king in order to serve as evidence for the very existence of a diviner, and that the message was not simply a fabrication of the reporting official, who may have had some particular motive for promoting a false report.[47] Surely *fraus pia*, "pious fraud", was no

[46] For the hair (or lock of hair—*šārtum*) and the hem of a garment (*sissiktum*) see Liverani 1977; Malul 1986; the latter suggests that not merely the hem but the entire garment (or rather, undergarment, covering the private parts) was involved; and see n. 47, below.

[47] Malamat 1956, pp. 81, 84; Malamat 1966a, pp. 225 ff. and notes. For other explanations, see Uffenheimer 1973, pp. 29–33; Ellermeier 1968; Moran 1969, pp. 19–22; Noort 1977, p. 83–86; and Craghan 1974, pp. 53 ff. Note in two documents (A. 455:25; and *ARMT* X 81:18) the illuminating but problematic addition appearing after the report on the despatch of the hair and the hem; in the latter: "let them declare (me) clean (*lizakkû*)"; according to Moran 1969a, pp. 22–23: ". . . it is the haruspex who 'tries the case' and it is his response that will in effect declare the prophetess clean." And cf. *ARMT* X, p. 267, *ad loc.*; Noort 1977, pp. 85–86. See Dalley *et al.*, 1976, pp. 64–65, No. 65—for initial evidence for an identical procedure outside Mari (at Tell al-Rimaḥ).

rarer in that period than it was later. This aspect also emerges from a long text (A. 15) in which the writer specifically states of a dreamer-prophet: "since this man was trustworthy, I did not take any of his hair or the fringe of his garment."[48]

The credibility of prophetic revelation was obviously a sensitive matter, not to be taken for granted. Thus it was often verified and confirmed by the accepted mantic devices, considered more reliable means than intuitive prophecy *per se*.[49] Alongside the obscure practice of sending the hem of a garment and a lock of the dreamer-prophet, we encounter the following features: Šibtu wrote to Zimri-Lim that she personally examined a prophet's message, prior to sending it on to him, and found the report to be trustworthy (*ARMT* X 6). In another letter, a lady of the royal household reported a vision, and advised the king: "Let my lord have the haruspex look into the matter . . ." (*ARMT* X 94). In a third letter, a woman implores the king to verify the vision of an *āpiltum* by divinatory means (*ARMT* X 81); the same woman advises the king, following the prophecy of a *qammātum* (see above, p. 85), to be alert and not to enter the city without inquiring of the omens (*ARMT* X 80).

In contrast, in Israel the prophetic word—whether accepted or rejected by the king or the people—was never subjected to corroboration by mantic means, but was vindicated by the test of fulfilment (cf. Deuteronomy 18:21–22; Ezekiel 33:33).

In sum, the problem of reliability existed wherever intuitive prophecy flourished. It concerned the Mari authorities no less than the biblical lawmakers and "true" prophets, from Moses to Jeremiah—all of whom sought a yardstick for measuring prophetic authenticity. In the words of one expert: "The prophets who preceded you and me from ancient times prophesied war, famine and pestilence against many countries and great kingdoms. As for the prophet who prophesies peace, when the word of that prophet comes to pass, then it will be known that the Lord has truly sent the prophet" (Jeremiah 28:8–9).

---

[48] Dossin 1948, p. 132; in l. 53 we read (with Oppenheim 1956, p. 195, and 1952, p. 134): *ták-lu*, "trustworthy" (rather than Dossin's *kal-lu*, a kind of official).

[49] Moran 1969a, pp. 22–23; Craghan 1974, pp. 41–42; and Saggs 1978, p. 141.

Bibliography

Anbar, M., (1975). "Aspect moral dans un discours 'prophétique' de Mari", *UF* 7, pp. 517–518.

——, (1981). in "Notes brèves", *RA* 75, p. 91.

Blenkinsopp, J., (1983). *A History of Prophecy in Israel*, Philadelphia.

Bottéro, J., (1974). In J.P. Vernant, *et al., Divination et Rationalité*, Paris, pp. 70–197.

Buber, M., (1950). *Der Glaube der Propheten*, Zürich.

Caquot, A. & Lemaire, A., (1977). "Les textes araméens de Deir 'Alla", *Syria* 54, pp. 189–208.

Charpin, D., (1985). "Les archives du devin Asqudum dans la résidence du chantier A", *MARI* 4, pp. 453–462.

Charpin, D. & Durand, J.-M., (1985). "La prise du pouvoir par Zimri-Lim", *MARI* 4, pp. 293–343.

——, (1986). "'Fils de Sim'al': Les origines tribales des rois de Mari", *RA* 80, pp. 141–183.

Cagni, L., (1995). *Le profezie di Mari*, Brescia.

Cody, A., (1979). "The Phoenician Ecstatic in Wenamun", *JEA* 65, pp. 99–106.

Craghan, J.F., (1974). "The *ARM* X 'Prophetic' Texts: Their Media, Style and Structure", *JANES* 6, pp. 39–57.

Daiches, S., (1909). "Balaam—A Babylonian *barû*", in *Assyrian and Archaeological Studies* (*H.V. Hilprecht Anniversary Volume*), Leipzig, pp. 60–70.

Dalley, S. *et al.*, (1976). *The Old Babylonian Tablets from Tell al Rimah*, Hertford.

Dietrich, W. *et al.*, (1976). (with Loretz, O. & Sanmartin, J.), *Die Keilalphabetischen Texte aus Ugarit*, Neukirchen-Vluyn.

Dossin, G., (1948). "Une révélation du dieu Dagan de Terqa", *RA* 42, pp. 125–134.

——, (1966). "Sur le prophétism à Mari", in *La divination en Mésopotamie ancienne*, Paris, pp. 77–86.

——, (1975). "Le songe d'Ayala", *RA* 69, pp. 28–30.

Durand, J.-M., (1982). "In vino veritas", *RA* 76, pp. 43–50.

——, (1984). "Trois études sur Mari", *MARI* 3, pp. 127–180.

——, (1988). *ARMT* XXVI/1, Paris (See List of *Archives Royales de Mari*, p. 240).

——, (1997a). "Les prophéties des textes de Mari", in J.G. Heintz (ed.), *Oracles et prophéties dans l'antiquité*, Strasbourg.

——, (1997b). "La divination par les oiseaux," *MARI* 8, Paris, pp. 273–282.

Ellermeier, F., (1968). *Prophetie in Mari und Israel*, Herzberg.

Ellis, M. De Jong, (1987). "The Goddess Kititum Speaks to King Ibalpiel: Oracle Texts from Ishchali", *MARI* 5, pp. 235–257.

Finet, A., (1982). "Un cas de clédonomancie à Mari", in G. van Driel *et al.* (eds.) *Zikir Šumim* (F.R. Kraus Festschrift), Leiden, pp. 48–55.

Fleming, D., (1993). "Two New Syrian Religious Personnel", *JAOS* 113 (1993), pp. 175–183.

Fronzaroli, P., (1997). "Les combats de Hadda dans les textes d'Ebla", *MARI* 8 (1997), pp. 283–290.

Gibson, McG. & Biggs, R.D. (eds.), (1977). *Seals and Sealing in the Ancient Near East*, Malibu, Calif.

Gnuse, R.K., (1984). *The Dream Theophany of Samuel*, Lanham, N.Y.

——, (1996). *Dreams and Dream Reports in the Writing of Josephus*, Leiden, pp. 34–100.

Hackett, J.A., (1984). *The Balaam Text from Deir 'Alla* (Harvard Semitic Monographs 31), Chico, Calif.

Hanson, J.S., (1978). "Dreams and Visions in the Graeco-Roman World and Early Christianity", in H. Temporini & W. Haase (eds.), *Aufstieg und Niedergang der Römischen Welt* II, 23/2, Berlin.

Haran, M., (1977). "From Early to Classical Prophecy: Continuity and Change", *VT* 27, pp. 385–397.
Hecker, K., (1986). Assyrische Prophetien, in *TUAT* II/1, pp. 56 ff.
Heintz, J.G. (ed.), (1997). *Oracles et Prophéties dans l'Antiquité*, Strasbourg.
Helck, W., (1971). *Die Beziehungen Ägyptens zu Vorderasien im 3. Und 2. Jartausend v. Chr.*, Wiesbaden.
Herrmann, S., (1965). *Die prophetischen Heilserwartungen im Alten Testament*, Stuttgart.
Hoftijzer, J. & Van der Kooij, G., (1976). *Aramaic Texts from Deir 'Alla*, Leiden.
Holma, H., (1914). *Die assyrisch-babylonischen Personennamen der Form quṭṭulu*, Helsingfors.
Hölscher, G., (1914). *Die Profeten*, Leipzig.
Hossfeld, F.L. & Meyer, I.L., (1973). *Prophet gegen Prophet*, Fribourg/Göttingen.
Huffmon, H.B., (1970). "Prophecy in the Mari Letters", *BA Reader* III, Garden City, N.Y., pp. 199–224.
——, (1992). "Ancient Near Eastern Prophecy", *The Anchor Bible Dictionary*, vol. 5, New York, pp. 477–482.
——, (1997). "The Expansion of Prophecy in the Mari Archives . . .", in ed. Y. Gitai, *Prophecy-Prophets* (SBL Scholars Press), Atlanta, GA, pp. 7–22.
Kammenhuber, A., (1967). "Die hethitische und hurrische Überlieferung zum 'Gilgameš Epos'", *Münchener Studien zur Sprachwissenschaft* 21, pp. 45–58.
Kraus, F.R., (1984). *Königliche Verfügungen in altbabylonischer Zeit*, Leiden.
Lafont, B., (1984). "Le roi de Mari et les prophètes du dieu Adad", *RA* 78, pp. 7–18.
Landsberger, B., (1915). Review of H. Holma, *Die assyrisch-babylonischen Personennamen der Form quṭṭulu*, *GGA* 117, pp. 363–366.
Lemaire, A., (1996). "Les textes prophétiques de Mari dans leur relations avec l'ouest", *Amurru* I, Paris.
Lindblom, J., (1962). *Prophecy in Ancient Israel*, Oxford.
Liverani, M., (1973). "The Amorites", in D.J. Wiseman (ed.), *Peoples of Old Testament Times*, Oxford, pp. 100–133.
Malamat, A., (1956). "Prophecy in the Mari Documents", *EI* 4, pp. 74–84 (Hebrew; English summary, pp. VI–VII).
——, (1958). "History and Prophetic Vision in a Mari letter", *EI* 5, pp. 67–73 (Hebrew; English summary, pp. 86*–87*).
——, (1966). "Prophetic Revelations in New Documents from Mari and the Bible", *SVT* 15, pp. 207–227 (see in present volume ch. 7).
——, (1980). "A Mari Prophecy and Nathan's Dynastic Oracle", in J. Emerton (ed.), *Prophecy—Essays G. Fohrer*, Berlin-New York, pp. 68–82 (see in present volume ch. 9).
——, (1987). "A Forerunner of Biblical Prophecy: The Mari Documents", in P.D. Miller, P.D. Hanson, S. Dean McBride (eds.), *Ancient Israelite Religion, Essays in honor of F.M. Cross*, Philadelphia, pp. 33–52.
——, (1989). (pb. edition 1992). *Mari and the Early Israelite Experience* (The Schweich Lectures, 1984), The British Academy, London-Oxford.
Malul, M., (1986). "'Sissiktu' and 'sikku'—Their Meaning and Functions", *BiOr* 43, pp. 20–36.
Margueron, J.C., (1982). "Rapport préliminaire sur la campagne de 1979", *MARI* 1, pp. 9–30.
——, (1983). "Rapport préliminaire sur la campagne de 1980", *MARI* 2, pp. 9–35.
——, (1984). "Rapport préliminaire sur la campagne de 1982", *MARI* 3, pp. 7–39.
McCarter, P.K., (1980). "The Balaam Texts from Deir 'Alla: The First Combination", *BASOR* 239, pp. 49–60.
Moran, W.L., (1969a). "New Evidence from Mari on the History of Prophecy", *Biblica* 50, pp. 15–56.
——, (1969b). "Akkadian Letters", *ANET* 3rd ed., pp. 623–632.
Nakata, I., (1982a). "Two Remarks on the So-called Prophetic Texts from Mari", *Acta Sumerologica* 4, pp. 143–148.

——, (1982b). Rezension zu: Noort, Edward, *Untersuchungen zum Gottesbescheid in Mari* (*AOAT* 202), 1977, *JAOS* 102, pp. 166–168.
Noort, E., (1977). *Untersuchungen zum Gottesbescheid in Mari* (*AOAT* 202), Neukirchen-Vluyn.
Oppenheim, A.L., (1956). *The Interpretation of Dreams in the Ancient Near East* (*Transactions of the American Philosophical Society* 46), Philadelphia.
Parker, S.B., (1993). "Official Attitudes toward Prophecy at Mari and in Israel", *VT* 43, pp. 50–68.
Parpola, S., (1983). *Letters from Assyrian Scholars to the Kings Esarhaddon and Assurbanipal II* (*AOAT* 5/2), Neukirchen-Vluyn, pp. 486–491.
—— (forthcoming). *Assyrian Prophecies* (*SAA* 9), Helsinki.
Petersen, D.L., (1981). *The Roles of Israel's Prophets*, Sheffield.
Rofé, A., (1979). *The Book of Balaam*, Jerusalem (Hebrew).
Ross, J., (1970). "Prophecy in Hamath, Israel and Mari", *HTR* 63, pp. 1–28.
Sasson, J.M., (1980). "Two Recent Works on Mari", *AfO* 27, pp. 127–135.
Schmitt, A., (1982). *Prophetischer Gottesbescheid in Mari und Israel*, Stuttgart.
Starr, I., (1983). *The Ritual of the Diviner* (Bibliotheca Mesopotamica 12), Malibu, Calif.
Van der Toorn, K., (1987). "L'oracle de victoire comme expression prophétique au Proche Orient ancien", *RB* 94, pp. 63–97.
Uffenheimer, B., (1973). *Early Israelite Prophecy*, Jerusalem (Hebrew).
De Vries, S., (1978). *Prophet against Prophet*, Grand Rapids, Mich.
Weinfeld, M., (1977). "Ancient Near Eastern Patterns in Prophetic Literature", *VT* 27, pp. 178–195.
Weippert, M., (1981). "Assyrische Prophetien der Zeit Asarhaddons und Assurbanipals", in F.M. Fales (ed.), *Assyrian Royal Inscriptions: New Horizons* (*OAC* 17), Rome, pp. 71–115.
——, (1985). "Die Bildsprache der neuassyrischen Prophetie", in H. Weippert *et al.* (eds.), *Beiträge zur prophetischen Bildsprache in Israel und Assyrien*, Fribourg & Göttingen, pp. 55–93.
—— & Weippert, H., (1982). "Die 'Bileam' Inschrift von Tell Der 'Alla", *ZDPV* 98, pp. 77–103.
Wilcke, C., (1983). "*ittāttim ašqi aštāl*: Medien in Mari?", *RA* 77, pp. 93 f.
Wilson, R.R., (1980). *Prophecy and Society in Ancient Israel*, Philadelphia.

PROPHETIC REVELATIONS IN MARI AND THE BIBLE: COMPLEMENTARY CONSIDERATIONS*

The greatest relevance and most promising results in a comparative study of the Mari documents and the Bible are inherent in the research of the nature of the tribal societies and their institutions.[1] Unquestionably, such a study may also render a considerable contribution in the realm of religious manifestations and ritual practice. Light has already been shed on such aspects as the covenant-making ceremony, the ban-enforcement as penalty for transgression and the more controversial concept of census-taking and ritual expiation.[2]

---

* The following abbreviations are used here:

** This article was originally published in: *Supplements to Vetus Testamentum*, 20 (1966), pp. 207–227 (under a slightly different title). A few paragraphs (their contents already dealt with in ch. 6) have been deleted.

AHw—W. von Soden, *Akkadisches Handwörterbuch*, I, Wiesbaden 1965.

ANEP—J.B. Pritchard, *The Ancient Near East in Pictures*, Princeton 1954.

ANET—J.B. Pritchard, ed., *Ancient Near Eastern Texts* etc.^{2}, Princeton 1955.

ARM—*Archives royales de Mari* (publiées sous la direction de A. Parrot et G. Dossin), Paris.

EI IV—A. Malamat, "Prophecy in the Mari Documents", *Eretz-Israel* (Archaeological, Historical and Geographical Studies), Vol. IV, Jerusalem 1956, pp. 74–84 (in Hebrew; English summary pp. VI f.).

EI V—A. Malamat, "History and Prophetic Vision in a Mari Letter", *Eretz-Israel*, Vol. V, 1958, pp. 67–73 (Hebrew; Eng. summary pp. 86* f.).

RA XLII—G. Dossin, "Une révélation du dieu Dagan à Terqa", *Revue d'Assyriologie* XLII, 1948, pp. 125–134.

Robinson Volume—G. Dossin, apud A. Lods, "Une tablette inédite de Mari, intéressante pour l'historie ancienne du prophétisme sémitique", *Studies in Old Testament Prophecy Presented to Th.H. Robinson*, Edinburgh 1950, pp. 103–107.

[1] A. Malamat, "Mari and the Bible: Some Patterns of Tribal Organization and Institutions", *JAOS* LXXXII, 1962, pp. 143 ff. and now *MEIE*, pp. 27–52; cf. P. Fronzaroli, "L'ordinamento gentilizio semitico e i testi di Mari", *Arch. Glott. Ital.* XLV, 1960, pp. 1 ff.

[2] See the respective studies of M. Noth, "Das alttest. Bundschliessen im Lichte eines Mari-Textes", *Gesammelte Studien zum Alten Testament*. München 1957, pp. 142 ff.; A. Malamat, "The Ban in Mari and in the Bible", *Biblical Essays—Proceedings of the 9th Meeting of Die Ou-Testamentiese Werkgemeenskap in Suid Africa*, 1967, pp. 40–49; E.A. Speiser, "Census and Ritual Expiation in Mari and Israel", *BASOR* CXLIX, 1958, pp. 17 ff. and for a contrasting view *Chicago Assyrian Dictionary*, Vol. IV, p. 6 (s.v. *ebēbu*).

One of the most remarkable disclosures of the Mari documents in the sphere of religious phenomena is the occurrence of intuitive divination which places Near Eastern prophecy in general and biblical prophecy in particular in a new perspective. This type of divination, which existed in Mari alongside the standard mantic practices prevalent throughout Mesopotamia, did not entail the operation of magical and oracular techniques; rather was it manifested in the experience of god's revelation. Unlike the usual run of priests and sorcerers, and especially the *bārû*, the expert in haruspicy,[3] who in the service of the court made their demands on the deity, the diviner-prophets of Mari were inbued with the consciousness of mission and took their stand before the authorities in a spontaneous manner and upon the initiative of their god.

It is these particular characteristics which have brought the diviner of Mari into greater proximity to the Israelite prophet[4] than any other divinatory manifestation in existence in the ancient Near East. Yet the all-too obvious gap is apparent in the essence of the prophetic message and in the destiny assigned to the prophet's mission. The Mari prophetic utterances have nothing comparable to the socio-ethical pathos or religious ideology, nor any semblance of national purpose, which distinguish biblical prophecy. In contrast the Mari oracle limits his address to the sovereign or to his representatives as individuals and more often than not voices demands of a material nature and of an unmistakable local patriotism. This apparent ideological abyss notwithstanding,[5] the utmost import is to be attributed

---

[3] For the cultic functionaries in Mesopotamia and their various techniques of divination see most recently A.L. Oppenheim, *Ancient Mesopotamia*, Chicago 1964, pp. 206 ff. Acceptance of the *bārû*, a man of learning and professional skill, as a kind of prophet or seer, as still maintained in various studies, is thoroughly unjustified. See, e.g., A. Haldar, *Associations of Cult Prophets among the Ancient Semites*, Uppsala 1945, pp. 1 ff. (and literature there.)

[4] In this respect no distinction should be made between the early ("primitive") and the late ("classical") prophets in Israel, a distinction which as such has been highly overrated ever since G. Hölscher's, Die Profeten, Leipzig 1914. See J. Lindblom, *Prophecy in Ancient Israel*, Oxford 1962, pp. 47, 105 ff.

[5] Considering the parallel features of biblical and ancient Near Eastern prophecy, Yehezkel Kaufmann emphasized the far greater significance of the former in the religion of Israel compared to the ephemeral role played by prophecy in any one of the pagan religions. See his *The Religion of Israel*, translated and abridged by M. Greenberg, Chicago 1960, pp. 212 ff. On the other hand, he underestimated the relevant importance of the Mari material, for it can no longer be maintained that "apostolic prophecy is an Israelite creation" and "was limited to the people of Israel" (pp. 214 f.).

to the phenomenon of intuitive divination and the very existence of the prophetic emissary among West Semitic tribes predating the Israelite prophets by centuries, despite the impossibility to determine the precise circumstances of this analogy.

Some regard the prophetic phenomenon as characteristic of the western cultural sphere extending across Palestine, Syria and as far as Asia Minor.[6] This viewpoint is based primarily on the existence of ecstatic prophecy which, in addition to the Bible, is attested sporadically throughout this region by such occurrences as a person obsessed by god in Hittite sources, a prophet in Byblos in the Egyptian tale of Wen-Amon and ecstatic personages in Syria described by classical writers.[7] Yet without attempting to divest Mari or Israelite prophecy of any ecstatic features, primacy must be given here to the sense of mission. Herein lies the actual validity and potency of this analogy above all others as seen from a phenomenological aspect.[8] Moreover, considering that the greater part of the population depicted in the Mari documents was closely related (ethnically and in semi-nomadic existence to Israel's ancestors) and that divine revelation is but one of various points of contact between Mari and Israel, is it not reasonable to assume a rather close relationship between these parallel manifestations? Granted this, prophecy in Mari apparently reflects the early budding of the later, brilliant prophetic flowering in Israel.

Six documents from Mari published between 1948–1954,[9] devoted to the appearance of diviners, have been under discussion by various

---

[6] See, e.g. Oppenheim, *op. cit.*, pp. 221 f., who points to the contrast of the god-man relationship in general between the western (including late Assyria) and the eastern (i.e. Mesopotamia proper) approach.

[7] On the ecstatic in Hittite documents, called *šiunianza*, see A. Goetze, *Kleinasien* (Kulturgeschichte des Alten Orients)^2, München 1957, p. 147. The plea for ecstatic divination as a universal phenomenon, not restricted to regional or ethnic boundaries, is made by J. Lindblom, "Zur Frage des kanaanäischen Ursprungs des altisrael. Prophetismus", *Von Ugarit nach Qumran* (*Festschrift O. Eissfeldt*), Berlin 1958, pp. 89 ff. and cf. now the first chapter of his book *Prophecy in Ancient Israel.*

[8] Cf. R. Rendtorff, "Erwägungen zur Frühgeschichte des Prophetentum in Israel", *ZThK* LIX, 1962, pp. 145 ff. and the studies on Mari prophecy mentioned below n. 10. The very existence of the Mari material, as is justly alluded to by the above author, tends to negate the oft-accepted assumption of the Canaanite origin of Israelite prophecy. This is further corroborated by the total absence of the prophetic phenomenon in the Ugaritic texts; for this see J. Gray, *The Legacy of Canaan*^{2}, Leiden 1965, p. 217. Yet Israelite prophecy may still have absorbed certain Canaanite features during its early stages.

[9] *RA* XLII, pp. 128–32; *Robinson Volume*, pp. 103–06; *ARM* II 40; III 40; 78; VI 45.

scholars, with due attention paid to biblical prophecy, including two studies in Hebrew by the present writer.[10] The documents consist of letters sent to Zimrilim, the last ruler of Mari, by his officials of high rank and legates. The diviners appear as emissaries of Dagan, deity of Terqa, of Adad, patron god of Kallasu, generally located in the vicinity of Aleppo, and the god Adad, of Aleppo proper (see ch. 9 below).[11] Save for one instance where the god reveals his message to a person by means of a dream (*RA* XLII), the subjects of the divine mission (including females as well) bear the specific title of diviner-prophet.

Two Akkadian terms, *muḫḫûm* (fem. *muḫḫūtum*) and *āpilum* (fem. *āpiltum*), are employed to designate the diviners, though a clear delineation of character of the two types is denied us because of paucity of material at hand. The former term, derived from a root meaning "to rave, to become frenzied", has long since become familiar to us in the form *maḫḫû(m)* as a temple functionary of possible ecstatic nature and inferior social status.[12] Mari usage, however, is restricted to the spelling *muḫḫûm*, a nominal pattern denoting some defect.[13] It

---

[10] *EI* IV, pp. 74–84; *EI* V, pp. 67–73 (this study dealing with the letter in the *Robinson Volume*, the former with the remaining five documents). For earlier studies (excluding *ARM* VI 45 published in 1954) note: M. Noth, "Geschichte und Gotteswort im Alten Testament", *Bonner Akad. Reden* III, 1949, repr. Gesammelte Studien zum A.T., pp. 230 ff.; W. von Soden, "Verkündung des Gotteswillens durch prophetisches Wort in den altbabyl. Briefen aus Mari", *WO* I, 1950, pp. 397 ff.; H. Schmökel, "Gotteswort in Mari und Israel", *ThLS* LXXVI, 1951, pp. 53 ff.; F.M. Th.de Liagre Böhl, "Prophetentum und stellvertretendes Leiden in Assyrien und Israel", *Opera Minora*, Groningen-Djakarta 1953, pp. 63 ff., also N.H. Ridderbos, *Israels Profetie en "Profetie" buiten Israel*, Den Haag 1955, pp. 14 ff., C. Westermann, "Die Mari-Briefe und die Prophetie in Israel", *Forschung am Alten Testament*, München 1964, pp. 171 ff. and cf. the bibliographical notes of G. Fohrer, *ThR*, N.F., XXVIII, 1962, pp. 306 f. Add the literature in ch. 6, n. 2.

[11] On this deity and his rise to prominence in the wake of West Semitic infiltration into Syria see now H. Klengel, "Der Wettergott von Ḫalab", *JCS* XIX, 1965, pp. 87 ff. In *EI* V, p. 70 and n. 5, I suggested the identification of Kallasu with a village of the same name mentioned in the census lists of Alalah, an identification now questioned by Klengel (p. 89). But, if the city of Alahtum (desired by Adad of Kallasu; cf. ch. 9) is actually to be identified with Alalah (as Durand now suggests) than our initial proposal is strengthened.

[12] On *maḫḫû* see S. Langdon, *JRAS*, 1932, pp. 391 f.; Haldar, *Associations of Cult Prophets*, pp. 21 ff.; V. Christian, *WZKM* LIV, 1957, pp. 9 f.

[13] For references see *ARM* XV, s.v. *muḫḫûm*: add *ARM* VI 45: 9, 15 (fem. forms). The term occurs also in a Mari ritual of the goddess Ishtar, G. Dossin, *RA* XXXV, 1938, pp. 6 (l. 22), 8 (l. 36). The same spelling is found in a Neo Assyrian vocabulary (E.F. Weidner *AfO* XI, 1936–37, p. 357, l. 20) and in an Old Babylonian lexical list of social classes (OB Lú A 23 f. = B 25 f.). The spelling *muḫḫûm* is not a phonetic variant of *maḫḫûm* (as assumed by von Soden, *WO* I, p. 400), but rather

is similar both in connotation and form to the Hebrew word *m^{e}šugga*ʿ, "possessed, mad", which in some biblical instances is applied as a synonym for prophet (II Kings ix 11; Jer. xxix 26; Hos. ix 7). It is worth noting that the person obsessed by the deity was often regarded as mad, owing to his eccentric and abnormal behaviour. Autosuggestion or even ecstatic stimulation (though there is no specific reference to this in Mari) rather than an innate disturbance, may well have accounted for such conduct. Evidence to this effect is to be found in the sober, purposeful statements of the *muḫḫûm* (and Israelite prophets) wherever they are transmitted in the documents.

While the mantic personage alluded to is closely akin to the *maḫḫû*, frequently mentioned in Akkadian sources, the *āpilum*, on the other hand, is intrinsic to the world of Mari and scarcely known outside it.[14] Recurrent reference to the latter is found in the epistle sent to Mari from the Aleppo area in northern Syria (*Robinson Volume*). In one of these references, in connection with the proclamation of the divine message, the title occurs in the plural (l. 24: *awīlē*^{meš}*āpilū*), indicating that these diviners acted in groups as well, similar to the prophetic band or coterie known from the Bible (1 Sam. x 5; xix 20; 1 Kings xx 35 ff.). In contrast, the *muḫḫûm*, in accordance with evidence available so far, always functions alone. The same letter tells of one *āpilum* engaged in the cultic framework of Adad of Kallasu, thus ranking him as a cult-prophet.[15] Another is mentioned as emissary of Adad of Aleppo, with a further reference to male and female visionaries of this category in Mari proper (ll. 29 f.; 41).

The latter fact is further corroborated in an administrative document from the Mari archives, listing, among others, an *āpilum* as

---

the form *quttul*, designating a (bodily) defect. For the form *quttul* (or *purrus*), corresponding to Hebrew *qiṭṭel*, in this sense see H. Holma, *Die assyrisch-babylonischen Personennamen der Form quttulu*, Helsinki 1914 (especially p. 8, citing an opinion by Landsberger and the latter's recension of Holma's book, *GGA* CXVII [1915], pp. 363–366). (Cf. above ch. 6, pp. 66 f.).

[14] *AHw*, p. 58, s.v. *āpilum*. With the exception of Mari only one true citation is recorded there (nos. 2 and 3 are irrelevant); for it see p. 212, n. 1.

[15] The activity of the *āpilum* centers around a sanctuary, possibly a tent-shrine (*maškānum*), *Robinson Volume*, ll. 26–28, 37–38; cf. *EI* V, pp. 69, 73 and below ch. 9.

Bible scholars, adherents of the still controversial "cult prophecy" school, might see in such affiliation of the *āpilum* yet another characteristic feature of early Hebrew prophets. On cult prophecy in Israel see especially S. Mowinckel, *Psalmenstudien* III: *Kultprophetie und prophetische Psalmen*, Kristiania 1923, pp. 14 ff.; Haldar, *Associations of Cult Prophets* (extremist in views); A.R. Johnson, *The Cultic Prophet in Ancient Israel*^{2}, Cardiff 1962, and the survey by H.H. Rowley, "Ritual and the Hebrew Prophets", *From Moses to Qumran*, London 1963, pp. 111 ff.

having received vestments from the royal court (*ARM* IX 22:14). This recourse of the *āpilum* to the royal palace is of considerable interest, although it does not bear out his direct access to the king, which is actually indicated in a source other than Mari.[16] In any event, this evidence brings the *āpilum* into greater proximity to the court prophets in the class of Nathan and Gad of David's entourage, or the Baal and Ashera prophets of Ahab. For the *muḫḫûm*, on the other hand, no direct contact with the palace is as yet attested.

One of the "prophetic" texts from Mari (*ARM* XIII 23) refers to a diviner spelled *a-ap-lu-ú-um* (*aplûm*) which may be another form for *āpilum*, Akkadian for "he who responds, respondent" (from *apālum*, "to respond"). On the other hand this new form is closer to terms denoting cultic or diviner personnel recorded in various lexical lists, appearing there in turn as quasi-synonyms for *maḫḫû* and *muḫḫû*(*m*).[17] If, indeed, the appellative *āpilum/aplûm* was derived from the Akkadian verb "to answer, to respond", then the title, as in the case of *muḫḫûm*, recalls biblical terminology pertinent to prophecy, as exemplified by the verb *ʿnh* and its derivatives.

The verb *ʿnh*, "to answer, to respond", is used repeatedly in the Bible for the response by God to an appeal by a prophet, or by any individual for that matter (1 Sam. xxviii 6 et *passim*). It is in turn employed by prophets entreating the deity for a divine sign or message as in the encounter of Elijah with the prophets of Baal on Mount Carmel, where both disputants appeal to the respective deities with the same formula "*Respond* to me, O Lord; *respond to me*"; "O Baal, *respond* to us" (1 Kings xviii 37, 26). The failure of the Baal prophets

---

[16] Reference is to an omen-text, *KAR* 460: 16 (cf. *AHw*, *loc. cit.*), where the apodosis reads: "the king will not receive the *āpilum* in his palace", inferring that normally the *āpilum* had access to the palace. It is true that in the "prophetic" documents of Mari the king's agents as a rule acted as intermediaries between the sovereign and the visionaries. Yet this may be coincidental, due to the fact that these documents are part of the royal correspondence between the king and his officials.

[17] For *apillû* and *aplû* designating cultic functionaries see *AHw*, pp. 57 and 58 (s.v. *aplu* II). The former is in addition attested in the lexical series HAR. gud B VI: 135 (published in 2 *R* 51, No. 2 and *CT* XVIII, Pl. 16 [Rm. 360]), where it is listed as the equivalent of the Sumerian term lú.gub.ba. (reference supplied by B. Landsberger). On the other hand this Sumerian term is at times equated with *muḫḫû* (see lexical lists mentioned p. 210 n. 4) and *maḫḫû* (see references Haldar, *Associations of Cult Prophets*, p. 21, n. 3 and in addition the synonym list igituḫ = *tāmartu*, l. 263, cf. B. Landsberger – O.R. Gurney, *AfO* XVIII, 1957–58, p. 84), rendering the latter synonyms of *apillû*. However, it is difficult to determine the correct relationship between the forms *āpilum*, *aplûm* and *apillû*, which cannot be explained merely as differences in spelling.

to elicit any reaction from their god is described in terms of: "But there was no voice, nor any *response* (*ʿōnæ*)" (*ibid.* and cf. Mic. III 7).[18]

These and similar passages illuminate the true nature of the *āpilum*-diviner. Though he may at times have answered questions put to the deity (as did the biblical prophets), his primary function was to proclaim, unbidden by others, the word of god.[19] True, the respondent in the Bible is generally God himself and not his prophet as in Mari; nevertheless, "to respond" is still the undisputed act of the biblical prophet as God's mouthpiece (cf. 1 Sam. xxviii 6, 15; Mic. vi 5 in reference to Balaam's oracles). The actual term "respondent", designating some kind of diviner-prophet, may even occur in the Bible. We refer to the obscure words *ʿēr wᵉʿōnæ*, "he who is aroused and he who responds" in Malachi ii 12, which there are parallel to "him that offers an offering unto the Lord of hosts", thus indicating functionaries associated with divine service.[20]

Owing to the unique character of the prophetic phenomenon in Mari, we may assume that the appellatives *muḫḫûm* and *āpilum* are Akkadian translations of West Semitic terminology, prevalent in the original dialects of the Mari scribes to denote types of diviner-prophets, which were cognates of such Hebrew terms as *nāḇîʾ*, *mᵉšuggaʿ*, *ʿōnæ*. If our conjecture is correct, the question remains why these scribes did not fall back on their original vocabulary, which they had done on other occasions, particularly in the sociological realm.[21] The acceptance

[18] Cf. ch. 6, pp. 68 ff. for additional examples. In this connection the Edomite name *Qwsʿnl*, appearing on a seal impression of the 7th century B.C. from Ezion-geber is of interest. This name may be interpreted as *Qws ʿānā lî*, i.e. the Edomite god "Qaus has answered me", according to B. Maisler (Mazar), *BASOR* LXXII, 1938, p. 13, n. 45.

[19] It is worth drawing attention here to a diviner known as *šāʾilu*, fem. *šāʾiltu*, "(s)he who asks questions, inquirer", who functioned as an expert in posing questions to the deity. See Oppenheim, *Interpretation of Dreams*, (cf. p. 221, n. 2) pp. 221 ff. The terms "inquirer" and "respondent", though seemingly antonyms, actually point to the contrast in function and divinatory properties of each type. The *šāʾilu*, acting *both* as inquirer and respondent, received the oracle by magical techniques, whereas the *āpilum*, on the other hand, achieved divine revelation without recourse to any mantic mechanics.

[20] For the above words, which have remained obscure so far, see, e.g. S.M.P. Smith, *Book of Malachi, Int. Crit. Com.*, Edinburgh 1912, pp. 50 f., 58 (and there renderings of the ancient versions and earlier efforts of the commentators to explain the passage). The verb *ʿûr*, "to awake, to be aroused", which yielded the designation *ʿēr* referring to a diviner, serves at times in the Bible like *ʿnh* to denote prophetic revelation, see, e.g. Zech. iv 1. Apparently it infers nocturnal visions occurring in a state of semi-wakefulness and not during deep sleep.

[21] Cf. M. Noth, *Die Ursprünge des alten Israel im Lichte neuer Quellen*, (Arbeitsgemeinschaft

or unacceptance of West Semitic loanwords may well depend upon the degree of adaptation of Mari society to its surroundings in the various spheres. While the contemporaneous Mesopotamian societal structure was utterly foreign to the patriarchal-tribal system of Mari, which meant a lack of a specific nomenclature in the Akkadian language, the Mari scribes might have found the highly ramified Akkadian lexicon pertaining to cultic affairs and divinatory personnel a more facile linguistic medium to cover their needs and concepts.

Following the general remarks on the character and terminology of Mari prophecy, we proceed with the investigation of the "prophetic" documents, published more recently in Volume XIII of the *Royal Archives of Mari*.[22]

ARM XIII 23 = XXVI/1 209

To my lord
speak.
Thus (speaks) Mukannishum
your servant. After I had offered sacrifice
to the god Dagan for the well-being of my lord
the *aplûm*-prophet of the god Dagan of Tuttul
arose and thus spoke
as follows: "O Babylon! Why
dost thou ever (evil)? I will gather thee
in the net!
[line erased by the scribe]
The houses of the 7 confederates
and all their treasures
I shall place
in Zimrilim's hand!"
Truly the *aplûm*-prophet of the god Dagan
arose (?) [a second time (?)]
and thus sp[oke]
Hammurabi. . . . (the remaining four lines have been lost)

für Forschung des Landes Nordrhein-Westfalen, Heft 94), Köln 1961; Malamat, *JAOS* LXXXII, pp. 143 ff.

[22] First published in *ARM* XIII: *Textes divers*, Paris 1964. The four letters in question are: No. 23 published by J. Bottéro, Nos. 112–114 published by J.R. Kupper. No. 113 has not been dealt with, as the fragmentary state of the prophetic message denies any clear comprehension. For a revised edition of these letters see Durand 1988 (*ARM* XXVI/1).

This document is a letter from the dossier of Mukannishum, a high-ranking official in the court of Mari. The writer reports to Zimrilim that upon completion of the sacrificial rite on behalf of his king there appeared before him a diviner designated *aplûm* (for this unique spelling see above n. 17). It is unclear what link if any exists between the offering and the diviner's appearance.[23] Worthy of note in this respect is the second instance recounting the prophetic mission of this type of mantic personage, where the author of the missive has prefaced the vision with a report on the delivery of cattle most likely for sacrificial purposes (*Robinson Volume* ll. 1–5). Two other previously published documents relate the oracular urgings upon royal officialdom to make oblationary offerings, in one case for the *manes* of a deceased king of Mari, father of Zimrilim (*ARM* II 90; III 40). Hence it is likely that the diviner in our document, emissary of Dagan, was involved in the process of sacrifice to the deity for the well-being of the Mari sovereign.

Dagan, as is well known, occupied a central position in the pantheon of the West Semitic tribes specifically in the Mari region. Thus we find on four occasions in the Mari documents that diviners are sent by this divinity (*RA* XLII; *ARM* II 90; III 40; XIII 114). Whereas the latter instances, however, refer to Dagan of the city of Terqa—our case is the first to mention a prophet of Dagan, the patron of the city of Tuttul. Most instructive is the fact that this deity had already been noted some five centuries earlier in the inscriptions of Sargon the Great.[24] In connection with the ruler's western campaign there is a reference to his worship of Dagan in Tuttul, the god who had granted him dominion over Mari and the lands west of it. This serves as evidence for the importance of Tuttul as a cultic center of Dagan and the deity's prominence in the Mari area. Additional testimony to the significance and influence enjoyed by this divinity, even in regions as far west as the Levantine coast, can now

[23] The ritual of sacrifice as related to the variegated mantic activity is obviously a recurrent phenomenon. Attention should be drawn to the explicit biblical evidence on the matter of offerings as preparatory to divine revelation; cf. altar construction and offering of holocausts in the Balaam pericope (Num. xxiii) and the Elijah-Baal prophets confrontation on Mount Carmel (2 Kings xviii 22 ff.). On Balaam see e.g., R. Largement, "Les oracles de Bile'am", *Mémorial du cinquantenaire* 1914–1964 (Travaux de l'institut cathol. de Paris, X), Paris 1964, pp. 46 f.; see now also W.C. Kaiser, "Balaam Son of Beor. . . ." in *Go to the Land I Will Show You* (FS D.W. Young), Winona Lake, IN, 1996, pp. 95–106.

[24] *ANET*, p. 268; cf. C.J. Gadd, *Camb. Anc. Hist.*, I (rev. ed.), chap. XIX, Cambridge 1963, p. 10.

be adduced from a new Ugaritic document. Among a listing of deities, we find *dgn ttlh* (the final letter apparently corresponding to the Hebrew locative *h*), i.e. Dagan (who turns) towards the city of Tuttul.[25]

The location of the aforementioned city of Tuttul has been identified with Tall Biʿa on the confluence of the Euphrates and Balih river and was excavated in the 1980s, and 1990s.[26] A southern Tuttul is to be identified with modern Hit lying on the Euphrates south of Mari near the Babylonian border. The western center,[27] in fact, was inestimably superior in importance during the Old Babylonian period to the southern locality. Evidence of its particularly esteemed position within the local Mari dynasty may be deduced from the titles of both Yahdunlim and Zimrilim "King of Mari, Tuttul and the land of Hana".[28]

In the course of his missive, the writer quotes the prophecy of the *aplûm* which is directed at the kingdom of Babylon. The short prophetic discourse undoubtedly reflects the deterioration of previously sound political relations between Hammurabi, king of Babylon and the ruler of Mari, both formerly in a state of mutual dependence. It was Hammurabi's growing urge for expansion to the north as well that led to a strained attitude between the two erstwhile allies on the eve of the conquest of Mari in the Babylonian king's 32nd regnal year.[29]

The oracular message is noteworthy for its poetic coloration, being similar in this respect to the prophetic burden of the *āpilum* as transmitted in the letter of the *Robinson Volume*. At the same time, the diviner's speech is more obscurely formulated than found elsewhere in the Mari prophecies, which may account for flaws at the hands of

---

[25] Ch. Virolleaud, *GLECS* IX, séance du 21 février 1962, p. 50. The complete document, *RS* 24.244, has been published under the heading "Šapaš la déesse du soleil et les serpents" in *Ugaritica* V, pp. 564 ff.

[26] For the above identification see G. Dossin, *RA* LXVIII (1977), pp. 25–34; for the excavation reports, E. Strommenger *et al.*, *MDOG* CXIX (1987), pp. 7–49 and the most recent one, *MDOG* CXXVII (1995), pp. 43–55. On this site have been discovered impressive OB levels and hundreds of Mari-like tablets.

[27] On the location of Tuttul see previously W. Hallo, *JCS* XVIII, 1964, p. 79; A. Goetze, *ibid.*, pp. 118 f. Hallo accepts the assumption of two western cities of the same name, one at the mouth of the Balikh river; the other he identifies with Tell Aḥmar, the site of later Til-Barsip, north of the great bend of the Euphrates. Goetze maintains the existence of a single site at Tell Aḥmar. For a western Tuttul, referred to in an economic document of the Ur III period see E. Sollberger, *AfO* XIX, 1959–60, pp. 120 ff.

[28] *F. Thureau-Dangin, RA* XXXIII, 1936, pp. 49, 53.

[29] On relations between the two neighbouring countries in the time of Zimrilim, as reflected in the Mari correspondence, cf. most recent discussion by C.J. Gadd, *Camb. Anc. Hist.*, II (rev. ed.), chap. V, 1965, pp. 10 ff. (and bibliographical notes).

the scribe in the letter under discussion (deletion of a syllable in l. 13; erasure of one sign in l. 10 and the whole of l. 11). Although the specific circumstances which gave rise to the diviner's appearance are unknown, and not all his statements are lucid, the general tenor of the oracle is readily comprehensible. There is the pronounced wrathful denunciation of Babylon and the tidings of salvation for Mari's ruler, conjuring up associations with some of the utterances of Israel's prophets. Biblical rhetoric is further called to mind by the similes in the oracle (also present in other ancient Near Eastern sources):

I shall gather thee in the net—a reference to the ensnaring of the enemy in the hunter's or fisherman's net by the deity. Evidence denoting the antiquity of this motif in Mesopotamia is readily apparent in the "vultures stele" of Eannatum, ruler of Lagash, dating to the middle of the third millennium B.C. The god of Lagash is shown smiting the defeated people with a mace held in his right hand, as they flounder about helplessly in a large net which he grasps in the left.[30] The accompanying inscription emphasizes repeatedly that the ensnaring in the net by the deity constitutes special punishment for violation of a treaty, an offense which is apparently the basis for our prophecy. Biblical imagery, especially in the case of the Later Prophets, is familiar with the theme of the defeated enemy being likened to creatures trapped in the net of the hunter or fisherman (Ez. xii 13; xvii 20; xix 8; xxxii 3; Ho. vii 12; Hab. i 15–17; Job xix 6).

The prophecy concludes on a note of encouragement to Zimrilim, and the deity's assurance that he (Zimrilim) would subjugate the seven confederates (a typological number) or allies of Babylon with all their possessions. These confederates may be an allusion to Babylon's royal vassals which numbered some ten to fifteen kings, according to a diplomatic report by Iturasdu, one of Zimrilim's agents.[31] It is also possible that the remark refers to tribal chieftains which may have come under Hammurabi's rule, in similar fashion to the "7 kings, the fathers (*abū*) of Hana (sic!)" (i.e. the seven Hanaean tribal heads) subjugated by Yahdunlim, ruler of Mari (Disc inscription, col. I: 15–18). In a formula similar to that of our letter, the god Dagan (referring to the deity of Terqa) proclaims elsewhere that, were the Mari sovereign to heed his command, the deity "would long ago have placed the

[30] For illustration and interpretation see A. Parrot, *Tello*, Paris 1948, pp. 95 ff.; Pl. 6; *ANEP*, No. 298. For inscription see G.A. Barton, *The Royal Inscriptions of Sumer and Akkad*, New Haven 1929, pp. 23 ff. For a stele with a similar scene, discovered in Susa, see in *ANEP*, No. 307.

[31] See below ch. 21.

'kings' of the Yaminites" in "Zimrilim's hand" (*RA* XLII, ll. 30–31). Here again the reference is to the chieftains of a tribal federation that had been actively opposing Mari domination.

The remainder of the letter is defective and its end completely missing. From the legible remains it appears however, that the diviner made a second appearance with an additional, curt address. In a previous document (*ARM* III 78:20 ff.), we also find the bearer of a prophetic message reappearing before the authorities, obviously because of the oracle's desire to increase the forcefulness of his message.

Our first document is of special significance, as it is one of the few Mari texts with an oracle concerning another people, proclaiming condemnation and doom in the manner familiar to us from the biblical prophecies against the nations. While the next document also contains a prophecy on Babylon (*ARM* XIII 114), only the opening is extant and, in this section at least, there is no such pathetic vision as in the prophecy hitherto discussed.

ARM XIII 114 = XXVI/1 210

[To my lord]
speak.
Thus (speaks) Kibri-Dagan
your servant:
On the day on which I send this my tablet
to my lord,
before the darkening of the mountain (i.e. at nightfall),[32]
a wife of a (free)man came to me
and as to the affairs of Babylon
thus she spoke to me as follows:
"The god Dagan hath sent me.
Send (a message) to thy lord.
Let him not be anxious and [ ]
Let him not be anxious.
Hammurabi,
[King o]f Babylon

(The reverse of the tablet is illegible. Along the edges are the words *ana ḫalaqišu*—for his loss).

[32] For the peculiar Akkadian expression cf. Kupper, *Syria* XLI, 1964, p. 111, n. 1. Since it is strange to refer to mountains in the Euphrates region, Durand deems that this expression originated with the Amorites, when still dwelling in the West (Syria and Lebanon).

The author of this, as of the two remaining "prophetic" epistles (*ARM* XIII 112, 113), is Kibri-Dagan, governor of Terqa under Zimrilim. The previously published correspondence of this official already contained three letters dealing with diviner-prophets (*ARM* II 90; III 40, 78). It comes as no surprise that "prophetic" documents are included in the correspondence of the governor of Terqa, a prominent centre of the god Dagan and the religious focus of the Mari kingdom. The deity's temple, mentioned in particular by one of the visionaries (*RA* XLII), undoubtedly served as focal point for prophetic activity. The unique feature, however, of the three recent documents, in contradistinction to their predecessors, where the diviners are designated *muḫḫûm* (in *ARM* II 90 the term is possibly to be restored in the lacuna of l. 16), is the lack of any such prophetic appellative for the bearers of the divine message. More explicitly put, they were no professional prophets but individuals designated merely as "youth", "(free)man" and "wife of a (free)man", typical examples of personal charisma, contingent neither upon class, sex nor age.

The prophecy in our letter is ascribed to the "wife of a (free)man" (*aššat awīlim*), an appellation intended to emphasize the trustworthiness of her personality and her message.[33] Nevertheless, as in the other Mari letters, Kibri-Dagan failed to specify the diviner's name. We have already mentioned in passing other instances of female oracles in the Mari documents. The female presence comes as no surprise in surroundings where women traditionally played a significant role as experts in cultic practices side by side with men. The innovation in our document lies rather in the fact that a woman has served as divine emissary without being a professional prophetess, while in previous texts female diviners were designated *muḫḫūtum* (*ARM* VI 45: 9, 15) or *āpiltum* (*Robinson Volume*, l. 30).

The Bible, too, knows prophetesses, such as Deborah the wife of Lappidoth (Jud. iv 4), Huldah the wife of Shallum, son of Tikvah, son of Harhas (2 Kings xxii 14) and Noadiah (Neh. vi 14). We may note that in the first two instances the biblical source sees fit to mention the fact of their married state as in the Mari case. In addition, a relatively high social standing is imputed to Huldah's spouse, who

[33] The compound usage *aššat awīlim* is rare, as *aššatum* itself denotes a married woman. Consequently, reference is to the wife of a nobleman. The same expression recurs several times in the Hammurabi Code; see G.R. Driver – J.C. Miles, *The Babylonian Laws*, II, Oxford 1955, Glossary, p. 365b.

bears the title of "keeper of the robes", an official of the temple or palace. Huldah's prophecy, as well, concerned itself with the fate of the sovereign (Josiah) and the monarchy, although in contrast to the Mari visionary, she was charged with seeking out the word of God on the initiative of the king, who sent a special delegation to her for this very purpose (2 Kings xxii 12 ff.).

This is the first occasion where the female oracle's words are transcribed verbatim. Fully conscious of the divine message she is about to impart to the authorities, she commences her prophetic address declaring: "Dagan has sent me", a formula also found in other Mari oracles (*ARM* II 90: 19; III 40: 13; and cf. *RA* XLII, l. 32). This fact testifies that amongst the Mari visionaries this typical message-formula had already taken root. A parallel formula, representative of Israelite prophecy as well,[34] is attested by Moses' proclamation before Pharaoh: "The Lord, the God of the Hebrews, sent me" (Ex. vii 16) and down to Jeremiah's address to the ministers: "The Lord sent me" (Jer. xxvi 12, 15). As in the former document, the prophecy relates to Babylon, with consoling words for Zimrilim uttered by the deity, undoubtedly owing to the mounting danger of Hammurabi to the Mari kingdom. This letter must, consequently, be dated to the last years of Zimrilim's rule. The urgency of the matter at hand is evinced both by the woman's appearance before the governor of Terqa at eventide and the latter's haste in transmitting her encouraging words to the palace that very day.

In the remaining two documents (*ARM* XIII 112, 113), a special category of divination is encountered—a prophetic revelation by means of a dream. As a medium of divine manifestation, the dream was widespread throughout the ancient Near East and above all in biblical sources. The relevant material (excluding the Bible) has been assembled by Oppenheim in his treatise on dreams in the ancient Near East.[35] In his classification of dream-types, one of particular interest to us is designated as the "message dream", i.e. where the intent of the deity is conveyed. There is need, however, for further

---

[34] For the approximation between the formula in Mari and in the Bible see M. Noth, *Gesam. Studien zum A.T.*, pp. 288 f.; C. Westermann, *op. cit.*, pp. 179 ff.; *idem, Grundformen prophetischer Rede*, München 1960, pp. 82 ff.

[35] A.L. Oppenheim, The Interpretation of Dreams in the Ancient Near East, *Trans. Amer. Philos. Society XLVI*, Philadelphia 1956, pp. 179 ff.; see now also R.K. Gnuse, *Dreams and Dream Reports in the Writing of Josephus*, Leiden 1996, pp. 34–100.

specific delineation between the bulk of dreams relating to the dreamer himself and to the type of dream whose message is meant for another subject. The Mari dream-reports belong to the latter group. This distinction is applicable to the Bible as well, for alongside visions pertaining to the dreamer (e.g. those experienced by the patriarchs and Solomon at Gibeon), is one containing a message to another person (cf. Num. xii 6; Jer. xxiii 25 ff.; xxix 8; Zech. x 2 and others).[36]

The visionaries of Mari, whose revelation was prompted by a dream, bear no particular title of diviner. They are referred to merely as "youth" (*ṣuḫārum, ARM* XIII 112) and "(free)man" (*awīlum*, ib. 113), the latter appellation also designating the sole dreamer known to us from previous documents (*RA* XLII, ll. 7, 40). With the exception of the "wife of a (free)man" (*ARM* XIII 114), whose appearance at dusk may hint at a nocturnal vision, approximating a kind of dreamer, the remaining cases of Mari prophecy invariably employ a specific title of diviner-prophet. This distribution is not a matter of coincidence, but its true significance lies in a phenomenological delineation between the professional oracle, privileged with direct revelation, and the dreamer of dreams.

A similar distinction is reflected in the biblical law: "If there arise in the midst of thee a prophet, or a dreamer of dreams" (Deut. xiii 2 ff.), and we are told of Saul: "the Lord did not answer him either by dreams or by Urim or by prophets" (1 Sam. xxviii 6; cf. v. 15). Jeremiah, as well, views the dreamers on one occasion as a distinct grouping within the visionary framework (Jer. xxvii 9). True, the dividing line is not always distinct concerning the ancient Near East in general, and the Bible, in particular, whose prophets occasionally resort to the dream as a source of divine inspiration (e.g. Num. xii 6). In the course of time, however, Israelite prophecy diminished the potency of the dream as a legitimate medium of divine revelation, as witnessed especially in the polemics of Jeremiah against the false prophets (Jer. xxiii 25 ff.).

---

[36] On dreams in the Bible see E.L. Ehrlich, Der Traum im Alten Testament, *ZAW, Beih.* LXXIII, 1953; A. Caquot in *Les songes et leur interprétation* (Sources orientales, II), Paris 1959, pp. 106 ff.; A. Resch, *Der Traum im Heilsplan Gottes*, Freiburg 1964. Contrary to Mari and the Bible, the Oppenheim collection of ancient Near Eastern dreams, as far as I can determine, has yielded only two examples of a message addressing itself to another person (pp. 249 f., Nos. 10 and 11, where the dream-report of a priest of Ishtar, respectively of a "(free)man" [*awīlum*], is meant for the king Ashurbanipal). Here again Mari and the Bible conform in using the dream for the purpose of prophetic mission.

ARM XIII 112 = XXVI/1 234

(Rev.) To my lord
speak.
Thus (speaks) Kibri-Dagan
your servant:
The god Dagan and the god Ikrub-Il are well;
the city of Terqa and the district is well!
(In the following line only isolated signs have been preserved.
Approximately six further lines are lost).
(Rev.) Thus he saw (a vision) as follows:
"Build not his house . . .[37]
If that house will be builded
I shall cast it into the river!"
On the day he saw that
dream he did not tell (it) to anyone.
On the second day he saw again
the dream as follows: "The god (it was who did speak)
'Build not this house;
If thou wilt build it I shall cast it
into the river!'" Now,
herewith, the hem of his garment
and a lock of hair of his head
I have sent
to my lord.
From that day (forward)
(that) youth
is ill.

The youth's dream may be relegated to the category of admonitions intended to forestall a specific act, in our case the construction of a building. We cannot account for the reason in opposing its construction, nor do we know the nature of the edifice itself, whether it was of a religious or secular character. What is clear is its intended establishment on the bank of the Euphrates. Fuller details may have been contained in the defective portion of the tablet, or perhaps had been familiar to the king of Mari, thereby obviating the need for elucidation by the Terqa commissioner. In any event, the dream-

[37] The Akkadian word here is *ḫaripam* which, Kupper, editor of this letter, considers to come from *ḫarābu*, "to lie waste" and translates: "ne (re)construisez pas cette maison *en ruines*(?)." Bottéro derives it from *ḫarāpu*, "to be early", meaning: "do not build *in haste*" (*ARM* XIII, p. 168). Accepting the derivation of the latter with a change of inference we may suggest translating: "do not build this house *too soon*", implying that the official delays date of construction.

message recalls the prophet Nathan coming before David on a mission concerning the construction of a House of God (2 Sam. vii 4 ff.). Nathan also achieved divine revelation in a nocturnal vision and on this occasion, too, God showed his disapproval of the planned construction. The youth's dream parallels essentially a prophetic mission related in previously published correspondence of Kibri-Dagan (*ARM* III 78). Here, too, the diviner (*muḫḫûm*) appeared before the governor of Terqa on a matter of construction (in this instance, the building of a gate) having been sent by the deity either to impede or, as we presume, to hasten the work (cf. *EI* IV, p. 79).

Of particular importance is the fact of the dream's recurrence and identity of content on both occasions. It appears that the first vision left the dreamer vague as to the full meaning of his experience which he dared not relate to a soul. It was only with the re-appearance of the dream the following night that he was fully convinced of the dream's message and of a mission thrust upon him by a divine source. We immediately call to mind the nocturnal manifestation concerning the doom of Eli's house revealed to Samuel, the boy, in the tabernacle at Shiloh (1 Sam. iii 3 ff.). However, in contrast to our Mari text, here the vision recurs four times, during the very same night, and Samuel transmits the portent only after Eli's insistent urging not to conceal anything from him.

Despite the contrasting circumstances, the significant fact underlying both cases is that these dreams, which bear a fundamentally auditory character (i.e. the deity's voice is actually heard), recur until the dreamer fully apprehends their inner import. This phenomenon becomes readily apparent once it is realized that both occurrences concern individuals whose youthful years precluded initiation into the mysteries of prophetic revelation.[38] Consequently, they were incapable of penetrating its actual core of meaning at the initial experience, as explained by the author of the Samuel story: "Now Samuel did not yet know the Lord, neither was the word of the Lord yet revealed to him" (ib. v. 7). It is true that Samuel had been engaged for some time in the sacred service and that the dream was revealed to him while sleeping in the Shiloh sanctuary. Nevertheless, there is no proof

[38] In this connection Jeremiah's prophetic call is particularly interesting, when it relates his hesitancy to accept the divine mission on the pretext of being a mere youth (Jer. i 6–7). On another parallel between Mari and 1 Sam iii—Eli's adjuration of Samuel and the so-called "Diviner's Protocol" from Mari (*ARMT* XXVI/1 1) see now V.A. Hurowitz, *VT* XLIV (1994), pp. 483–497.

in this instance, and even less so in the Mari case, to the effect that the dream was the result of a wilful incubation which the dreamer had anticipated.[39] (On the "prophetic" dream see also above ch. 6, pp. 74 ff.)

After a verbal transcription of the dream, Kibri-Dagan informs the king that he has sent him the youth's fringe or hem of garment (*sissiktu* in Akkadian) and a lock of hair. A similar procedure is related in two previous documents: 1) Bahdilim, the prefect of the Mari palace, in a memorandum sent to the king concerning the prophecy of a certain female diviner (*muḫḫūtum*), encloses "her hair" (implying a curl of hair) and the hem of her garment; 2) an official named Iturasdu reports to his lord a divine message revealed once again in a dream. The letter concludes by stating that the official is unable to send the visionary along to the king and emphasizes "because he is a *trustworthy* man I have not taken his hair nor the hem of his garment" (*RA* XLII, l. 53).[40]

On this peculiar practice see our previous treatment of these documents (*EI* IV, pp. 81, 84 and now ch. 6, pp. 77 f. above). In this context we noted the biblical story of David coming upon the unattended Saul in the cave, where he cut the hem of his pursuer's robe (1 Sam. xxiv 4 ff.). In his review of *ARM* VI M. Noth mentions the same parallel and while attributing to the hem/hair motif the power to control a person, sees in it primarily a magic-religious significance.[41] The more important factor, however, remains the legal symbolism of exercise of power over an individual through possession of his personal articles, as suggested by various scholars.[42]

---

[39] See Ehrlich, *op. cit.*, pp. 45 ff. In one of the new Mari documents mention may have been made of a "youth of (the goddess) Ishtar", i.e. a servant in the Ishtar temple, in the event that the reference to *ṣuḫār Ištar* does not imply a proper noun (*ARM* XIII 150: 5 and the editor's note on p. 174). To relate a similar assumption to the "youth" in our document, namely his having served in a Terqa temple, cannot find support in the missive.

[40] Translation of passage is in accordance with Oppenheim, *Interpretation of Dreams*, p. 195. Instead of Dossin's reading *kal-lu*, a kind of official, this keyword should read *ták-lu*, "trustworthy", as proposed by Oppenheim, *JNES* XI, 1952, p. 134.

[41] *JSS* I, 1956, pp. 327 ff. For the Saul-David episode in the light of the cuneiform evidence on the usage of *sissiktu* (hem of garment) see J. de Fraine, "Fimbria vestimenti", *VD* XXV, 1947, pp. 218 ff. As to the ritual significance occasionally attached to a lock of hair among the Semites, see J. Henninger, "Zur Frage des Haaropfers bei den Semiten", *Wiener Schule der Völkerkunde*, Wien 1956, pp. 349 ff. The examples cited there, however, are irrelevant to our discussion. Furthermore, in our instance the taking of hair and seizure of cloak are inseparable.

[42] Dossin, *RA* XLII, p. 134. For the ramified and widespread usage of the hem

of a garment as a juridical symbol in the Mari documents see J.M. Munn-Rankin, *Iraq* XVIII, 1956, pp. 91 f.; G. Boyer, *ARM* VIII, pp. 161 f. The significance of *sissiktu* in symbolizing personality has been stressed repeatedly by P. Koschaker, see especially *Über einige griechische Rechtsurkunden* etc. (Sächsische Akad. der Wissenschaften; Philol.-Hist. Klasse, I), Leipzig 1931, pp. 111 ff. There on pp. 116 f. two exceedingly interesting incantation texts are quoted, recording a ritual of a substitute offering for a sick person, whereby the cut-off hair and hem serve in his stead to free him of his disease (*KAR* 42:27 f. and E. Ebeling, *Tod und Leben* etc., Leipzig 1931, p. 56, l. 26). For more recent literature see above ch. 6, p. 78 nn. 46 and 47.

8

EPISODES INVOLVING SAMUEL AND SAUL AND THE PROPHETIC TEXTS FROM MARI*

A. *Circuit of Several Towns by a Diviner*

In *ARM* 26/1, 88 [= *ARM* 5, 65:15–28] (Durand 1988: 32 f., 226 f.), Asqudum, the chief diviner at the Mari palace in the Old Babylonian period (on this person see Durand 1988: 71–228) writes to Yasmah-Addu, the viceroy of Mari, *inter alia* about his visit to four towns in order to perform extispices there for the well-being of their inhabitants (cf. Cryer 1994: 202 f.). The towns are Saggarātum (on the lower Habur river), Terqa (near the confluence of the Habur and Euphrates), Ṣuprum (south of Terqa) and finally Mari, the home-base of Asqudum. All the above sites are located in the heartland of the Mari kingdom. We do not know the frequency of Asqudum's rounds, but his extispicy for Saggarātum was valid for six months (l. 19).

Turning to the Prophet Samuel, the Bible reports that he made annual rounds to four major towns, all of them the seat of sanctuaries, within the tribal area of Benjamin, the heartland of Israel: Bethel, Gilgal, Mispah, where Samuel administered justice to the people of Israel. "Then he would return to Ramah, for his home was there and there too he would judge Israel" (1 Sam. 7:16–17; Smith 1899: 54 f.; McCarter 1980: 148; Klein 1983: 69 f.).

Thus, we have in Mari and in the Bible an analogue of the functions and activities of a major cultic personage, who made the rounds to four places, although Asqudum covered larger distances than Samuel. The mention of just *four* cities in the circuits of each one of the diviners may not be coincidental. We know, at least with regard to Mari, that a "quartet" of places may indicate a stable, administrative unit or district (cf. Durand 1997:202).

---

* This article will also be published in: *Hesed we Emet: Studies in Honor of E.S. Frerichs*, eds. J. Magnes and S. Gitin, Crown University Press, Providence, RI, 1998 (forthcoming).

B. *Asses Gone Astray*

One of the best-known tales in the First Book of Samuel concerns the lost asses of Kish, Saul's father. Kish asks Saul to return the missing animals to him (1 Sam. 9:3 ff.) (Hertzberg 1960: 60 ff.; Klein 1983: 86). Saul, in the company of a servant, searched for the asses throughout the region of Benjamin as well as Ephraim, but in vain. The servant drew the attention of Saul to the fact that in the vicinity of their wanderings dwelt a prophet (i.e. Samuel), who might know where to find the asses and a visit to him might be beneficial (on the remuneration given to the prophet see Malamat 1989: 62 f.). Indeed, the asses were found, but the real purpose of the encounter between Samuel and Saul was to appoint the latter as king of Israel. Saul sought asses and "found" kingship.

The reality of asses going astray must have been a frequent phenomenon, but it is reported only rarely. A noteworthy parallel to the biblical tale is the Mari text A. 629, *ARM* 26/1, 63 (Durand 1988: 206 f.). Again Asqudum, the diviner, addresses King Zimri-Lim. The text first reports that Zimri-Lim had acquired an ass. Then it records that other asses had been lost, a fact confirmed by an inquiry of Asqudum. The latter's asses were in Qaṭṭunan, a distant provincial town in the north of the Mari kingdom. Zimri-Lim should know that the asses of another person had also been lost. The parallel situation is obvious. Asses at times went astray and search parties were sent out in order to return the missing animals.

C. *An "Old Man" as Diviner—Prophet*

In a fragmentary letter included among the dream prophecies by J.-M. Durand in *ARM* 26/1, 230 (Durand 1988: 469 f.) an old man (lú šu.gi) is mentioned in a temple of Dagan. While not named, the addressee must have been Zimri-Lim. We shall base ourselves on the reading and restorations of the text by J.M. Sasson, without adhering to his conclusions (Sasson 1995: 292–297). The report states: "[Thus a woman . . .] in her dream (Durand)/vision (Sasson): an old man was dwelling at Dagan's shrine." ([*maška*]*nātum*; for a West Semitic term meaning shrine, Hebrew "tabernacle," see Malamat 1980: 72: tent-shrine. Durand restores [*sikka*]*nātum*. "betyl" of Dagan) (ll. 1–2). Indeed, we may occasionally consider lú šu.gi as an additional epithet for a visionary, a prophet or the like. [Before Itur-M]er during prostration he (the old man) said: "I told you [ ] all of you are dead, but you will not listen to my words" (ll. 3–5). In the continuation of the letter various deities are mentioned dealing with the old man's vision. Sasson suggests that the old man addressed a divine council and complained that he was ignored (by the deities?).

In the light of the biblical parallels, the document may be reporting a prophecy or a vision rather than a dream (as already suggested by Sasson) and thus should be removed from the section in *ARM* 26 in which it has been placed. First comes to mind the seance at Endor and the femal necromancer (*baʿalat ōb*) (Tropper 1989: 225 f.; Kleiner 1995; Schmidt 1995). She consults the ghost of the prophet Samuel on behalf of King Saul (1 Sam. 28:7–19; Hertzberg 1960: 177 f.). The appearance of the dead prophet according to the witch of Endor likened that of "an old man" (LXX: "erect," based on Hebrew *zāqēp/ūp* instead of MT *zāqēn*, "old") "coming up and he is wrapped in a robe" (v. 16). As in Mari, in the biblical episode it was a woman who envisaged an old man, the ghost of the prophet Samuel. Also similar to Mari, the Bible stresses the fact that Saul did not hearken to Samuel's words and thus the latter utters a prophecy of doom.

Beyond the Samuel cycle, in 1 Kings 13:11–32, a legendary account attributed to the time of King Jeroboam of Israel, we hear of an anonymous prophet, who is designated *zāqēn*, "old man" (vv. 11, 29). This prophet resided at the cult place Bethel (Noth 1968: 298 ff.) and took care of another holy man, the *ʾīš hāᵉlōhīm*, man of God, coming from Judah. Finally, there were in the time of the desert wanderings the seventy old men of Israel (*zᵉqēnīm*; usually translated "elders" of Israel, i.e. a group of Israelite leaders), whom Moses gathered, around the tent-shrine. There, they started to prophesy (Num. 11:24–25).

It appears from Mari and the Bible that occasionally men of old age had the capacity of a visionary or even of a prophet.

Bibliography

Cryer, F.H., (1994). *Divination in Ancient Israel and its Near Eastern Environment*, Sheffield *JSOTSS* 142.
Durand, J.-M., (1988). *Archives épistolaire de Mari* I/1 (= *ARM* 26/1), Paris.
——, (1997). *Documents épistolaires de Mari* 1 (LAPO), Paris.
Hertzberg, H.W., (1960). *Die Samuel Bücher* (ATD), Göttingen.

Klein, R., (1983). *1 Samuel* (WBC), Waco, Texas.
Kleiner, M., (1995). *Saul in En-Dor—Wahrsagung oder Totenbeschwörung?* (Erfurter Theol. Studien 66).
Malamat, A., (1980). "A Mari Prophecy and Nathan's Dynastic Oracle" in *Prophecy* (FS G. Fohrer), Berlin, pp. 68–82.
——, (1989). "Parallels between the New Prophecies from Mari and Biblical Prophecy: II. Material Remuneration for Prophetic Services," *NABU* 1989/89 (pp. 63 f.).
McCarter, P.K., (1980). *1 Samuel* (Anchor Bible), Garden City, N.Y.
Noth, M., (1968). *Könige* I (BKAT), Neukirchen.
Sasson, J.M., (1995). "Mari Apocalypticism Revisited" in eds. K. van Lerberghe and A. Schoors, *Immigration and Emigration within the Ancient Near East* (FS E. Lipiński), Leuven, pp. 285–298.
Schmidt, B.B., (1995). "The 'Witch' of En-Dor" etc., in eds. M. Meyer and P. Mirecki, *Ancient Magic and Ritual Power*, Leiden, pp. 111–129.
Smith, H.P., (1899). *The Books of Samuel* (ICC), Edinburgh.
Tropper, J., (1989). *Nekromantie* (AOAT 22), Neukirchen.

9

A MARI PROPHECY AND NATHAN'S DYNASTIC ORACLE*

One of the most interesting "prophetic" texts (the second to have been published already in 1950) is of particular relevance for a comparative study with prophecy in the Bible. The document in question (A. 1121) was published by G. Dossin only in transliteration and (French) translation.[1] In the meantime it (our text A below) was collated and edited by B. Lafont, who, upon a suggestion of J.-M. Durand, made a join with the small fragment A. 2731 (our text B below);[2] the latter fragment was also published originally by G. Dossin, only in French. Since the initial publication, various translations and treatments have appeared, mostly in the general context of Mari prophecy.[3] Amongst these is a specific study by the present author (published in Hebrew, with a brief English abstract), giving a Hebrew translation of the document, with a discussion of the text, its historical background and its implications for biblical prophecy.[4]

One facet with which we have not previously dealt has curiously been unappreciated till now (except for some passing remarks): the nature of the prophecy in this document as a "dynastic oracle," and its impact on the study of the parallel material in the Bible. It is this

---

* This article was originally published in: J. Emerton, ed., *Prophecy—Essays for G. Fohrer*, *BZAW* 100 (1980), pp. 68–82.

[1] In A. Lods, Une tablette inédite de Mari, intéressante pour l'histoire ancienne du prophétisme sémitique, in: *Studies in Old Testament Prophecy Presented to T.H. Robinson* (H.H. Rowley, ed.), 1950, 103–107.

[2] See B. Lafont, Le roi de Mari et les prophètes du dieu Adad, *RA* 78 (1984), 7–18. We shall deal below with the two texts separately to keep the format of our original publication.

[3] See W. von Soden, *WO* 1 (1947–52), 403; H. Schmöckel, *ThLZ* 76 (1951), 55; G. Rinaldi, *Aevum* 28 (1954), 1–9; J.J. Roberts, *Restoration Quarterly* 10 (1967), 124 f.; F. Ellermeier, *Prophetie in Mari und Israel*, 1968, 48–53; H.B. Huffmon, *BA* 31 (1968), 106 f. (= *BA* Reader 3, 1970, 204 f.); W.L. Moran, *ANET*[3], 1969, 625 and E. Noort, *Untersuchungen zum Gottesbescheid in Mari* 1977; see p. 153, index s.v. A. 1121 and A. 2731; see now L. Cagni, *Le profezie di Mari*, 1995, No. 35, pp. 88–90 (Italian translation and annotations).

[4] A. Malamat, History and Prophetic Vision in a Mari Letter, *Eretz-Israel* 5 (1958), 67–73 (Hebrew; English Summary on pp. 86* f.).

facet which occupies our attention here, our ultimate aim being a comparison with Nathan's oracle on the Davidic dynasty, in II Sam. 7, also referred to as Yahwe's covenant with David.

As the basis of our discussion, we present an English translation of the major fragment of the Mari document, with brief annotations. This is followed by an English translation of the smaller fragment of the letter (A. 2731).[5] It is thus of considerable aid in restoring and providing certain details missing there—including the salutation mentioning Nur-Sin, Zimri-Lim's "ambassador" at Halab (Aleppo) as sender and the king of Mari himself as recipient. For convenience, we shall henceforth refer to these two texts as A and B, respectively.

A
(A. 1121)

(Commence with verso of text B [p. 110] and continue:)

Concerning [the delivery of] the *zukrum*,
Alpan, in the presence of Zuḫatnim, Abi-Šadi and [. . .]
spoke to me, as follows: "[Deliver] the *zukrum*;
also deliver the cattle. My lord, in the presence of [. . .]-men,
told me to deliver the *zukrum*, as follows:
'Never shall he break (his agreement) with me.'
I have brought witnesses for him. Let my lord know this.
Through oracles, Adad, Lord of Kallassu,
[spoke] to me, as follows: "Am I not
[Ad]ad, Lord of Kallassu, who
reared him (the king) between my loins and restored him to the throne
of his father's house? After I restored him to the throne
of his father's house, I have again given him a residence.
Now, since I restored him to the throne of his father's house,
I will take from him an estate.
Should he not give (the estate),
am I not master of throne, territory and city?
What I have given, I shall take away. If (he does) otherwise, and
satisfies my desire, I shall give him throne upon throne,
house upon house, territory upon territory,
city upon city.
And I shall give him the land

[5] See G. Dossin's French translation in: *La Divination en Mésopotamie ancienne*, 1966, 78 (where the fragment is erroneously designated as A. 2925; cf. *ARM* XVII/1, 29) and now Lafont, *RA* 78 (above n. 2).

from the rising (of the sun) to its setting."
This is what the *āpilū*-diviners said, and in the oracles
it "stands up" constantly. Now, moreover,
the *āpilum*-diviner of Adad, Lord of Kallassu,
is standing guard over the tent-shrine of Alaḫtum to (be) an estate.
Let my lord know this.
Previously, when I was residing in Mari,
every word the *āpilum*-diviner or *āpiltum*-diviner
told me, I would report back to my lord.
Now that I am living in another land,
that which I hear and which they tell me,
would I not communicate to my lord?
If ever anything remiss should occur,
let not my lord speak thus, as follows:
"The word which the *āpilum*-diviner has spoken to you—while over your tent-shrine
he is standing guard—why have you not
communicated to me?" Herewith I communicate (it)
to my lord. Let my lord know this.
Moreover, the *āpilum*-diviner of Adad, Lord of Ḫalab,
came [to Abu]ḫalum and spoke thus to him,
[as follows:] "Communicate to your lord
(broken off; speech of the god missing)

[from the rising (of the sun)] to its setting,
[it is I] who will give (it) to you."
[This] is what Adad, Lord of Ḫalab,
told me in the presence of Abuḫalum.
Let my lord know this.

Annotations to Text A

ll. 1–7 Our suggested punctuation here remains conjectural, and is in part contrary to that of G. Dossin.

l. 1 *CAD* Z, 153, translates *zukrum* as "pasture-land (?)". But this otherwise unknown word more probably denotes a male animal, as G. Dossin claims. It is difficult, however, to decide whether *zukrum* connotes "oxen" (as G. Dossin seems to hold), or "stud bull" or possibly "rams/he-goats". For the word *lâtu* (in l. 4), paired with *zukrum* here, does not only designate the fem. pl. "cows" (pace G. Dossin), but also "cattle" collectively (*CAD* L, 218). For a *zukru* festival at Emar see now D.E. Fleming, *The Installation of Baal's High Priestess at Emar*, 1992, 239 ff.

l. 2 Regarding Zuḫatnum, a high official at Mari during the reign of Zimri-Lim and, *inter alia*, emissary ("chargé de missions") to Halab, see now *ARM* XVI/1, 244.

l. 4 A new examination of the text of this letter (cf. J.G. Heintz, *Biblica* 52, 1971, 546) has led to the reading of the last preserved words in this line as *awī[le^{m}]^{eš} ù[...* (= ... "men"), rather than the published reading *šarr[āni^{m}]^{eš} ù[...* (= "kings and ..."). "Men" may refer to the representatives of a certain city, or rather may serve as a determinative signifying tribal chieftains or the like.

l. 6 Here, Alpan (this PN, as well as the PN Abi-Šadi, are safely read by Lafont seems to be quoting the words of his lord (the king of Mari, or the author of the letter?). It is also possible that the subject of this sentence is a god, who would never break his covenant with the ruler.

l. 8 *ina têrētim*, "through oracles," is preferable to "through visions," as in our earlier (Hebrew) translation. W.L. Moran translates: "at (the inspection of) omens" (by the *āpilū* mentioned below?).

l. 11 The words here refer to the king of Mari. The usual translations of *paḫalli* (lit. "my testicles") are, euphemistically, "genoux", "Schoss", "thighs", etc., which blur the realistic imagery which the speaker had in mind. The god Adad is here depicted primordially in the form of a bull. In Mesopotamian art, Adad is sometimes shown standing upon the back of a bull, or even personified as a bull. Our view has been accepted by W. Moran, *op. cit.* (n. 3), 625 n. 27.

l. 13 *ašar šubti*, lit. "dwelling-place", here referring to the palace.

ll. 15, 27 *niḫlatum*, translated by us as "estate", is taken by G. Dossin as a place name, an alleged town Niḫlatum near Halab. The appearance of this word in l. 27, defined by the post-determinative KI, might tend to support this assumption, though it is by no means decisive. First, the usage of KI is not restricted to toponyms, but it may be affixed to other geographical designations as well. Furthermore, in l. 15 the KI is missing, and in l. 27 it might simply be a scribal error, influenced by the place name Alaḫtum, mentioned immediately before. As a matter of fact, in the other text (cf. J.G. Heintz, *op. cit., ad. loc.*), *niḫlatum* actually occurs without the KI. Following upon a discussion with B. Landsberger, we suggested in our Hebrew article (and cf. my remark in *JAOS* 82, 1962, 149) that this is a West Semitic idiom for an "estate", "hereditary property", "patrimony"—an interpretation now generally accepted. The noun *niḫlatum* (and cf. *ARM* I 91: 6'; V 4:5), and the verbal form *naḫālum*, "inherit", "apportion", attested in several Mari documents, do not exist in standard Akkadian. But in turn these forms do have cognates in Hebrew (*năḥ^{a}lā* and *naḥăl*), as well as in Ugaritic (*nḥl*; and see below, p. 120). They should be added to the various other West Semitic terms in Mari relating to tribal heritage (cf. *MEIE*, pp. 48–52). The noun *naḫalu* is also found as a West Semitism in the Akkadian documents from Ugarit (cf. *PRU* III, 109, No. 16.251:7).

l. 17 *epi/erum*, "territory", "land", is not a West Semitic term, strictly speaking, as G. Dossin holds—cf. *CAD* E, 189b. It occurs in the documents from Alalaḫ, level VII, originating in approximately the same period and area as our letter. There, too, it occurs in combination with the words "house" and "city", as in our ll. 20–21 below (cf. Wiseman, *AT*, Selected Vocabulary, s.v. *epirum*).

ll. 20–21 The syntactic structure X upon (*eli*) X, Y upon Y, and so forth, seems to be of West Semitic character. For similar examples in biblical Hebrew (e.g. Jer. 4:20), Phoenician (Azitawadda I, 6–8) and Aramaic (Sefire I B, 30), cf. J.C. Greenfield, *JSS* 11 (1966), 103 ff.

l. 23 The idiom *ṣitiša . . . erbiša*, "from the rising (of the sun) to its setting", i.e. from east to west, is parallel to the expressions in Hebrew: *mimmôṣaʾ ûmimmăʿarab* (Ps. 75:7; and cf. Ps. 50:1, 113:3, Isa. 45:6, Mal. 1:11); in Phoenician: *lmmṣʾ šmš wʿd mbʾy* (Azitawadda A II, 2/3); and in Aramaic: *mn mwqʾ šmš wʿd mʿrb* (Panamu, l. 13).

l. 24 The *āpilum* (fem. *āpiltum*, pl. *āpilū*), lit. "answerer" (derived from the Akkadian verb *apālum*, "to answer"), designates a divinatory prophet or some sort of cultic functionary. This sense is attested in Mari only, cf. *CAD* A II, 170a. For a discussion of the significance of the *āpilum*, see our remarks in ch. 6, 67 ff. and below, pp. 113–116.

l. 25 *ittanazzaz*, from *izuzzum* (W. von Soden, *GAG*, 154, § 107, 8b; *AHw*, 410), "to stand", in the Gtn form (iterative), signifying "continuously, constantly standing". Generally this verb has been translated here as if the *āpilū*-diviners were the antecedent of the verb, consequently the verb is emended and read as a plural, and it is assumed that the prophets continuously resided at the site of the oracle. Thus G. Dossin: "or ils [?] se tiennent continuellement dans les oracles"; W.L. Moran: "they are constantly appear(ing) at the omens"; and our own Hebrew translation, rendered into English: "they insist upon (or stand by) the vision". W. von Soden, without emending the verb to the plural, translates: "hält er sich immer wieder bei den Orakeln auf". However, the antecedent of *ittanazzaz* is not *āpilū*, but rather *annitam*, "this matter". Thus H.B. Huffmon: "It continues to stand up in the extispices", as well as our present rendering: "and in the oracles it (*annitam*) 'stands up' constantly".

l. 27 The true connotation of *maškānum* as used in our letter (here and in l. 37) seems to have eluded those who have translated it according to one of its usual Akkadian meanings ("region", "threshing-floor", "dépôt"; cf. *CAD* M I, 369 ff.). It would seem, however, that it is used here in the specialized meaning of its Hebrew cognate, the biblical *miškan*, "tent-shrine", "tabernacle". If so, this is yet another illustration of West Semitic influence on vocabulary and religious practice at Mari, especially in the "prophetic" letters there. It must be noted, however, that in the Bible, too, threshing-floors proper were used as cultic places; cf.

II Sam. 24:18 ff. (David's altar at the threshing-floor of Araunah), and I Kings 22:10 (the prophets at the threshing-floor near the gate of Samaria).

ll. 27, 37/38 The idiom *maškānam . . . inaṣṣar*, "stand guard over the tent-shrine", has its equivalent in the biblical (*šamăr*) *mišmæræt miškan*, "keeping watch over the tabernacle" (e.g. Num. 1:53; and cf. II Kings 11:5). For the biblical phrase, see J. Milgrom, *Studies in Levitical Terminology*, I 1970, 8 ff. Lafont, however, reads *inazzar*, "claim (the tent-shrine)".

This new interpretation of the words *maškānum* and *niḫlatum* thus yields: ". . . the *āpilum*-diviner . . . is standing guard over the tent-shrine . . . to (be) a (sacred) estate".

l. 37 The conjunction *ū* introduces a circumstantial clause and would yield the best sense if translated "while" (cf. A. Finet, *L'accadien des lettres de Mari*, 1956, 225 f., § c, d). W. von Soden translates (p. 403): "Das Wort ⟨des Gottes⟩ [supplying *ša ilim*] sagte der 'Beantworter' dir, während er deine Tenne (?) bewacht."

ll. 3'–4' The speaker, of course, is the *āpilum*-diviner of Adad.

B
(A. 2731)

"To my lord, speak: Thus Nur-Sin, your servant. Once, twice, five times have I communicated to my lord concerning the delivery of the livestock to Adad and concerning the *niḫlatum* which Adad, Lord of Kallassu, demands from you. (Reverse; insert text A:)

'Am I not Adad, Lord of Ḫalab, who has raised you . . . and who made you regain the throne of your father's house? I never demand anything of you. When a wronged man or woman cries out to you, stand and let his case be judged.[6] This is what I demanded from you, and what I have communicated to you, you will do. You will heed my word and the land from the ri[sing (of the sun) to its setting] and the land of . . . [I will give you]'. This is what the *āp*[*ilum*-diviner of Adad, Lord of Ḫalab spoke to me."]

Each of these texts originally contained two oracles intended for Zimri-Lim—in both texts, the first by Adad, Lord of Kallassu, and the second by Adad, Lord of Halab. The first oracle is preserved in its entirety in text A, and the second oracle survives in text B. The

[6] Based on G. Dossin's transliteration of this one sentence, in M. Anbar, *UF* 7 (1975), 517 f., who cites as a biblical parallel Jer. 22:3a. For further parallels of prophetic utterances on kingly obligations and conduct, cf. Jer. 21:11–12; 22:15–16.

damaged state of the first seven lines in text A precludes a clear understanding of the precise matter there. In the light of text B, however, it is evident that the passage relates to the oracle following, and that the animals to be delivered were apparently intended for sacrifice.[7]

The relationship between the two gods, whether they are merely two aspects of a single Adad or truly separate deities, is not clear, for we know practically nothing of the locale of Kallassu, which is generally considered to be in the vicinity of Halab, if not an actual quarter of that city, sacred or otherwise.[8] In any event, though both deities claim to have restored Zimri-Lim to his throne, there is an interesting difference between the two in the demands put to him: in both texts, the Lord of Kallassu claims a *niḫlatum*, while in B (the relevant passage in A is broken) the Lord of Halab presses for a just hearing for the downtrodden, as we encounter in a newly published document; see ch. 14.

A brief analysis of the historical context of these texts can now add certain details which have been made known since our previous (Hebrew) treatment of the matter.[9] Adad's oracle must be interpreted against the backdrop of the evolving ambivalent political relationship between the land of Yamḫad (with Halab as its capital) and Mari, after Zimri-Lim's accession.[10] Though the general picture is obscure, we now know that Zimri-Lim (after almost two decades of exile in Yamḫad?) succeeded in regaining the throne of Mari after forcing out Yasmaḫ-Adad, the Assyrian viceroy.[11] He was aided by Yarim-

[7] For the offering of sacrifice prior to the delivering of an oracle, see *ARM* XIII 23, 4 ff. (where the diviner is designated *aplûm*, a variant of *āpilum*), and A. 455 (G. Dossin *op. cit.* [above, n. 5], 79 f.).

[8] On Adad of Halab, see H. Klengel, *JCS* 19 (1965), 87 ff.; and Adad of Kallassu, *ibid.*, 89. For Zimri-Lim's devotion to Adad of Halab, see his year formula, No. 20, G. Dossin, *Studia Mariana*, 1950, 57; and cf. *Syria* 19 (1938), 115 n. 3, for an oracle obtained by one of Zimri-Lim's functionaries at Halab. See now also *ARM* XIV, 9, where Yaqqim-Adad, governor of Saggarātum, assures Zimri-Lim that sacrifices will be offered to Adad, Lord of Halab, in every town of his district. On the significance of Adad of Halab concerning Zimri-Lim's enthronement at Mari, see below ch. 14.

The tablets recently discovered at Ebla (only 70 km south of Halab) may attest a long-standing tradition of prophecy in the Halab region, over half a millennium prior to Mari, as shown, by the words there for prophet (*nabi'ūtum*, Hebrew *nabî'*) and ecstatic (*maḫḫūm*); cf. G. Pettinato, *BA* 39 (1976), 49.

[9] See above, n. 4.

[10] On relations in general between Yamḫad and Mari, see H. Klengel, *Geschichte Syriens im 2. Jahrtausend v.u.Z.*, I 1965, 102 ff.; III 1970, 146 ff., and cf. P. Artzi and A. Malamat, Orientalia *NS* 40 (1971), 86 ff. (ch. 19 below).

[11] For Zimri-Lim's recovery of Mari, see a very fragmentary victory stele published

Lim, king of Yamḫad (who, at one stage or another became his father-in-law). To this effect, we now have the final publication of a letter (A. 1153) in which Zimri-Lim quotes Yarim-Lim as having said: "Is it not I who made Zimri-Lim regain his throne, who consolidated his strength and the foundation of his throne?" (ll. 8–10). Later in the letter, Zimri-Lim addresses his "father"—that is, his suzerain, Yarim-Lim: "It is my father who made me regain my throne; it is he himself who strengthened me and fastened the foundation of my throne" (ll. 24–25).[12] This immediately recalls the similar phrasing of Adad, Lord of Kallassu (A: 9–13) and Adad, Lord of Halab (B), surrogating for Yarim-Lim of Yamḫad, or rather, Yarim-Lim standing proxy for the deity.

Mari's inferior status vis-à-vis Yamḫad, at least at the time of these oracles, is further emphasized by the harsh tone of Adad, Lord of Kallassu, towards Zimri-Lim, threatening to depose him if he does not fulfill the deity's demand. But we can learn of the looseness of Yamḫad's superiority from the fact that, even after the five appeals to Zimri-Lim noted in B, the deity's ultimatum was ignored—regardless of whether these events were in the days of Yarim-Lim or under his son and successor, Hammurapi.[13]

The crux of the matter lies in the nature of the object demanded by Adad, Lord of Kallassu—the *niḫlatum*. Although its precise meaning here is elusive, it may well have been some sort of estate, real or otherwise; here, coveted as it is by a deity, it would have been dedicated to sacred purposes—perhaps a temple precinct or even the sanctuary itself. This can further be inferred from A: 26–27, which states that "the *āpilum*-diviner of Adad, Lord of Kallassu, is standing guard over the tent-shrine at Alaḫtum, to (be) a *niḫlatum*". That is, the tent-shrine was apparently an interim, anticipatory expedient to be superseded by the eventual *niḫlatum*.

---

by G. Dossin, *Syria* 48 (1971), 1 ff.; and cf. J.M. Sasson, *RA* 66 (1972), 177 f. For an allusion to Yasmaḫ-Adad's flight from Mari, see *ARM* X, 140.

[12] Cf. G. Dossin, *La voix de l'opposition en Mésopotamie*, 1973, 179–183; for earlier reports on this document, cf. *Bull. Acad. Royale Belgique (Classe des lettres . . .)* 38 (1952), 235; *Proceedings, 23rd Congress of Orientalists*, 1954, 121 f.

[13] The death of Yarim-Lim and the accession of Hammurapi at Halab must have occurred about the middle of Zimri-Lim's reign. For the date in terms of Zimri-Lim's year formulas (i.e. his tenth year, at least), see now M. Birot, *Syria* 55 (1978), 342. Our texts A and B are certainly not from early in his reign, as sometimes contended, since Nur-Sin had resided at Mari for a period prior to his appointment to Halab (see A: 29–31).

Alaḫtum, site of the tent-shrine, was perhaps situated near Halab or between Halab and Yamḫad's border with the kingdom of Mari. This town appears in the Mari documents, in three published instances.[13a] In addition to our text A, an administrative text (*ARM* IX, 9) records a shipment of oil from Alaḫtum, sent to Mari by Nur-Sin, Zimri-Lim's "ambassador" to Halab—and a letter (*ARM* X, 176) notes Mari ladies at Alaḫtum, in the presence of several junior clerks (*ṣuhārū*). More revealing are several unpublished texts, sent by Nur-Sin to Zimri-Lim, kindly brought to my attention by Professor G. Dossin.[14] These letters (A. 1257, A. 1496 and A. 4445) show that Alaḫtum had been ceded to Zimri-Lim by Hammurapi of Aleppo who, in the meantime, had succeeded Yarim-Lim to the throne of Yamḫad (about the middle of Zimri-Lim's reign). In one letter, it is reported that "Hammurapi constantly pesters me concerning the construction of the city of Alaḫtum",[15] and he entreats Zimri-Lim to provide the necessary funds as well as masons for that purpose. Can we thus presume that the oracle in A (and B) was invoked to induce Zimri-Lim to provide Adad, Lord of Kallassu, with a tangible estate at Alaḫtum, in stead of the tent-shrine there? Or was this *niḫlatum* to be located at Kallassu, in or near Halab—or even at Mari itself? Only further evidence will tell.

Turning now to the *āpilu*-diviners—an intrinsic and specific part of the Mari milieu—in A we find them, female as well as male (A: 30), as spokesmen for deities, acting also in groups (A: 24), like the groups of prophets in the Bible (cf. I Sam. 10:5, 19:20; I Kings 20:35 ff.).

We have summarized our views on the *āpilum* and the implications for biblical prophecy, especially in ch. 6, pp. 67 ff. and 7, pp. 87 ff.[16] Here, we may note briefly that an *āpilum*-diviner apparently received

---

[13a] It may also appear in *ARM* X, 9:12, spelled *A-la-i-tum*, as suggested by J. Sasson, cited by M.C. Astour, "The Rabbeans: A Tribal Society...", *Syro-Mesopotamian Studies* 2/1 (1978), 4; Astour locates Alaḫtum on the right bank of the Euphrates, between Emar and the Baliḫ confluence (cf. his map on p. 3). But for *a-la-i-tum* as "city resident" see now G. Dossin *ARM* X *ad loc.* and p. 253.

[14] Personal communication, dated 19. X. 1979. For Alaḫtum see also Lafont, *op. cit.* (n. 2), pp. 14–18; and now Durand, who is inclined to identify this site with the city of Alalaḫ, *ARMT* XXVI/3 (forthcoming).

[15] This passage in A. 1496, ll. 5–7, reads: *a-na ka-a-ia-an-tim Ḫa-m[u-ra-pí]/aš-šum a-lim A-la-aḫ-tim/ba-ni-e-em ú-da-ab-ba-ba-an-ni.* Cf. also G. Dossin's report of a text concerning the transfer of Alaḫtum to Zimri-Lim, the appointment of new officials there, and the poor condition of the palace buildings there (see A. Pohl, *Orientalia, NS* 22, 1953, 108).

For the cylinder-seal of Nur-Sin, "servant of Zimri-Lim", see W. Nagel, *AfO* 18 (1958), 323 f.

[16] See also E. Noort *op. cit.* (above, n. 1), 142, index, s.v. *āpilum, āpiltum*; and

the oracles while serving at a tent-shrine, within a cultic framework (A: 37–38). Therefore, in biblical terms he can be considered a "cult-prophet". The very meaning of the Akkadian word *āpilum*, "answerer", "respondent", further recalls biblical terminology concerning divine revelation—i.e. the Hebrew verb *ʿnh*, "to respond", frequently employed for divine responses to prophetic appeals. Significantly, this Hebrew verb is not restricted to specifically solicited responses from the divinity, but may at times refer to revelatory messages *per se*.

Admittedly, the biblical text often makes no mention of any intermediary in such contexts, but the "answerer" must have been a diviner or some other mortal messenger of God. Furthermore, peculiar appellatives for cultic functionaries are noted in Mal. 2:12—*ʿer wᵉʿonǣ* "arouser and answerer" (sic). In Mic. 6:5, referring to Balaam's oracles, we read—". . . what Balak king of Moab devised and what Balaam the son of Beor *answered* him". In this last context, the recently published wall inscriptions from Deir ʿAlla (late 8th–7th century B.C.)—which tell of visions of Balaam son of Beor—mention an *ʿnyh*, "she who answers", that is, a female diviner—in effect, an *āpiltum*.[17] The Aramaic Zakur inscription (*ca.* 800 B.C.) also employs this same root: "Baʿalshamayn answered me (*wyʿnny*) . . . through seers and through diviners" (side A, ll. 11–12).[18]

Hence, the prime function of the *āpilum*/*āpiltum*-diviner appears to have been to reveal unsolicited divine messages, though he or she may occasionally also have been the medium for responses to enquiries

---

L. Ramlot, Le prophétisme, *Dictionnaire de la Bible, Suppl.* VIII, 1972, 884 ff. and most recently Durand in J.-G. Heintz, *Oracles et prophéties dans l'Antiquité*, 1997, pp. 125 ff.

On pp. 130–131 Durand mentions a new Mari term for diviner and he postulates that this term is a West Semitic equivalent to the Akkadian *āpilum*, i.e. *hayyādum, hiādum* (cf. Hebrew *ḥīdā, ḥūd*), a "diseur" (in French translation).

[17] Cf. the editio princeps, J. Hoftijzer and G. van der Kooij, *Aramaic Texts from Deir ʿAlla*, 1976, 174, I:13, translating (p. 180): "she who transmits divine messages"; and the reference there to *āpiltum*, p. 212 (citing our interpretation). For such an interpretation, cf. also H. Ringgren, Balaam and the Deir ʿAlla Inscription, in: *I.L. Seeligmann, Volume III*, 1983, 93–98. The word *ʿnyh*, however, could also mean "the poor one (fem.)", as preferred by A. Caquot and A. Lemaire, *Syria* 54 (1977), 200.

The biblical Balaam seems particularly close to the *āpilum*-diviners of our two Mari texts. He and Balak repeatedly sacrificed and constantly tended the oracle (Num 23:3. 6. 14 ff. 29); cf. M. Weinfeld, *VT* 27 (1977), 186 f. In any event, Balaam should not be compared with the Mesopotamian *barû*, as has frequently been done, since the latter was expert specifically in haruspicy, but was not distinctly a prophet or seer.

[18] For the tie between Mari prophecy and that at Hamath in Zakur's time, cf. J.F. Ross, *HThR* 63 (1970), 1–28 and cf. above ch. 6, pp. 69 f. for further details with regard to this paragraph.

addressed to the deity (as sometimes were the biblical prophets).

Since our earlier treatments of prophecy at Mari, four additional Mari prophetic texts have become known, containing messages revealed by *āpilum/āpiltum*-diviners: A. 4260 (only through a French translation); *ARM* X, 9; *ARM* X, 53; and *ARM* X, 81.[19] These instances shed light on Nur-Sin's statement (our A: 29–31) that, while still resident at Mari, he had had contacts with such diviners there. A. 4260 is addressed to Zimri-Lim by an *āpilum*-diviner (of Shamash at Sippar) himself, without any lay intermediary—a unique occurrence in the Mari prophetic texts. In *ARM* X, 9, an *āpilum*-diviner comes to the palace gate to convey his message to the queen, Shibtu, for delivery to Zimri-Lim. These and other factors[20] show that the *āpilū*-diviners were in more intimate contact with the royal palace than any other type of diviner-prophet at Mari. This relationship brings the *āpilū* into closer analogy with the biblical court-prophets of the type represented by Gad and Nathan. With this, we arrive at the principal theme of our discussion, that is, the bearing of the Mari documents quoted above (our A and B) on similar prophetic messages in the Bible, specifically Nathan's oracle concerning the kingship.

Nathan's prophecy on the Davidic dynasty, often known as the "Davidic Covenant", should preferably be regarded as a dynastic oracle. The text of this prophecy, in II Sam. 7:1–17, is paralleled (with minor variations) in I Chr. 17:1–15; its poetic counterpart appears in Ps. 89, an interpretative exposition of the original,[21] while Ps. 132 would seem to be a poetic reflection of the same oracle. It has been the subject of a voluminous literature—especially since L. Rost's pioneer study in 1926.[22] The specific problems of the textual analysis

[19] For A. 4260, cf. G. Dossin *op. cit.* (above, n. 5), 85. For the other letters, cf. now the improved renderings by G. Dossin (in collaboration with A. Finet), Correspondance féminine, *ARM* X, 1978.

[20] See *ARM* IX, 22:14, where an *āpilum* is listed as receiving a garment from the royal stores.

[21] For the assumption that all three biblical sources are different recensions of an original source, and for an attempt to reconstruct that source, see J.L. Mc-Kenzie, The Dynastic Oracle: II Sam. 7, *ThSt* 8 (1947), 187–218. But for the literary dependence of Ps. 89 on II Sam. 7, see, e.g., N.M. Sarna, in A. Altmann, ed., *Studies and Texts* I: *Biblical and Other Studies*, 1963, 29–46. A divergent view regards Ps. 132 as containing the earliest conception of the "Davidic covenant"; see F.M. Cross, *Canaanite Myth and Hebrew Epic*, 1973, 232 ff., esp. 233.

[22] L. Rost, *Die Überlieferung von der Thronnachfolge Davids*, 1926, 47–73 (Nathanweissagung). Of the vast literature on II Sam. 7, we shall mention only some of the more recent books, which can also be consulted for the earlier literature, including articles and commentaries: R.A. Carlson, *David the Chosen King*, 1964, 97–128; R.E.

of II Sam. 7—such as the various literary strata, the Deuteronomistic redaction and the dating of the several compositional layers—are beyond our present scope, and can be consulted in the literature noted above. Suffice it here to say that the prophecy *per se* comes from the period of the United Monarchy, with a Davidic nucleus and an adaptation under Solomon.

An oft-applied comparison with extra-biblical sources perceives this literary type of prophecy as a sort of *Königsnovelle* on the Egyptian pattern.[23] This has rightly been refuted, most recently by T. Ishida,[24] who instead looks toward Mesopotamia, drawing on comparative material from the neo-Assyrian and neo-Babylonian royal inscriptions. He intimates even a possible early West Semitic tradition underlying Nathan's oracle.[25] In our present study, we focus upon the relevant comparative material in Mari and in the Bible, neither implying nor excluding the diverse possibilities of influence.

Nathan's oracle displays several basic elements held in common with our Mari prophecy, despite several other distinctly contrasting features. Amongst the latter, the promise of Adad, Lord of Kallassu, is conditional upon Zimri-Lim's meeting the deity's demand, whereas the solemn pledge given to David is unconditional, for even if David strays from the way of the Lord, God "will not take my steadfast love from him" (II Sam. 7:15 and cf. Ps. 89:33–37 [MT v. 34–38]; but see the conditional reinterpretation in Ps. 132:12). In other words, the one is obligatory while the other is promissory.[26] Another

---

Clements, *God and Temple*, 1965, 56 ff.; P.J. Calderone, *Dynastic Oracle and Suzerainty Treaty*, 1966; N. Poulssen, *König und Tempel im Glaubenszeugnis des Alten Testaments*, 1967, 43–55, 118 ff., 171–174; F.M. Cross *op. cit.* (above, n. 21), 241–265; T. Veijola, *Die ewige Dynastie. David und die Entstehung seiner Dynastie nach der deuteronomistischen Darstellung*, 1975, 68–79; T.N.D. Mettinger, *King and Messiah*, 1976, 48–63; J. Bright, *Covenant and Promise*, 1977, 49 ff.; T. Ishida, *The Royal Dynasties in Ancient Israel*, 1977, 81–117; K. Ruprecht, *Der Tempel von Jerusalem*, 1977, 62–78; B. Halpern, *The First Historians*, 1988, 164 ff. Cf. also the literature in the following notes and see the recent commentaries P.K. McCarter II *Samuel* (AnBi), 1984, 190–231; H.J. Stöbe, *Das zweite Buch Samuelis* (KAT) 1994, 207–230.

[23] See S. Herrmann's study entitled "Die Königsnovelle in Ägypten und Israel", *WZ Leipzig* 3 (1953/54; *Ges.-sprachwiss. Reihe*, I), 51–62 and now "2 Sam VII in the Light of the Egyptian Königsnovelle—Reconsidered" in ed. S.R. Groll, *Pharaonic Egypt*, 1985, 119–138. Among his many adherents is, recently, M. Görg, *Gott-König-Reden in Israel und Ägypten*, 1975, 178–271.

[24] T. Ishida *op. cit.* (above, n. 22), 83 ff.; and cf., e.g., E. Kutsch, *ZThK* 58 (1961), 137–153, esp. 151 ff.; and more recently T. Veijola *op. cit.* (above, n. 22), 71 f.

[25] T. Ishida *op. cit.* (above, n. 22), 92.

[26] For terminology, see, e.g., M. Weinfeld, *JAOS* 90 (1970), 184–203; *idem, IDB*

fundamental contrast appears in the eventual divine rejection of David's intention to build a temple, whereas Adad was adamant in the fulfilment of his desire by Zimri-Lim (see A: 15 ff. and B).

Despite such divergences, there is much common ground, and the distinctive parallel patterns reveal a typology of dynastic oracles; the common features can be outlined under the following headings:

Motif	*Adad, Lord of Kallassu* (A. 1121 [A], A. 2731 [B])	*Yahwe, Lord of Hosts* (II Sam. 7:1–17)
(a) Installation	"(I) restored him to the throne . . ." (A: 10–11)*	"I took you from the pasture . . . that you should be prince over my people" (v. 8)
(b) Father-son imagery	"(I) reared him* between my loins . . ." (A: 11)	"I will be his father and he shall be my son" (v. 14)
(c) Tent-shrine	*maškānum* (A: 27, 37)	*ʾohæl* and *miškan* (v. 6)
(d) Sanctuary as house or estate	*niḫlatum* (A: 15; B)	*băyit* (v. 5. 6. 13; cf. *năḥᵃlā*, Ex. 15:17, Ps. 79:1)
(e) House as palace/dynasty	*ašar šubti* (A: 13); *bītum* (A: 20)	*băyit* (v. 11. 16)
(f) Throne	*kussû* (A: 11 f., 19)*	*kisseʾ* (v. 13. 16)
(g) Land/kingdom	*epirum* (A: 20); *mātum* (A: 22)	*mămlākā* (v. 12. 16)
(h) Extent of rule	Spatial: "from the rising (of the sun) to its setting" (A: 22–23)*	Temporal: *ʿăd ʿôlâm*, "for ever" (v. 13b. 16)

* Theme employed by Adad, Lord of Halab, in second oracle in A and B.

Suppl. Vol., 1976, 188–192 (s.v. Covenant, Davidic). M. Weinfeld employs the term "grant" for the unconditional form of the covenant with David, but "treaty" for the conditional type. And now cf. J.D. Levenson, *CBQ* 41 (1979), 208 f. Several scholars assume that the Davidic covenant (that is, Nathan's oracle) was originally conditional, but that it became unconditional as the result of later reinterpretation; see, e.g., M. Tsevat, *HUCA* 34 (1963), 71–82; and now F.M. Cross *op. cit.* (above, n. 21), 241 ff., and in both the relevant biblical passages. In contrast, for an original, unconditional covenantal royal ideology, see T.N.D. Mettinger *op. cit.* (above, n. 22), 276 ff.

(a) In either case the installation of the king marked the beginning (David) or renewal (Zimri-Lim) of a dynasty.

(b) This is a conventional metaphor throughout the ancient Near East for the relationship between deities and mortal rulers, as well as between overlords and their vassals. The metaphor takes on a legal connotation, for it implies the legitimation of the ruler. This imagery appears in the Bible for the Israelite king in general, in Ps. 2:7; for Solomon, in our oracle (cf. also I Chr. 20:10; 28:6); and for David, in Ps. 89:26–27, where the motif is further developed, the king becoming the "firstborn" of God.[27] The metaphor in text A from Mari remains unique, however, and implies a much more graphic imagery (see the annotation to A: 11).

(c) If we are correct in our assumption that the *maškānum* in A has a specialized West Semitic connotation (see the annotation to A: 25), then it refers to the sacred abode of the deity, as does the *mšknt* in the earlier literary stratum at Ugarit (in the epics, such as *UT* 128 [*CTA* 15]: III: 19; 2 Aqht [*CTA* 17]: V: 32–33), and the tabernacle in the Bible. Such tent-shrines served primarily in semi-nomadic societies, precisely as noted in Nathan's oracle: "I have not dwelt in a house since the day I brought up the people of Israel from Egypt to this day, but I have been moving about in a tent for my dwelling" (v. 6). This biblical tabernacle or the Tent of Meeting was not merely a cultic shrine, housing the Holy Ark, but served also as an oracular pavilion.[28] This is clearly attested concerning Yahwe's theophany before the Israelites and his revelation to Moses (cf. Ex. 33:7–11, Num. 14:10 ff.; 16:19 ff., Dtn. 31:14–15), and by the seventy elders prophesying at the Tent of Meeting (Num. 11:16–17); and surely this was the case with the *āpilum* in text A as well.

(d) In both Mari and Israel, with the consolidation of the monarchy, an ideological reorientation occurred away from the erstwhile "tent" tradition towards a "house" tradition; in other words, the temporary, mobile shrine came to be replaced by a more elaborate

[27] See the apt remarks by G. Fohrer, *Geschichte der israelitischen Religion*, 1969, 138 ff., justly divorcing this metaphor from the notion of divine descent or adoption, and regarding it merely as an expression of legitimation of rule. Similarly, F.C. Fensham, *Near Eastern Studies in Honor of W.F. Albright* (ed. H. Goedicke), 1971, 130 f. For the father-son imagery, cf. also M. Weinfeld, *JAOS* 92 (1972), 469; *idem, IDB Suppl.* Vol., 190 f.; and T. Ishida *op. cit.* (above, n. 22), 108 f.

[28] Cf. Y. Kaufmann, *The Religion of Israel* (transl. and abridged by M. Greenberg), 1960, 183 f.; M. Haran, *Temples and Temple Service in Ancient Israel*, 1978, 264 ff.; and cf. *Encyclopaedia Biblica*, V 1968, 542 f., s.v. *miškān* (Hebrew).

installation, a permanent structure within an actual, sacred precinct.[29] This finds expression repeatedly in Nathan's oracle, the term *băyit* (v. 5, 6, 13) referring there specifically to a temple; as we have seen, the intended *niḫlatum* in Mari (text A) most probably also referred to real estate, including a structure proper. Significantly, the Bible, too, applies the cognate term *năḥ*ᵃ*lā* (see annotation to A: 15, 27)[30] to Yahwe's permanent abode, as in the Song of the Sea, in Ex. 15:17: ". . . on thy own mountain [*hăr năḥ*ᵃ*latkā*; that is, "the mount of thy estate"], the place, O Lord, which thou hast made for thy abode, the sanctuary. . . ." While the *năḥ*ᵃ*lā* of God generally refers to the Holy Land or to His People, the Israelites, here it points to the Temple Mount in Jerusalem, just as the term is paired with the Holy Temple in Ps. 79:1. Elsewhere, too, *năḥ*ᵃ*lăt Yahwe* is restricted to some specific locale, as in II Sam. 20:19, where it refers to the town of Abel Beth-Maacah. This meaning of *niḫlatum/năḥ*ᵃ*lā* is greatly supported by the Ugaritic mythological texts, which several times designate the divine abode as a *nḥlt.* Of particular relevance to the biblical context is the reference to Baal's holy abode as *ǵr nḥlty*, "the mountain of my *nḥlt*" (*UT* ʿnt [*CTA* 3] III: 27, IV: 64), while the abode of Kothar and Khasis, as well as of Mot, is denoted *ʾarṣ nḥlth*, "the land of his *nḥlt*" (*UT* ʿ*nt* [*CTA* 3] VI: 16; 51 [*CTA* 4]: VIII: 13–14; 16 [*CTA* 5]: II: 16).[31]

(e) The exegetes on II Sam. 7 have generally noted the word play on *băyit*, referring here to both "temple" (v. 5) and "palace" (v. 11): "Would you build me a house (i.e. temple) to dwell in? . . . the Lord will make you a house (i.e. palace)." They also recognize the double meaning of *băyit* as both "palace" and "dynasty". Such a twin usage is found also in Mari, in our text A where *bītum* denoted "palace" in standard Akkadian usage but, under West Semitic influence, came to denote "dynasty" as well, in the phrase *bīt abīšu*, "his father's house", appearing in this sense in several Mari texts.[32]

---

[29] For the age-old "tent" tradition as against the innovative "house" tradition in Israel, see F.M. Cross *op. cit.* (above, n. 21), 231 ff.; and cf. W. Brueggemann, *JBL* 98 (1979), 169 f.

[30] For the *năḥ*ᵃ*lā* in the Bible, cf. *Encyclopaedia Biblica* V, 815 f., s.v. (Hebrew); and *THAT* II, 55 ff. For this term, its verbal form *năḥ*ᵃ*l* and its counterparts at Mari, see A. Malamat, *JAOS* 82 (1962), 147–150 and now *MEIE*, 48–52.

[31] For the references, see C.H. Gordon, *Ugaritic Textbook*, 1965, 443, No. 1633. For the Ugaritic pair *qdš—nḥlt*, "sanctuary"—"estate, patrimony", as well as its biblical correspondents, cf. *Ras Shamra Parallels*, I (ed. L.R. Fisher) 1972, 324, No. 484.

[32] Cf. T. Ishida *op. cit.* (above, n. 22), 101; *CAD* B, 282 ff., s.v. *bītu* 1. temple, palace; 6. royal house; *CAD* A/1, 73 ff., s.v. *abu* A, in *bīt abi* 1. family. The latter surely also includes the sense of "dynasty", usually denoted in Akkadian by *palû*.

(f) The throne was obviously the symbol par excellence of regality, and thus it is emphasized in both texts, figuratively and literally. In another Mari prophecy directed at Zimri-Lim (*ARM* X, 10:13–15), we read: "Kingship, sceptre and throne are sound".[33]

(g) The Bible employs here the Hebrew term *mămlākā*, "kingdom", while the Akkadian used different terminology, expressed by *epirum*, "territory", and *mātum*, "land"—specifically geographical terms. This difference in conceptualization is brought out even more boldly in the next point.

(h) Both the Mari oracle and Nathan's prophecy end with a climactic declaration of divine grace to be bestowed upon the king. In the Mari text, it is to manifest itself spatially, the royal domain is to be extended to the ends of the earth. This favour is distinctly imperial in design, as is the promise, several lines earlier, of palaces, territories and cities. In Nathan's oracle, however, Yahwe's pledge is decidedly in temporal terms, assuring the perpetuation of the Davidic dynasty: "your house and your kingdom shall be made sure for ever before me; your throne shall be established for ever" (v. 16; and cf. Ps. 89:5, 30, 37 f. [MT]).[34] This contrast is representative of the divergent Mesopotamian and biblical world-views, a broad and fascinating subject in itself.

---

[33] The reading *qa-ma-at*, "firm" ("sont solides"), has now been confirmed by Dossin, *ARM* X (1978), 10:15, and p. 254, superseding the previous readings, e.g., *CAD* K, 591b.

[34] For the theological implication of *ʿăd ʿôlam*, cf. *THAT* II, 228 ff., s.v. *ʿôlam*, and the literature there. According to I.L. Seeligmann, *Pĕraqim* 2 (1969–1974), 302 ff. (Hebrew), the notion of the perpetuity of the Davidic dynasty in Nathan's oracle is a late, tendentious addition, making it a divine charter for the Israelite monarchy.

10

PARALLELS BETWEEN THE NEW PROPHECIES FROM MARI AND BIBLICAL PROPHECY*

I. *Predicting the Death of a Royal Infant*

An abundance of new prophecies from Mari, published recently by J.-M. Durand in Volume Twenty Six, Part One of the series of Mari documents,[1] presents a challenge for comparative study with biblical prophecy.[2] From among the various parallels, alongside numerous differences, which can be pointed out on the basis of leafing through the new material, we have chosen two which are of particular interest from several aspects. Let us first examine a prophecy the like of which occurs only once each at Mari and in the Bible.

Infant mortality in antiquity, including that of kings' children, seems to have been quite commonplace, so that reporting it would have been a trivial matter. However, as is demonstrated by two examples, one from Mari and the other from the Bible, exceptional circumstances were liable to warrant the description of such calamities. We cite here the Mari document (initially published in *ARM* X 106 and newly collated in *ARM* XXVI 1 no. 222)[3] in its entirety, noting that although it is damaged on the left side it can be restored with reasonable certainty:

To Dariš-libūr
say:
Thus (says) Ušareš-ḫetil
your [son]—

---

* This article was originally published in: *Nouvelles Assyriologiques Brèves et Utilitaires*, 4 (1989), pp. 61–64.

[1] J.-M. Durand, *Archives Royales de Mari* (*ARM*) XXVI/1 = *Archives Épistolaires de Mari* (*AÉM*) I/1 Paris 1988.

[2] Concerning previously known prophecies from Mari and their comparison with biblical material see my synopsis "A Forerunner of Biblical Prophecy: The Mari Documents," in *Ancient Israelite Religion* (*Essays is Honor of F.M. Cross*, eds. P.H. Miller *et alii*), Philadelphia 1987, pp. 33–52, and ch. 6 above.

[3] Durand, *op. cit.* (n. 1), No. 222 (A. 3724), pp. 451 ff. and see as well the notes on the Akkadian text and cf. p. 403 top.

[concerning the daughter o]f the Queen
(the prophesier) has become en[tranced] (i.e. prophesied):
"[The daughter] of my lo[rd]
[will not live].
[Presently s]he shall di[e]
She was born on [. . .]
[x] x x x"
[At that time] Irra-gamil
[became] entranced (i.e. prophesied).
[Thus h]e (said)—
["She will not li]ve".
[Before the ki]ng reaches Mari
tell him that
the said daughter has died
so that he will be aware.
Perish the thought that upon entering Mari
the king
will (then) hear
about the death of that daughter
and will be taken (aback)
and deeply distressed.

Dariš-libūr, to whom the letter is addressed, occupied a position senior to that of the sender, and is a well known official[4] at the palace of Zimri-Lim, the last king of Mari. The message transmitted in this letter has the purpose of carefully informing the king of the tragic news that the baby girl recently born by his wife has died. The name of the king's spouse is not stated explicitly, although the title *bēltum*, "Lady" seems to indicate that it was his first ranking wife. The name of the prophesier, Irra-gamil, is known from other documents, in which he explicitly bears the title *muḫḫûm*, namely "ecstatic prophet" (or: literally "lunatic", equivalent to the Hebrew *mešuggaʿ*, sometimes used as a designation for prophets).[5] The present document does not use the nominal title, but contains nonetheless the verbal form *maḫû* in the N stem which means "to prophesy, to get excited, to become entranced" (lines 6 and 13). At issue is the prediction of the death of a baby girl. The point of the letter and having the news conveyed to the king before he enters the palace at Mari is to spare him from expressing pain and grief in the presence of the royal entourage and courtiers.

[4] See *ARM* XVI, p. 87, s.v. Dariš-libūr.
[5] For this type of prophesier see A. Malamat, *op. cit.* (n. 2), p. 39; Durand, *op. cit.* (n. 1), pp. 386–388 and ch. 6, pp. 66/7 above.

The document from Mari brings to mind at first glance, even if only superficially, an episode which occurred about 750–800 years later at the court of king David, in which a prophet was involved in announcing the death of the king's offspring (II Samuel 12:13–23).[6] In contrast to the event at Mari, Nathan's appearance before David and his prophecy of disaster have a blatantly moral impetus—the king's adultery with Bathsheba, who eventually became the queen and first ranking wife in the kingdom. Such an ethical motive and the idea of retribution usually set the Bible apart when compared with the prosaic, pragmatic reports known from Mari.

Despite all the differences in circumstances, and although one text speaks of a son and the other of a daughter, there are certain parallels between the two incidents. In both cases the death of the king's child is connected with a prophetic vision, and in both the king is confronted by the senior administration (note the elders of David's House, *ziqnēy bēytô; ibid.* vs. 17). To be sure, at Mari the officials intentionally forewarn the king of the Jobian news, while in the Bible the notables attempt to conceal the disaster (*ibid.* vs. 19). Even so, it seems that the *raison d'être* in both cases was actually identical—concern for the public behavior of the king in time of misery and grief. At Mari, restraint and self control were to be assured, whereas in the Bible, loss of control over the emotions, even to the point of self degradation, was not prevented.

II. *Material Remuneration for Prophetic Services*

It is reasonable to assume that prophesiers and prophets of all sorts depended on material support from their customers who were in need of a divine word. At Mari documentation concerning such matters has reached us in two forms: palace lists and official correspondence.

The palace lists enumerate, among other things, officials, professionnals and types of prophets, sometimes supplying the names of the individual. In many cases the lists included notes recording the

[6] See the commentaries to the Second Book of Samuel such as H.P. Smith, *The Books of Samuel* (ICC), Edinburgh 1899, p. 325; H.W. Hertzberg, *Die Samuelbücher* (ATD), Göttingen 1960, pp. 258 ff.; P.K. McCarter, *II Samuel* (Anchor Bible), Garden City, N.Y., 1984, pp. 296 ff.; H.J. Stöbe, *Das zweite Buch Samuelis* (KAT), Gütersloh 1994, pp. 295 ff.

granting of goods to the prophesier, usually changes of clothes or silver jewelry.[7]

References to prophesiers earning clothes are found in *ARM* IX 22:14; XXI 333:34'–35'; XXII 167:8', and 326:6, 10 (this text mentions a female prophesier who received in addition to a garment two head covers); XXIII 446:9', 19'.[8] Of unique character is XXV 142:12–15. This passage mentions not only a silver ring allotted to the prophesier, but spells out as well the event occasioning the remuneration: "when (the prophesier) reported a vision to the king".[9]

Turning from the lists to the new letters included in *ARM* XXVI 1, we find that two of them make explicit reference to male or female prophesiers demanding payment. In text 199:40 and 53, a female prophesier is mentioned who bears the title *qammatum*[10] and appears in the name of Dagan of Terqa. For her prophetic word she charges a special type of garment and a golden nose ring. These items were paid out to her by the writer of the letter, whereas the woman reported her prophecy to the high-priestess in the temple found in the Mari palace. Also in letter 203:14'–19', a *qammatum* type prophesier earns a large garment of unclear nature. To these documents we may add letter 206:18–27 (published previously in *ARM* XIV 8). In this case the prophesier is a *muḫḫûm* and in exchange for his prophecy of Zimri-Lim's salvation he demands that he be clothed in a suit of clothes—a request complied with by the writer of the letter.

When the prophetic revelation is spontaneous or is initiated by the deity, or, to be more specific, when the prophet speaks in the name of the god and addresses the king or the authorities without being asked, it is only natural that the prophecy is delivered free of charge. For this reason, biblical prophecy, which is usually of the latter type, alludes only on rare occasions to compensation for the prophet. Indeed, any profit for prophesying seems to have fallen into disrepute, cf. Amos 7:12 and especially Micah 3:11, who rebukes among the leading elements in society also ". . . prophets (who) divine for pay." Furthermore, even in such cases where the prophet is approached, as in the above mentioned Mari prophecies, he

[7] See in brief Durand, *op. cit.* (supra, n. 1), pp. 380 f.
[8] For references see Malamat, *op. cit.* (supra, n. 2), p. 39.
[9] See H. Limet, *ARM* XXV, Paris 1986, p. 47.
[10] For this document see Durand, *op. cit.* (supra, n. 1), pp. 426 ff. For the title *qammatum* in place of the previous reading *qabbātum* see *ibid.*, p. 396.

does not demand payment but is given a present by those who employ him.

For example, Jeroboam's wife presents the prophet Ahiah in Shiloh with various items of food—ten loaves, some wafers and a jug of honey—so that he will inquire of the Lord concerning her son who has fallen ill (I Kings 14:1–4).[11] On another occasion King Jeroboam himself tries to entice an anonymous "man of God" to come to his house, certainly so that he will inquire for him concerning his own well being. The king promises to feed him and give him a gift (*ibid.*, 13:7 ff.), but the prophet refuses in accordance with YHWH's command. In the Elisha cycle, the prophet goes to Damascus when Ben-Hadad, king of Aram, is sick (II Kings 8:7 ff.). Hazael suggests that the king visit the prophet and take along some tribute so that Elisha will inquire of the Lord: "Will I recover from this illness?". The tribute, as described in the biblical hyperbole consisted of "forty camel-loads of all the bounty of Damascus." Nonetheless, the prophet's words are gloomy, announcing that the king is destined to die.

In two other cases, the items given the prophet are suits of clothes and/or pieces of silver, as they are at Mari. When Naaman, the army commander of Aram Damascus, turns to Elisha to be cured of the skin inflammation afflicting him (II Kings 5:11), the prophet refuses to accept any compensation whatsoever (vs. 16). But his squire Gehazi, who fancies the presents which Naaman has brought with him (cf. vs. 5), runs after him, unknown to his master, in order to collect the payment customarily intended for the prophet (vs. 20–27). Gehazi demands a talent of silver and two changes of clothes, supposedly for two lads from the prophetic guild, and his request is granted. Gehazi is punished by Elisha for this deception, being afflicted himself with the skin disease. The other incident is more ancient, dating to the time of Saul, before he was king, and Samuel the prophet. It is integrated into the popular tale of searching for the asses lost by Saul's father, Kish (I Samuel 9:1 ff.).[12] Saul's attendant lad suggests locating

---

[11] For this and the following examples from I–II Kings see the commentaries such as: A. Šanda, *Die Bücher der Könige* (Exeg. Handbuch zum AT) I Münster 1911, pp. 363 f.; II 1912, pp. 40–46; E. Würthwein, *Die Bücher der Könige* (ATD), *1. Könige 1–16*, Göttingen 1977, p. 175; *1. Kön. 17–2. Kön. 25*, 1984, pp. 298–303; J.A. Montgomery (ed. H.S. Gehman), *The Book of Kings* (ICC), Edinburgh 1951, pp. 266–271, pp. 373–378; J. Gray, *I & II Kings* (OTL)², London 1970, p. 336, pp. 504 ff.

[12] For this chapter see the commentaries on Samuel mentioned above, supra note 6 and see ch. 8, p. 103.

the missing beasts by going to the "Man of God", for he will certainly be able to point out the proper way to recover the lost animals. Saul remarks that it would be proper to present a *tešûrāh*[13] to the prophet, but none is available. The lad saves the day by suggesting "I happen to have a quarter-shekel of silver. I can give it to the man and he will tell us about our errand" (vs. 7–9).

All the cases from Mari and the Bible lead to the conclusion that when a prophetic vision is "ordered" the prophets could expect to earn material compensation for their services.

[13] This hapax legomenon, meaning "gift" and derived from the root *ŠWR* meaning "to see" has an exact interdialectical equivalent in Akkadian *tāmartu*, "gift," which is derived from *amāru*, "to see". On this word and its Akkadian parallel see S. Paul, "1 Samuel 9,7: An interview Fee", *Biblica* 59, 1978, pp. 542–544, and independently H.R. Cohen, *Biblical Hapax Legomena in the Light of Akkadian and Ugaritic*, (SBL Dissertation Series), Scholars Press, Missoula 1978, pp. 25, 30.

11

NEW LIGHT FROM MARI (*ARM* XXVI) ON BIBLICAL PROPHECY*

A Prophet's Need for a Scribe

Documentation of divine messages, especially when ordered by God, is not unusual among the biblical prophets (see e.g., Isa. 8:1; Ezek. 37:11; Hab. 2:2). The reverse procedure, however, i.e., a prophet petitioning a scribe, on his own initiative, to record the prophet's message, is indeed a rare event. Hence we have but a single instance of this procedure in both the Bible and Mari.

The outstanding case in the former is the well-known account of the prophet Jeremiah and his amanuensis, Baruch, the son of Neriah.[1] On several occasions Jeremiah, or the narrator, specifically mentions the scribe Baruch taking dictation from the prophet's mouth.[2] The key passage is Jer. 36:4: "Then Jeremiah called Baruch ben Neriah and Baruch wrote upon a scroll at the dictation of Jeremiah all the words of the Lord which he had spoken to him" (and cf. Jer. 45:1). Presumably, Baruch was from the outset a person of some eminence and a colleague of the professional royal scribes in Judah circa 600 B.C. This status may be deduced also from the publication of a bulla reading: "(Belonging) to Berekyahu son of Neriyahu the scribe (*hspr*)".[3] In this seal-impression the full form of the scribe's name is stated, whereas the Bible uses the hypocoristicon.

---

* Originally published in: *Storia e Tradizioni di Israele* (in Onore di J.A. Soggin), eds. D. Garrone e F. Israel, Brescia 1991.

[1] See, e.g., the following commentators on Jeremiah: R.P. Carroll, *Jeremiah*, Philadelphia 1986, pp. 662 ff.; A. Weiser, *Der Prophet Jeremia*, Göttingen 1960, pp. 234 ff.; W. Rudolph, *Jeremia*, Tübingen ³1968, pp. 231 ff.

[2] On Baruch and his relationship to Jeremiah, see in particular J. Muilenberg, "Baruch the Scribe", *Proclamation and Presence* (*Essays in Honour of G.H. Davies*), eds. J. Durham and J.R. Porter, London 1970, pp. 224 ff. On writing in the 1st millennium B.C. see A.R. Millard, "An Assessment of the Evidence for Writing in Ancient Israel," *Biblical Archaeology Today* (ed. A. Biran), Jerusalem 1985, pp. 301–312.

[3] The bulla was published by N. Avigad, see his *Hebrew Bullae from the Time of Jeremiah*, Jerusalem 1986, pp. 28 f. and cf. p. 130 and now his *Corpus of West Semitic Stamp Seals* (rev. by B. Sass), Jerusalem 1997, pp. 175 f.

Moreover, Jeremiah commands his scribe to read the scroll before an audience in the Temple (Jer. 36:5–6) and later in the royal quarters, at the office of the court scribe (vv. 12 ff.). Naturally, the court officials in Jerusalem were inquisitive of the actual procedure of the dictation and asked Baruch: "Tell us how did you write all these words? Was it at his dictation?" Baruch answered them: "He dictated all these words to me, while I wrote them with ink on the scroll" (Jer. 36:17–18).

The main question for us is, of course, why the prophet required a scribe at all to whom he could dictate his messages. Ruling out the assumption that Jeremiah was illiterate, we are left with speculative explanations, such as the presumption that the prophet at this particular time had no free access to the Temple, not to mention the palace.[4] In any event, nowhere else in the Bible do we hear of a prophet availing himself of another person in order to dictate his prophecies.

There exists now, however, a comparable instance, at least in principle, in the recently published documents from Mari. The case in point is the letter of a high official, perhaps a military commander of King Zimri-Lim, by the name of Yasim-El, who writes to his lord from the north-eastern sphere of the Mari kingdom. We quote the passage of the letter relevant to the prophetic activity (*ARM* 26/2, no. 414):[5]

Another matter: Atamrum, the respondent
of the god Shamash, came here and thus he spoke to me
as follows: "Send me a competent and discrete
scribe that I have (him) write down
the message of Shamash to the king".
That is what he told me. I have sent Utu-kam
and he wrote this tablet; that man
has appointed witnesses.
Thus he (the prophet) said to me as follows:
"Send this tablet urgently
and the exact wording of the tablet
let him (the king) carry out".
Now, I have sent this tablet
to my lord.

[4] Cf. Muilenberg, *op. cit.* (n. 2), pp. 227 f.; Rudolph, *op cit.* (n. 1), p. 233.

[5] Published by F. Joannès, "Lettres de Yasîm-El," *Archives Royales de Mari* XXVI/2, Paris 1988, pp. 294/5 and cf. J.-M. Durand *ARM* XXVI/1, p. 391. Scribes were employed also with regard to Neo-Assyrian prophecies; see S. Parpola, *SAA* 9, forthcoming (there Prophecy No. 6).

Yasim-El reports to Zimri-Lim that a prophet designated "answerer" or "respondent", a well-known type of diviner in the Mari documents,[6] approached him requesting a scribe in order to take down a message of the god Shamash for the king. The Akkadian spelling for "scribe" here ("the son of the tablet house" referring to a school or rather, academy) indicates an expert in the scribal craft, apparently of an official status.[7] Furthermore, the scribe would have served as a confidant of the prophet, not unlike Baruch with regard to Jeremiah. The dictated message concerned matters of a secret nature, presumably important political or military issues, intended for the king's ear only.[8] Moreover, the message seems to have been of utmost urgency to the Mari ruler.

As stated above, we have here a singular case in the prophetic corpus of Mari of a prophecy dictated to a scribe and, furthermore, in the presence of witnesses. In all other instances, the prophet delivers his message orally, usually to royal officials or governors, who would then pass on a written report to the king of Mari. Even if scribes may have officiated as intermediaries in other cases, we have no allusion to their existence elsewhere.

There may be several explanations for our extraordinary episode, such as the illiteracy of the prophet who, in this case, had no proper person to address orally. More reasonable is the assumption that Atamrum was not familiar enough with the Babylonian language and perhaps spoke a foreign dialect in the heavily populated Hurrian environment. Thus, a scribe was selected to render the prophecy into proper standard Akkadian for the royal scribes at the Mari palace.[9] An alternate explanation might lie in the very contents of the message, which may have been of utter secrecy, and thus prevented from being delivered orally.

---

[6] The prophetic title *āpilum*, "*respondent*", occurs relatively frequently at Mari. On this kind of prophet see J.-M. Durand, *ARM* XXVI/1, Paris 1988, pp. 338 ff. and A. Malamat, *MEIE*, pp. 86 f.

[7] The Akkadian reading for scribe employs here the exceptional form: lú-dumu é ṭup-pi, rendered by, e.g., B. Landsberger, *JCS* 9 (1955), p. 125 n. 125, as scribe of the royal administrations, military scribe.

[8] This may be deduced perhaps from the fact that the prophet does not deliver his message to the general Yasim-El in order that it be passed on to the king.

[9] For the problematic and unresolved issue of the original dialects spoken by the prophets see A. Malamat, ch. 6, p. 65 above.

Selecting a Campaign Route by Oracle

In an additional letter of Yasim-El (*ARM* 26/2, no. 404)[10] the application of an oracle is again attested, having its parallel in biblical prophecy. This time the divinatory means alludes to a military affair—the specific manner of an army advance. Yasim-El in his lengthy report records, *inter alia*, the military designs of Atamrum, king of Andariq (and not the prophet, his namesake mentioned in the previous section). This kingdom is located to the north-east of Mari in the Jebel Sinjar region.[11]

Atamrum, together with several of his vassal kings and an auxiliary army of 500 soldiers, is on his way to Mari. Atamrum has previously turned down an offer to assist Babylon and decides to hold negotiations with Zimri-Lim. The particular route to be taken in order to reach Mari, however, remains undecided. The relevant section of the text reads (ll. 81–85):

> He (Atamrum) will arrive [either via] Saggaratum or via Terqa [or via Ma]ri. Concerning the three routes [ ] he is going to arrange [an oracular inquiry] and [if his gods render their consent], it is that (particular) route which shall be seized and he will arrive at my lord. May my lord [know about it]!

The significance of selecting the right route is elusive. No prophet is mentioned here and in the lacuna of the tablet a word for oracle has been suggested by the editor.[12] Indeed, in the cuneiform sources diviners or mantic devices, per se, frequently occur in the reporting of army movements. In a similar instance of an alternative concerning three routes in the advance of a campaign, Pharaoh Thutmosis III (first half of the 15th century B.C.) depends on a more rational means of strategic character in order to attack Meggido in Palestine.[13]

The Bible makes only one mention of an episode similar to the above incident, not surprisingly in a Babylonian context. Yet the contrast lies in the choice of the target—in Mari all three routes lead

---

[10] Published by F. Joannès, "Lettres de Yasim-El", *Archives Royales Mari*, XXVI/2, Paris 1988, pp. 260–263.

[11] Cf. *ARM* XVI/1, p. 5, s.v. Andariq and there bibliography.

[12] I.e.: *te-re-tim*; see also *AHw*, p. 1350, s.v. *têrtum*.

[13] See his Annals in Karnak, *ANET*³, pp. 235b f. For another attestation in Mari of a road junction parting into three alternative routes to the West, see J.-M. Durand: "Les trois routes de l'Euphrates à Qatna à travers de desert", *MARI* 5 (1987), pp. 159–167; cf. *ARM* XXVI/2 500, ll. 16–27 (selection between two routes).

to the very same objective, the capital city, whereas in the Bible each route proceeds to a different place. When referring to Nebuchadnezzar's campaign to the kingdom of Judah in 589 B.C., Ezekiel describes the advance of the Babylonian army halting at the junction of roads. The relevant passage reads[14] (Ezekiel 21:24–27 [MT; NJPS; RSV 21:19–23]):

> And you, O mortal, choose *two* roads on which the sword of the king of Babylon may advance, both issuing from the same country; and select a spot, select it where roads branch off to [two] cities. (25) Choose a way for the sword to advance on Rabbah of the Ammonites or on fortified Jerusalem in Judah. (26) For the king of Babylon has stood at the fork of the road (*ēm ha-derek*), where *two* roads branch off, to perform divination: He had shaken arrows, consulted teraphim, and inspected the liver (*rāʾāh baʾ-kābēd*). (27) In his right hand came up the omen (*ha-qesem*) against Jerusalem . . . (Hebrew terms supplied).

The description refers, outwardly, to the performance of a symbolic action by the prophet, as if to set up signposts at the fork of the road, pointing to Rabbath Ammon, on the one hand, and Jerusalem, on the other. Yet in contradistinction to most commentators, this prophecy is certainly not entirely imaginary, but rather, based on a realistic, concrete background. Without entering here into a complex textual analysis, our passage deals with Nebuchadnezzar's dilemma upon reaching a junction along the main route (most likely at Damascus). Which direction should his army pursue, the more eastern route leading to Rabbath Ammon or the western (or right hand)[15] route towards Jerusalem? The decision is reached by consulting an oracle traced through various mantic means. Three such devices, well-known in ancient divinatory performances, are enumerated: The shaking of (inscribed?) arrows, the inquiring, by means of teraphim, and the inspection of the liver, i.e. by means of hepatoscopy or extispicy.[16] In particular, the last practice was common in Mesopotamia especially in the military realm.

---

[14] See, e.g., the following commentaries on Ezekiel: W. Eichrodt, *Der Prophet Hesekiel*, Göttingen 1966, pp. 195–197; G.A. Cooke, *Ezekiel* (ICC), Edinburgh 1936, pp. 231–238; W. Zimmerli, *Ezechiel* I, Neukirchen-Vluyn 1969, pp. 481–489; M. Greenberg, *Ezekiel 21–37* (AnBi), 1997, pp. 426–430.

[15] On the possible magical significance of the "right hand" as a benevolent sign, see now M. Greenberg, "Nebuchadnezzar at the Parting of the Ways: Ezekiel 21:26–27," in *Ah, Assyria* . . . (FS H. Tadmor), eds. M. Cogan and I. Eph'al, Jerusalem 1991, pp. 267–71.

[16] For divination through the inspection of the liver of an animal see recently I. Starr, *The Rituals of the Diviner*, Malibu 1983. See there also on the significance of the "right" versus "left" side in examining the liver, pp. 60 ff.

The oracle points to the road leading to Jerusalem, a move which conforms fully with strategical considerations, favouring an initial attack on the stronger target (i.e. Jerusalem), rather than on the weaker one (Rabbath Ammon). Ezekiel must have been familiar with the operational designs of Nebuchadnezzar as well as with the political constellation of the West where Ammon was the closest, or only ally of Judah and thus also an adversary of Babylonia.[17]

[17] E.g. A. Malamat, The Last Years of the Kingdom of Judah, *The Age of the Monarchies-Political History* (*WHJP* IV/1), Jerusalem 1979, p. 215.

12

THE SECRET COUNCIL AND PROPHETIC INVOLVEMENT IN MARI AND ISRAEL*

Among the recently published documents from the Mari archives (*ARM*, vols. 26/1–2)[1] there are five letters that mention a state body in the nature of a secret assembly or council, for which the biblical term סוד is appropriate. In the discussions on these letters some additional as yet unpublished documents are referred to. The Akkadian term for the secret assembly here is *pirištum*, a word known for some time but whose meaning as an assembly or council has not been elucidated.[2] It apparently is a cognate of the Targumic Aramaic פְּרִישְׁתָּא and Mishnaic Hebrew word פְּרִישָׁה, i.e., separation and isolation.[3]

First, let us list the Mari documents: *ARM* 26/1, no. 101 (p. 266 and cf. pp. 237/8); no. 104 (p. 270 and cf. pp. 21, 237/8); no. 206 (pp. 434 ff., cf. p. 381). In vol. 26/2, see no. 307 (p. 64); and no. 429 (p. 329). Here we shall deal only with the three documents in the first volume for they alone are connected with the diviners who attend the secret council or are removed from it. And this is precisely our concern in the comparison between Mari and the Bible.

In document 26/1, no. 101, Ḫali-Ḫadun and Ilu-shu-naṣir, two diviners (see the phenomenon of a pair of diviners below), complain together to Zimri-Lim, King of Mari, that Ibal-pi-Il, the Mari ambassador in Babylon, is conspiring against them. He will not provide them with sheep for performing hepatoscopy (liver-divination) for the

* This article was originally published in R. Liwak und S. Wagner, (eds.), *Prophetie und geschichtliche Wirklichkeit im alten Israel* (FS S. Herrmann), Stuttgart 1991, pp. 231–236. The English biblical texts are from the Revised Standard Version, 1952, unless indicated otherwise.

[1] See J.-M. Durand *et alii*, *ARM* XXVI/1–2 (= *AÉM* I/1), Paris 1988.

[2] *AHw* II, 866, s.v. *pirištum* "Geheimnis", i.e. secret, but neither this nor any other dictionary entry carries the sense of a secret assembly, and this warrants renewed investigation of the various Belegstellen.

[3] M. Jastrow, *A Dictionary of the Targumim, the Talmud Babli and Yerushalmi, and the Midrashic Literature*, New York 1950, 1228, s.v. פְּרִישָׁה, "separation", etc.; G.H. Dalman, *Aramäisch-Neuhebräisches Handwörterbuch zu Targum, Talmud und Midrasch*, Frankfurt 1922, 399, s.v. פְּרִישָׁה; cf. J. Levy, *Wörterbuch über die Talmudim und Midraschim*, Bd. IV, Berlin/Wien [2]1924 (Nachdruck Darmstadt 1963), 144: "Absonderung".

oracle for the army's safety. The diviners are therefore turning to the king so that he may order the ambassador to do his duty. Furthermore, Ibal-pi-Il expels the diviners from the secret council (or סוֹד, in biblical terminology) of King Hammurabi in Babylon. The diviners protest against the ambassador: "Ibal-pi-Il drove us out, and we are no longer parties to the secret council, no longer enter the palace with him. He detests us. . . ." In other words, the diviners are perturbed that they can no longer fulfill their function and request the king of Mari to right the wrong. However, it may be that the rejection by the ambassador was not arbitrary but a result of conflicting interests between the high official in question and the diviners.

In connection with this document, J.-M. Durand, the editor, cites two as yet unpublished tablets (p. 267/8). M. 6845: "In sum: 23 men sit in the presence of the king in the secret council." A second document deals with a complaint: "Why did we expel you from our Lord's secret council? It is required that our Lord keep a record of those of his servants that 'hear' (i.e. that are present at the meeting of) my Lord's secret council."

The second document, no. 104 (and also cf. p. 21) is a letter from Ibal-pi-Il to Zimri-Lim that deals with a prophecy meant for the king. As in the Bible, here too we have the connection of a diviner and the secret council or סוֹד. In Mari, what is said relates to state secrets whose intent is hidden, and such also seems to be the case with the biblical prophets. The letter mentions (by name) three generals in the army of Ishme-Dagan, the sworn enemy of Mari, of the rival Assyrian dynasty and heir of King Shamshi-Adad. The army generals make their way into the secret council of Hammurabi, the Babylonian king, and thus receive information of the diviners' oracles revealed in closed session. Here too, the preparation for an oracle by the diviners is spoken of, but this time Ibal-pi-Il does provide the sheep needed for the performance. This time, also, two diviners are mentioned together—Ḫali-Ḫadun (whom we have already met) and Inib-Shamash. The appearance of a pair of diviners is characteristic in connection with the secret council, perhaps in order to support the testimony emerging from the omens and to present it properly. In order to keep the disclosure of the omens, which concern state or military secrets, from hostile ears, Ibal-pi-Il removes the Assyrian officers from Hammurabi's council. As for the diviners, they not only report the omens in the closed circle but also interpret them and their significance for the king of Mari.

Finally, no. 206 is a letter to Zimri-Lim from Yaqqim-Adad, the Mari governor in the city of Saggaratum on the lower Habur. At first, he reports on a bizarre, and for us hair-raising, occurrence of a prophet bearing the title of *muḫḫûm* of the god Dagan, i.e. an ecstatic prophet serving as an emissary of Dagan, who carries out a symbolic action at the city gate of Saggaratum.

The city gate is often the prophesier's area. His pronouncements and actions there are documented both at Mari and in the Bible; the palace gates at Mari (see preceding prophetic documents) and at Babylon are also mentioned in this connection (*ARM* 26/2, no. 371, p. 178 and cf. part 1, pp. 340, 402). But, in particular, the gates of the city of Mari are mentioned (part 1, no. 208, p. 437 and the preceding document), as well as the city of Terqa (part 1, p. 450, no. 222-bis), and, in the document discussed here, the gate of the city of Saggaratum. And when, in the Bible, the phrase "who reproves in the gate" occurs in two of the prophetic books (Isa. 29:21; Amos 5:10), it is undoubtedly referring to the prophet positioned at the gate rebuking the people.

The prophet of our letter tears asunder a live sheep (cf. Jud. 14:6) and eats (*akālum*) a chunk of it raw, with the city elders crowded around, watching the vulgar performance. The prophet interprets the word *eating* as similar to or identical with the word pestilence, *ukultum*, which is to break out in the land.[4] The prophecy, then, is based upon a play on words, a phenomenon also found in biblical prophecy.[5] The prophet continues: "demand of the different cities that they return the sacred things (*assakum*). The ones who will act violently should be expelled from the city." The letter ends: "The omens which he (the prophesier) revealed to me are not secret (*simištum*)[6]. Indeed, he disclosed the omens in the assembly of the elders (i.e., in a public forum)."

---

[4] One of the nominal derivations from the verb *akālum*, "eat" (line 9) is *ukultum* which Durand translates as "dévorement" (la peste), i.e., plague, pestilence. On text No. 206 and its symbolism see most recently Heintz in: *Oracles et Prophéties dans l'antiquité* (ed. J.-G. Heintz), Strasbourg 1997, 202 ff.

[5] About plays on words in biblical prophecy, both positive and negative as in Mari, see, for example, the visions in Jer. 1:11–12: ". . . I see a rod of almond ('שָׁקֵד') . . . for I am watching ('שֹׁקֵד') over my word to perform it"; Amos 8:1–2: ". . . behold a basket of summer fruit (קָיִץ) . . . the end ('קֵץ') has come upon my people Israel."

[6] On the word *simištum* (line 32), Durand notes that it is absent in the Akkadian dictionaries, and that it is derived from the root *SMŠ*, a root mentioned in Mari as a verb meaning "to hide", "to conceal".

The omens were thus made known to the public, in contradistinction to the other instances.

As stated in the documents thus far, prophets and diviners are involved in the secret council in one form or another, whereas in the other documents (in vol. 26/2) there is no mention as noted, of this phenomenom, and we will therefore not deal with them here.

Unlike many other topics, the comparison of Mari and Israel in this matter of ours is rather vague and forced, for we are dealing here with two different planes on which the secret council is active. In Mari, the council is an actual, earthly, secular body that, first and foremost, is a royal-state institution functioning alongside the ruler or governor, and the like; whereas, in the Bible, in most instances, what we have is a heavenly assembly headed by the Deity, i.e., here we are on the theological plane. There is no doubt that this plane is a projection of the earthly, real council.[7] In the Bible, too, the members of the divine council are almost without exception prophets (alongside heavenly beings). To be sure, even in the Bible, in a few instances, we have a national council or convocation but, even then, the main participants are God or his spokesmen—the prophets. In order to understand the essence of the inner, closed council that is called סוֹד in the Bible, and in order to ascertain its apparatus and activity, we must draw an analogy not only from source to source but also from the earthly-royal plane to the heavenly-divine one—an analogy that is complicated and rather risky.

The word סוֹד, as is known, is mentioned in the Bible in two different but closely inter-related meanings. In the opinion of most scholars, the concept of סוֹד in the sense of something hidden and concealed, is not, contrary to first impression, the basic meaning of the word. Its basic meaning is derived from the other sense: a "secret council", an inner, closed circle.[8] Indeed, in the Bible, as in the case of Mari, we shall deal with סוֹד only in the sense of a secret council.

---

[7] On סוֹד in the Bible, see the summation by H.-J. Fabry, *ThWAT* V (1986), 775–782, s.v. סוֹד *sôd*, and the detailed bibliography there. And, in particular, on the prophet's participation in the סוֹד, see H.W. Robinson, "The Council of Yahwe", in *JThS* 45 (1944), 151–157; M.E. Polley, "Hebrew Prophecy Within the Council of Yahwe", in: *Scripture in Context* (eds. C.D. Evans *et alii*), Pittsburgh 1980, 141–156; M. Saebø, *ThHAT* II (1976), 144–148, s.v. סוֹד *sōd*. Cf. also the recent remark by R.P. Gordon, "From Moses to Mari . . .", in: *Of Prophets' Visions* . . . (FS R.N. Whybray), eds. H.A. McKay *et alii*, Sheffield 1993 (*JSOTS* 162), pp. 63–79.

[8] See the literature in note 7 above, especially *ThWAT* V, 777.

The verbs used to indicate presence in the council are also parallel in the two sources: "I did not sit in the סוֹד" (Jer. 15:17) and in the Akkadian *wašābum* (see above), and especially "For who among them has stood in the סוֹד" (Jer. 23:18), *i/uʾzuzzum*, "stand", in Akkadian. This verb serves in various contexts in both Akkadian and Hebrew, also to indicate service before a high authority and participation in an assembly in general (not necessarily in a סוֹד).

The term סוֹד as an assembly is used in the Bible some fifteen times, in most instances connected with prophecy and prophets. Perhaps the most outstanding instance is Jer. 23:18: "For who among them has stood in the council of the Lord to perceive and to hear his word?"[9] The words are directed at the contrast and rift between the true prophets, found in the council of the Lord (cf. Amos 3:7), and the false prophets (terms which, incidentally, are found not in the Bible itself but in the later sayings of the Sages), who have no part in the secret, heavenly assembly. Thus, the truth is absent from their words and they utter false prophecies. Therefore Jeremiah continues his discourse in which he completely denies the false prophets' presence in the סוֹד (Jer. 23:22): "But if they (the false prophets) had stood in my council, then they would have proclaimed my words to my people, and they would have turned them from their evil way and from the evil of their doings." Another relevant passage about the false prophets and their absence from the סוֹד is found in the Book of Ezekiel (13:9): ". . . the prophets who see delusive visions and who give lying divinations; they shall not be in the council of my people, nor be enrolled in the register of the house of Israel. . . ." The approximation to Mari is greater here because the council does not indicate a theological concept but an earthly body—the people of Israel, or in my opinion, a limited, intimate circle within the people to which the admission of the false prophets is forbidden and prevented. They are not even listed in the register of the Children of Israel, referring to a kind of citizens' roster.[10]

סוֹד appears in different phrases in the books of Psalms and Jeremiah

---

[9] On this verse and verse 23 of the same chapter, see the latest detailed commentary on the Book of Jeremiah: W. McKane, *Jeremiah* 1 (*ICC*), 1986, 576, and on the term סוֹד there (581). In verse 22, the author translates סוֹדִי as commonly, "my secrets", i.e. the false prophets did not acquire the hidden words of the Deity; but, here too, the interpretation of the "secret assembly" from which these prophets were absent, is preferable (as in the *NJPS*).

[10] See commentaries on the Book of Ezekiel, and especially: M. Greenberg, *Ezekiel*, 1–20 (AnBi 22), 1983, 237; W. Zimmerli, *Ezechiel*, *BK* XIII/1, 1969, 292.

with the precise meaning not always being clear: "סוֹד of the holy ones" (Ps. 89:8[7]) and "סוֹד of the upright" (Ps. 111:1)—apparently the angels or the children of God, heavenly figures; "סוֹד of the wicked" (Ps. 64:3[2])—followed by the parallelism, "evildoers"; "סוֹד of young men" (Ps. 6:11), "סוֹד of merrymakers" (Ps. 15:17)—an intimate group of young people. Once "סוֹד" appears in the Book of Job (19:19) in a phrase translated as "All my intimate friends", referring to those present at an assembly who, says Job, abhor and despise him as, in Mari, Ibal-pi-Il detests the two diviners participating in the secret council.

The general importance of the last two texts that mention the concept of סוֹד as an assembly or an intimate circle is clear, though they do not sufficiently clarify the assembly's purpose. In both instances, it is a real, earthly סוֹד. In Gen. 49:6, Jacob's blessing, it is said of the tribes of Simeon and Levi: "O my soul, come not into their council (סוֹד); O my spirit, be not joined to their company. . . ." In our opinion, the "council" spoken of here is none other than the joint assembly of the two tribes, an institution of the tribal covenant, for the opening (previous) verse begins: "Simeon and Levi are אַחִים," i.e. brothers in the sense of allies. The second verse containing the term סוֹד, Ps. 83:4[3], can be interpreted in a number of ways: "They lay crafty plans (סוֹד) against thy people; they consult together against thy protected ones. . . ." One may assume that these words are spoken apparently during a military consultation in an inner, closed assembly. Almost certainly the reference is to the enemies of Israel, enumerated as the chapter continues, who had convened in a סוֹד to form an alliance (v. 6 [5]) in order to carry out their military plots against the Children of Israel. This may also be the purpose of the earlier verse and elsewhere, exactly as in Mari (26/1, no. 206).

The term סוֹד is always mentioned in the Bible in a static manner, without detailing how matters were handled within the assembly. However, there are in the Bible, unlike at Mari, detailed descriptions of heavenly assemblies, though with no connection to the term סוֹד. Included among these are the classic visions of Isaiah's call to prophecy (Isa. 6) or the introduction to the Book of Job (Ch. 1), where (v. 6) the "sons of God came to present themselves before the Lord and Satan also came among them." Especially instructive for our concern is the section on the prophet Micaiah the son of Imlah during the war of Ahab and Jehoshaphat against Aram (I Kings, 22).[11] On the

---

[11] For example, see: E.C. Kingsbury, "The Prophets and the Council of Yahwe",

eve of the military expedition, the two kings meet at the threshing floor "at the entrance of the gate of Samaria" (v. 10), precisely like the event in the last Mari document mentioned above (*ARM* 26/1, no. 206).

Ahab assembles four hundred prophets in the vicinity of the gate to seek out the fate of the military venture and, most likely in the name of the Lord, they prophesy a brilliant victory for the forces of Israel. Furthermore, the text emphasizes that their prophecy was "with one accord" (v. 13). Jehoshaphat is not satisfied with this biased, unequivocal prophecy and wants further prophetic opinion, i.e., further examination of the prophecy of the four hundred, a resort to a kind of counter-prophecy.[12] Micaiah ben Imlah, prophet of the Lord, is summoned. He, as we know, prophesies the complete opposite of the society of prophets; that is, he foresees the total defeat of Israel, based upon the word of the Lord (verses 15 ff.). It may be that here too, as in the Mari documents, we have two groups of prophets functioning side by side, even though these groups are generally represented by a single prophet. Only as things continue does the biblical description transfer to the heavenly scene and the divine assembly in which Micaiah is a visionary participant (v. 19 ff.).[13] The Lord is sitting on His throne with the heavenly host standing on His right and left, as is customary in the king's council. A divine dialogue begins, as a result of which the spirit of falsehood accepts the mission of misleading all the prophets (i.e., the aforementioned four hundred). Obviously, we have here a typical description of the divine סוֹד which, as we have said, is nothing other than a derivative of the earthly-royal סוֹד.

Perhaps we can assume that God's words were often imparted to

---

JBL 83 (1964), 279–286; J. Gray, *I & II Kings* (OTL), London ²1970, 443 ff.; E. Mullen, *The Assembly of God*, Chico 1980, 205 ff.; A. Rofé, *The Prophetical Stories*, Jerusalem 1988, 142–152.

[12] The checking of the prophecies by another prophet or by mantic means is a universal phenomenon. On Mari, see A. Malamat, *MEIE*, 95 ff.; I. Starr, *The Rituals of the Diviner*, Malibu 1983, 4 ff.

[13] A. Rofé, *op. cit.* (n. 11), also discusses the difference between the nature of the source of the typical prophecy of Micaiah, on the one hand, and that of the four hundred prophets, on the other. The former gained his prophecy by virtue of the divine סוֹד, i.e., by means of an audio-visual experience. The other prophets were visited by the spirit only, a spirit (evil) sent from the divine סוֹד, hence presumably we have here a lower degree of prophetic inspiration. A. Rofé posits that, in time, this distinction caused a split among the prophets—a camp of the true prophets ("members of the סוֹד") and the false prophets.

the true prophets via their presence in the heavenly assembly (cf. Amos 3:7), even when the word סוֹד is not in the biblical text. The heavenly council certainly served as a source of inspiration and a conduit for transmitting the divine message, just as Ezekiel, for example, achieved his prophecy by means of a scroll which the Lord fed the prophet (Ezek. 3:1–3);[14] Isaiah, through the Seraph's touch upon his lips (Isa. 6:7); and Jeremiah, via God's touching his mouth: "and the Lord said to me, 'Behold, I have put my words in your mouth'" (Jer. 1:9).

---

[14] On the premise that the divine assembly was a sort of vehicle for the transmission of prophetic visions, see, for example M.E. Polley, *op. cit.* (n. 6), 149.
On Ezekiel's eating of the scroll, see the commentaries mentioned above in n. 10: M. Greenberg, *op. cit.*, 67 f., 73; W. Zimmerli, *op. cit.*, 77 and ch. 13 below.

13

NEW MARI DOCUMENTS AND PROPHECY IN EZEKIEL*

We shall examine, first and foremost, the relatively new documents from Mari, which have been published over the last few years in two volumes: Archives royales de Mari 26/1 and 2 (see notes 4 and 5). These short studies will discuss divination both in Mari and in the Book of Ezekiel.[1]

A. *The Power of God's Hand*

We shall first examine the material from Mari and then turn to the Book of Ezekiel. The Akkadian expression equivalent to the biblical "be" (often translated as "come") or to the expression "be strong" of "God's hand" is *qāt ilim* (or ŠU *ilim*) with the verb added, and is also found in Mesopotamian literature outside Mari. In contrast to most of the instances in the Bible as well as in Mari, the expression in Akkadian literature is usually connected with adversity, such as some kind of calamity or sickness.[2] Indeed, this meaning is also commonly found in the West Semitic region, such as in the documents from Tall al Rimaḥ, which were likewise composed in the Akkadian language, close to the Mari period. One of the documents from Tall al Rimaḥ mentions two youths who were struck, one after the other, by the hand of the deity: ". . . The young man (i.e. the second youth) who is afflicted by the 'hand of god' is continually ill" (No. 65, l. 16 ff.).[3] The young man was, without doubt, a diviner, as testified by

---

* This article has not been published in English. For a version in Hebrew see: M. Cogan *et al.* (eds.), *Tehillah le-Moshe* (FS M. Greenberg), Winona Lake, IN, 1997, pp. 71–77.

[1] I have discussed another parallel prophecy in Mari and Ezekiel (Ez. 21:24–27) in the FS dedicated to J.A. Soggin, *Storia e Tradizioni di Israele* (Brescia 1991), 188 ff., above ch. 11.

[2] *CAD* Q (1982), 186 a a, s.v. *qātu, qāt ilim.*

[3] See S. Dalley *et alii, The Old Babylonia Tablets from Tall al Rimah* (British School of Archeology in Iraq 1976), 64, No. 65: 14–19.

the custom of cutting his hair and the hem of his garment—a custom common in Mari among diviners, both men and women (see ch. 6, pp. 78 f. above). Compare the case of this young man, who prophesied and fell sick, with the Mari archives themselves, *ARM* 13, 112. The illness, in such cases and in others, no doubt involved an ecstatic experience undergone by the diviner. In the new documents from Mari, collected in volume 26/1,[4] the raising/use of the deity's hand is mentioned in six incidents (and in an additional incident mentioned in volume 26/2), either the hand of a specific god or of an unnamed god, and usually in a favourable sense, i.e. without causing sickness. We shall present these incidents in the order in which the documents have been collected.

1) In *ARMT* 26/1 No. 83, the sense is unfavourable, that is, affliction is intended. Asqudum, the chief expert (*bārû*) in divination at the palace at Mari, sends a letter to his lord, Yasmah-Addu, who was the ruler of Mari at that time. These are his words: "The oracle I consulted (has said) 'The hand of Ashtar of Radan' from the city of Ekallatum. The goddess put pressure/oppressed her (the woman) . . . until she (the woman) went to the city of Ekallatum her sickness did not lose its grip (on the woman, whose name is mentioned at the beginning of the letter)" (ll. 9–16). Here, as in several other incidents, the hand of the deity could cause ill health, to the extent that the expression "the hand of god" was itself used as a synonym for sickness. 2) Document No. 84. The correspondents here are the same as those in the preceding document, but this time there is no touch of the "divine hand" (*qāt–ilutim*; on this perplexing morphology, see note d on the interpretation of the document) causing harm or ill-health. 3) Document No. 136. The writer informs Yasmah-Addu that he has examined the entrails (of a sheep) again and again, to procure the recovery of the Lady Beltum (*beltum* = mistress) who was the First Lady of the palace at Mari at that time and was, apparently, the wife of Yasmah-Addu, having been brought from the city of Qatna in the West. It was inferred from the oracle that the princess's sickness was not caused by "the hand of god", but that she had merely fallen ill with a high fever; the writer points out that her life is not in danger.

[4] J.-M. Durand, *ARM* 26/1 = *AEM* I/1 (Paris, Editions Recherche sur les Civilisations, 1988).

4) Document No. 260. This letter is also addressed to Yasmah-Addu. It begins with a passage about "the hand of god". This time the "hand" has become relaxed. It does not strike with affliction, but is serene and calm. Now, no one has died on the day "the hand of god" was raised, although previously an epidemic had been raging and, in one day, ten adults and five children had died.
5) Document No. 264. A high official writes to the ruler of Mari: "See how 'the hand of god' which (found rest) on earth was conciliatory", i.e. "the hand of god" moved with favourable intention.
6) Document No. 265. At the end of the letter under discussion, there is a postscript stating that "the hand of god" was relaxed and calm and that the palace of Mari was at peace.
7) In addition to the above examples, the expression "the hand of god" may be found in volume 26/2, No. 371, lines 9–12.[5] This is a "prophetic" letter sent to king Zimri-Lim, in which there appears a diviner, with the title of *āpilum* (= respondent),[6] of the god Marduk, who ceaselessly warns: "Isme-Dagan will not escape from the hand of Marduk!"

In the above letters from Mari concerning "the hand of god", two categories should be mentioned: in the one the raised hand causes disaster and even death; in the other, "the hand of god" does not bring harm, but rather, it is beneficial to people or to the earth. It is possible that this second category is not typical of the Akkadian view of the world, but is characteristic of the culture of the Western regions (including, *inter alia*, Mari and the Bible).

In the Bible the phrase "the hand of God" (YHWH, and only once *ᵉlōhā*, Job 19:21) is mentioned many times, involving various functions, such as in the Exodus from Egypt and the wanderings of the Ark of the Covenant in 1 Samuel. However, here we shall confine ourselves to discussing the expression only in connection with prophecy and the arousal of prophetic vision[7] as testimony to one of the uses of the phrase in Akkadian. In particular, we shall focus our attention

---

[5] D. Charpin in *ARM* 26/2 (Paris, ERC 1988), 177–179.

[6] On the term *āpilum* see A. Malamat, ch. 6, pp. 67 f. Cf., e.g., D. Charpin, "Le contexte historique et géographique des prophètes . . . à Mari", *Bulletin Canadian Society for Mesopotamian Studies* 23 (1992), 21–2.

[7] On the hand of God in the Bible in connection with prophecy, see J.J.M. Roberts, "The Hand of Yahwe", *VT* 21 (1971), 244–251; A.S. van der Woude in E. Jenni/C. Westermann, *THAT* I (1971), 672–673; P. Ackroyd in *ThWAT* III (1982), 448–449.

on the Book of Ezekiel, which is notable for the wide use of the expression (seven times), more often than in any other book of the Prophets.

Let us now consider the readings in the Book of Ezekiel, 1:3; 3:14, 22; 8:1; 33:22; 37:1; 40:1; and compare 13:9.[8] In these verses, two different verbs are used in connection with "the hand of God"—first, the verb היה "be/was" (often translated as "came" in the New JPS translation): "and the hand of the Lord came upon him there" (1:3); "Then the hand of the Lord came upon me there" (3:22); "Now the hand of the Lord had come upon me the evening before . . ." (33:22); "The hand of the Lord came upon me" (37:1; 40:1). The second verb is חזק "be/was strong", "hold/held firmly", and describes the powerfulness of the prophetic vision; see, for instance, "A spirit seized me . . . while the hand of the Lord was strong upon me" (3:14). In this connection, attention should be drawn to Isaiah 8:11: "For this is what the Lord said to me, when He took me by the hand . . ." the intention here is that being given God's hand imparts strength. Only once, in connection with prophecy in the Book of Ezekiel, is the verb נפל "fall/fell" used: "and there the hand of the Lord God fell upon me" (8:1; the Septuagint gives the translation here, also, as "was").

In sum, three different verbs are used in expressions related to the spiritual awakening of Ezekiel and usually come as a direct prologue to the prophetic words which are pronounced after his arousal. The expression concerning God's hand stops near the point at which the prophetic vision, or some action on the part of the prophet, is expected.[9] As for the prophet himself, it is possible that he underwent an ecstatic experience, but that does not mean, apparently, that he completely lost his senses or that his speech was confused.

While in Akkadian (especially beyond the borders of Mari) the hand of the deity usually signified disaster, the same is true of a few instances in the Bible; however, in the prophecies contained in the Bible proper, this is, at the most, a marginal trend. The disaster motif is found, in particular, in the non-prophetical books of the Bible, e.g., "then the hand of the Lord will strike your livestock . . ." (Ex. 9:3); ". . . the hand of the Lord was against them to their undoing . . . " (Judges 2:15); "For the hand of God (*ᵉlōhā*) has struck me!"

---

[8] See M. Greenberg, *Ezekiel 1–20* (Anchor Bible), Garden City, N.Y. 1983, 41–42, 166, 236–237; W. Zimmerli, *Ezechiel* I (*BK* XIII, Neukirchen 1959), 47–50.

[9] Cf. Roberts, *op. cit.* (above, n. 7), 251, and the theological dictionaries mentioned in n. 7.

(Job 19:21). As stated, this last citation is the only instance in the Bible in which the divinity is mentioned in a general connotation, unconnected with a specific event. This is in contrast to Mari, as we have seen above; the divine hand usually acted benignly, bringing calm and tranquility.

The external difference between Mari and biblical prophecy lies in the purpose of the expressions discussed above. In the Bible, as already stated, the expression serves as an introduction to the prophecy and is not mentioned within the actual prophecy itself, whereas in Mari the expression is found also as a formula within the actual divination itself and is, in fact, used more extensively than would be an introductory technical formula.

B. "*. . . and make them into one stick*" (Ez. 37:19)

The prophecy pronounced immediately after the Vision of the Dry Bones in the Book of Ezekiel foresees a symbolic event involving two cuttings or twigs from a tree, which the prophet must take in his hand. God commands the prophet to hold the sticks together in his hand to form one stick, an act symbolizing the future unification of the two divided parts of the people—the House of Judah and the House of Joseph (Ez. 37:15–22).[10] The two parts of the people are in exile and, according to the prophet's vision, will return to the Land of Israel. The joining of the two twigs is described in a metaphor as follows: "Bring them close to each other, so that they become one stick, joined together in your hand . . . and make them into one stick; they shall be joined in My hand" (*ibid.*, 17–19). The sticks are thus joined in the prophet's hand. Here we have a metaphor of recognized importance both for Egyptian findings as well as for Akkadian expressions in Mari documents, as we shall see forthwith. The prophet concludes: "I will make them a single nation in the land. . . . Never again shall they be two nations, and never again shall they be divided into two kingdoms" (*ibid.*, 22).

There are analogies to this prophecy in Egyptian paintings which illustrate the joining and pressing together of plants and stems as a

[10] On this prophecy, see especially W. Zimmerli, *op. cit.* (above, n. 8), II, 903–912, and Greenberg, *Ezekiel 21–37* (AnBi), 1997, 752 ff.

symbol of the unification of Upper and Lower Egypt.[11] Moreover, in this connection, attention should be drawn too to the prophecy of Neferti regarding the unification of the two parts of Egypt.[12] However, it is now possible to present an instructive parallel example in the new documents from Mari, although at first glance the similarity is not obvious. There was a symbolic custom in Mari, apparently based on actual diplomatic practice with regard to state unification, in which the representatives of the two parties intertwined their fingers. Each party (people or places) had to wind his fingers round the fingers of the other "and they became one finger". (Maybe the command contained in the Biblical expression "*tāqa qap*" can be understood in this light.) Although one document from Mari describing this custom was published in 1950 (*ARM* 2, 21:11–12), other documents from Mari in vol. 26:2 can now be added to this example, describing four similar instances.[13] We shall present them below in the order in which they appear in *ARM* 26:

1) Document No. 392, lines 29–30: "If Atamrum (a high official in Mari) does it, then he and I will swear an oath from the bottom of our hearts, we will be one finger once again";
2) Document No. 438, line 22: "Why do you divide one finger into two?" (the words suggest the violation of a treaty);
3) Document No. 449, lines 14–15: "The cities of Mari and Babylon were one house and one finger";[14]
4) Document No. A. 4206, lines 11–12 (the tablet has not yet been published, but the passage treated here was included in vol. 26:2 by Charpin): certain people or places "are one finger".[15]
5/6) To these examples must be added document No. A. 4026, line 12, and document No. A. 2326, lines 8–13: "Hana (i.e. the nomads) and the land of Idamaraṣ have always been (as) one finger and one heart.

---

[11] See, e.g., B.J. Kemp, *Ancient Egypt* (London–New York 1991), 28, fig. 6; and *ibid.*, description of tying together of lotus flower and papyrus leaf.

[12] For a comparison with Neferti's prophecy, see N. Shupak, "Egyptian 'Prophecy' and Biblical Prophecy . . .", *Jaarbericht* 31 (1989–90), 32 f.

[13] Charpin *et alii*, *ARM* 26/2 (Paris 1988) and cf. note by W.L. Moran, *NABU*, 1989/4, No. 100, in which he draws attention to all the instances quoted and rightly assumes that the intention is to conclude a treaty.

[14] A similar expression for a treaty between two cities or kingdoms was discovered in a letter from Uruk, sent by King Anam to King Sinmuballit, Hammurabi's father: "Uruk and Babylon are one house"; see A. Falkenstein, *BaM* 2 (1963), 56 ff., col. II 2, III 25.

[15] On this quotation see Charpin, *ARM* 26/2, 225, text 392, n.g.

Now, why should the finger be divided in two?"[16] The expression "one heart" is significant here, because it is usually not found in this context in Mari; however, it is found twice in the Bible, although there it can mean "of one mind". Note: ". . . with whole heart (literally 'one heart') . . . to make David king over all Israel" (1 Chr. 12:39); ". . . making them of a single mind (literally 'heart') to carry out the command . . ." (2 Chr. 30:12).

It may well be assumed, from all the examples quoted above, that the symbolic act of intertwining and joining fingers was intended to signify a link, unification or a treaty, between two parties. In Ezekiel such ties were symbolized by the pressing together of two twigs in the palm of the hand, like illustrations of a similar nature in Egyptian paintings.

C. *Prophesying in the Bible by means of Eating a Scroll, and in Mari by Drinking a Beverage*

Ezekiel is the only prophet whose vision results from the swallowing of a scroll, written on both sides, which is fed to him by God: ". . . eat this scroll, and go speak to the House of Israel . . . I ate it . . ." (Ez. 3:1 ff. and cf. *ibid.*, 2:8–10). Here is the description of a mystifying event in which the prophet obeys a divine command, swallows the scroll which fills his belly (*ibid.*, 3:3) and endeavours to digest the words written on it, which are the words of God.[17] The scroll contains the prophecies which the prophet will proclaim to his people. In Jeremiah, too, mentioned once, is the vision of eating God's words: "When Your words were offered, I devoured them . . ." (Jer. 15:16). It is possible that the motif is the same in both books, but in Jeremiah it is general and is not connected to the prophet's call, whereas in Ezekiel it is detailed, of a definite, plastic nature, and comes at the end of the section dealing with the prophet's call.

Both Jeremiah and Isaiah receive their call solely through the divine touch. In Jeremiah 1:9, God puts out His hand and touches Jeremiah's mouth; in Isaiah 6:6–7, one of the seraphs touches the prophet's

[16] See Durand, *MARI* 6 (1990), 50, A. 4026; and see Charpin, *MARI* 7 (1993), 175, A. 2326.

[17] Cf. M. Greenberg (above, n. 8), 67–68; W. Zimmerli (above, n. 8), 78–79.

lips, although this time it is done with the purpose of taking away Isaiah's sin and purifying him. It is possible to find a parallel to this gesture in some of the new prophecies from Mari, but the expression used in this connection is "chin touch"[18] where the symbolic touch involved, apparently, not only the deity but, more importantly, a human hand.

Turning again to Ezekiel and comparing his swallowing of the scroll with the Mari divinations, we come across one, or maybe two, instances in the Mari documents of the enigmatic custom of someone being offered a drink, the ingredients of which are undefined, in order to induce the drinker to prophesy. The most outstanding document in this respect is *ARM* 26/1, No. 207 (A. 996).[19] Without entering into a discussion on the complete contents of the document, which are also important for other matters, let us examine the text in the lines relevant to our subject. Queen Šibtu (some read the name as Šibtu or Šipṭu), the wife of Zimri-Lim, in connection with a military campaign being waged by her husband against his enemies, declares: "I gave drink (*aš-qi*) to the signs for male and female (or it is possible, according to Durand, that a man and a woman themselves acted as signs) and I have enquired into the matter" (lines 4–6). Scholars are also divided over the kind of drink offered. Durand is of the opinion, and apparently rightly so, that the reference is to wine and, therefore, the drink must have been alcoholic (for instance, an intoxicating liquor) for the purpose of creating an atmosphere conducive to prophetic arousal.

A similar incident is to be found in vol. 26/1, No. 212.[20] It comprises Šibtu's answer to her husband about the oracle concerning Hammurabi, king of Babylon. Šibtu declares: "As for Babylon, I have given drink to the signs and have enquired into the matter. That man (Hammurabi) is plotting many things against this country, but he will not succeed" (lines 1–2). Here, also, a liquid was offered to

[18] *suqtam ilput*. Cf. Durand, *ARM*, 26/1, 378 and n. 13; cf. 281, 379, 433 (and see now M. Guichard, *Mém. NABU* 3, Paris 1994, p. 271). The editor cites four instances of this custom, some of which, however, are not connected with prophecy. Another gesture is the touching of the throat, practised in Mari, as is well known, when making a treaty.

[19] See (above, n. 4), pp. 435–436. The document was first published in *ARM* 10, No. 4; cf. *idem*, J.-M. Durand, *RA* 75 (1982), 43–50; *MARI* 3 (1984), 150–156; C. Wilcke, *RA* 77 (1983), 93; J.M. Sasson in *Mém. NABU* 3, p. 308.

[20] Pp. 440–441 and cf. J.M. Sasson (previous note), p. 308.

be drunk, which perhaps contained the "signs", i.e., the events occurring in the future, but no details are given of those bearing the message, in contrast to the previous prophecy.

In spite of all the differences between the vision involving, on the one hand, the feeding of a scroll to Ezekiel by the Deity, and on the other, the offering of a drink to a man and a woman by someone of flesh and blood, as described in the prophecies from Mari, the enigmatic practice in both instances acted as some kind of stimulant to arouse prophetic powers.

14

A NEW PROPHETIC MESSAGE FROM ALEPPO AND ITS BIBLICAL COUNTERPARTS*

J.-M. Durand recently published an intriguing document from Mari (A. 1968), namely, a letter by Nur-Sin, Mari's ambassador to Aleppo, to his lord Zimri-Lim (Durand 1993; for another letter of Nur-Sin regarding a prophecy of Adad see ch. 9 above).[1] The letter contains a relatively lengthy prophecy by Abiya, a prophet, designated the "respondent" or "answerer" (*āpilum*) (Malamat 1989: 86–87; Charpin 1992a: 21–22) for the God Adad (or Addu), the great deity of Aleppo (Klengel 1965). Thus we have here a Western prophecy, but what is "Amorite" about it is difficult to say.

The prophet utters the words of his deity concerning the rulers of Mari, past and present, who were more or less dependent on the kingdom of Aleppo. I shall present here the entire prophecy, and divide it into sections which seem to have no organic connection.

A. First, similar to *ARMT* I 3, in the famous letter of Yasmah-Adad to a deity, the fortunes of the individual Mari rulers are outlined (Charpin and Durand 1985: 297–98, 339–42). There, as in the present prophecy, Yahdun-Lim, the first king of Mari, was granted "all the countries" by the deity, but was then accused of abandoning the god and consequently was rejected by him. Yahdun-Lim's country was taken away and given to Šamši-Adad, the major king of the rival Amorite dynasty, which established itself in Assyria (cf. ch. 15 below). But the same harsh fate as Yahdun-Lim's now befell his successor Šamši-Adad. In the following lacuna in the tablet the name was surely mentioned of King Zimri-Lim, who drove the Šamši-Adad dynasty out of Mari and reigned as the last king of Mari. (For details of the actual expulsion, see Sasson 1972; Charpin and Durand

* This article was originally published in: A.G. Auld (ed.), *Understanding Poets & Prophets* (FS G.W. Anderson), *JSOT* Supplements 152, 1993, pp. 236–241.

[1] I thank Professor J.-M. Durand for supplying me with a galley of his article prior to its publication in *MARI* 7. D. Charpin cites *en passant* this document in a recent paper (Charpin 1992b: 3, 6, 10). Professor P. Artzi kindly read a draft of my paper and commented on it.

1985: 319–22; for the further events, cf. Charpin 1992b. 4–5.)

B. Then the text continues: "I have restored you [= Zimri-Lim] to the throne of your father and the weapons, with which I have beaten the Sea (*ti'amtum, temtum*), I have given you".

Adad, whose authority lies in the defeat of the Sea, is the patron deity of Zimri-Lim, whom he appointed king of Mari (for a similar prophecy see Malamat 1980; Lafont 1984), thus reflecting the superior status of the land of Yamhad (capital Aleppo) to the kingdom of Mari. The motif of a struggle between the storm-god and the sea-god, which is entirely novel to the Mari documents, has already been referred to in some preliminary remarks (Charpin and Durand 1986: 174). The motif is well attested to at Ugarit (Bordreuil and Pardee 1993), as well as in the Bible and even in the talmudic literature. In classical sources may be found sporadic references to a sea-deity (for the entire subject see Malamat 1989a: 107–12 and ch. 3 above). But nowhere in this context do we hear of any weapons to be delivered by a god to a king. (For an additional instance in the Mari documents [unpublished] where Adad's weapons were sent to Zimri-Lim who deposited them in the temple of Dagan at Terqa, see Durand 1993: 53. These might be apt illustrations for Th. Jacobsen's hypothesis of a West-East transfer in the Amorite period, in his case of course, in the spritual realm; Jacobsen, 1968).

C. And then: "I have anointed you with the oil of my luminosity (*namrirrūtum*) and nobody can withstand you". The anointment rite, which signifies the divine component of a king's coronation, is known in the ancient Near East, especially in the Bible (see below), but the references to it are relatively rare (Kutsch 1963). In Mari this is the first occurrence of the royal rite, which, with due reservation may have been an Amorite custom (see above ch. 2, p. 18 and n. 19). Several instances seem to occur in connection with the Hittite kings, in Ugarit as well as in the El-Amarna letters (*EA* 34.47–53; 51.5–9). May we conceive of the cases mentioned as in some way forerunners of the biblical ceremony?

D. "Hearken to a single word of mine: When somebody who cries out to you for judgment says: 'They wronged me', stand up and let [his case be] judged; render him justice. This is what I desire from you." The god has the power to make certain demands of the king and singles out his desire for justice. The same motif of rendering justice already occurs in an earlier published prophecy from Aleppo (A. 2731, to be joined to A. 1129; cf. Lafont 1984; Malamat 1980 and ch. 9 above) and thus seems to be characteristic of the god and the prophets (the "respondents") of his city. Whereas the Mari prophecies generally focus on material demands, here are rare instances of moral, ethical commands particular to Adad of Aleppo (Malamat 1989a: 79 in contrast to p. 83; Anbar 1975). And finally:

E. "When you participate in a campaign, by no means set out without consulting an oracle. When I, in an oracle of mine, should be favourable, you will set out on a campaign. If it is not so, do not pass the gate [of the city?]."

This procedure, as expected, is widespread, not just at Mari, the deity demanding that a military campaign be determined by mantic means (e.g. Durand 1988: 44–46; 1987: 163–67 [ll. 66–70]). Thus this device (here unusually recommended by a prophet) is mentioned in many Mari letters (e.g. *ARMT* 26/1, nos. 7, 27, 97, 117, 119, 160; see also texts in 26/2).

F. *Epilogue.* The prophecy terminates with a statement found frequently in the prophetic Mari letters: "This the *āpilum* said to me. Now [a lock of] his hair and the hem of his garment I send them to my lord [i.e. Zimri-Lim]." Various explanations have been put forward for this strange custom (for my own position, regarding these two personal items as a sort of "identity card" of the prophet, see my most recent statement in ch. 6, pp. 78–79.

* * *

Turning now to the Bible, we find counterparts to each of the motifs, although not to a continuous single literary unit as in Mari. Let us outline them according to the sections into which we divided the Mari prophecy:

A. The transfer of a country or kingdom from one ruler to another, because the deity has been neglected, is best expressed in the biblical episode of Saul and David. Here also it is a prophet, Samuel, who acts on behalf of the deity. The two most explicit biblical passages relating to our issue are: "And Samuel said to him [to Saul], 'The Lord has torn the kingdom of Israel from you this day, and has given it to a neighbour of yours, who is better than you'" (i.e. David, 1 Sam. 15:28); ". . . for the Lord has torn the kingdom out of your hand, and given it to your neighbour David. Because you did not obey the voice of the Lord . . ." (1 Sam. 28:17–28). In Mari and Israel a similar ideology regarding the behaviour of royalty is manifested (see ch. 15 below).

B. Unlike Mari, in the biblical monotheistic faith there is no place for a separate sea-deity next to Yahweh. But there are in the Bible certain echoes of the early existence of such a deity, although the latter has already been degraded to a Sea monster (Eissfeldt 1966; Cassuto 1975: 70 ff.] who revolts against the God of Israel and is subdued by him. For this motif in the Bible, see, for example, Isa. 51:9–10; Jer. 5:22; Ps. 74:13–14; Job 7:12 (and see Bingen 1992; Day 1992 and ch. 3, pp. 30–31 above).

C. The anointment of a king in Judah and Israel is a significant component of the coronation ceremony (Kutsch 1963; Weisman 1976; de Jonge 1992). In descriptions of six or even seven royal enthronements there is an express reference to this element: Saul (1 Sam. 9:16); David (1 Sam. 16:13 etc.); Absalom, trying to usurp the throne (2 Sam. 19:11); Solomon (1 Kgs. 1:34 etc.), Jehu of Israel (1 Kgs. 19:16 etc.), Joash (2 Kgs. 11:12); and finally Jehoachaz (2 Kgs. 23:30). To these cases must be added the anointing of Hazael, king of Damascus, by the prophet Elisha (1 Kgs. 19:15). Also indicative here is the term *māšiaḥ*, the anointed one, attributed in the Bible, *inter alia*, to King Cyrus, the Persian.

D. Demanding just and moral behaviour from the king is common to biblical prophecy, whereas in Mari there are only two prophecies on this theme (see above). As for the Bible (see in general Whitelam 1979: 29–37), let us cite Jeremiah's sermon concerning the conduct of the last Judahite rulers: "Execute justice in the morning and deliver from the hand of the oppressor" (Jer. 21:12); "Thus says the Lord: "Do justice and righteousness, and deliver from the hand of the oppressor him who has been robbed. And do no wrong or violence to the alien . . .'" (Jer. 22:3). Concerning King Josiah we have a specific statement made by Jeremiah that this king afforded help to the poor and needy (Jer. 22:15).

It is of interest to note that whereas in Mari the motifs C and D are simply set one after the other, in the Bible they are organically intertwined. See Ps. 45:7 (MT v. 8): "You love righteousness and hate wickedness. Therefore God, your God, has anointed you with the oil of gladness above your fellows." The king's anointment is here a consequence of his righteous behaviour towards the people, the logical but reverse sequence of the Mari prophecy. Similarly, it is possible that D and E are intertwined in the demand of the people of Israel for a king (1 Sam. 8:20).

E. Conducting a military campaign or a peaceful march following either an oracle or a prophecy are both attested to in the Bible (Christensen 1975). For the use of an oracle, see the passages in the book of Numbers: "At the command of the Lord the people of Israel set out, and at the command of the Lord they encamped" (Num. 9:18); and still more expressly, "And he shall stand before Eleazar the priest, who shall inquire for him by the judgment of the Urim [i.e. the oracle] before the Lord; at his word they shall go out, and at his word they shall come in, both he and all the people of Israel within the whole congregation" (Num. 27:21). See also 1 Sam. 23:35 on a razzia of David during his pre-monarchic days.

For the command of a prophet, let us take one instance out of several, namely, the war of King Ahab against the Arameans of Damascus. There, in contradiction to the 400 prophets who were unanimously in favour of war, the prophet Micaiah alone, upon divine inspiration, opposed the Israelite initiative (1 Kgs. 22:6–28; cf. Rofé 1988: 142–52). As for the earlier periods, see the biblical motif of the *heilige Krieg* and the use of the Ark of Covenant in warfare.

Our comparison between the Mari prophecy and the Bible has focused only on the major points; nevertheless it has shown a strong affinity between the two corpora—Mari and the Bible. The prophecy from Aleppo, which represents the West, is exceptional in its high standard of theological and moral contemplation, but the real breakthrough in this respect came only with the Bible and especially with the Great Prophets.

Bibliography

Anbar, M., (1975). "Aspect moral dans un discours 'prophetique' de Mari", *UF* 7:517–18.

Bingen, T., (1992). "Fighting the Dragon", *SJOT* 6:139 ff.

Bordreuil, P. and Pardee, D., (1993). "Le combat de Ba'alu avec Yammu d'après les textes ougaritiques", *MARI* 7:63–70.

Cassuto, U., (1975). *Biblical and Oriental Studies*, II (Jerusalem: Magnes).

Charpin, D., (1992a). "Le contexte historique et géographique des prophéties . . . à Mari", in *Bulletin SCEM* 23:21–31.

——, (1992b). "Mari entre l'est et l'ouest . . .", *Akkadica* 78 (Mai-Aout): 1–10.

—— and Durand, J.-M., (1985). "La prise du pouvoir par Zimri-Lim", *MARI* 4:293–343.

—— and Durand, J.-M., (1986). "Fils de Sim'al . . .", *RA* 80:141–83.

Christensen, D.L., (1975). *Transformation of the War Oracle in Old Testament Prophecy* (Harvard Dissertations in Religion, 3; Missoula, MO: Scholars Press).

Day, J., (1992). "Dragon and Sea", *The Anchor Bible Dictionary*, II (New York: Doubleday): 228–31.

Durand, J.-M., (1987). "Histoire du royaume de Haute-Mésopotamie", *MARI* 5: 155–98.
——, (1988). *ARMT* 26/1 = *AEM* I/1.
——, (1993). "Le mythologème du combat entre le dieu de l'orage et la mer en Mésopotamie", *MARI* 7:41–6.
Eissfeldt, O., (1966). "Gott und das Meer in der Bibel", *KS*, III, 256–64.
Jacobsen, Th., (1968). "The Battle between Marduk and Tiamat," *JAOS* 88: 104–108.
Jonge, M. de, (1992). "Messiah B, C—Anointed King(s)", *The Anchor Bible Dictionary*, IV (New York: Doubleday): 777–80.
Klengel, H., (1965). "Der Wettergott von Halab", *JCS* 19:87–93.
Kutsch, E., (1963). *Salbung als Rechtsakt im Alten Testament und im alten Orient* (*BZAW* 87; Berlin: de Gruyter).
Lafont, B., (1984). "Le roi de Mari et les prophètes du dieu Adad", *RA* 78:7–18.
Malamat, A., (1980). "A Mari Prophecy and Nathan's Dynastic Oracle", in J. Emerton (ed.), *Prophecy: Essays Presented to G. Fohrer* (*BZAW*, 150; Berlin: de Gruyter): 68–82.
——, (1989a). *Mari and the Early Israelite Experience* (Oxford: Oxford University Press).
——, (1989b). "Parallels between the New Prophecies from Mari and Biblical Prophecy" (I–II), *NABU* 1989/4:61–63.
——, (1991a). "New Light from Mari on Biblical Prophecy", *Festschrift J.A. Soggin* (Brescia): 185–90 (cf. ch. 11 above).
——, (1991b). "The Secret Council and Prophetic Involvement in Mari and Israel" (V), *FS S. Herrmann* (Stuttgart): 231–36 (cf. ch. 12 above).
Rofé, A., (1988). *The Prophetical Stories* (Jerusalem: Magnes).
Sasson, J., (1972). "Zimri-Lim's March to Victory", *RA* 66:177–78.
Whitelam, K.W., (1979). *The Just King* (*JSOTSuppl.* 12; Sheffield: *JSOT* Press).
Weisman, Z., (1976). "Anointing as a Motif in the Making of the Charismatic King", *Biblica* 57:378–98.

15

DEITY REVOKES KINGSHIP – TOWARDS INTELLECTUAL REASONING IN MARI AND IN THE BIBLE*

While the notion of divine rejection of kingship and its transfer to another ruler is also found in other ancient Near Eastern sources,[1] we shall restrict ourselves here solely to the Mari archives and to Biblical Israel. At Mari, thus far, three (or possibly four) documents explicitly contain such a notion, which appears to be the result of theological-political reasoning and as such is germinal to intellectual argumentation. It is unique in the Old Babylonian period and seems to bear an Amorite stamp.

We shall first examine the Mari documents, beginning with one from Aleppo, published recently by J.-M. Durand in *MARI* 7. This text (A. 1968), a letter from Mari's ambassador to Aleppo, Nur-Sin, contains a prophecy for King Zimri-Lim.[2] The prophet (an *āpilum*) speaks in the name of Addu (Adad), the great god of Aleppo, who was a universal deity, and thus, the prophecy is of a Western nature, as are the other documents discussed here. Prior to the actual contents of the divine message, the prophet reviews the earlier history of Old Babylonian Mari, outlining the fortunes of the individual rulers in a sort of theological discourse.

---

* This paper will also be published in: "Deity Revokes Kingship in Mari and in the Bible", *Proceedings of the 43rd RAI* 1996, Prague (forthcoming).

[1] For several such sources see, e.g., E.A. Speiser, The Idea of History in Ancient Mesopotamia, in eds. J.J. Finkelstein and M. Greenberg, *Oriental and Biblical Studies*, Philadelphia 1967, pp. 270–312. Immediately there comes to mind the so-called *Weidner Chronicle*, which sets out a scheme of the change-overs of the Mesopotamian dynasties, according to the piety or impiety of the relevant king; see A.K. Grayson, *Assyrian and Babylonian Chronicles*, Locust Valley 1975, Chronicle 19. Recent finds at Sippar have shown that the *Weidner Chronicle* was part of a longer piece, a literary letter supposedly from one OB ruler to another. See K.N.H. Al-Rawi, "Tablets from the Sippar Library I", *Iraq* 52 (1990), 1–13. This composition also originated in the 18th century B.C. and thus is proximal to the Mari Period. See now B.T. Arnold, in ed. A.R. Millard, *et al., Faith, Tradition & History*, Winona Lake, IN, 1994, pp. 129–148.

[2] *MARI* 7 (1993), pp. 41 ff. See on this prophecy A. Malamat, in ed. A.G. Auld, *Understanding Poets and Prophets* (*Essays in Honour of G.W. Anderson*), Sheffield 1993 (*JSOTS* 152), pp. 236–241 (see ch. 14 above). On Aleppo see now H. Klengel, "Die historische Rolle der Stadt Aleppo ...", in ed. G. Wilhelm, *Die orientalische Stadt ... 1. Intern. Coll. des DOG*, Saarbrücken 1997, pp. 363 ff.

The first true king of Mari, Yahdun-Lim, was granted "all the countries" by the deity and was promised that nobody would challenge his rule. But later, the king was accused of abandoning the god. Consequently, Yahdun-Lim was rejected by Addu (Adad) and his country was wrested from him and given to King Samsi-Addu of a rival Amorite dynasty. The real offense of Yahdun-Lim lay in the shifting of his alliance from Aleppo (capital of Yamhad) to Ešnunna. Charpin assumes that additional offenses committed by Yahdun-Lim consisted of his attack on the Yaminite tribes, who were then allied to Aleppo, and his conquest of the city of Emar from the ruler of Aleppo, Sumu-Epuh, father and predecessor of Yarim-Lim.[3]

Yet, the same harsh fate as befell Yahdun-Lim was also suffered by his successor at Mari, the rival king Samsi-Addu. There follows in the tablet a lacuna, in which the name was surely mentioned of Zimri-Lim who was, apparently, the son of Yahdun-Lim and last king of Mari (*ca.* 1775–1761 B.C. according to the Middle Chronology). As is known from various Mari sources, Zimri-Lim expelled from the city of Mari Yasmah-Addu,[4] son of Samsi-Addu, who was appointed by his father viceroy of Mari. Our text continues, with the prophet proclaiming in the name of Addu concerning Zimri-Lim: "I have restored you to the throne of your father . . . I have anointed you with the oil of my luminosity[5] and nobody can withstand you" (ll. 1'–5').

A Mari document similar in nature to the above, but siding with the rival dynasty of Samsi-Addu at Mari, is the celebrated letter composed by Yasmah-Addu, viceroy or governor of Mari, to a deity whose name is broken in the text (G. Dossin, *ARMT* I 3). That the letter was addressed by Yasmah-Addu to a deity was first recognized by B. Landsberger, who suggested that the god was Dagan.[6] In a new collation and reworking of this letter, Charpin and Durand have restored the name of the deity as (Ner-)gal,[7] but the god may have been Addu (^{d}IM), as in the aforementioned document. Presumably,

[3] Cf. D. Charpin, *Mémoires de NABU* 1 (1992), p. 38.

[4] E.g., J. Sasson, *RA* 66 (1972), pp. 177 f.; D. Charpin and J.-M. Durand, *MARI* 4 (1985), pp. 319 ff.

[5] *Namrirrūtum*; Durand understands this word in the sense of (oil of) victory; *op. cit.* (n. 2), pp. 53 f.

[6] See B. Landsberger, *apud* A.L. Oppenheim, *JNES* 11 (1952), p. 130.

[7] For a new collation and annotated translation of *ARMT* I 3, see Charpin and Durand, *op. cit.* (n. 4), pp. 293–298, 339–342.

the present letter, too, was composed in response to a prophecy.[8] This letter starts, in contrast to A. 1968, with a generation prior to Yahdun-Lim and Samsi-Addu, i.e. their ancestors Yagid-Lim and Ila-Kabkabu, the founding fathers of the two dynasties. At first, the deity favored the "Lim" dynasty, which kept the divine norms (l. 7: me), but later Yagid-Lim is accused of committing a crime, i.e., breaking the treaty with Ila-Kabkabu.[9] Consequently, Yagid-Lim was punished by the deity, "marching at the side of Ila-Kabkabu," who defeated his rival. Yagid-Lim also committed an offense against Samsi-Addu and thus lost the benefaction of the god to the rival dynasty, which was now established at Mari (see below).

The passage which follows is unclear as to whether the subject of the events is Yahdun-Lim or his son (or younger brother) Sumu-Yamam, an ephemeral figure who reigned after his father (or elder brother) only some two years. Thus, we are not certain whether the following sentences (ll. 4'–12') are to be applied to Yahdun-Lim, as we believe, or rather to Sumu-Yamam, as assumed by others and lately by Charpin—Durand. "[The god's] temple which former kings had [built], he tore down and built a palace.[10] [The god] called him to account, and his own servants (or vassals) killed him . . ." as punishment for his "sacrilege". Instead of the word palace Charpin—Durand read "house of his spouse", i.e. a harem. At any rate, the king is accused of transforming a palace sanctuary, or a part thereof, into a building of a profane nature, thus desecrating a sacred area.

---

[8] Charpin and Durand *op. cit.* (n. 4), p. 293; for the historical background see the brief remarks by Durand in *Documents épistolaire* . . . 1 (LAPO), Paris 1997, pp. 43 f.

[9] In the *editio princeps* (*ARMT* I 3), ll. 6, 12, 14, 18, 3', 15', 16', the spelling is *qullulu*, "to offend" from *qalālu* "to slander", cf. *CAD* G, p. 132a. This reading has been accepted by E.A. Speiser, *op. cit.* (n. 1), pp. 293 f., 296. But the spelling *gullulu*, "to commit a sin" is preferable, cf. Landsberger, *WZKM* 57 (1961), p. 11, n. 47, and cf. *CAD* G, pp. 131 f., citing *inter alia* our document.

[10] L. 10': G. Dossin read *bīt ḫilāni* which is unacceptable, the expression occurring only in the first millennium; Landsberger read É-GAL, "big house," i.e. palace, *JCS* 8 (1954), p. 35, n. 28 (cf. N. Naaman, *RA* 76 [1982], p. 191), while Charpin and Durand (n. 4) read É DAM-NI, "house of his spouse."

We present here a few additional annotations to "The Letter to a God:" *ARMT* I 3, l. 14: *telk/qema tašalšu* is an hendiadys, meaning "you took the matters in your hand;" differently, *CAD* L, p. 135: "you have learned (about it) and have questioned (him)"; l. 25': in the beginning of the line restore *šarrānu*, "kings", near the end of the line read with W. von Soden: *mātam*, "land (acc.)" (*Orientalia* 21 [1952], p. 76), implying that while the former kings aspired to lands which were not their own, Yasmah-Adad asked only for his life and offspring; l. 28': *inīka lā tanašši*, lit.: "you did not raise your eyes", in the sense of "you did not watch" (and see Hebrew Ez 18:6, 15 ועיניו לא נשא).

The king's demise may have been brought about by a court conspiracy or rather by military defeat, fighting against rebellious vassals, as Charpin and Durand surmise. Subsequently, Samsi-Addu took over the Mari kingdom and appointed his younger son Yasmah-Addu as governor or viceroy.

A similar pattern of transferring kingship from one ruler to another (in this case within the same dynasty) appears in a new Mari letter, published again by Durand in the same article as our initial document.[11] The letter is a response to Zimri-Lim by an unnamed high official who had earlier sent a message concerning Yarim-Lim, king of Aleppo. The correspondent undoubtedly cites Yarim-Lim: "Zimri-Lim has expelled his enemies! Now, he firmly insists on his demands. Sumu-Epuh (former king of Aleppo), my father, having respected Samsi-Addu, obtained (all) that he desired. Once he (Sumu-Epuh) came close to (= besieged) the kingdom which Addu gave to Samsi-Addu. (Thus), Sumu-Epuh, my father (as punishment), did not attain the fullness of old age. You made him attack the land which Addu had given to Samsi-Addu, (thus) god Addu made him (Sumu-Epuh) perish. Until now the heart of Addu has not been vexed with me." To quote Durand: "Such conceptions that tend to attribute universal royalty to Addu of Aleppo can be easily explained when coming from the mouth of the king of Yamhad" (MARI 7, p. 56). Yarim-Lim of Aleppo seems to have recognised that he himself and his father did not respect King Samsi-Addu.[12] The latter, consequently, precipitated the early downfall of Sumu-Epuh, father of Yarim-Lim, according to an unpublished letter of Dariš-Libur to Zimri-Lim (A. 4251).[13]

Finally, a fairly similar example of this genre appears in a fragmentary letter (now A. 3006), already referred to by Ch.F. Jean as early as 1939, concerning the repeated crimes of the tribe of the Lullu against several Mari kings.[14]

---

[11] See *MARI* 7 (1993), pp. 55 f. (A. 4251).

[12] Durand (*MARI* 7, p. 55) refers in this context to a contrastive example from Mari, *ARMT* XXVI/1, No. 196. This is a prophecy concerning a heavenly judgement, where Dagan of Terqa threatens to cause the downfall of Tišpak, the god of Ešnunna, a sort of deicide.

[13] The continuation of the letter is severely broken (cf. *MARI* 7, p. 65, n. 60); see Durand "Culte d'Addu d'Alep" in *ARMT* XXVI/3 (forthcoming).

[14] Ch.F. Jean, Excerpta . . . Mari, *RÉS* (1939), p. 66, #7, nn. 3 and 4 cites only a few lines of the letter; but see now Charpin-Durand, *op. cit.* (n. 4), p. 297, n. 22, who published the entire letter.

Now we may turn to the Bible, adducing two extraordinary incidents from the beginning of the Davidic dynasty, while choosing to ignore the several overthrows of kingship in Northern Israel, since they do not explicitly display the above pattern. The two well-known incidents relate to King Saul and David, and to King Solomon and Jeroboam, respectively.

The kingship of king Saul, together with that of his offspring, was abrogated in favor of the future King David,[15] since the former was accused of committing various, specified sins, at least according to the Deuteronomistic redaction of the First Book of Samuel. As in Mari, the events evolved through the agency of a prophet, in our case the Prophet Samuel; also similar to Mari (where Addu anointed Zimri-Lim in A. 1968, l. 5), David was anointed by Yahweh through the intermediary of Samuel (1 Sam. 15).[16] The key-passage reads: "The Lord has this day torn (. . . קרע מעליך) the kingship over Israel away from you (i.e. from Saul) and has given it to another who is worthier than you (i.e. David)" (1 Sam. 15:28; New JPS; this translation is used henceforth).[17] This verse is self-explanatory. The motif is foreshadowed in 1 Sam. 13:13–14 and a comparison may be made with 1 Sam. 28:17.[18]

The verse revoking the kingship of Solomon, also edited by the Deuteronomist, is almost identical with the verse about Saul and David; the verses are certainly dependent on each other.[19] The Lord

---

[15] On the rejection of Saul as king see the commentaries on 1 Sam (below n. 17) and in particular S. Yonick, *Rejection of Saul as King of Israel*, Jerusalem 1970; D. Jobling, *JBL* 95 (1976), pp. 367–376, and H. Donner, *Die Verwerfung des Königs Saul*, Wiesbaden 1983, V. Ph. Long, *The Reign and Rejection of King Saul*, Atlanta, GA, 1989. Cf. A. Popovic, *The Election and Rejection of Saul*, Rome 1994.

[16] On the entire chap. 15 of 1 Sam and its relation to further texts, see A. Weiser, *ZAW* 54 (1936), pp. 1–28; D.M. Gunn, *The Fate of King Saul*, Sheffield 1980, chap. 3; and F. Foresti, *The Rejection of Saul in the Perspective of the Deuteronomistic School* (*A Study of 1 Sam 15 and Related Texts*), Rome 1984.

[17] See the commentaries on 1 Samuel, e.g.: H.J. Stoebe, *Das erste Buch Samuelis*, Gütersloh 1973, p. 195; P.K. MacCarter, *1 Samuel*, Garden City, N.Y., 1980, pp. 264 f.; J.T. Willis, *First and Second Samuel*, Austin, TX, 1982, pp. 158 f. On Saul's rejection see also J.H. Grønbæk, *Die Geschichte vom Aufstieg Davids*, Copenhagen 1971, pp. 37–68.

[18] Cf. the commentaries on 1 Sam (n. 17); and add A. Caquot and Ph. de Robert, *Les livres de Samuel*, Genève 1994, p. 180.

[19] See the commentaries on 1 Kings, e.g.: A. Šanda, *Die Bücher der Könige* I, Münster 1911, p. 319; J.A. Montgomery, *Kings* (*ICC*), Edinburgh 1951, pp. 241 f.; J. Gray, *1 & 2 Kings* (rev. ed.), London 1970, pp. 279 f. (on v. 11) and 296 f.; M. Noth, *Könige* I, Neukirchen 1968, pp. 250 (v. 11) and 259 f. (and there on the problematic

addresses Solomon: "Because you are guilty of this [= this is with you]—you have not kept My covenant and the laws which I enjoined upon you—I will tear (קרע אקרע . . . מעליך) the kingdom away from you and give it to one of your servants (i.e. Jeroboam)" (1 Kings 11:11, and cf. *ib.* 14:8 and 2 Kings 17:21). Here too, as in the case of Saul and David, a prophet was certainly an intermediary, i.e. Ahija of Shilo. The kingship of Solomon was revoked because he abandoned Yahweh for other deities, late in his reign. He had not walked in "My ways or done what is pleasing to Me, or kept My laws and rules as his father David did" (1 Kings 11:33). Young Jeroboam inherited most of David's and Solomon's kingdom, ten tribes out of eleven or twelve.

In sum: Mari and the Bible display similar historiographic patterns in the revocation of kingship and the choice of a successor ruler. Even the Mari examples are not bare records but interpretative accounts like the biblical parallels. The theological reasoning in both is based on a specific cause, inherent in the behaviour of the king—obeying the deity on the one hand or committing an offense against it on the other. The application of the principle of causality in depicting the events, or in other words in historiography is, no doubt, a significant step towards an intellectual grasp of history.[20]

---

division of the kingdom of Israel into 11, respectively 12 parts). Cf. now also Ch. Schäfer-Lichtenberger, *Josua und Salomo*, Leiden 1995, pp. 341–351.

[20] See Speiser, *op. cit.* (n. 1) and e.g., J.J. Finkelstein, "Mesopotamian Historiography," *Proceedings American Philosophical Society*, 107 (1963), pp. 461–472; on the doctrine of causality in near Eastern and biblical historiography cf. A. Malamat, *VT* 5 (1955), pp. 1–12. For a general treatment of the above remarks see, e.g., A.O. Lovejoy, in ed. H. Meyerhoff, *The Philosophy of History*, Garden City, N.Y. 1959, pp. 173–188; E.H. Carr, *What is History?*, London 1961, esp. chap. 4: "Causation in History."

PART THREE

CUSTOMS AND SOCIETY

16

A RECENTLY DISCOVERED WORD FOR "CLAN" IN MARI AND ITS HEBREW COGNATE*

As expected, the word *lîmum* at Mari, "clan, tribal unit," has finally appeared. The Lim names were exclusively divinized family names and did not refer to real deities. In several new Mari texts, the West Semitic word *lîmum* is attested. It is a cognate of Ugaritic *l'im* and of Hebrew *lĕ'ōm* "clan, tribe, people". In Akkadian *lîmum* also means "the figure 1000, a multitude". The Biblical Hebrew word *'elep* "1000" is also a synonym for "clan" and is thus a semantic parallel to Akkadian, including the Akkadian of Mari.

Since the very beginnings of the Mari discoveries in the 1930s, various personal names have appeared that incorporate the theophoric element Lim, such as Yahdun-Lim and Zimri-Lim, the kings of Mari, and Yarim-Lim, the ruler of Aleppo, and many more.[1] Outside Mari as well, Lim names are plentiful, mostly in the Old Babylonian Period. Recently, some earlier Lim names have also appeared at Ebla, spelled there *li-im*.[2] Yet the deity Lim proper, that is, outside personal names, has so far not been attested. Thus we may have in "Lim" only a divinized name, rather than a real deity. The case is similar to that of the name Hammurapi or Ammurapi, where Hammu (*ʿammu*) is again exclusively a divinized family or clan, but not an actual deity.

Accordingly, the Lim names, like the Ammu names, never carry the DINGIR determinative, perhaps a sign of their weakened theophoric character, denoting a deity of lower rank. Lim is never written in Mari with a Sumerogram and always with a syllabic spelling, such as *li-um, li-im* (see n. 4).

Surprisingly, Durand and Marello have now published new Mari letters attesting to a West Semitic word *lîmum*, spelled syllabically *li-im*, meaning a "clan or a tribal unit". In one instance in the Marello

* This article was originally published in: Zevit, Z., Gitin, S., Sokoloff, M. (eds.), *Solving Riddles and Untying Knots* (Festschrift J.C. Greenfield), 1995, pp. 175–179.

[1] On Lim in short, see M. Krebernik, "Lim," *RLA* 7.25ff. For the above Lim names and many others, see M. Birot, *ARM* 16/1 (1979), Noms de personnes. See also I.J. Gelb *et al.*, *Computer-Aided Analysis of Amorite* (AS 21; Chicago 1980), 145–46.

[2] E.g., A. Archi, "Die ersten zehn Könige von Ebla," *ZA* 76 (1986), 213–17.

letter (A. 1146, line 21),[3] silver was passed on to a clan. In a second instance (line 24) the clan is said to have been assembled in its entirety in the city of Hen, which was situated in a seminomadic environment on the Upper Habur. Certain other aspects of this document are also of interest, but they lie outside the scope of this note. The Durand letter mentions the annihilation of a certain clan or tribe (M. 6060).[4] A further recent occurrence of *lîmum* is still unpublished (A. 2090), but both Durand and Marello refer to it.[5] The clan in question was situated in the country of Zalmaqum and migrated from there to the lowland.

Lîmum has occurred previously in lexical texts, where it is parallel to the noun *nîrum*, also meaning "a clan".[6] The synonym now appears in a Mari text, published by Lafont.[7] The text contains a list of people, including the idiom *nîrum*, referring twice to a large number of women. Text 12 records 70 mí *ni-ru-um*, and text 19 mentions a *ni-ru-um* of 74 women. These were perhaps not simply groups, but rather formal assemblies or even clans.

It is of interest that in Ugarit, or rather, Ugaritic, we encounter the vocable *l'im* (*'alep* with *ḥîreq*), also referring to a people or clan,[8] a form identical with the Mari word. On the other hand, the archaic and poetic expression *lĕ'ōm* (pl. *lĕ'ummîm*) for a tribal unit or even an entire people[9] is frequently attested in biblical Hebrew. Like the Hebrew kinship groups *gôy*, *'ummâ*, *ḥeber*, and *'amm*, thus *lĕ'ōm* in time came to expand its scope to encompass entire peoples or nations, contrary to its original narrow gentilic sense as still attested at Mari. While at Ugarit the Mari vowel of *lîmum* is retained, in the Bible it changes to *o/u*, like *m'id* "much" in Ugaritic and *mĕ'ōd* in Hebrew. *Lîmum* has hardly any connection with the biblical archaic form *lmw* (Deut. 32:3, etc.)[10] or with the personal name Lemuel, Lemoel (*lmw'l*)

---

[3] P. Marello, "Vie nomade," *Mémoires NABU* 1 (1992), 115–25.

[4] J.-M. Durand, "Precurseurs syriens . . .," *Marchand, diplomates et empereurs* (*Mélanges P. Garelli*) (Paris 1991), 50–53.

[5] Durand, *ibid.*, 53; Marello, "Vie nomade," 119, e.

[6] *CAD* N/2, 263 s.v. *nîru* E; *CAD* L, 198 s.v. *lîmu* C.

[7] B. Lafont, "Le *ṣâbum* du roi de Mari," *Miscellania babyloniaca* (*Mélanges M. Birot*) (Paris 1985), 174 (no. 12), 176 (no. 19).

[8] C.H. Gordon, *UT* 426b.

[9] *HALAT* 2.488; *TWAT* 4.411 ff. The word *lĕ'ummîm* appears once in the Bible as the name of a specific tribe (Gen. 25:3).

[10] *HALAT* 2.505. But see E. Lipiński ("Le Dieu Lim," in *15e Rencontre assyriologique internationale* [Liège 1967], 150–60), who equates *lmw* with Lim and takes it as an

(Prov. 31:1, 4), as sometimes assumed[11] (unless we propose a metathesis). In the Bible we apparently have not only an etymological parallel with Mari but also a semantic one. *Lîmum* in Akkadian, including Mari Akkadian, also stands for the number 1000,[12] which may designate a multitude.[13]

Now, one of the common synonyms in the Bible for a clan or a tribe is *ʾelep*.[14] The most common explanation of *ʾelep* is 1000. Thus *lîmum* may be equivalent not only to *lĕʾōm* but also to *ʾelep*. The concept of 1000, a typological number for multitude, may represent a tribe or clan, or perhaps, more precisely, the military potential of these entities.

Addendum: On *lîmum* and *damum* (blood kinship) in Mari and Ebla, see now M. Bonechi, "Lexique et idéologie royale à l'époque proto-syrienne," *MARI* 8 (1997), 477 ff.

---

epithet of the God of Israel. Cf. similarly C. Dossin, "À propos du dieu Lim," *Syria* 55 (1978), 327–32.

[11] Cf. recently S.C. Layton (*Archaic Features of Canaanite Personal Names in the Hebrew Bible* [Atlanta 1990], 190–91), who translates "Lim is God" instead of "God is for him" or the like.

[12] *AHw* 553b; *CAD* L 197.

[13] Cf., e.g., *Recueil É. Dhorme: Études bibliques et orientales* (Paris 1951), 70.

[14] *HALAT* 1.58 s.v. אלף III; D.R. Meyer and H. Donner (eds.), *Wilhelm Gesenius: Hebräisches und Aramäisches Handwörterbuch über das Alte Testament* (18th ed.; Berlin 1987), 68 s.v. אלף III; J. Pedersen, *Israel: Its Life and Culture* (London 1926 [repr. 1946 as 4 vols. in 2]) 1.50. For the typical biblical passages with *ʾelep*, see above and in S. Bendor, *The Social Structure in Ancient Israel*, Jerusalem 1996, 94–97.

17

A NOTE ON THE RITUAL OF TREATY MAKING IN MARI AND THE BIBLE*

Many years ago a Mari letter was published giving details of the preparations necessary for making a treaty between two parties (*ARM* II 37).[1] This letter had been sent to Zimri-Lim, king of Mari, by Ibal-Il, the king's representative in Ida-Maraṣ, situated on the Upper Habur river. For the purpose of concluding a treaty between the Hanaeans (the nomadic population) and the people of Ida-Maraṣ, the latter brought to Ašlakka (a city in Ida-Maraṣ) a puppy and a goat[2] to be slaughtered in a religious ritual. From the continuation of the tablet, it seems that these animals were not suitable for sacrifice in the eyes of the Mari authorities and Ibal-Il ordered the foal of a she-ass to be offered instead. By sacrificing the foal, peace was established between the Hanaeans and the people of Ida-Maraṣ.

Two more letters of Ibal-Il have recently been published (in *MARI* 7), dealing with the same matters, one (A. 1056) containing almost the exact wording of the above document (see below).[3] The other document (A. 2226) mentions Išme-Addu, governor of the city of Ašnakum (also situated in Ida-Maraṣ), as well as the Elders in various cities in Ida-Maraṣ. According to this document, a puppy and a goat were also brought for the purpose of making a treaty, but the

---

* This article was originally published in: *Israel Exploration Journal* 45 (1995), pp. 226–29.

[1] C.-F. Jean: *Lettres diverses (transcrites et traduites)* (= *Archives Royales de Mari* II), Paris 1950, pp. 82–83. Now cf. also A. Finet: Le sacrifice de l'âne en Mésopotamie, in J. Quaegebeur (ed.): *Ritual and Sacrifice in the Ancient Near East*, Leuven 1993, pp. 135–141.

[2] Puppy = *mērānum*; goat = *ḫazzum* (a West Semitic term which in Akkadian is *enzum*). The interpretation of *Chicago Assyrian Dictionary* H, p. 128, is unacceptable (from the word "lettuce" [*ḫassa*], or "leafy bough"), as is that of G.E. Mendenhall: Puppy and Lettuce in Northwest-Semitic Covenant Making, *BASOR* 133 (1954), pp. 26–30; for the accepted interpretation, cf. W. von Soden: Neue Bände der Archives Royales de Mâri, *Orientalia* 22 (1953), p. 197; M. Held: Philological Notes on the Mari Covenant Ritual, *BASOR* 200 (1970), pp. 39–40; D. Charpin: Un Souverain ephémère en Ida-Maraṣ: Išme-Addu d'Ašnakkum, *MARI* 7, Paris 1993, p. 184, n. 11.

[3] Charpin (above, n. 2), pp. 182–186, Nos. 7, 8, 9.

delegate of the king of Mari again replaced them by the foal of a she-ass in order to perform the treaty-making ritual in a fitting manner.

Document A. 1056, which is more or less identical with *ARM* II 37, differs from it with regard to the kinds of animals brought to the ritual. While goats were brought in both cases, a calf was brought in the latter, instead of a puppy.[4] These animals were then replaced—following the Mari delegate's demand—by the foal of a she-ass. The difference in the animals' names in Akkadian is very slight: young dog, puppy = *mērānum*, whereas young bull or calf = *mērum*.[5] If there is no mistake in the cuneiform writing (omitting *an*), here is another animal which the local population considered suitable for the ritual of treaty making, but which was declared unfit by the authorities of Mari. In the eyes of the people of Mari, a proper peace treaty could be made only by slaughtering the foal of a she-ass.[6] Further testimony is provided by the West Semitic formula *ḫayaram qatālum*, "slaughtering an ass", which sometimes indicates the making of peace even without the performance of a ritual. It may be surmised, however, that on the outskirts of the kingdom of Mari other animals were also used in the peace-making ritual.

Treaty making, as described above, had its origins in West Semitic customs, and indeed, two episodes in the Bible describe treaty making by means of the dismemberment of animals.[7] The better-known one is the Covenant of the Pieces made between God and Abraham: "And the Lord said unto him 'Bring me a heifer three years old[8]

---

[4] J.M. Sasson (Isaiah LXVI 3–4a, *VT* 26 [1976], pp. 199–205, see pp. 204–205) surmises that the use of a dog in treaty making was accepted practice among the Hurrians, a neighbouring people to the West Semites in Ida-Maraṣ. See *ibid.*, similar customs among the Hittites, the Greeks and the Romans.

[5] See debate in Charpin (above, n. 2), p. 186, nn. 7–8, and Durand, *Documents épistolaires*... 1 (LAPO), 1997, pp. 444 f. and n. c, who prefers the reading "chiot" (puppy).

[6] See list of references to this ritual in the Mari texts up to 1990 (one of these references is from Tell al-Rimaḥ [see below, n. 12]): D. Charpin: *Mélanges Jean Perrot*, Paris 1990, pp. 116–117, n. 35. Now add a new Mari reference, end of text A. 2692 + 3288; see J.-M. Durand: *Mémoires de NABU* 3 (*Mém. M. Birot*), Paris 1994, p. 92, n. 24. In addition, there is a similar reference in the Ishchali tablets (beyond the Tigris), published by S. Greengus (1979), text 326:35; according to the reading of F.R. Kraus, there is mentioned "a foal of an ass" and not "a lion"; see now S. Greengus, *JAOS* 108 (1988), pp. 154–155.

[7] For a comparison between Mari and the Bible, see M. Noth: Das alttest. Bundschliessen im Lichte eines Mari Textes, *Gesamm. Studien zum Alten Testament*, Munich 1966, pp. 142–154.

[8] The meaning of Hebrew *mĕšullaš*, fem. *mĕšullešet* is "tripled; of three parts" (Koh.

and a she-goat three years old and a ram three years old and a turtle-dove and a young pigeon'. And He brought all of these and cut them in two and laid each half over against the other, but He did not cut the bird in two"[9] (Gen. 15:9–10). A number of animals are mentioned here, including a heifer and a she-goat, as in the above-mentioned documents from Mari. There is no biblical reference to an ass or the foal of a she-ass in connection with treaty making.

With regard to the other treaty recorded in the Bible—made between King Zedekiah, his officers and the people at the time of the Babylonian siege of Jerusalem, with the intention of freeing the slaves inside the city[10]—only a calf is mentioned, as in the new document from Mari (No. 9); however, the Jerusalemites later violated the treaty—possibly because the Babylonian siege on the city had been eased—and against this treachery the prophet Jeremiah protests: ". . . the men who . . . did not keep the terms of the covenant which they made before me, I will make like the calf which they cut in two and passed between its parts: the princes of Judah and the princes of Jerusalem . . . who passed between the parts of the calf" (Jer. 34:18–19). It would seem that the ritual of this covenant, performed only with a calf, was the original custom, whereas the one described in the Covenant of the Pieces in Genesis, in which a number of other

---

4:12), hence: "three years old", when said of a young and tender animal. See, e.g., C. Westermann: *Genesis, BK* I/2, Neukirchen 1981, pp. 251, 267–268. On the Covenant of the Pieces and for comparisons of treaties made by West Semites, see G.F. Hasel: The Meaning of the Animal Rite in Genesis 15, *Journal for the Study of the Old Testament* 19 (1981), pp. 61–78. See *ibid.*, for the connection between the two covenants, in Genesis and in Jeremiah (cf. A.S. Kapelrud: The Interpretation of Jeremiah 34, 18 ff., *Journal for the Study of the Old Testament* 22 [1982], pp. 138–140).

[9] In referring to the above animals, the verb *wayĕbattēr* ("and he cut") is used in the *piʿel* form, but the *qal* form, *lô bātar* ("he did not cut") is used in reference to the bird. This phenomenon is well known both in Hebrew and in Arabic; an object (as well as a subject) in the singular is at times accompanied by a verb in the *qal* form, whereas an object (as well as a subject) in the plural is accompanied by a verb in the *piʿel* form. See A. Malamat: *MEIE*, p. 49.

[10] On this episode, see, e.g., W. Rudolph: *Jeremiah* (HAT), Tübingen 1968 (3rd ed.), pp. 223–224, and cf. *ibid.*, the reference to the treaty made in the eighth century B.C.E. between Aššur-Nirari V, king of Assyria, and Mattiʿel from Bit Agusi in Syria. See also Kapelrud (above, n. 8). A similar treaty is mentioned in the documents from Alalaḫ in northern Syria; in particular, document No. 456 mentions that the local king swore an oath to the gods and at the same time performed the ritual slaughtering of a lamb. On a recent comparison between the Covenant of the Pieces and the Covenant of Zedekiah, see R. Hess: The Slaughter of Animals in Gen. 15:8–21, in R.S. Hess *et al.* (eds.): *He Swore an Oath, Biblical Themes from Genesis 12–50* (FS D.J. Wiseman), Cambridge–London 1993, pp. 55–65. For both Covenants and the Mari parallels cf. also the remarks and literature of D.B. Weisberg, *MAARAV* 7 (1991), pp. 264–67.

animals besides the heifer were brought to sacrifice, should be considered a later addition.[11]

While in Mari and elsewhere[12] an ass was mainly used in the ritual of treaty making, other animals, principally calves, were used in the Bible, as was the custom in certain provincial places in the Mari kingdom. It may be assumed that the ass, an unclean animal in the Bible, was considered unfit for treaty making, as it was in the sacrifice of the firstlings.[13] The firstling of an ass was not sacrificed to God in the same way as other animals, but was either redeemed by a lamb or had its neck broken, cf. Exodus 13:12–13: ". . . You shall set apart unto the Lord all that first opens the womb. . . . And every firstling of an ass you shall redeem with a lamb; and if you will not redeem it, you shall break its neck". Nevertheless, the element common to all the rituals discussed here is the use of young, tender animals.[14]

---

[11] See S.E. Loewenstamm: Zur Traditionsgeschichte des Bundes zwischen den Stücken, *VT* 18 (1968), pp. 500–506.

[12] Evidence of this practice at Tell al-Rimaḥ, which was close to Mari both in time and place, may be found in the tablet published by S. Dalley *et al.*: *The Old Babylonian Tablets from Tell al Rimah*, London 1976, pp. 12–13, No. 1:37–40.

[13] See, in general, on the firstling of unclean animals, G. Brin: *Studies in Biblical Law*, Sheffield 1994, pp. 196–208.

[14] Cf. A. Malamat: Mari, in *Enṣ. Miqr.* IV, Jerusalem 1962, Col. 575 (Hebrew).

18

IS THERE A WORD FOR THE ROYAL HAREM IN THE BIBLE? THE *INSIDE* STORY*

It is rather surprising that the Hebrew Bible has no specific term for the royal women's quarters within the palace, that is, the harem. Admittedly, there are the general terms *bayit* "house" in connection with Solomon's separate house, which he built for Pharaoh's daughter (1 Kgs. 7:8, 9:24), and the *bêt hannāšîm* at the Persian court, mentioned in the book of Esther (2:3, 9, 11, 13, 14). Now, at least some of the kings of Judah and Israel, such as David, Solomon, and Rehoboam, married many wives. Even the "Law of the King" attests to polygamy, since it warns the Israelite rulers against too many spouses (Deut. 17:17). Thus, we may assume that in the palaces of Jerusalem and in the capital cities in the Northern Kingdom special quarters were set aside to accommodate royal ladies, similar to the harems throughout the ancient Near East and later in the Islamic and Ottoman Empires.[1] The Hebrew word **harmôn*, used in Modern Hebrew under the influence of Arabic for harem, appears once in the Bible, in Amos 4:3, although in the peculiar form *haharmônâ* (with *hē locale*), which is obscure and is generally taken as a toponym.[2]

Thus we need to look for an alternative word in the Bible for harem, one denoting the physical realm of the women's quarters deep within the palace. A possible solution is suggested by the Akkadian sources, especially the Mari documents from the Old Babylonian Period (eighteenth century B.C.E.). There the Akkadian term *tubqum*, meaning "corner", at times actually refers to the interior parts of the

* This article was originally published in: Wright, D.P., Freedman, D.N., Hurvitz, A. (eds.), *Pomegranates and Golden Bells* (FS J. Milgrom), Winona Lake, IN, 1995, pp. 785–87.

[1] On Assyria, see E. Weidner, "Hof- und Haremserlasse assyrischer Könige," *AfO* 17 (1954–56), 257–93. On harems in recent times (of the Ottoman Empire), see now A.L. Croutier, *Harem: World behind the Veil* (New York: Abbeville 1989). On the harem in the Bible in general, see R. de Vaux, *Les institutions de L'Ancient Testament* (2 vols.; Paris: Du Cerf. 1958), 1,177 ff.

[2] See, e.g., *HALAT* 243, s.v. הרמון ("unexplained"). See also the recent commentaries on the book of Amos: F.I. Andersen and D.N. Freedman, *Amos* (*AB* 24A; Garden City, N.Y.: Doubleday 1989), 419, 425 (*harmôn* is a place name beyond Damascus); and S.M. Paul, *Amos* (Hermeneia; Minneapolis: Fortress 1991), 135–36.

palace containing the harem.[3] A conspicuous example of the latter is mentioned in a Mari source, referring to a harem in the city of Ashlakka (north of Mari), where, *inter alia*, one of King Zimrilim's daughters resided (*ARMT* 10 74:11 ff.). The king of Ashlakka made her stay in a corner and made her hold her cheeks in her hands and she complains that in this posture she looks like a fool or an idiot.[4] The term *tubqum* occurs again in a recently published letter from King Šamši-Adad to his son, the viceroy of Mari, concerning the arrival of a princess from Qaṭna in Middle Syria at Mari (A. 4471:7, 28).[5]

The above term is particularly apt, since the harem was deep within the palatial structure or in the corner of the building, some distance from the palace gate. These circumstances are illuminated by the archaeological and architectural evidence of the majestic palace at Mari proper and elsewhere.[6] That the *tubqum* must have occupied a considerable area may be assumed by the estimate that King Zimrilim's harem included some 175–200 women, as well as their entourage.

A similar picture emerges apparently from the Bible, where an idiom is used as a substitute for the official term for the living space of the royal women. Our assumption is that the word *pĕnîmâ* fulfills this purpose and twice occurs in the Bible to signify the harem.[7] The prime example of this usage is in the hymn about the wedding of an anonymous Israelite king in Ps. 45:14–15 (MT): "The royal princess, [following the Hebrew text, add: (with)] all (her) belongings, her dress

[3] See J.-M. Durand and J. Margueron, "La question du harem royal dans le palais de Mari," *Journal de Savants* (Oct.–Dec. 1980), 253–80. On *tubqum*, see also *AHw* 1365 ("Ecke, Winkel"). For general remarks on the Mari harem, cf. B.F. Batto, *Studies on Women in Mari* (Baltimore: Johns Hopkins University Press 1974), 8–36 (chap. 1) and now N. Ziegler, *Le harem de Zimri-Lim, Mém NABU* 5, Paris 1997 (unavailable to me).

[4] See G. Dossin (and A. Finet), *ARMT* 10 (Paris: Geuthner 1978), 112–13. For an additional instance, see J.M. Durand, *ARMT* 21, 398:39 (here the form of the relevant word is *tubuqtum*).

[5] See J.M. Durand, *MARI* 6 (1990), 291–93.

[6] See Durand and Margueron, "La question," 279–80 and figs. 3–7 for Mari. For additional sites, see figs. 1, 2. For the textual documentation, see J.M. Durand, "L'organisation de l'espace dans le palais de Mari...," *Le système palatial en Orient, en Grèce et à Rome: Actes du colloque de Strasbourg, 19–22 juin 1985* (ed. F. Lévy; Travaux du Centre de recherche sur le proche-orient et la Grèce antique 9; Leiden: Brill 1987), 80 ff.

[7] I alluded to this assumption already in a footnote in *Mari and the Early Israelite Experience* (London: British Academy/Oxford University Press 1989), 11 n. 29. There I also referred to the Middle Assyrian term *bitāni* "interior apartments in a mansion" and specifically to the Amarna letters, where *bitāti* (*EA* 29:32) clearly signifies a harem.

embroidered with golden mountings, is led *inside* [and from there; A. Malamat] to the king; maidens in her train, her companions are presented to you."[8] At first glance the word *pĕnîmâ* "inside, interior" could refer to the palace as such (in one case regarding the palace of King Hezekiah; cf. 2 Chr. 29:18), but on closer examination it specifically refers to the harem proper. Besides mentioning the princess and her belongings (*kĕbûdâ*), the text describes how the princess is led forth to the king (from the "inside"), robed in royal apparel and accompanied by her entourage of maidens (Ps. 45:15). The custom of escorting a royal bride from the harem to the king is illustrated by the story of Queen Vashti, wife of Ahasuerus, who was commanded to appear before the king in all "her beauty" (Esth. 1:9–17).

Another instance of *pĕnîmâ*, presumably identifying a harem, occurs in 2 Kgs. 7:11–12, in the passage one of the Aramaean-Israelite wars: "The gatekeeper called out and the news was passed on *into* the king's palace (in Samaria). The king (of Israel) rose in the night and said to his courtiers . . ." (NJPS).[9]

We may surmise that here too the word *pĕnîmâ*, "into, inside", alludes to the women's quarters rather than to the palace *per se*, as the above translation and many commentators have it. It appears that the king passed the night in the harem, presumably in a separate chamber, and it is there that the upsetting news reached him.

In sum, the appellation *pĕnîmâ*, like the term *tubqum* in Mari, has its own logic and denotes the harem, since the latter was usually located in the innermost parts of the palace, if only for security reasons. Indeed, throughout history until modern times the harem has been a secluded, well-guarded unit. As in many other cases, an informal expression supplants a technical term.

---

[8] For the usual meaning of this passage, consult commentaries on the book of Psalms, such as: A.A. Anderson, *The Book of Psalms* (NCB; 2 vols.; Grand Rapids, Mich.: Eerdmans 1972), 1.353; D.W. Rogerson and S.M. Mackay, *Psalms 1–50* (*CBCOT*; Cambridge: Cambridge University Press 1977), 21–22; M. Dahood, *Psalms I* (*AB* 16; Garden City, N.Y.: Doubleday 1979), 275. In contrast, the *RSV* rightly translates here *pĕnîmâ* "in her chamber". Various medieval exegetes also come close to suggesting that "interior" refers to the palace, but not specifically to the harem; e.g., Ibn Ezra, *ad loc.*

[9] For the common interpretation, see such commentaries on 2 Kings as: A. Montgomery, *A Critical and Exegetical Commentary on the Books of Kings* (ICC; Edinburgh: T. & T. Clark 1951), 387; G.H. Jones, *1 & 2 Kings* (*NCBC*; 2 vols.; Grand Rapids: Eerdmans 1984), 2.437; T.R. Hobbs, *2 Kings* (*WBC*; Waco: Word 1985), 86–93; A. Šanda, *Die Bücher der Könige* (2 vols.; *EHAT*; Münster: Aschendorffscher 1911–12), 2.61. The latter commentary compares our term to an Egyptian usage, referring *inter alia* to a palace but not to a harem *per se*.

19

THE CORRESPONDENCE OF ŠIBTU, QUEEN OF MARI IN *ARM* X*

I

The latest volume to appear in the series of the "*Archives Royales de Mari*" (Vol. X), edited by G. Dossin, is devoted entirely to feminine correspondence.[1] To date, only the cuneiform copies are accessible; the corresponding volume containing the transliterations and French translation is still forthcoming.[2] However, while anticipating the companion volume, which will undoubtedly attract a wider audience, it is only appropriate to examine a substantial portion of these documents as they contain an abundantly rich mine of information on female activity in the Mari realm. Such an investigation, even in part, may at the same time reveal the potential significance and impact of the new material on the study of women of rank in the ancient Near East in general.

The present volume contains 179 letters which were either sent by women of the palace of Mari or dispatched to them; no other such variegated correspondence has been found elsewhere in the ancient Near East. Outstanding here is the correspondence of the wives of Zimrilim, the last king of Mari (*ca.* 1780–1760 B.C.E. according to the middle chronology), in particular that of his chief spouse Šibtu. The dossier of this queen contains seventeen letters addressed to her husband, twenty which she received from him, and at least sixteen additional communiqués from high ranking officials or other

* This article, written together with Prof. P. Artzi, is the result of the authors' combined study in autumn 1969 of *ARM* X containing only the autographed copies of the tablets. This article was originally published in: *Orientalia* 40 (1971), pp. 75–87 and remains here practically unchanged. A few items in this paper are now outdated, while our translation of the Mari document should be checked against the official publication of *ARMT* 10.

[1] G. Dossin, *Archives Royales de Mari: La correspondance féminine* (*TCL* XXXI, Paris 1967). Quotations from the Mari archives are cited by volume and number (No.) of document, except for *ARM* X, where usually only the number of the document is given.

[2] Several documents touching upon prophecy contained in this volume have already been discussed extensively; see *infra* n. 19.

personalities, including one letter from her father. A study of Šibtu's correspondence depicts her as a very active and highly influential person in the kingdom of Mari, far-removed from the status of a woman confined to the royal harem. This stately individual may serve as a paragon for women of royal stature in other parts of the Near East, including Israel. We shall, however, neither be concerned here with a comparative study, e.g. with court women in the Assyrian or Hittite kingdoms, in Ugarit or the Bible,[3] nor shall we enter into a detailed discussion of the manifold problems arising from reading Šibtu's correspondence.

There is no doubt that Šibtu's personal traits and her exceptional ability to cope with both administrative and political matters was instrumental in aiding her toward her advancement to a position of prime importance. But, first and foremost, her unique status derived from her royal descent as the daughter of Yarimlim, king of Yamḫad, who lived at its capital Aleppo.[4] Her father was the most powerful ruler in the West and also apparently, for a time, in all of Mesopotamia. At any rate, he held a position superior to Zimrilim. Šibtu's cylinder seal, two fragmentary imprints of which survive on clay sherds, bear witness to her lineage.[5]

The entire legend of the seal is cited in one of the letters in the new volume (No. 119), already previously communicated by Dossin (see n. 4). The author of the letter, apparently Zimrilim, asks the queen to dispatch to him a document, bearing her seal: (1') [*i-na ku-nu*]-[*uk*]-*ki-ki* (2') [*ša*]SAL *Ši-ib-t*[*u*] (3') DUMU.SAL (= *mārat*) *Ia-ri-im-li-im* (4') *aš-ša-at Zi-im-ri-li-im* (5') *ša-aṭ-ru ku-un-ki-ma* IM.GU.X[6] (6') *pí-iq-di-ma* . . .—"(1') [with] your seal on which (2') "(lady) Šibtu, (3') the daughter of Yarimlim, (4') the wife of Zimrilim", (5') is written, seal (it) and in the dossier (?) (6') enclose it. . . ."

---

[3] From many points of view the closest comparative material to Mari is found at Ugarit. Concerning the queen and other palace women there, now see in addition to *PRU* III and IV, J. Nougayrol, *Ugaritica* V (Paris 1968), 134 ff.; 261 ff.

[4] For a first report on Šibtu see G. Dossin, "Šibtu, reine de Mari", *Actes du XXIe congrès des orientalistes* (Bruxelles 1949), 142 ff. On King Yarimlim, see *infra*, pp. 187 ff. and n. 28.

[5] See A. Parrot, *Mission archéologique de Mari* II: *Le Palais—Documents et Monuments* (Paris 1959), 167 f.; 254 (*ME* No. 69, 181); Fig. 103, Pl. XLVI.

[6] Regarding the reading of the compound logogram IM.GU.X (where the final sign is broken) several possibilities suggest themselves: The GU sign may have been mistakenly copied for GÚ; or perhaps we should emend the spelling: IM.GID (!).DA. In both cases the most probable Akkadian reading is *liginnum* ("tablet with one column") denoting "dossier". See *ARM* VII, No. 120: 4', 12', 29', 39'; and cf. *AHw* 552: "Aktennotiz".

Concerning the circumstances of Šibtu's marriage to Zimrilim the following contention, put forth by Dossin, is generally accepted (see n. 4): after the murder of his father Yaḫdunlim, and the capture of Mari by Šamši-Adad, Zimrilim escaped to Aleppo. During his exile he was given in marriage to the daughter of Yarimlim, his patron, with whose endeavors (after some 20 years), he reascended the throne of Mari which had been reconquered from Assyrian domination. Admittedly, no proof has yet been discovered to authenticate this hypothesis. It may, however, project a most interesting light on the unusually close bond between the future king and his spouse whose fate proceeded from the former's humble days in exile.

In addition to Šibtu's seal, at least one letter to Zimrilim and an economic text, listing her among court women at Mari supplied with cuts of mutton from the palace (*ARM* VII No. 206:6'), were published prior to the appearance of the new volume. Šibtu's letter to Zimrilim (*ARM* II No. 116) parallels in content one of the new letters (No. 19), informing her husband that she is sending him a choice selection of garments and weapons (the text speaks of bows). On the other hand, it is necessary to emphasize that the author of a second letter with a similar name, *Ši-ba-tu(m)* (*ARM* II No. 115), should not be identified with Šibtu, as becomes apparent from the new volume, containing two additional letters from this same woman (Nos. 94–95).[7]

Three letters written by a person called *be-el-et ma-tim* (always written syllabically), "the lady of the land", pose a special problem. This rare and significant title appears at a later period in a theophoric personal name from Nuzi (^{d}*Ištar-bēlet-māti*). Especially noteworthy is the use of this term with explicit reference to the country, applied to several queens in the El-Amarna correspondence and in a Hittite letter.[8] According to Dossin, the bearer of this title at Mari is Queen

---

[7] Contrary to Dossin's earlier opinion (cf. n. 4), p. 142, n. 2. In the Table of Contents in *ARM* X he now reads the name of this woman as Šimatu(m). Against this reading see Moran (*infra*, n. 19), pp. 44 f. The name Šibtu perhaps means "the old woman" (*šībtu* with long *i*), used as an affectionate name. On this possibility, see F. Delitzsch, *Sumerisches Glossar*, 242, s.v. AMA.SÍG = *šībtu*; A. Falkenstein, *Sumerische Götterlieder*, 1 (Heidelberg 1959), 57, 76; and now *MSL* XII 128:79.

[8] Ramses II addresses the Hittite queen Puduḫepa as follows: *atti* SAL *bēltum ša māt Ḫatti* (*KBo* I, 21:12). Taduḫepa, daughter of Tušratta, king of Mitanni, and wife of Amenhotep III, is called: NIN-*et* (= *bēlet*) *māt Miṣri; ana bēlti* (*māt*) *Miṣri; ša* (*māt*) *Miṣri bēlassu* (*EA* 19:17–19; 20:9, 16). Tušratta, writes to Tiy, the Queen Mother in Egypt and widow of Amenhotep III: "*ana* [SAL *Teje*] NIN (= *bēlet*) (*māt*) *Miṣri* (*EA* 26:1). In the caption of a letter to Amenhotep IV he also greets the Queen Mother: *ana* SAL *Teje ummīka* NIN (= *bēlet*) (*māt*) *Miṣri* (*EA* 28:7). See for all these references and the personal name from Nuzi mentioned above, *CAD* B 190.

Šibtu, Zimrilim's chief wife (cf. n. 4, and *ARM* II 239; XV 156). This identification remains doubtful, however. In previously published (*ARM* II No. 117), as well as in new correspondence (No. 20), the woman who refers to herself as *bēlet mātim* addresses Zimrilim without adhering in the salutatory formula to the subservient status *amatkama*, "your maidservant". This is in open contrast to the standard formula, which occurs without exception in all of Šibtu's letters to her husband. This implies that *bēlet mātim* held a very prominent position in theory at least, higher than that of an ordinary wife of the king. It may have paralleled the status enjoyed by the *g*ᵉ*bīrā* in the Bible—the "first lady" in the kingdom. Just as in the monarchies of Israel and Judah the designation *g*ᵉ*bīrā* usually referred to the Queen Mother[9] and just as Tiy, the Queen Mother in Egypt (as Amenhotep III's widow), had borne the corresponding title (cf. n. 8), it is possible that in Mari too, *bēlet mātim* actually designated Zimrilim's mother, the widow of King Yaḫdunlim. There is, however, no proof in the Mari texts to support our assumption. In a third letter (No. 28) *bēlet mātim* writes to an official named Yassi-Dagan, requiring him to send her a rare and expensive garment. Again we are bewildered as to the identity of this mysterious woman.

In this connection we should mention a prominent woman, now known from the new documents, by the name of Tarišḫattu, whose eminent position is clearly reflected in two letters of Volume X. In one (No. 114) she addresses Šibtu without any introductory formula such as "my lady" or "your maidservant". Moreover, upon closing she calls Šibtu: "my daughter", an expression not to be taken literally here, but rather in keeping with the protocol, as a mere indication of the writer's standing. In the second letter (No. 104) she writes to a man, of whose name only the latter element (Dagan) is preserved, in which she calls herself "your mother" (*ummaka*). Here also, the term should not be accepted verbatim but, rather as the designation of a superior rank.[10] Because of the great interest of the letter to Šibtu we quote it here in full (*ARM* X, No. 114):

---

[9] For a detailed study on this subject, see H. Donner, "Art und Herkunft des Amtes der Königinmutter im Alten Testament", *Festschrift J. Friedrich* (Heidelberg 1959), 105 ff.; cf. R. de Vaux, *Ancient Israel* (New York 1961), 117 ff., and the literature, p. 528.

[10] For the salutatory formulae in Akkadian letters in general see E. Salonen, *Die Gruss- und Höflichkeitsformeln in babylonisch-assyrischen Briefen* (*StOr* 38, Helsinki 1967).

(1) *a-na* SAL *Ši-ib-tu* (2) *qí-bí-ma* (3) *um-ma* SAL *Ta-ri-iš-ḫa-at-tu-ma* (4) *a-wa-tam ki-a-am eš-me um-ma-a-mi* (5) SAL.TUR *Be-el-ta-ni i-na Ma-ri* (KI) (6) *a-na Ki-ib-ri-(d)Da-gan a-bi-ša* (7) *ki-a-am iq-bi um-ma-a-mi* (8) SAL *Ta-ri-iš-ḫa-at-tu iš-pu-ra-am-ma* (9) *in-ṣa-ba-ti-ia ù* ḪAR KÙ.BABBAR-*ia*[11] (10) *ú-ḫa-am-mi-ṣú* (11) *an-ni-tam eš-me-ma* (12) *li-ib-bi ma-di-iš* (13) *iz-zi-iq* (14) *i-nu-ma an-ni-tam e-ep-pé-šu* (Rev.) (15) *ṭe₄-mi a-i-ša-am*[12] *ú-bi-il* (16) *a-ga-na* DUMU *ši-ip-ri-ia li-il-li-kam* (17) *ú-lu-ma ka-ni-ki li-id-di-nu-nim* (18) *ša i-nu-ma aš-pu-ra-am-ma* (19) *su-ba-ti*[13] "*ša*" SAL.TUR *ša-a-ti i-na qa-bi-ia* (20) *ú-ḫa-am*]-*mi-ṣú a-wa-tam ša-a-ti* (21) *ú-ul i-di ú-ul eš-me-ma* (22) *šum-ma i-na ki-na-tim-ma* (23) *ma-ar-ti at-ti ù ši-ri-ia* (24) *ta-ra-am-mi-ma* (25) LUGAL *šu-uš-mi-ma* (26) *an-ni-tam la an-ni-tam* (27) *ṭe₄-ma-am ga-am-ra-am* (Tr.) (28) *me-ḫe-er ṭup-pi-ia šu-bi-lim*

(1) To the lady Šibtu (2) say: (3) Thus (said) the lady Tarišḫattu: (4) I have heard words (of slander) as follows: (5) The young woman Beltani, (who is) in Mari, (6) to her father Kibri-Dagan (7) said as follows: (8) "The lady Tarišḫattu sent to me (a messenger) (9) and my earrings and ring-money (= "silver rings")[11] (10) were removed by force". (11) I have heard this and (12) my heart is greatly (13) wounded. (14) When I would have done this (Rev.) (15) I would have been insane (lit.: where would my mind lead?) (16) Very well. My messenger will come there (17) and let them give him a sealed document (18) (which would testify) as to whether when I sent (a previous messenger to her) (19) the rooms[13] "of" that young woman were actually looted (20) in accordance with my command! Of this matter (21) I am not aware, I did not hear. (22) If truly (23) you are my daughter and you love (24) my health (= flesh), then (25) you will convey (this matter) to the king, and (26) whatever the case may be (27) a complete report (Tr.) (28) send to me as a reply to my letter.

The specific circumstances concerning the robbery of Beltani's jewelry and money (does this refer to her dowry?) mentioned in the letter are unknown and we cannot determine if a wider legal implication

[11] On the earring see *CAD* A/II 144 f., s.v. *anṣabtu, inṣabtu.* Concerning the silver rings (ḪAR KU.BABBAR) note: Sumerian ḪAR is Akkadian *sēweru/sewēru*, "ring". On the Sumerian, see E. Sollberger, *The Business and Administrative Correspondence under the Kings of Ur* (New York 1966), 131, No. 300: ḫa-ar. Since the scribe expressly specified the word ring by "silver", we must assume that this is not ordinary jewelry but rather refers to "ring money"; see the discussion in *ARM* VII 320 ff. and cf. S.R. Driver – J.C. Miles, *The Babylonian Laws* 1 (Oxford 1952), 365; J. Renger, *ZA* 58 (1967), 161.

[12] On this accurate spelling see *CAD* A/1, s.v. *ajīšam; ajīšamma*, lexical section.

[13] The spelling *subati* for standard *šubati* points to the phonetic shift š/s, peculiar to the West Semitic idiom of Mari. See A. Finet, *L'accadien des lettres de Mari* (Bruxelles 1956), 18. Although it is possible to read the initial sign as an "untidy" *šu* (cf. *ARM* XV No. 203), the internal evidence of our letter rather points to the proposed reading *su* (cf. the different forms of *šu* in ll. 14, 25 and 28).

should be ascribed to this matter. However, Tarišḫattu's superior position is evident from her letter. A special messenger through whom she is able to give "commands" is at her behest, and moreover, as mentioned previously, she appeals to Queen Šibtu as "my daughter". A further possible factor enhancing the importance of the described encounter lies in the name of Beltani's father, Kibri-Dagan, who quite possibly is Mari's well-known governor of the district of Terqa (concerning whom, see below).

II

Before concerning ourselves with Šibtu's extensive correspondence with her husband, we shall discuss her exchange of letters with the high officials of the Mari administration. In the new volume there is only a single communiqué (No. 27) sent by Šibtu to an official, Darišlibur, who was in charge of the precious metals of the palace (cf. *ARM* VII 232; IX 327). On the other hand, it contains a group of at least thirteen letters from different officials to Šibtu (Nos. 152–164), dealing with administrative and even political and military affairs, thus proving that in such matters direct ties evolved between officialdom and the queen. The salutatory formula in these letters is *ana bēltīi̯a*, "to my lady!", and once, *ana bēltim*, "to the lady!" (No. 153).

Most of the officials are known previously from the Mari texts, for example Iturasdu, who served as Mari's representative in the city Naḫur and later held a high position at the court of the capital. His two letters addressed to the queen have been preserved in a very fragmented condition (Nos. 152, 154).[14] In contrast, the letter of Kibri-Dagan, Zimrilim's governor of Terqa (situated on the Euphrates seventy kilometers north of the metropolis), has been preserved intact (his otherwise extensive correspondence comprises *ARM* III and part of volume XIII). We learn from his letter (No. 153) that Kibri-Dagan was requested to do a personal service for the queen who had sent him a message (*našpartum*) to clarify in a matter of days, the reason for the "heartache" (*muruṣ libbim*) of a certain woman. As much as this request seems insignificant it characterizes Šibtu, nevertheless, as a queen who took a personal interest in the affairs of individual

[14] The better preserved of the two letters, No. 152, has already been published by J. Bottéro, *RA* 52 (1958), 173 ff.

royal subjects. This same tendency is expressed in other instances as well (cf. above Tarišḫattu's request to Šibtu), as in No. 160. This time the queen acts through her confidant Šubnalu, "the inspector" (he bears the title GÌR, for which cf. *ARM* VII No. 74 and pp. 175–76), to secure the release of several women who were imprisoned as hostages for a debt (SAL *nipût* PN).[15]

The letters of Meptum and Ḫaliḫadun deal with political and military affairs. Meptum, the governor of the southern and eastern border districts of the kingdom of Mari, passes intelligence on to the queen, which he has gathered with the assistance of the frontier guard (*bazaḫātum*) under his command (No. 155). He informs her that the guard reached the gate of the city of Kakkulātum on the Middle Tigris: (9) *ṭe-em li-ib-bi ma-at Èš*-[*nun*]-*na*[(KI)] (10) *aš-ta-al-šu-nu*—"(10) I asked them (9) for a report on the interior of Ešnunna". He received a report, confirmed by similar intelligence gathered from the vicinity of the city of Ekallātum on the Tigris—a considerable distance north of Kakkulātum—on the movement of an army (apparently from Ešnunna) numbering 1500 men toward (or possibly along) the bank of the river (Tigris?).

Again, Ḫaliḫadun, who was Mari's governor in the area of the Upper Baliḫ, writes to the queen concerning his activities among the tribes dwelling on the northern fringes of the kingdom (No. 157). He was commissioned by Zimrilim, who was then in the city of Ašlakka in the vicinity of Naḫur, to go to the area of the tribes of Numḫû and Yamūtbāl (*ana ḫalaṣ Numḫû u Yamūtbāl*). His task was to establish peace between these tribes—known from the Mari texts and other sources of the Old Babylonian period—and Qarnilim who ruled in one of the nearby cities:[16] (12) *sa-li-ma-*[*am*] (13) *ù dam-qa-*[*tim ina*][17] (14) *bi-ri-it* (15) *Qar-ni-li-*[*im Nu-um-ḫu-u* (?)] (16) *ù Ia-mu-ut-*[*ba-lim aš-kun*]—"(12) Peace (13) and good relations[17] (14) between (15) Qarnilim, [Numḫû (?)] (16) and Yamūt[bāl I have established]".

[15] On the term *nipûtum* "prisoner for debt", see now *AHw* 792 (Schuldhäftling) and *ARM* IX 316. This term refers to hostages taken from the debtor when unable to repay his loan. This practice is also known from legal documents and the legal codes of Ešnunna and Ḫammurabi; see Driver-Miles, *Babylonian Laws*, I 210 ff.; A. Goetze, *The Laws of Eshnunna* (New Haven 1956), 68 ff.

[16] The tribes of Numḫû and Yamūtbāl are mentioned together also in other documents from Mari; cf. J.-R. Kupper, *Les nomades en Mésopotamie au temps des rois de Mari* (Bruxelles 1957), 216 ff.; D.O. Edzard, *Die "Zweite Zwischenzeit" Babyloniens* (Wiesbaden 1957), 106. On Qarnilim, who was apparently the king of Ašnakkum, see *ARM* XV 153.

[17] On the term *damqātum* "good things, good relations" in the context of treaties,

It seems that the close ties and the good relations prevailing between Šibtu and the high officials of Mari were brought about by the complete confidence which Zimrilim placed in his wife and the active part she played in state affairs. Several letters between the king and queen bear witness to this close partnership, examples of which we will now present.

III

In contrast to the formal and businesslike tone characteristic of the correspondence between Šibtu and the functionaries, several private letters from Šibtu to Zimrilim stand out for their intimate content and feminine touch. Particularly moving is a short message in which the queen informs her husband of the happy news that she has given birth to twins (No. 26):[18] (1) [*a-na be-lí-ia*] (2) [*qí*]-*bí*-[*ma*] (3) *um*-[*ma*] SAL [*Ši-ib*]-*tum* (4) *amat*-[*ka-a-m*]*a* (5) *tu-i-mi a*[*t-ta-a*]*l-da* (6) *1 māram ù mārtam* (7) *be-lí lu-ú ḫa-di*—"(1) [To my lord] (2) say: Thus (said) [Šib]tu (4) [your] maidservant: (5) I have [just given] birth to twins (6)—a son and a daughter. (7) May my lord rejoice!

The close contact between the royal couple continued, even when Zimrilim traveled great distances on inspection tours in the provinces or on military expeditions. Šibtu's concern for her husband and her hope for victories over his enemies is a recurrent theme in her communiqués, as presented in the following letter (No. 17): (5) *be-lí na-ak-ri-šu* (6) *li-ik-šu-dam-ma* (7) [*i-na š*]*a-lim-tim ù ḫu-ud li-ib-bi-im* (8) [*a-n*]*a Ma-ri*(KI) *li-ru-ba-am*—"(5) May my lord (6) conquer his enemies (7) and safe and sound and in joy of heart (8) may he return [to] Mari". The subsequent lines display concretely the wife's concern for her husband. She tells of having sent him a coat and another garment made by herself and requests that the king wear them (*ana idīšu liškun*, "may he put them on his shoulder [= sides]").

Šibtu's continual concern for her husband's welfare reveals a fur-

---

see W.L. Moran, *JNES* 22 (1963), 175, who adduces several examples from the Mari documents. For a similar use of the corresponding Hebrew term "*ṭōbā, ṭōbōt*" see e.g. D.R. Hillers, *BASOR* 176 (1964), 46 ff. and A. Malamat, *BiAr Reader* 3 (New York 1970), 196 f.

[18] On this and the following letter see already A. Parrot, *Séance publique annuelle des Cinq Académies* (25.10.1966) (Paris 1966), 10; A. Malamat, *Qadmoniot* 1 (1968), 84 (Hebrew).

ther significant aspect of the queen's activity, i.e. in the realm of religion and specifically in the inspection of omens, a practice common in the Mari texts. She frequently consulted haruspices that omens be taken (*tērtam šūpušum*) in order to seek the word of the gods on Zimrilim's fate, in particular with the purpose of directing his movements on the battlefield or to safeguard him in other precarious situations; see, e.g. letter No. 11: (7) [*i-na*] *re-eš wa-ar-ḫi-im* (8) [*te*]*-re-tim a-na šu-lum be-lí-ia* (9) [*ú-*]*še-pi-iš-ma* (10) *ṭe-em* [*te-re-et*(?) *š*]*u-lum be-lí-ia* (11) *ša-al-ma*—"(7) [On] the day of the new moon—(8) an inspection of the omens for the welfare of my lord (9) I commanded to be made (10) and the report [of the omens] (with regard to) the welfare of my lord (11) is favorable". However, Šibtu entreats the king to take care of himself: "May he act in accordance with the true sign from the mouth of the god" (*ittum ša kittim ša pī ilim bēlī līpuš* [ll. 15–17]).

Moreover, the king's reaction to his wife's preoccupation with the examinations of omens are displayed in several of his letters to Šibtu, e.g. No. 124: (18) *aš-šum ṭe-em te-re-tim ša ta-aš-pu-ri-*[*im*] (19) *um-ma at-ti-ma te-re-tim a-na šu-lum be-lí-ia* (20) *ú-še-pi-iš-ma nakiru a-na qá-at be-lí-ia* (21) *mu-ul-*[*li*] . . .—"(18) Concerning the report (of the inspection) of the omens which you sent (19) and thus you (said): The omens, which for the welfare of my lord (20) I commanded to make (resulted in the response): The enemy into the hands of my lord (21) be delivered. . . ." Subsequently the king confirms that the enemy has actually fallen into his hands and he requests the queen to inform him about the welfare of the palace in Mari (ll. 18–25).

Another method of divination peculiar to Mari, as is well attested from previously published documents, is the phenomenon of prophecy, which places these sources in close proximity to the corresponding biblical manifestation. Many reports from Šibtu to her husband dealing with matters of his fate are based on revelations of this type. As these letters (Nos. 4, 6, 7, 8, 9, 10) have already been the subject of detailed studies we shall not concern ourselves with them here.[19]

---

[19] For a preliminary survey of these letters see G. Dossin in *La divination en Mésopotamie ancienne* etc. (*XIVe Rencontre assyriologique internationale*, Paris 1966), 77–86. The most comprehensive study is W.L. Moran, "New Evidence from Mari on the History of Prophecy", *Bib* 50 (1969), 15–56. On prophecy in the Mari documents and its relationship to biblical prophecy, see A. Malamat, *ErIs* 4 (1956), 74–84; 5 (1958), 67–73; 8 (1967), 231–240 (all three in Hebrew); *VT Supplement* 15 (1966), 207–227; F. Ellermeier, *Prophetie in Mari und Israel* (Herzberg 1968); H.B. Huffmon, *BiAr* 31 (1968), 101 ff.

Since the queen took an active part in palace life and in the organization of the court, most of the correspondence between Šibtu and her husband revolves around subjects of an administrative nature. In these affairs Šibtu acted on a par with the high functionaries in Mari, such as Baḫdilim, the prefect of the palace. Admittedly, it is difficult to distinguish, for the present, between the functions and spheres of authority of the queen and the various palace officials, as likewise the delineation of activities among the officials themselves remains unclear.[20] Obviously, to Šibtu were relegated the duties of "a matron" of the palace and at the same time she was entrusted, as an intimate of the king, with matters that were both delicate and confidential in nature. From the large amount of material a few examples will suffice to demonstrate the wide range of activities and occupations in which she indulged.

In letter No. 12, the queen informs Zimrilim of a confidential and, quite likely, secret mission. According to her husband's instructions Šibtu chose several reliable controllers (LÚ.MEŠ *ebbū*, l. 8),[21] who were attached to a special envoy of the king. Their mission was to gather "tablets", i.e. documents, wherever the king's envoy would direct them. In one place the delegation entered an administration building (*bīt tērtim*, l. 26; perhaps an "embassy"; on this term see *ARM* VII 230; XV 273). There the delegation took crates of documents (GI.PISAN, l. 27) and transfered them to Mari. The queen reports that the documents are now being kept by her until the king's return in compliance with his instructions.

From letter No. 126, sent by Zimrilim to Šibtu, we may learn of the queen's activity in directing labor forces in the palace. In accordance with the king's request she selected women—the text refers to females designated *ugbabtum*, i.e. priestesses of low rank (cf. *ARM* VII 245)—and sent them to the "weaving house" (*bīt išparāti*). In fact, the administrative texts from Mari mention several times expert female weavers serving in the palace (see, e.g. *ARM* IX No. 24, col. 4:18; No. 25:38; No. 27, col. 5:43 and cf. XIII No. 21:9'–16').

---

[20] Cf. P. Garelli, *Le proche orient asiatique* (Paris 1969), 266 ff., based on the studies of J.-R. Kupper, "Baḫdi-Lim, préfet du palais de Mari", *Bull. Acad. Roy. Belg., Classe de lettres* 40 (1954–56), 572 ff.; M. Birot, "Les lettres de Iasîm-sumû", *Syria* 41 (1964), 25 ff.

[21] On this official acting as a confidant see *CAD* E 3, 2a. It is noteworthy that a further letter of Šibtu to Zimrilim (No. 7:12) mentions several bearers of this title, who were apt to serve as royal guards in time of danger; cf. Moran, *Bib* 50 (1969), 30 ff.

Of special interest is Zimrilim's letter No. 134, which details his instructions to Šibtu regarding the allocation of an inheritance. The king received from his wife the "tablet of property" (*ṭuppi bašītim*, l. 4)[22] of Bunuma-Addu (perhaps to be identified with the king of Niḫriya, a vassal kingdom of Mari on the Upper Tigris). Zimrilim entrusts his wife with the execution of the inheritance of the deceased according to the following stipulations: (5) *e-nu-ut bītim ka-la-ša še-em ma-li i-ba-aš-šu-ú* (6) 50 *ikû eqel be-er-tim ù kasap ilāni-šu* (= KÙ.BABBAR DINGIR.MEŠ-*šu*)[23] (7) *ma-li ša ta-aš-pu-ri-im wa-aš-še-ri-ma* (8) *i-na* 21 *awēlī-šu* (LÙ.LÙ.MEŠ-*šu*) *ši-it-ti-in a-na bītī-šu* (9) *li-id-di-nu-ma ša-lu-uš-tam a-na ekallim li-il-qú-ú* (10) *ù imērī narkabtī-šu a-na (d) Šamaš-i-in-ma-tim*[24] *na-ad-nu* . . .—"(5) All of the household utensils, as much grain as there is, (6) 50 *iku's* of choice land and his 'silver of the gods',[23] (7) the full (amount) which you wrote to me—release and (8) among his 21 men two-thirds (of the property) to the household (servants) (9) shall be given and a third shall be taken for the palace (10) and the asses for his chariot are given to Šamaš-inmatim. . . ."[24]

Three letters from Zimrilim to Šibtu deal with shipments of wine which were either received for the palace or which the palace intended to forward to another destination (Nos. 131, 132, 133). These communiqués serve as a good illustration of the business transactions or rather, exchange of gifts, between the various royal houses, a customary procedure in international relations. According to the first two letters (Nos. 131–132), the sender of the wine is Ḫammurabi who, most likely, is identical to the (future) king of Yamḫad, the son and heir of Yarimlim and brother of Queen Šibtu. This conjecture is based upon the fact that, in the Mari documents, Yamḫad is known as an exporter of wine to the palace of Mari (see *ARM* VII, No. 238 and pp. 268/9; IX No. 33 and p. 271). Moreover, an economic document, a sort of bill of lading, preserved in the Mari archives, bears the following message: "5 (?) jars of wine has sent Ḫammurabi, the son of Yarimlim, for the 'house of the wine jars' (i.e. the wine

---

[22] On this term cf. *CAD* B 139.

[23] On *kasap ilim*, which either denotes "finest silver" or silver reserved for the gods, occurring only in Mari and in an Amarna letter from Cyprus, see *CAD* I/J 98, 1e.

[24] This personal name, which means "The-god-Šamaš-is-the-eye-of-the-land", is attested also in Old Babylonian documents from Ur; see *Ur Excavation Texts* V (London 1953), 60 b.

cellar in the Mari palace; *ARM* IX, No. 33)". Letter No. 131 speaks of a special variety of wine called *karānum sāmum*, "red wine".[25] It appears to have been of such an expensive quality that Zimrilim requested his wife to watch personally over the filling of the wine casks and to hand them over afterwards to Baḫdilim, who was in charge of the palace. In a third letter, No. 133, Zimrilim instructs his wife to dispatch a consignment of wine to Babylon, as "Ḫammurabi, the king of Babylon, has written to me concerning the wine" (l. 3). The above documents evidence the fact that the Mari palace engaged as an intermediary in wine consignments, just as it played an active role in transit trade in general.

The royal pair, in their exchange of letters, are occasionally concerned with various troubles which befell the capital. Once Šibtu reported to her husband on a natural disaster (letter No. 25): (6) . . .*u₄-um 24*-KAM (7) *ša-mu-um* (8) *ki-bi-it-*[*tum*] (9) *i-na Ma-ri* (KI) *iz-nu-un* (10) *i-na li-ib-bi* (11) *i-kí-im ša be-lí* (12) *i-pu-šu* (13) *mu-ú* 1 *qanûm* (= GI) (14) *iz-z*[*i-iz-zu-ni*]*m*—"(6) On the 24th day (of the month) (7) the rain's (8) largest amount (9) fell in Mari. (10) In midst (11) the canal which my lord (12) has built (13) there is 1 *qanû-* (height; cf. the biblical measure *qāne*) of water (14) standing".

Letters Nos. 129–130 deal with a woman afflicted with an apparently contagious disease. In letter No. 129, the king instructs his wife on preventive measures to be taken in order to curtail the spreading of the disease: (4) *eš-me-e-ma* SAL *Na-an-na-me* (5) *sí-im-ma-am*[26] *mar-ṣa-at* (6) *ù it-ti ekallim* (7) *ma-ga-al wa-aš-ba-at-ma* (8) SAL.MEŠ *ma-da-tim it-ti-ša-ma* (9) *i-sa-ab-bi-ik*[27] (10) *i-na-an-na dan-na-tim šu-uk-ni-ma* (11) *i-na ka-ás i-ša-at-tu-ú* (12) *ma-am-ma-an la i-ša-at-ti* (13) *i-na kussî ša úš-ša-bu* (14) *ma-am-ma-an la úš-ša-ab* (15) *ù i-na eršim* (= GIŠ.NÁ) *ša it-ti-il-lu* (16) *ma-am-ma-an la it-te-e-el-ma* . . .—"(4) I have heard that the woman Nanname (5) is sick with the *simmum*-disease[26] (6) and with the palace (personnel) (7) she spends a lot of time (8) and many women (9) she afflicts (= infects?) with herself.[27] (10) Now give strict orders:

---

[25] On this variety of wine, cf. *ARM* IX 271 (§ 40a). On *sāmum*, "red" see now B. Landsberger, *JCS* 21 (1967), 140 f.

[26] On this disease (or rather its symptoms), whose exact nature is undetermined, see provisionally Driver-Miles, *Babylonian Laws*, II 249 f. (preferring the reading, *ṣimmum*), and F.R. Kraus, *JESHO* 12 (1969), 210. Since writing this paper it has come to our notice that letter No. 129 appeared in a French translation (differing slightly from our interpretation); cf. A. Finet, *AIPHOS* 14 (1954–57), 129.

[27] Von Soden derives this word from the Hebrew root *ś/sbk*, German: "verflechten", and considers it here a Canaanism in the sense of "(Die Kranke) setzt sich dazwi-

(11) from the cup from (which) she drinks (12) no one else should drink; (13) on the chair (on which) she sits (14) no one else should sit (15) and on the bed (on which) she lies (16) no one else should lie. . . ."

As already noted, the queen took an active part in affairs of state, far beyond her duties in the royal household, particularly in the king's absence from the capital. Thus, one of Šibtu's (?) letters to her husband (No. 5) deals with Suma-ila, the representative of the Numḫû tribe (on this tribe see letter No. 157 quoted above, p. 181 and n. 16), and the convocation of the assembly of this same tribe's leaders (*puḫur qaqqadātīšunu*, l. 11), as well as the oath which they took. Likewise the queen dispatches to her husband regular reports on the current welfare of the capital, Mari, while conversely, Zimrilim, for his part, continuously informs her of his victories over his enemies and the state of his army, e.g. letters Nos. 121–124, the last one already mentioned above (p. 183).

In conclusion, Queen Šibtu presents herself to us as a woman of exemplary virtue, a "woman of valor" (*ēšet ḥayil*) to use a biblical expression, and a true partner to her husband-king.

IV

Finally, we will examine two letters (Nos. 151, 156) concerning Šibtu's ancestral home in North Syria, which were no doubt sent from there to Mari. The fact that the salutatory formula in these letters does not contain any formality except for the name of the woman (*ana* SAL *Šibtu qibima umma* PN, "To the lady Šibtu say: Thus (said) so-and-so") attests to the high rank of both authors. Hence Yarimlim, the author of the first letter (No. 151), is undoubtedly none other than the renowned king of Yamḫad, Šibtu's father. As mentioned in the beginning, Yarimlim was one of the central figures of his time, perhaps of similar stature as the kings Šamši-Adad I of Assyria and Ḫammurabi of Babylon, who elevated the North Syrian kingdom of Yamḫad to one of the major forces on the international scene of the Old Babylonian period.

With the exception of one letter sent to the king of the Trans-Tigridian city of Dēr, the correspondence of Yarimlim has not yet

---

schen"; see *Or* 38 (1969), 432. The meaning, however, seems to be here "to afflict other women with the sick person".

been published, and only some preliminary details have been made known to date.[28] Hence, despite its personal character, the new document is a welcome addition to the repertoire of this North Syrian ruler. As this letter raises many interesting points, it is thus desirable to present it in its entirety (*ARM* X, No. 151):

(1) *a-na* SAL, *Ši-ib-tu* (2) *qí-bí-ma* (3) *um-ma Ia-ri-im-li-im-ma* (4) *aš-šum* A.ŠÀ (= *eqel*) *du-un-nim*[29] *ša Ḫa-ma-nu i-ri-šu* (5) *ta-aš-pu-ri-im um-ma at-ti-ma* (6) *ki-ma Ḫa-ma-nu zi-bi*[30] A.ŠÀ (= *eqlim*) *id-di-nu* (7) *i-na-an-na Ḫa-at-ni-*(*d*)IM (8) *zi-bi li-*[*id*]*-di-in-ma* A.ŠÀ (*eqlam*) *ša-a-tu* (9) *li-ri-iš an-ni-tam ta-as-pu-ri* (10) A.ŠÀ (= *eqlam*) *ša-a-tu ú-ul a-na-ku ad-di-in* (11) LÚ ENGAR[31] (= *ikkarum*) *Ba-lu-ia*[32] *id-di-in-ma* (12) *ar-ka-nu* LÚ ENGAR *iq-bi-im-ma* (13) [*l*]*i-ib-ba-ti-šu am-la*[33] (14) *ki-ma Ba-lu-ia id-di-nu* (15) [*A*]. *ŠÀ ra-ma-ni-šu e-ki-im-ma* (16) GIŠ APIN(?) *i-ia*$_8$-<*u*>*-um i-ri-iš* (17) *ù wa-ar-ka-at* A.ŠÀ *ša-a-tu* (18) *ú-ul pa-ar-sa-at*(!) A.ŠÀ ḪI.A (19) *mu-úš-ke-nim*[34] *i-na i-ta-at* (20) A.ŠÀ *šu-a-tu i-ba-aš-ši* (21) *ù* LÚ ENGAR *ma-ga-al-*[*ma*] *iḫ-*[*šu*]*-úš-ma* (22) *a-na Ḫa-ma-nu id-di-in i-na-an-na a-nu-um-ma* (23) *a-na* LÚ ENGAR *aš-pu-ur* (24) *wa-ar-ka-at A.ŠÀ li-ip-ru-ús* (25) A.ŠÀ ḪI.A *mu-úš-ke-nim li-be-er-ma*[35] (26) [*a/i-n*]*a* É.GAL-*lim* (= *ekallim*) *ša ra-ma-ni-ia* (27) [*m*]*a-li ma-ṣú-ú* (28) [*a-n*]*a Ḫa-at-ni-*(*d*)IM (29) *li-id-di-nu.*

(1) To Šibtu (2) say: (3) Thus (said) Yarimlim. (4) With regard to the *irrigated* field[29] which Ḫamanu has plowed (5) you wrote to me and thus you (said): (6) "Just as Ḫamanu gave an offering[30] from the field (7) now (also) Ḫatni-Addu (8) shall give an offering, and that field (9) let him plow!"—so you wrote. (10) But I did not allot that field! (11) The head-man of the farmers,[31] Baluya,[32] alloted (that field). (12) And (when) afterwards the head-man of the farmers reported to me (about

[28] On the letter to the king of Dēr, see G. Dossin, *Syria* 33 (1956), 63 ff. On King Yarimlim, see Dossin, *Bull. Acad. Roy. Belg., Cl. lettres*, 38 (1952), 289 ff.; S. Smith, "Yarim-Lim of Yamḫad", *RSO* 32 (1957), 155 ff.

[29] The word *dunnu* has several meanings (see dictionaries). Here it seems to be connected with irrigation installations, such as a dam or a water course with reinforced side walls. See *CAD* D 84/5, 2b (s.v. *danānu*); Driver-Miles, *The Assyrian Laws* (Oxford 1935), 502; G. Cardascia, *Les lois assyriennes* (Paris 1969), 274 (we accredit this last reference to Father R. Tournay).

[30] The translation "offering" is based on the suggested reading *zību* for ZI-BI, here meaning a food-offering; see *CAD* Z 105 f., s.v. *zību* A. Etymologically the word is identical with Hebrew *zbḥ*, but its Akkadian usages are different. Apparently the text here refers to an offering of agricultural produce, a kind of tax which the farmer paid to the palace.

[31] The reference is to an overseer of extensive agricultural property; cf. *CAD* I/J 53, 3: farm bailiff.

[32] The form of the personal name Baluya (= Baʿal with the diminutive ending) instead of the common spelling Baḫl—in the Mari onomasticon is noteworthy. This form is peculiar to Syria also at a later period as attested to in the El Amarna letters (*EA* 170:2) and in Ugarit (*PRU* IV 284:8).

this) (13) truly, I became furious at him.[33] (14) (For), when Baluya made this allocation (15) he usurped the field on his own (16) and he plowed with my own plow (?). (17) But (the legal status) of that field (18) was (even) not investigated! The landed properties of (19) the *muškēnu*[34] are situated (20) on the perimeter of that field. (21) Thus the head-man of the farmers acted very much in haste (22) by allocating (the aforementioned field) to Ḫamanu! Therefore, now (23) I have sent a message to the head-man of the farmers: (24) Let him investigate (the legal status of) the field. (25) Let him establish the legal position[35] of the landed properties of the *muškēnu* (26) and (if necessary), from my own palace (27) let the full value (of compensation) (28) be given (29) to Ḫatni-Addu!

Yarimlim, in his letter to Šibtu explains, in quite an apologetic tone, why he cannot comply with her request to transfer a property—the text apparently deals with a piece of land which had excellent irrigation facilities—from the possession of Ḫamanu to that of Ḫatni-Addu, the latter most likely a protégé of the queen. The reason is that the overseer of the farmers had already given the field over to Ḫamanu without the consent of Yarimlim. Despite the fact that the overseer illegally appropriated the title to the land, he involved the king personally, as is to be concluded from Yarimlim's words, l. 16: "and he plowed with my own *plow*" (if the somewhat dubious sign has actually to be read APIN, "plow"). This statement may be taken either literally, referring to a symbolic act or merely as an idiomatic expression denoting the seizure of rights of the landed property. Moreover, there arose a suspicion that the property of the *muškēnu*, i.e. the simple serfs dependent on the court, was interspersed with the land in question. Therefore the king informs Šibtu that he ordered the negligent official to check the legal situation of the property under dispute. On the one hand, the rights of the *muškēnu* must be clarified and honored (cf. their complaint in *ARM* II No. 55:31–32). And on the other, Ḫatni-Addu must be compensated from the royal treasury,

---

[33] On *libbātu*, "anger", see *AHw* 548. The Akkadian idiom interestingly finds its parallel in the Hebrew phrase מָה אֲמֻלָה לִבָּתֵךְ in Ez. 16:30: "How am I filled with anger" (misinterpreted in the English translations of the Bible, e.g. AV: "how weak is thine heart"); and cf. Donner-Röllig, *KAI*, vol. II 286.

[34] For the term *eqel muškēnim* see *Laws of Ešnunna* § 12. It recurs in *ARM* II, No. 61:25, significantly to our context alongside the term *eqel ekallim*, "field of the palace". For the abundant literature on the social status of *muškēnum*, which cannot be dealt with here, see W. Rölling, "Gesellschaft", *RLA* III/4 (Berlin 1966), 235.

[35] On the meaning of the verb *bâru* in the D stem cf. *CAD* B 127, 3: *burru* "to establish the true legal situation".

since apparently he, too, had possessed rights to that land.

Although the specific circumstances surrounding the contents of the letter and its legalistic background are elusive, it bears witness, nevertheless, to the continued interest and even intervention of Mari's queen in the affairs of her native land—in the case of our letter, concerning the cultivation of a piece of land. This fact ties in with the assumption proposed previously on other grounds, that Zimrilim possessed some landed property in Yamḫad;[36] however, it is not clear whether Zimrilim inherited this property as a patrimony or received it as a grant during his exile in Northern Syria. Whatever the case, our letter illuminates some interesting facets of the institution of the monarchy in the Old Babylonian period, or to use the biblical terminus technicus, *mišpaṭ hammelek*, "the manner of the king". Without further pursuing here this most intriguing theme, we may merely state that Yarimlim, like other Old-Babylonian kings, did not possess the prerogative to transfer property rights from one person to another arbitrarily.

The other letter to Šibtu was sent by Dadiḫadun (No. 156), who, although his exact identity and functions elude us, must have been a person of high standing, as appears both from the present letter and from other information in the Mari archives. Thus the governor Kibri-Dagan attributes to Dadiḫadun's arrival at Terqa enough importance to inform the king of Mari about it in two communiqués (*ARM* XIII No. 123 and shortly after *ARM* III No. 45). Even more indicative of his rank is Dadiḫadun's letter to Zimrilim, testifying to his rule over many villages, apparently in the vicinity of the western bend of the Euphrates, which acknowledged the suzerainty of the king of Mari (*ARM* II No. 61).

Since Dadiḫadun's letter to Šibtu is severely damaged on its right side, we will only give it cursory treatment. The letter apparently deals with a family disagreement which developed between Šibtu and Ḫammurabi, the latter being no doubt Yarimlim's son and the brother of Mari's queen (see above, p. 138), who by now had most likely succeeded to the throne at Aleppo. Proof for the assertion that we

[36] This possibility may be surmised on the basis of a letter sent to Zimrilim from Aleppo, dealing with prophecy (published by G. Dossin in *Studies in Old Testament Prophecy presented to Th.H. Robinson* (Edinburgh 1950), 103 ff.); see A. Malamat, *JAOS* 82 (1962), 149 and for an historical analysis of this letter pertaining to our subject *idem*, "History and Prophetic Vision in a Mari Letter", *ErIs* 5 (1958), 67 ff. (Hebrew).

actually deal here with the ruler of Aleppo is to be found in the fact that Dadiḫadun addresses Ḫammurabi in this letter in the name of "the god Addu, lord of A[leppo]" (l. 10).[37] From the rest of the letter it appears that Dadiḫadun was able to convince Ḫammurabi that a third party caused the family controversy and in that way succeeded in reconciling him and Šibtu. The letter thus concludes on a happy note and the invocation of Šamaš, the god of justice: (30b) *ki-ma a-na-ku* (31) *a-bu-ut-ki aṣ-ba-tu*[38] (32) (d)UTU (= *Šamaš*) *a-bu-ut a-wa-ti-ia* (38) *li-iṣ-ba-at*—"(30b) Just as I (31) interceded on your behalf[38] (32) (so) may the god Šamaš intercede (33) on my behalf!"

[37] On the god Adad of Aleppo see H. Klengel, *JCS* 19 (1965), 88 ff. Note the significant passage ll. 10–11 of our letter: *aš-šum* (*d*)IM *be-el ḫa-*[*la-bi*] *ù ilim*(*lim*) *ša a-bi-*[*ka*]—"by the name of (the god) Addu, lord of A[leppo] and the *god of [your] father*". This is the second occurrence of "the god of the father" in the Mari texts, the other contained in a letter from the king of Qatna (*ARM* V, No. 20:16). Both originate from the West, as do all the other references to this type of deity (mentioned in the Cappadocian tablets, in the temple inventories from Qatna and in an Amarna letter from this same place, as well as in the Ugaritic texts); hence their special significance for the biblical conception of "the god of the fathers", referred to chiefly in the patriarchal narratives.

[38] For the expression *abbūtam ṣabātum*, literally "to take the position of fatherhood", i.e. to intercede on behalf of someone, see *CAD* Ṣ 24, 8a–b. For a corresponding idiomatic phrase in post-biblical Hebrew see *Manual of Discipline* II, 9: לוא יהיה לכה שלום בפי כול אוחזי אבות "And may you have no peace from the mouth of all intercessors (*'ōḥᵃzē 'bwt*)" (Our attention was drawn to this passage by Prof. G.B.A. Sarfatti). In Akkadian the verbs *aḫāzu* and *ṣabātu* at times are used synonymously, see *CAD* s.v. *aḫāzu; ṣabātu* (lexical sections).

20

THE GREAT KING
A PRE-EMINENT ROYAL TITLE IN CUNEIFORM SOURCES AND "IN" THE BIBLE*

1. *Introduction*

Along with his contributions to cuneiform and biblical studies, Bill Hallo pioneered and established the systematic study of the royal titles in cuneiform civilization.[1]

The present writers, induced by long-standing, common interest to improve the understanding of the ancient Near Eastern royal title "The Great King"[2] (abbreviated: GK), benefited greatly from two basic facts in Hallo's study (although the treatment of this specific title is beyond its boundaries). First, the royal political title is a reliable indicator of the rank and prestige achieved by a ruler; this prestige was bestowed on the basis of success in internal and international activities. Secondly, the title "king" (Sumerian: lugal; Akkadian: *šarru*) underwent from its very inception in central/southern Mesopotamia, gradual ascendancy and then primacy.[3]

Collecting and evaluating various data and studies, we reached the (we hope not erroneous) conclusion that, besides the comprehensive handbook of Seux,[4] there is no monograph on our subject.

---

* This article, written together with Prof. P. Artzi, was originally published in: Cohen, M.E., Snell, D.C., Weisberg, D.B. (eds.), *The Tablet and the Scroll* (FS W.W. Hallo), CDL Press, Bethesda 1993, pp. 28–38. It remains here practically unchanged.

[1] William W. Hallo, *Early Mesopotamian Royal Titles, AOS*, New Haven 1957 (abbreviated: Hallo).

[2] See Table 2.5.1.

[3] See also the observations of F.R. Kraus in *Le Palais et la Royauté* (ed. P. Garelli), Paris 1974, p. 251.

[4] M.-J. Seux, *Épithètes Royales Akkadiennes et Sumériennes*, Paris 1967 (abbreviated: Seux). See also the recent book of M. Liverani, *Prestige and Interest, International Relations in the Near East ca. 1600–1100 B.C.E.*, Padova 1990, pp. 68 ff. (abbreviated: Liverani); W.L. Moran, *The Amarna Letters*, Baltimore and London 1992, p. 3 n. 2 (abbreviated: *EAMr*).

2. *Historical Survey*

2.1 *A pre-Sargonic forerunner (ca. 2370 B.C.E.)*

The royal title: "The Great Ruler (by the decision) of Enlil."[5] This title, containing the augmentation gal (= great) after the title ensi, "ruler," stands in the second position in the titulary of two kings of pre-Sargonic Mari (northern Mesopotamia; see 2.3): Lamgi-Mari[6] and Ikū(n)-Šamaš. More significantly, it appears also in second position in the titulary of Lugalzagesi after the title "Lord of Uruk, King of Ur."[7]

The best explanation of the use of the augmentation by Lugalzagesi has been proposed by A. Poebel and F. Thureau-Dangin: the aim of this augmented title of priestly origin, combined with the political title ensi (= territorial ruler) is to validate his political authority, bestowed upon him by the god Enlil. Founder of an "empire-core" state, Lugalzagesi turns, equipped with this title, towards the still unaligned rulers of Sumer aiming at their acceptance of his peaceful, federative leadership.[8]

As with the southern pre-Sargonic political configurations, we may assume that also the "North," pre-Sargonic Mari (cf. 2.3), was active in establishing federal formations; here the eminent power-status of Ebla should also be taken into account.[9]

---

[5] ensí.gal.$^{(d)}$Enlil, Seux, p. 399.

[6] Lamgi-Mari: J.R. Kupper & N. Karg, *RLA* 6, p. 446; Ikū(n)-Šamaš: J.R. Kupper, *RLA* 5, p. 46. For a different reading of the royal PNs cited, see now I.J. Gelb and B. Kienast, *Die Altakkadischen Königsinschriften des dritten Jahrtausends v. Chr.*, *FAOS* 7 (Stuttgart), 1990, p. 9, *MP* 17; see also the observations of Pomponio, *SEL* 8 (1991), p. 143 and of Krebernik, *ZA* 81/1 (1991), p. 139.

[7] Lugalzagesi: Hallo, p. 19; Å. Westenholz, *RLA* 7, pp. 155 ff.

[8] Priestly origin of the title: Hallo, pp. 35 ff.; political value of the augmented title: Seux, p. 399, note 128 with literature. This title was used also by Sargon (but afterwards discontinued). We prefer the assumption of A. Poebel to that of Thureau-Dangin, indicating not an imperial title but primacy; see Th. Jacobsen, *Towards the Image of Tammuz*, 1970, pp. 153–154; cf. with a different emphasis, Å. Westenholz, in *Power and Propaganda* (ed. M.T. Larsen), Copenhagen 1979, p. 109 (status of "Great King," but still without the actual title; cf. our Ch. 3).

[9] Cf. as a figurative sign of aspiration: the head-dress of Lamgi-Mari, *RLA* 6, p. 446; E. Strommenger, *Mesopotamien*, 1962, pl. 100: "golden-helmet hairdress," imitation of the actual helmet of Meskalamdug ("King of Ur"; Hallo, p. 150), see also the helmet on the head of Eannatum, ruler of Lagaš ("King of Kiš"; imperial title; cf. Hallo, pp. 21 ff.) depicted on the "Stela of Vultures," Strommenger, pl. 68.

For Ebla see: J. Renger, *Ebla 1975–1985* (ed. L. Cagni), Napoli 1987, pp. 293–311; G. Pettinato, *ibid.*, pp. 19–35.

2.2 *A note on the absence of the title GK in the Middle Old Babylonian Period (Hammurabi)*

Contrary to the intensive activity around the emerging title GK in the north and the northwest (see 2.3; 2.4), there is no data on its use in the documentation in the south, in spite of the fact that—at least in a transitory period!—the states of the north, south, east and west were organized into identical federal configurations of "power blocks" (cf. 2.3 Mari). There are, on the other hand, clear indications of a search for appropriate royal attributes which express the prestige of Hammurabi as the versatile head of an Empire (not federation, because the aim of the South is complete unity). To cite but one example: the Law-Stele of Hammurabi, Prologue, col. iii 1 16: "The god (or: the divine one) among all the kings, the wise of the wisest."[10]

2.3 *šarru rabû at Mari*

The use of the idiom *šarru rabû* ("Great King") at Mari is attested to about ten times.[11] It occurs more or less about the same time in Ḫatti, designating King Anitta as LUGAL.GAL (but in a copy of his inscription of some 200 years later, see 2.4).

As for Mari, the appellative *šarru rabû* designates almost always King Šamši-Adad I of the "Assyrian" dynasty, ruling for some time over Mari. Yet we are not certain if the expression refers to an epithet of veneration or already to a distinct royal title. The former meaning seems to be more acceptable.

The most conspicuous case at Mari, often cited in scholarly discussions, is a letter from Tarīm-Šakim to Yasmaḫ-Adad, son of Šamši-Adad I and viceroy of Mari. The writer designates Šamši-Adad as *šarru rabû* (*ARM* V 28–31), while in the correspondence between Išme-Dagan, the elder son of Šamši-Adad I and his future heir, and Išhi-Adad of Qaṭna, the king of a western state in Middle Syria, the

---

[10] *i-lu* LUGAL-*rí* = *ilu šarrī* (*pluralis unitatis*); this epithet aggrandizes and "modernizes" the Old Akkadian epithet DINGIR Agade ("The god of Akkad"), Seux, p. 389; for a different interpretation see *AHw*, p. 372, *illum* 1, "*etwa auserlesen*" (but see *CAD* I/J, *illu* A and *illatu* A with *CAD* N/1, *nasqu*: not "choicest" but "playmate"). For the PN *Hammurabi-ilī*, see now Stol, *SEL* 8 (1991), p. 205.

[11] J.-M. Durand, *Précurseurs syriens aux Protocoles néo-assyriens*, in eds. D. Charpin & F. Joannès, *Marchands, Diplomates et Empereurs* (FS Garelli), Paris 1991, pp. 54–63. The author publishes two new instances of Great King(s) and refers in the footnotes to the previous ones.

latter addresses Išme-Dagan, attempting a better commercial deal: "You are a great king" (*ARM* V 20:7). Išme-Dagan is likely to have inherited from his father, as legitimate successor, the epithet "great king." Nevertheless, it seems that GK here is referred to in a rhetorical ironic mode, expressing disappointment; cf. *EA* 7:26 f.; 16:13.

There are four occurrences of *šarru rabû* in the economic texts published by J. Bottéro in *ARM* VII, records of foodstuff for the royal table, all referring to Šamši-Adad as indicated by D. Charpin and J.-M. Durand,[12] whereas K.R. Veenhof[13] opts for Išme-Dagan: *ana qāt šarrim rabîm*, i.e., for the disposition of the great king.

Of special interest in these records is the document published by D. Charpin in MARI 3, p. 92, no. 59: "for the messenger of the great king, Ikūn-pî-Ašar," the latter being a royal official. Perhaps in this instance the appellative *šarru rabû* already takes on the meaning of a distinct title. In order to explain the application of the idiom *šarru rabû* to Šamši-Adad, Charpin and Durand draw attention to the relatively vast expansion of his kingdom, extending to the east (ruled by Išme-Dagan) and west (ruled by Yasmaḫ-Adad).[14] Hence this title is first and foremost the result of territorial aggrandizement, including dominion over vassal kings (cf. 2.4).

To the above references we can now add two new attestations of *šarru rabû* published recently by Durand.[15] The interesting fact in both cases is that the idiom occurs in the plural form—great kings. In A. 230:7 the spelling is LUGAL-*ri-a-ni*. The plural form *-ānu* (*šarrāni*) is conceived by Durand to mean "great kings,"[16] and not as individual kings or even minor kings, as usually surmised;[17] thus his explanation remains doubtful. However, this letter is of special significance, not only for the use of the plural of "king," but also as an apt illustration for Itūr-Asdu's famous sermon listing the five great powers (*šarru dannu*) of his time in Mesopotamia and Syria (A. 482).[18] Itūr-Asdu addresses

[12] Charpin-Durand, *MARI* 4 (1985), p. 301, n. 37; Durand (above, n. 11), p. 63, n. 143. The texts in addition to those cited above are: *ARM* VI 28; XVIII 107; XXVI 14, 62, 181, 218.

[13] See *MARI* 4 (1985), p. 209, while M. Anbar is wavering between the two candidates; see *Reflets de deux Fleuves* (*Mélanges A. Finet*), Leuven 1989, p. 12b.

[14] Cf. *MARI* 4 (1985), p. 301 and n. 37.

[15] Durand (above, n. 11), pp. 54 (A. 230), 57 (A. 4215).

[16] *Op. cit.* (above, n. 11), p. 54, n. 113.

[17] See W. von Soden, *GAG* §61 i (*eine Anzahl einzelner Könige*).

[18] Published only in transliteration and translation by G. Dossin, *Syria* 19 (1938), pp. 17 ff. For an English translation cf. W. Moran in *ANET*³, p. 628; K. Balkan,

in the name of Zimri-Lim various unaligned, petty kings (*šarrāni*) in order to convince them to join a strong power, meaning obviously King Zimri-Lim, and thus flourish. Now A. 230 describes a dialogue between Asqur-Adad, king of Karana, and the populace in order to encourage him to join Zimri-Lim "who is our lord and father." Thus both situations here are alike, the populace in each instance being pushed to join a great power, in these instances Zimri-Lim, whose political standing becomes more elevated by such accomplishments (cf. 2.4). Incidentally, Zimri-Lim is once called *šar kiššatim*, "king of the world" (*ARM* 26/2, no. 409:12), a title also given to Šamši-Adad I.

Finally, Durand published in the same article[19] one more document mentioning the great kings (LUGAL.MEŠ *ra-ab-bu-tum*) (A. 4215:11). Here the word "great" is written syllabically and there is no doubt about the translation of the idiom. The lines relevant to us are: Yasīm-Dagan, a general, replies to Šunuḫraḫalu (the "prime minister" of Zimri-Lim, 1.16): ". . . I am 'despised', yet before the great kings, with whom I am in constant touch, my person (*lit.* head) is honored." The "great kings" refer here to the highly-valued kings, Zimri-Lim and Hammurabi, mentioned in 1.8.

In summary, the term discussed here is already prevalent in the political conscience and in the linguistic usage of the Mari Age, but it is still not a standard title as in Anatolia about this time and in later periods (see 2.4).

2.4 *The stages of emergence and standardization of the title GK in the West: Hittite Anatolia and Northern Syria (1900–700 B.C.E.)*

2.4.1 We have just seen at Mari in northern Mesopotamia (2.3) the emergence of the concept of the GK, and even clear signs of its administrative formalization through the "elevation"/upgrading of the senior ruler to the rank of GK, but without his own formal, documented, standardized use of the title.

We call attention to a similar development in the West in the late Old Babylonian period: the rulers of the "Great Kingship" of Jamḫad/Ḫalab, one of the leading states of the period, never use the title GK; on the other hand, its king is "elevated" to this title by the

---

Letter of King Anum-Hirbi . . . (= below, n. 23), pp. 27 f. and cf. A. Malamat's treatment of this document in *JQR* 76 (1985), pp. 47–50 (below, ch. 21).

[19] Cf. Durand (above, n. 11), p. 57.

administration of his federal dependent state, Alalaḫ—as in Mari.[20]

As will be shown below, we are standing here on the threshold of the "First Circle" of northern emergence of the title Great King.

2.4.2 Let us now return to the inception, the process of emergence of the title in Anatolia.

We agree with Starke[21] that the title "Great King" (LUGAL.GAL) is "*vermutlich eine hettitische Wortschöpfung*" only in the sense of standardization, a prime example of the special Hittite faculty of "*Ordnungsprinzip*," of legal thinking. This qualified disagreement is based on the follow-up to the process.

The process was initiated by the close contacts, commercial and other, between the Old-Assyrian Kingdom and the Anatolian local rulers, through the local Anatolian formalization of the Old-Assyrian secondary royal title *rubā'um*, "prince" (Sumerian: NUN).[22]

The growing political-commercial strife among the local rulers led soon to a further step: systematization; a ruler of the first order is termed *rubā'um*; the lesser, petty, dependent kingdoms are ruled by kings, a collective designation in pl.: *šarrāne* (the term for "small king"; see 2.5).[23] Moreover, the intensification of the power struggles between able rulers and their dependents led to a momentous change—the appearance of the title: "The Great Prince" (*rubā'um rabi'um*).

We know only of two "Great Princes,"[24] indicating that the focal point in the contents of the new augmented title (cf. 2.1) was the

---

[20] The kingship of Alalaḫ was created by Jamhad/Ḫalab; see D. Wiseman, *The Alalakh Tablets*, London 1953, no. *1, document belonging to Alalaḫ level VII of the late Old Babylonian period. On the "Great Kingship of Jamhad" see *CAH* II 1[3], pp. 30 ff.; H. Klengel, *Geschichte Syriens* 1963, I, pp. 102 ff.; especially, p. 145c), AT *269 mentioning LUGAL.GAL = The King of Jamḫad; see Landsberger, *JCS* 8 (1954), p. 53, n. 90, stressing the significant evidence of AT *376 (cf. Klengel, pp. 173: 127; 217: 29), and pointing out that the kings of Jamhad themselves use only the title "king."

[21] *ZA* 67 (1977), p. 288.

[22] For this title see M.T. Larsen, *The Old Assyrian City-State and its Colonies*, Copenhagen 1976, pp. 121 ff.

[23] K. Balkan, *Letter of King Anum-Ḫirbi of Mama to King Warshama of Kanish*, Ankara 1957, pp. 25 ff.; on Balkan's view about the identity of content of the plural-form "kings" with the Old Babylonian-Mari usage of this form, see Balkan, p. 27 and cf. our 2.3.

[24] Seux, p. 251, n. 97, second entry; the augmentation is always written (in the formal titles) with GAL as in LUGAL.GAL. Taking into account with Larsen (*op. cit.*, n. 22) that *rubā'um* in its Old-Assyrian definition was virtually a northern equivalent of *šarru*, king (sing.), the basic equation with *šarru rabû* is inherent. Moreover, for the transformation of the title, to be discussed presently, see S[a] Vocabulary Boğazköi,

concentration of territorial power and leadership. Here appears Anitta, ruler of Kuššar and (later) Neša, as a central figure. Chronologically he is a contemporary of the Middle Old Assyrian-Babylonian period (*ca.* 1800;[25] cf. our 2.3). With Anitta, the title "Great King" makes its first appearance in the famous "Anitta Inscription."[26] Written in Hittite, this document describes Anitta's march to the peak of sole leadership in (central) Anatolia. While in his contemporary local inscriptions Anitta uses the title Great Prince,[27] in the "Inscription" he appears (after his victory)[28] as LUGAL.GAL. A delicate problem faces us: The "Inscription" is known only from a relatively later, Old-Hittite Kingdom edition/copy (*ca.* 1600).[29] Therefore, since this title is in continuous use by the Hittite Kings (see below, 2.4.3), we may judge the use of the title GK in the "Anitta Inscription" as a modernization, which is needed for the endorsement of continuous prestige and legality of the Hittite royal dynasty.

But, perhaps, there is another answer. We propose the possibility that Anitta himself wished to break with the local Anatolian system described above, and, by the application of the title GK, wanted to integrate the Anatolian realm into the international scene (cf. 2.3). The solution was again, in the Hittite way of reasoning, to normalize and standardize the appellative GK, already known in the north of Mesopotamia (see 2.3). Thus, we suppose, by closing the "First Circle," which began its turn from Assyria to Anatolia (for the "Second Circle" see 2.5), Anitta tried to be a part of the "central" international power-situation (see also below, in relation to Muršili I).

Fragment H, *MSL* 3, p. 59, 6': . . . *rubû* = LUGAL-*uš* (= Hittite **haššuš*; see *FHWB*, p. 64). (See also Fragm. 1, p. 61, note to line 10).

[25] O.R. Gurney, *CAH* II 1³, 232 ff.; Balkan, *Observations on the Chronology of the Karum Kaniš*, Ankara 1955, pp. 41 ff., esp. p. 44. See also V. Donbaz, *Studies in Honor of Özgüç*, (Ankara), 1989, p. 88.

[26] CTH², no. 1 (p. 2); E. Neu, *StuBoT* 18 (1974); H. Schmökel, *Kulturgeschichte des Alten Orient*, Stuttgart 1961, pp. 335–337; Gurney (note 25), p. 248; Güterbock, *ZA* 44 (1938), p. 141; Otten, *MDOG* 83 (1951), pp. 39, 44; H. Cancik, *Grundzüge der hettitischen und alttestamentlichen Geschichtsschreibung*, Wiesbaden 1976; Steiner, Or. Ant. 23 (1984), pp. 53 ff.

[27] I.J. Gelb, *Inscriptions from Alishar and Vicinity* (*OIP* 27), Chicago 1935; Texts I (p. 19); 49 (p. 50). In the first document Anitta is *rubā'um*; in the second: *rubā'um rabi'um* (cf. also Balkan, *op. cit.*, n. 6).

[28] In the Anitta Inscription the title LUGAL, "king," opens the story. Then in line 41 appears the title LUGAL.GAL. Between these lines there is a brilliantly organized historical narrative of Anitta's advancement (cf. Steiner, *op. cit.*, n. 26, p. 55, and n. 15), conferring upon himself the title GK. For further, very important, details see literature in notes 26 and 29.

[29] Cf. Steiner (*op. cit.*, n. 26).

2.4.3 It is clear that the Hittite Royal House from *ca.* 1650 to its very end almost constantly used the overlordship-title GK, even when it was overshadowed by the emerging title of glorification "My Sunship".[30] As we learn from recent studies, this continuity was preserved down to the last moments of existence of the neo-Hittite kingdoms, long after the disappearance of the Empire.[31]

Standardized, the title is used always in first position: "KN, the GK, [the Sun], King of the land of Hatti, the Hero, beloved of the God DN."[32]

The central, Hittite concept of the title GK is: continuous, inherited leadership in Anatolia and then, in the period of the Empire (see below and 2.5), leadership of and dominion over dependent states.[33] In this latter period the title was permitted to be used as well by the kings of Karkemiš, as members of the Hittite royal family and, chiefly, as direct overseers of the affairs of the North Syrian dependents.[34] Moreover, a new format of state treaty was developed to ensure, in the spirit of a uniquely Hittite interpretation, a cohesive relationship between the Great King and his dependents.[35]

2.4.4 In the present article we cannot discuss in more detail the process of consolidation of the Hittite form of the Great Kingship which was characterized above in 2.4.3. But for our special purpose—the development of the title GK—it is important to point out that this consolidation had already begun early in the period of the Old-Hittite Kingdom (*ca.* 1600) by Hattušili I (see above) and especially by his

---

[30] For the Hittite royal titulary see, besides Seux, Hatice Gonnet, "La titulature royale hittite au IIᵉ millénaire avant J.-C.," *Hethitica* III (1979), pp. 3–108. The title LUGAL.GAL is discussed on pp. 18–19, then in the royal list pp. [32] ff. It is to be stressed that the title GK was "renewed" (supposing that the title of Anitta is genuine; see above) by Hattušili I (the first important king of the Old Hittite Kingdom); see Gonnet, p. 35, n. 23. The glorifying title "Sun" ($^{(d)}$UTU-*ši*) appears for the first time also in Hattušili I's titulary (Gonnet, p. 19 and p. 35, n. 27); A. Goetze, *Kleinasien*, 1953, p. 89.

[31] J.P. Hawkins, "Kuzi-Tešub and the 'Great Kings' of Karkemiš," *AnSt* 38 (1988), pp. 99–108.

[32] A. Goetze, *Kleinasien*, 1953, p. 88. For the last element see Hallo, p. 137.

[33] Cf. Gurney, *The Hittites*, Penguin Books, 1952, p. 64; cf. our 2.5.

[34] H. Klengel, *Geschichte Syriens* I, pp. 43, 83 and n. 138 (= *PRU* IV, p. 138:20'). Cf. above, n. 31.

[35] See with comprehensive literature: A. Altman, "The 'Deliverance Motif' in the 'Historical Prologues' of Suppiluliuma I's Vassal Treaties," *Bar-Ilan Studies in History* II, Ramat Gan 1984, pp. 41–76; *I Trattati nel Mondo Antico* . . ., ed. by L. Canfora, M. Liverani, C. Zaccagnini (Roma), 1990.

grandson and heir, Muršili I. Operating on a wide front, Muršili I achieved the first involvement of the Hittite Great Kingship in international affairs by destroying the last vestiges of the Old Babylonian political power: (a) the destruction, and virtual inheritance, of the "Great Kingship" of Ḫalab (see above 2.4.1); (b) then, the demise of the First Dynasty of Babylon (cf. 2.2; 2.3) by the "sack of Babylon" in *ca.* 1595.[36] While the involvement of the GK, Anitta, mentioned above, is no more than mere assumption, the invasion was part of the preparation for the advent of a new age, a new stage in the history of the title GK; see 2.5.

2.4.5 The value of the title GK is also apparent during the period of temporary Hittite decline. In the period of the Middle Kingdom (1480–1380) its use also declines and returns to its standard use only by Šuppiluliuma I, founder of the Empire.[37] Moreover, it is significant that the rulers of the emerging Hurrian state of Mitanni did not use the title GK before the Age of the Amarna archive (2.5): King Parattarna, who began to extend Mitannian rule during the Hittite temporary decline, was "elevated" (see 2.3) to the (ancient) title LUGAL *dannu*, "mighty king," by no other than his most important western vassal, Idrimi, King of Alalaḫ; cf. 2.4.1.[38]

Thus, around 1400 the title GK appears as a credible indicator of the internationally eminent standing of a certain ruler (cf. our Ch. 1, Introduction).

2.5 *The transformation of the title "Great King" in "The (Extended) Age of the Amarna Archive"* (= AAA, *ca.* 1460–1200 B.C.E., or: the closing of the "Second Circle" in the development of the title GK (see: 2.5.4)).

2.5.1 See Table 2.5.1 for an illustration of the transformation of the title GK and its diffusion over the entire Near East—in the format of a multilingual dictionary.[39]

---

[36] C.J. Gadd, *CAH* II 1³, pp. 224 ff. For the Ḫalab Treaty (*ca.* 1330) which opens with a historical reconstruction of the former status of the Great Kingship of Ḫalab—now a dependent of the Great King of Hatti—see Liverani, p. 75; N. Na'aman, *JCS* 32 (1980), pp. 34 ff.

[37] See data in Gonnet (*op. cit.*, note 30).

[38] Klengel, *RHA* 36 (1978), p. 92, 1.1.

[39] See Nougayrol, *Ugaritica* V, especially p. 234, 13'–14'.

Table 2.5.1

1. *Sumerogram*	2. *Akkadian (Assyria and Babylonia)*	3. *Hatti*	4. *Egypt*	5. *Hurrian*	6. *Ugarit*	7. [*Bible, First Millenium*]	8. [*Aramaic Royal Inscriptions, First Millennium*]
LUGAL.GAL*	In the international correspondence = 1	In the State and international documents = 1	In the international correspondence = 1	International correspondence of Mitanni = 1	In Akkadian correspondence = 1 (the King of Hatti and of Karkemiš)[5]		See note 8 below
	= Akkadian: *šarru rabû*[1]	Hittite form: unknown. Hieroglyphic: KING + GREAT[2]	= Egyptian term: *pꜣ ḥqꜣ ʿꜣ*[3]	Hurrian equivalent: PN EN.GAL = *Ibri-talma/i*[4]	Ugaritic translation: *mlk rb*[6] (cuneiform: *malku*)	*melek rab* *melek gādōl*	

Notes:

* Surprisingly not documented in lexical texts (see note 24, last entry).
1. In this period not written phonetically; cf. 2.6.2.
2. Gonnet (*op. cit.*, no. 30), p. 18; see also note 24.
3. Edel *Ägyptische Ärzte* . . ., 1976, pp. 17 and 135; Lorton, *The Juridical Terminology* . . ., 1974, p. 62.
4. Laroche, *Glossaire de la langue Hourrite*, 1980, p. 85, s.v. *ewri.*
5. Nougayrol, PRU IV, p. 263, s.v. *šarru.*
6. E.g., Virolleaud, PRU II, p. 34, n. 18, lines 2, 7, and 22–23.
7. J. Greenfield, see note 86; for Biblical-Aramaic forms see 2.7.
8. KAI 216 (*Sam'al*) 10, 11: מלכן רברבן בעלי כסף ובעלי זהב; 222, (Sfire) B, 7: מלך רב.

2.5.2 For a definition of the "(Extended) Age of the Amarna Archive" (= AAA): it was observed[40] that this age is identifiable by a series of common factors creating the third[41] International Age of the ancient Near East, encompassing the entire subcontinent (Elam re-enters only towards the second part of the period).[42]

2.5.3 The AAA opens with an unparalleled scene: while the northwestern intervention of the Hittite Great King (cf. 2.4.4) was futile in promoting formal international relations, the tremendous success of the southwestern Eighteenth Dynasty of Egypt, extending up the Euphrates to the northeast under Thutmose III and repulsing Mitannian power (see above 2.4.5), opens an age of peaceful relations with the surrounding "Great Kings" (see below), expressed by diplomatic delegations to Egypt. The result is: a meeting of the Great Powers of the four quarters of the Near East.[43]

2.5.4 These two tables (Table 2.5.1 and the Table of Helck, see our n. 43) lead us to the central question: how did this revolution come about and what was its program, the change in the concept and practice of the title, and political institution, GK, which made possible this new age of coexistence?

As in the case of truly decisive historical turning points, the answer is simple and direct: all the political powers of "Great Kingships" reached a common conclusion, expressing the "objective spirit" of the new era,[44] that "hegemony" is now impossible; the powers are in political balance. On the other hand, there is a long, interconnected series of needs which call for coexistence and even much more cooperation. Therefore, the "Second Circle" became closed: *The Western concept of "Great Kingship" merges with Eastern international principles.*

The West is represented by the Hittite concept of the Great Kingship, as characterized in 2.4.3. Practically the same concept is present in Egypt, now building its Empire, as indicated by the Amarna corre-

---

[40] P. Artzi, *Bar-Ilan Studies in History* [1], 1978, pp. 34–36; H. Tadmor, *Symposia* (ASOR 75th Anniversary), 1979, pp. 1 ff.

[41] Cf. M. Weinfeld in *I Trattati* (cf. n. 35), p. 175, n. 1.

[42] R. Labat, *CAH* II 2[3], pp. 384 ff.

[43] See chronological Table of delegations, coming from Assur, Babylon, Hatti, Alašia (and lesser kingdoms), from the 24th year of Thutmose III on: Helck, *Beziehungen* . . .[2], 1971, p. 167, n. 144.

[44] Cf. W. Dilthey, *Patterns and Meaning in History*, edited by H.P. Rickman, Harper Torchbooks 1961, esp. pp. 66–68.

spondence from Byblos, a Mediterranean port-city with long-standing, close connections with Egypt, addressing Pharaoh as GK.[45]

The bountiful Eastern "dowry," introduced into this "political marriage-alliance" of East and West, is an accurate selection from the accumulated heritage of a thousand year cuneiform(-Mesopotamian) experience in international relations. This selection is headed by the principle of "equality," expressed by the corresponding Akkadian term *miḫru*[46] and "mutuality," expressed by the terms *aḫu*, "brother," *aḫḫūtu*, "brotherhood," and *atḫūtu*, "reciprocity."[47] The implementation of these two principles means "recognition."

Thus the political experience of all the Near East cooperates in order to create a new era, which, in all vicissitudes, persisted until 1200 B.C.E. (see literature in note 40).

2.5.5 **parṣu*[48] *ša šarrāni rabûti* or *"The Code of Norms and Customs" for "Great Equal Kings," as documented in the cuneiform sources of the AAA:

> Preliminary note: (a) the aim of this subchapter is to demonstrate through Stages I, II, III and IV the ramifications of obligations binding together the GK's of the AAA; (b) almost every instance of the themes and *termini* appearing in this section finds its continuity or parallel in a great number of Near Eastern, including biblical, sources; we can cite only a sampling here. For a fuller picture consult: P. Kalluveettil, *Declaration and Covenant*, 1982.

Stage I

The standard position of the title GK in the titulary used in the address-formula of the international state-correspondence: it follows immediately after the PN of the ruler, as in the Hittite scheme (see 2.4.3); then the national geographical identification-title and the

[45] P. Artzi, *JNES* 27 (1968), p. 165, n. 18.

[46] *CAD* M/2, p. 57 2, a); see there also as Akkadogram in Hittite texts (Hittite term: *annauali*); V. Korošec, *International Relations According to Cuneiform Reports from the Tall-al-Amarna and Hittite State Archives* (English summary of an article written in Slovenian 1950), 3; Liverani, p. 70.

[47] M. Weinfeld, *Heidelberger Studien zum Alten Orient* 2 (1988), pp. 345–348; Liverani, pp. 197 ff.

[48] *AHw*, p. 836; Goetze, *Kizzuwatna*, 1940, p. 28 (*KBo* I 14, r. 6); cf. below, n. 62.

status of recognized-equality-title follow: "your brother." The principle of symmetry (as part of courtesy between equals; see below, Stage III 1; 2) is strictly observed. Examples: EA 16 (from Assyria to Egypt), II 1–4: "To RN, the GK, K. of Egypt, my brother . . . [from] RN, King of Assyria, GK, your brother"; KUB 3, 25 (+ 27; CTH^2, 162; from Egypt to Hatti) 1–3: "From RN, the GK of Egypt . . . to RN, the GK of Hatti, my brother."

Stage II

Recognition-equality-mutuality (= "brotherhood"): The first stages of mutual recognition of rank and merger of concepts occurred obviously around the years 24/33 of Thutmose III (cf. note 43): the arrival of delegations from Hatti and Kassite Babylonia—and a second delegation from Assyria to Egypt (see below). During the whole period a "pyramid" of equal states emerges; at the peak: the two "Suns" and "Great Kings"—Hatti and Egypt—characterized also by the careful and persistent use of the title, followed by the slightly less equal, and because of that paranoid, Kassite-Babylonian Royal House. This Babylonian "lesser" equality is reflected in the split of international "political public opinion" around the question: "Is the King of Babylonia a GK or is he not?" as we learn from a letter of Puduhepa, the "Great Queen," Queen of Hatti, wife of Hattušili III and mother of Tuthalija IV (*ca.* 1270).[49]

There are at least four special cases of variations in the history of the title GK in the AAA; each case produces a special lesson. We mention three of them only briefly: Mitanni: after the reconciliation with Egypt in the time of Amenhotep II, Mitanni becomes one of the Great Equal Kingships thanks to its geopolitical importance for Egypt against Hatti, bolstered by marriage-alliances. Then Mitanni, mistakenly, overestimates the importance of this latter component and loses the political-military support of Egypt in the time of its final confrontation with Hatti.[50]

Alašia-Cyprus, actually a business partner in delicate geopolitical

---

[49] *KUB* XX 38, CTH^2 176; W. Helck, *JCS* 17 (1963), pp. 87 ff.; for the entire picture of changes in Kassite-Babylonia's international position see P. Artzi, "Kurigalzu II and His Elamite Campaign (paper delivered at the 36ème *RAI*, Gand 1989; forthcoming).

[50] Cf. Klengel, *RHA* 36 (1978), p. 110.

position, never uses the title GK, satisfying itself with "brotherhood."[51]

Arzawa, a Western Anatolian kingdom which returned to temporary independence during the Hittite weakness, is "Brother," and never was accorded the title GK by Egypt, exercising cautious policy.[52]

Contrarily, the fourth case, Assyria, represents the aggressive, "new" partner and natural pretender to the status of Great King (cf. 2.3). This country of long historical-international tradition and dormant potential is engaged in a war of two hundred years to re-enter the international scene as a Great Equal King.

At the inception of the AAA Assyria is a formal dependent of Mitanni; exactly because of this situation, Assyria is the first to initiate contact with victorious Egypt (see Table Helck of our n. 43). Then in the period of the archive itself, towards its end, Aššur-uballiṭ I, the founder of the Middle Assyrian Kingdom, is fully recognized by Egypt as a Great King.[53]

But this new position of Assyria arouses a new storm: Assyria is from now on in direct confrontation with Hatti, the sharing partner of the Mitannian partition; Hanigalbat, the old-new post-Mitannian state, becomes a "buffer" between Assyria and Hatti: the Great King against the "upstart" who is already recognized by Egypt and later by Babylonia. The ensuing, long diplomatic-military campaign, eloquently documented, is concluded only around 1255(!) by the Hittite recognition of the King of Assyria as a "Great (Equal) King."[54]

Similar to "equality and brotherhood" (see n. 47), "mutuality, reciprocity, and sharing between (Great) Kings" was also defined in the correspondence of the AAA. Here the proverb of Burnaburijaš II, King of Kassite Babylonia, stands out,[55] with its elegant formulation,

---

[51] P. Artzi, (above, n. 40), p. 29, n. 5.

[52] *EA* 31 and 32; *EAMr*, pp. 101–103; Heinhold-Krahmer, *Arzawa* . . ., T. Heth 8 (1977).

[53] For the emergence of the Middle Assyrian Kingdom see Liverani, p. 71 with n. 29. In *EA* 16:27 the key problem of the emendation is not definitely resolvable: v. Soden, *Orientalia NS* 21 (1952), p. 434, proposes—in Assyrian style: *šanināku* ("I am equal") while we prefer—with J. Friedrich, cited by C. Kühne, *Chronologie* . . ., 1973, p. 78, n. 389: *meḫrēku* (see above), a term consistent with the international usage of the period; see EAMr.

[54] For the documentation of the Assyrian-Hittite military campaign see: P. Machinist, *BBAO* II (1982), pp. 265–267; A. Harrak, *Assyria and Hanigalbat*, 1987, pp. 138–189; cf. Chart p. 188 and I. Singer, "The Battle of Nihriya and the End of the Hittite Empire," *ZA* 75 (1985), pp. 100–123; A. Goetze, *CAH* II 2^3, p. 258; Szemerényi, *Oriens Antiquus* 9, (1945), pp. 120–123; C. Kühne and H. Otten, STuBoT 16, 1971 (Šauškamuwa Treaty).

[55] *EA* 11: 21–22.

utterly different from the sharp arguments of the commercially minded "Northern" Aššur-uballiṭ I, in *EA* 16 (see literature in note 40). Nevertheless, the "message" is the same, in the spirit of the period. Because of the intentional disuse of the term GK, this proverb reaches a level of almost abstract generalization, saying (in free translation): "Between Kings 'Brotherhood', 'Goodwill/Friendship', 'Peace', and 'Courteous Relations' are in strict relation to the amount and weight of 'precious stones, silver and gold' [sent/exchanged as various kinds of 'gifts']." Thus, in *EA* 11 a thousand years of international cuneiform experience becomes a common denominator between the Great Equal Kings of all the Near East.[56]

Stage III

The norms of correct behavior between Great Kings in the AAA (and after):[57]

Norm 1: Establishment of relations, formulated in the international state letters; combination of selected themes from the Amarna and Hittite state letters; sequence: (a) address: symmetrical royal titles and status-designation of equality; secular[58] greetings; (b) historical arguments of persuasion, based on precedents; the writer declares that the relations between the two parties are dynastically long-standing[59] and are based on three operative principles: *aḫāmiš ṭabānu*,[60] we are always "good" to each other, we are firm friends and well-wishers; *dabābu*, we are ready to arrive at agreements through talk;[61] we are

[56] On "gifts" (*šulmānu, šūbultu, etc.*) see C. Zaccagnini, *Lo Scambio dei Doni nel Vicino Oriente durante I Secoli XV–XII*, 1973.

[57] Along this list of norms consult the pioneering presentation of Brinkman, "The Monarchy in the Time of the Kassite Dynasty," in P. Garelli ed., *Le palais et la royauté*, 1974, pp. 397 ff.

[58] Without mentioning any deity; this observation is an addition to the still incomplete study of the international greeting-formulas in the AAA (see E. Salonen, *Die Gruss- und Höflichkeitsformeln . . .*, 1967, pp. 61 ff., also *EAMr*, p. xxiii).

[59] Key term is *abu*, "father," and extensions: (fore-)fathers, earlier (great) kings of the dynasty.

[60] Perhaps alluding to actual treaties now lost; cf. W.L. Moran, *JNES* 22 (1963), pp. 77–78. For Hebrew equivalent *ṭōbāh*, referring to treaty-terminology see A. Malamat, *Biblical Archaeologist Reader* 3, 1980, pp. 196–198.

[61] A term already used in the Hamazi letter of Ebla; see literature in n. 47; see *CAD* D, p. 3, *dabābu* s., c) 3, "agreement" and *dabābu* verb, p. 8, 3, b), "to come to an agreement" (through negotiations).

always ready to satisfy the material needs, wishes (*ḫišiḫtu, mēreš/štu*) of our brother, by sending/receiving/exchanging equitable gifts (cf. note 56).

Norm 2: You must never "elevate," upgrade (cf. 2.3; 2.4) yourself above your brother![62]

Norm 3: You must prefer personal relations, "love," "loyalty" (?) over colliding interests in your international relations; you must fulfill your obligations, binding you and your dynasty, *vis-à-vis* your brother GK.[63]

Norm 4: You are your brother's keeper (cf. Gen. 4:9)! You must help him in his distress.[64]

Norm 5: "Life-Cycle-Diplomacy" (see below, note 71): You must carefully apply all these norms on the occasion of the following events: beginning of rule/coronation,[65] festival,[66] palace/temple-building,[67]

---

[62] One of the key cases is *EA* 42, a Hittite state letter, which needs much additional research and restoration. In this letter it is stated that the King of Egypt transgressed the *parṣu* (see our note 48) by the letter-formulation described by the Hittite King as *šumka eli šumīja*, "Your name over my name"; it seems that the complaint is raised against the asymmetric use of the royal status titles. In another letter, Raamses II refutes quite courteously the accusation of Hattušili III that he wrote to him *akî ardi*, "as to a servant." It seems, with Goetze (see below), that because of the circumstances of his ascendance to the throne, Raamses II did not congratulate him properly (see below, 5th Norm), or denied him the proper titles, even brotherhood? (see 1st Norm).

Literature to *EA* 42: *EAMr*, pp. 115–116. To the Ramesside letter: A. Goetze, *JCS* I (1947), pp. 241–251; *id.*, *CAH* II 2^3, p. 257; see some other cases in Liverani, pp. 70–71.

[63] Sample: *EA* 9: Basing himself on historical precedent (of doubtful basis) and on international common law combined with "love"/"loyalty," Burnaburijaš II implores his brother, the King of Egypt, to expel Assyrian merchants now doing business in Egypt, because they are his servants and dependents; cf. Liverani, p. 72, n. 32; p. 198, n. 10. (The request was denied; see above on the Egyptian recognition of Assyria. To international common law, applied in this letter, see the case already presented by Anum-Hirbi; see literature in note 23.)

[64] Sample: Aššur-uballiṭ I, King of Assyria, intervenes as a relative and ally to ensure the continuity of the Kassite dynasty by killing the illegal king and putting the legal heir, Kurigalzu II, on the throne of his father without exploiting his situation (A.K. Grayson, ABC, p. 159, Chronicle 21, "Synchronistic History," 8'–17').

[65] Sample: *EA* 33:9–18; 34:50–53: King of Alašija to the King of Egypt; *KBo* I, 14, rev. 5b–10: King of Hatti to the King of Assyria, setting down the rules (*parṣu*) on the occasion of coronation; cf. our n. 48. I Kings 5:15 (Hiram to Solomon); see regarding the Septuagint variation (anointing; cf., e.g., above, Alašija): J. Katzenstein, *Tyre*, 1973, pp. 96–97.

[66] Festival: *EA* 3:18, 20, complaint of the Babylonian King for not sending an invitation and presents for a state-festival. *EAMr*, p. 8, n. 8: one of the *sḏ* festivals of Amenhotep III.

[67] New Temple/Palace; sample: *EA* 5. Pharaoh to the King of Babylonia: furniture for his "new house(s)" (= É.GIBIL); see in general: *EAK* II, p. 1389, s.v. *dullu*, building

marriage-alliance,[68] sickness,[69] and death[70] (for the last event cf. also 4th Norm).[71]

Stage IV

Political rules for the personal use of the Great Equal King:

Rule 1: Keep your international correspondence in good order—important documents of the past must be preserved![72]

Rule 2: Keep your communications open not only for imperial administration, fiscal and police/military actions, but for trade and mainly for the use of the diplomatic service![73]

Rule 3: You must be able to find solutions to relieve international obstacles/problems which may arise in relation to Rule 2.[74]

---

operations of the State. *EA* 16:16b–18: The King of Assyria requests gold for the "New Palace" (*ekallu eššetu*; cf. Borger, *EAK* I, pp. 26; 28 ff.; Grayson, *ARI*, 1972, p. 45, n. 5).

68 Marriage(-alliance): for this huge topic see Artzi in *La Femme dans le proche Orient Antique* (ed. J.M. Durand), Paris 1987, pp. 23 ff., and mainly, F. Pintore, *Il matrimonio interdinastico nel Vicino Oriente durante i secoli XV–XIII*, Roma 1978; for Israelite-Egyptian marriage-alliance see A. Malamat, our nos. 86 and 93.

69 Sickness: sample: *EA* 7:8–25, Burnaburijaš II complains that Pharaoh did not ask immediately about his health; see in general, E. Edel, *Ägyptische Ärtzte und ägyptische Medizin am Hettitischen Königshof*, 1976.

70 Death: see P. Artzi, "Mourning in International Relations," *Mesopotamia* 8 (*Death in Mesopotamia*, ed. by B. Alster), Copenhagen 1980, pp. 161–170.

71 On the theory of "Life-Cycle-Diplomacy" see literature in notes 68 (Artzi) and 70.

72 Sample: *KBo* I 10, obv. l. 52: . . . *amatama ša aḫū'a išpuru lukîn*; translation (with A.L. Oppenheim, *Letters from Mesopotamia* 1967, p. 143): ". . . should my brother send me a message, I retain every word" (cf. *CAD* K, p. 163, 2').

73 Samples: *EA* 7:73–82 and *EA* 8. The King of Babylonia demands juridical punitive action and compensation from the robbers/murderers of his merchants, adding in *EA* 8:33 the warning: if you will not act according to these demands, the result will be *ina birīni mār šipri iparras* "there will be no more diplomatic exchange between us!" For the diplomatic service see A. Meier, *The Messenger in the Ancient Semitic World*, (Atlanta, GA), 1988; D. Elgavish, *The Emissary and His Mission: The Diplomatic Service in the Cuneiform Sources and in the Bible*, Ph.D., Bar-Ilan, 1989 (in Hebrew; English summary, vol. I, pp. I–VIII); Y.L. Holmes, *JAOS* (1975), pp. 376–381.

74 Sample: *EA* 16:37–42 and 52–55: Aššur-uballiṭ, Great King, announces to Pharaoh a new system of safety on the international roads. See P. Artzi in: *Ah Assyria . . . Presented to Hayim Tadmor*, Jerusalem 1990, pp. 254–325; "The International Royal Trade-court at Karkemiš," H. Klengel, *Mesopotamia* 8, Copenhagen 1980, pp. 189–197.

Rule 4: You must behave as a Great Equal King![75]
Rule 5: Learn about your peers![76]

2.6 *The first millennium: partial decline of the title GK*

Preliminary note: for Section 2.6 consult Seux.

2.6.1 In Assyria of the first millennium only two genres of state documents use the title GK: royal inscriptions and colophons. This development began already in the second part of the second millennium, still in the AAA. Aššur-uballiṭ I (see above) never uses the title GK in his local inscriptions, while he is "re-elevated" to the title *šar kiššati* (last used by Šamši-Adad I and Zimri-Lim; see 2.3) by the Babylonian scribe Marduk-nadin-aḫḫe, son of Marduk-uballiṭ(!), at the end of the prayer/blessing section of his votive inscription.[77]

It is a post-AAA King, Aššur-bēl-kala (son of Tiglat-pileser I), a

[75] Autobiography and "apology" of Hattušili III, the "Great King," concerning his behavior and policy towards traditional friends, "vassals," and enemies; see translation of passage in A. Goetze, *CAH* II 2^3, p. 257. *KBo* I 10: Hattušili III, the Great King to his brother Kadašman-Enlil II, the Great King (special stress; 0., 2); from 36b ff.: the problem of communication between the two countries: H. refutes the Babylonian apologetic argument that the communication between Babylonia and Hatti was interrupted because of (a) the interference of the Ahlamu nomads; (b) especially, the possibility that the King of Assyria will refuse permit of passage. The refutation appears in o., 38b–39a: *šarrūt šarrūtika aḫū'a ṣeḫrēta*, "In royal authority/power, my Brother, are you 'small'?!" (not a "Great King," but a "Small King" of a dependent state; for the term "Small King" [LUGAL.TUR, **šarru ṣeḫru*] see: Goetze, *Hattušiliš (III)*, 1925, p. 124; Harrak, *Hanigalbat*, p. 148: *KUB* XIII 103 o., 27'–28': The King of Assyria rose from a LUGAL.TUR to a LUGAL.GAL; Liverani, p. 68). We add here, that in our opinion, these *termini* are not 'technical' ones (Liverani) but reflect a classification of international power-status in the tradition of cuneiform international relations.

Rhetorical answer of Hattušili III to his own question: 0., 49b–51: *aḫū'a šarru rabû attā u ina littūti lu kašdāta* "(But), my Brother, you are a GK and you are destined for a long and successful life!"

For *KBo* I 10 in general: full transliteration and translation in T. Heth 16, 1989, pp. 281–300 by Albertina Hagenbuchner; on the historical background: A. Goetze, *CAH* II 2^3, p. 258 *et passim.*

[76] In our opinion the royal (even private) cuneiform libraries in the West served not only to teach the writing and the language itself—cf. the Egyptian reading-dots in *EA* 356–7—but to know and understand the theological ideas and political aims of "heavenly" and "earthly" leaders of the Mesopotamian and Hittite world. For the "Library" of Amarna see D.O. Edzard, *Proceedings of the Ninth World Congress of Jewish Studies (1981), Plenary Sessions, Bible and ANE* (ed. by M. Goshen-Gottstein), Jerusalem 1988, pp. 27–33; for Hattuša see H.G. Güterbock, *ZA* 42 (1934), pp. 1–91; 44 (1983), pp. 45–149; G. Beckman, *JCS* 35/1–2 (1983), pp. 97–114.

[77] *IAK*, p. 40, XVII, 2, r. 15; Grayson, *ARI*, p. 43, 278.

ruler in the period of Assyrian weakness under Aramaic stress, but nevertheless the last of the second millennium Assyrian kings still active in the West, who reintroduces the title in the sequence: "Great King, King of the World, King of Assyria,"[78] a combination of the AAA and Assyrian traditions.

After this period the title GK becomes a standard part of the neo-Assyrian royal titulary in the following order:

"RN, GK, Strong King, King of the World, King of Assyria."[79] This titulary, we suggest, was built historically and stylistically in a manner to unite all facets of the Assyrian royal international prestige, in rising sequence; the last one is the sum total of all, the Empire. The difference between the AAA-sequence and the Assyrian one of titles is, therefore, programmatic, diametrically opposite; see below 2.6.2 (Cyrus).

There are, however, two instances which show that the title still had its reduced significance: (1) the use of the title by two kings of Urartu-Ararat (Seux, p. 299), a far echo of the AAA?; (2) although, as was just noted, the title GK is now standardized in the neo-Assyrian titulary, the fact that this particular title was used in Hebrew translation under the walls of Jerusalem may show that its Western meaning of domination (see 2.4.3) was not lost; see 2.7.[80]

2.6.2 Neo- and Late Babylonian Period: The rulers of the early pre-Chaldean Neo-Babylonian period (1150–625 B.C.E.), occupied by the task of post-Kassite revival and then by a fight for independence from Assyrian rule, had no interest in the message of the title GK and preferred the more hereditary, programmatic *šar kiššati*.[81]

In the period of the Chaldean dynasty and Empire (625 onwards) this use continues, this time with justification. Then, suddenly, Nabunaid, the last Chaldean dynast, uses the title GK again: Nabonid

---

[78] *ARI* 2, p. 47, 212 (emendation). Cf. Borger, *EAK* I, p. 142; *ARI* 2, p. 58, 264; p. 59, 273; in the West: p. 55, 248.

[79] See the observations and tabulations of Chaim Cohen, "Neo-Assyrian elements in the first speech of the Biblical *rāb-šāqê*," *Israel Oriental Studies* IX, 1979, pp. 38–39; for the use of the title GK in colophons see H. Hunger, *Babylonische und assyrische Kolophone* (*AOAT* 2), 1968, nos. 317–344, *passim*.

[80] Of course, the rhetorical aspect of the biblical formulation of *rāb-šāqê*'s speech must be taken into account; but one is reminded here of the epigraphical evidence for the title *melek gadōl*; see 2.7, and n. 89.

[81] J.A. Brinkman, "The Early Neo-Babylonian Monarchy," in *Le Palais et la Royauté*, 1971, pp. 411–412.

(Nabunaid) n. 1, Restoration of the Sin-temple in Ḫarran: col. i 1–2 (partly normalized):[82]

> *anāku* N., LUGAL (= *šarru*) *ra-bu-ú*, LUGAL *dannu*, LUGAL *kiššati*, LUGAL *Bābili*, LUGAL *kibrāti erbitti*
>
> I, N., the GK, the mighty King, King of the World, King of the Four Quarters (of the World).

Here appears a combination of neo-Assyrian, imperial Babylonian, and Old-Akkadian royal titles; see partly above, 2.6.1. This renewed inclusion of the title GK may be one of the symbols of the renaissance-program of this last ruler of Babylonia.

This inheritance of titles reappears in the "Cyrus Cylinder" at the opening of the Persian-Achaemenid Period (539 on), Cyrus Cylinder 20:

> *anāku Kuraš*, LUGAL *kiš-šat*, LUGAL.GAL, LUGAL *dannu, šar Bābili, šar (māt) Šumēri u Akkadi, šar kibrāti erbittim....*

With an inverted order between the leading titles and a further historical enlargement in the series ("King of Sumer and Akkad") the continuity is clear; moreover, in the new sequence of titles, *šar kiššati* now occupies the place of the title GK in the Hittite titulary; see 2.4.3.[83]

The use of the title GK continues (without *šar kiššati*) in the titulary of Darius I, Xerxes, and Artaxerxes I–II–III (521–338).

Lastly, the titulary of the Seleucid King Antiochus I, Soter (279–261 B.C.E.); Cylinder, col. i 1–2: *A*., LUGAL.GAL-*ú* (= *rabû*), *šarru dannu, šar kiššati, šar Bābili, šar matāti* (= "King of Countries")...."[84] Nevertheless, as Oelsner notes, this use is rare and an exception.[85]

The cuneiform usage for *ca.* fifteen-hundred years of the title GK reached its end.

Note a Middle Babylonian exception: during the reign of Adad-šuma-uṣur, one of the last kings of the Kassite Dynasty, (cf. Brinkman, *ZA* 59 (1969), pp. 233–238; Tadmor, *JNES* XVII (1958), 129–141), "Babylonia managed to gain a temporary ascendancy over Assyria" (Brinkman); as attested in Harper letter *ABL* 924:3, the Babylonian king uses the title GK; see Brinkman, *A Political History of Post-Kassite Babylonia*, 1968, p. 87, and n. 453.

[82] Nabonid (Nabunaid): Langdon, *NAB*, p. 218; Tadmor, *AS* 16, pp. 351, 358.

[83] Cyrus: Weissbach, *KA* 1, Cyrus (Kyros), pp. 4–5, 20; Tadmor, "The Historical Background of the Decree of Cyrus," *'Oz le-David* (FS David Ben-Gurion), Jerusalem 1964, pp. 451 ff. (Hebrew).

[84] Antiochus I, Soter, Weissbach, *KA*, pp. 132–133.

[85] J. Oelsner, *Materialien zur Babylonischen Gesellschaft und Kultur in Hellenistischer Zeit*, Budapest 1986, p. 271, e.

2.7 *The title GK in the Bible*

In the Hebrew Bible two idioms occur for "Great King," both apparently calques deriving from Akkadian *šarru rabû: melek gādōl* and *melek rab*.[86] While the first seems to be a direct translation from Akkadian (or rather Assyrian), the second may have penetrated the Hebrew language via Ugaritic or Aramaic where, in both, the expression *mlk rb* is used for "Great King"; see Table 2.5.1, 6, 8.

There is no evidence, so far, that the title GK was used at all by the Kings of Judah and Israel (but see below). The title, on the one hand, is reserved for the Assyrian king, as in Rabshakeh's speech referring to Sennacherib (2K 18:19, 28 = Isa. 36:4, 13) (cf. 2.6.1). On the other hand, the idiom is used and apparently originated in the theological sphere as one of the epithets of the God of Israel (Mal. 1:14; Ps. 47:3; 95:3), an apt title for the incomparable divine king. The plural *mĕlākīm gĕdōlīm* (Ps. 136:17), here in parallelism to *mĕlākīm ʾaddīrīm* (v. 18) and *mĕlākīm ʿăṣumīm* (Ps. 135:10), is applied to Sihon and Og, the Amorite kings in Transjordan in proto-Israelite times.[87] In this semi-legendary context of Israel's conquest of Transjordan the idiom "Great Kings" is of a poetical rather than a realistic stance.

Of interest is a further occurrence of "Great King," symbolic rather than real, in Ecclesiastes 9:14: "There was a little city with few men in it and to it came a great king, who invested it and built mighty siegeworks against it."[88] The phraseology here may indicate a play on words, contrasting the great king with a little city and few men. The imagery here reflects a somewhat grotesque situation mocking the great king, the symbol of power and then praising wisdom.

Finally, note the words *melek gādōl* in Hebrew script on a Nimrud

---

[86] On the various epithets of the divine king, i.e. God, and the mortal king in the Bible, see recently M.Z. Brettler, *God is King—Understanding of an Israelite Metaphor*, Sheffield 1989 (*JSOTSS* 76), especially pp. 30 f., 68 ff. For earlier remarks see J.C. Greenfield in the *4th World Congress of Jewish Studies* I, Jerusalem 1967, pp. 118 f. (Table 2.5.1, 7) and cf. A. Malamat in *Studies in the Period of David and Solomon* (ed. T. Ishida), Tokyo 1982, pp. 196 f.

[87] The epic hymn deals with the exodus, conquest and settlement in Canaan, specifying explicitly only the Amorite kings Sihon and Og; cf., e.g., H.J. Kraus, *Psalmen*, vol. 2, 4, Neukirchen 1972, p. 902.

[88] See commentaries on Ecclesiastes 9:14. Some assume that the great king here refers to Antiochus III ("The Great"); cf. L. Levy, *Das Buch Qoheleth*, Leipzig 1912, pp. 30 f. The English renderings of the Hebrew Text are taken throughout this paper according to *NJPS* (= *A New Translation of the Holy Scriptures*, the Jewish Publication Society).

Ivory of the late 8th century B.C.E.[89] But since these are the only words remaining on the fragment, we are unable to ascribe them to a title either of an Israelite king or of an Assyrian potentate.

The other royal title in the Bible for "Great King" is *melek rab*, which presumably represents a stylistic stratum different from that of *melek gādōl*. This idiom appears to be also of a more archaic nature, finding its way into Biblical Hebrew via Ugarit or Early Aramaic, where *mlk rb* is attested (for the Aramaic, note the Sefire Inscription I B 7 from Northern Syria;[90] cf. Table 2.5.1, 8). It is thus the heritage of a Western tradition in contrast to *šarru rabû* or *melek gādōl*. But whereas the latter terms carry a super-regional quality (cf. 2.4; 2.6.1), *melek rab* functions in a more limited regional framework.

The first instance of this title appears in Ps. 48:2 [MT 48:3], where the word "great" in the idiom קרית מלך רב, "a city of the great king", has been taken almost unanimously as an epithet for God, who is characterized here as the great king of Jerusalem. Although God is the dominant figure in this Psalm in connection with his city Jerusalem, we claim[91] that it is King Solomon who is referred to here, our assertion being also based on the next instance in the Bible where the idiom occurs. *Rab* in the above passage, as well as elsewhere (cf. Jer. 50:41), has sometimes been interpreted not as "great" but as "numerous," that is "many kings," indicating also the exceptionally lengthy Davidic dynasty.[92] But there remains still the possibility of translating the idiom in Jer. 50:41 as "mighty kings," and not "many kings."

The second occurrence, strengthening our assumption concerning the first one, is the Aramaic passage in Ezra 5:11, which undoubtedly refers in retrospect to Solomon's building Jerusalem and beautifying it: ומלך לישראל רב בנהי ושכללה. In other words, a title applied to Solomon alone of all the kings of Israel and Judah evokes a particular category of a major potentate, the overlord, which later history was to call "emperor" and the like.[93] Perhaps the grandiose title

[89] Published by A. Millard, *Iraq* 24 (1962), pp. 45 ff.; cf. our n. 80.

[90] See J.A. Fitzmeyer, *The Aramaic Inscriptions of Sefire*, Rome 1967, pp. 16–17, 61; cf. Table 2.5.1, 8.

[91] Thus already Malamat in *Studies* (above, n. 86), p. 197.

[92] See, e.g., A. Berlin, *JBL* 100 (1981), pp. 90–93.

[93] For the expansion and the vast international relations of Solomon's kingdom, favoring for this ruler the title Great King, see Malamat in *Studies* (above, n. 86), pp. 189–204.

is the result of a lengthy process in which courtiers and political leaders, as well as historiographers, participated. King David did not assume this title,[94] although in I Chron. 17:8b we read: "Moreover, I will give you renown like that of the greatest men on earth." It is most likely that early Western traditions penetrated the royal Israelite court under Solomon. Of all the Hebrew kings it is he who bears the title GK in a later Greek source in the Sibylline Oracles (11:80). In Biblical Aramaic we also find די כל מלך רב ושליט, "for a great king and ruler" (Dan. 2:10).

Finally, most unusual is the form in the Book of Hosea (5:13; 10:6), *melek yārēb*, referring to an Assyrian ruler in relation to the Kingdom of Israel (Tiglat-pileser III?). The form *yārēb* is most likely related to the same word in Syriac "(to become) great."[95] The strange form perhaps reflects a North Israelite linguistic usage, a feature not uncommon in Hosea. Usually, the commentators emend *melek yārēb* to *malkî rab*.[96]

The Bible is, of course, not the last source mentioning the royal title "Great King"; it is rather the impetus for the future usage of this epithet. Indeed the title flourishes in the Persian and Hellenistic periods[97] and beyond, throughout European history from Alexander the Great to Czar Peter the Great (cf. 2.6.2, end).[98]

3. *Conclusions*

We are aware of the need to deepen our presentation on the history of the royal title Great King, especially as to the following aspects:

---

[94] See in this connection the passage in I Kings 1:47: "May God make the renown of Solomon even greater than yours (*i.e.*, of David), and may he exalt his throne even higher than yours!"

[95] Cf. Greenfield in the *4th World Congress* (above, n. 86), p. 119; S. Paul in Y. Avishur and J. Blau, eds., *Studies in the Bible and Ancient Near East* (FS S.A. Loewenstamm), Jerusalem 1978, pp. 313 f. and n. 34 (Hebrew).

[96] E.g. the commentary of F.I. Andersen and D.N. Freedman, *Hosea* (Anchor Bible), Garden City, NY, 1980, pp. 413–414 (*yārēb* is an incorrect division of *malkî rab*). For retaining the term *yārēb*, see E.M. Good, *JBL* 85 (1966), pp. 277 f.; H.L. Ginsberg, *Encyclopedia Judaica* vol. 8 (1971), pp. 1010–1024.

[97] For the Hellenistic Period (also referring to earlier times), see most recently D.C. Duling, *JBL* 110 (1991), pp. 296 ff., and see still the pioneer treatment by E.R. Bevan, "Antiochus III and his Title the 'Great King'," *JHS* 22 (1902), pp. 241–244.

[98] For Europe, see the short monograph of T. Schieder, *Über den Beinamen "der Grosse"—Reflexionen über historische Grösse*, Rheinisch-Westfälische Akademie der Wissenschaften (G 271), 1984.

- A closer investigation of the emergence of the title, especially in the north and northwest of the Near East;
- A detailed analysis of the relationship of the title with other royal titles;
- A systematic investigation of the influence of the Great Kingship as a political institution, on statecraft, on dependent states, and on international relations;
- The theological aspects of the Great Kingship;
- Its transmission into Hellenistic and post-biblical Jewish thought and literature;
- The causes, reasons and methods of applying the attribute "Great" in relation to individual political figures from its earliest inception (cf. note 8) to the present (cf. 2.7, end and note 98).

21

ʿAMM LᵉḆĀḎĀḎ YIŠKŌN: A DIPLOMATIC REPORT FROM MARI AND AN ORACLE OF BALAAM*

The status and position of Old-Babylonian Mari within the sphere of Mesopotamia and Syria are reflected in a tantalizing document which, though often quoted, has not yet been published in full.[1] Indeed, Mari was not the only kingdom or hegemony in the region. The text sums up the political situation as it appeared to one high official of Mari. It is a letter addressed to Zimri-Lim, the last king of Mari (*ca.* 1775–1760 B.C.), by Itur-Asdu, then the king's agent in the city of Naḫur (biblical Nahor). It is a high-level diplomatic report, which presents an overview of the political situation of the day and reveals five major states besides Mari.[2] On the king's instructions, Itur-Asdu called a meeting of the various local sheikhs or petty kings (*šarrānu*) in the land of Tarmanni[2a] located to the north of Mari, taking advantage of the occasion of a festival of the goddess Ishtar. The meeting was apparently held with the intention of inducing the sheikhs to conclude covenants with Mari—a practice often associated with sacrificial ceremonies, particularly those for Ishtar.

Itur-Asdu's report reads as follows: "With regard to what my lord wrote here to the sheikhs, saying, 'Come to the sacrifice in honor of Ishtar'—I gathered the sheikhs of Tarmanni and conveyed this message to them: 'There is no kinglet (*šarru*) who is strong (*dannu*)[3] by

* This article was originally published in: *The Jewish Quarterly Review*, 76 (1985), 47–50 (Memorial M. Held).

[1] Published only in transliteration and translation by G. Dossin, *Syria* 19 (1938), 117 f. Reported already by Dossin in the *Comptes Rendus* of the Académie des Inscriptions, 1937 (Jan.–Mar.), 17–18. The first English translation, a partial one only, was given by W.F. Albright, in *BASOR* 67 (1937), 27; a fuller one by W. Moran may now be found in *ANET*[3], p. 628.

[2] It is noteworthy that Assyria does not figure among the current powers in the region; this may have reflected the specific political situation at that very moment, after Zimri-Lim had recovered his throne at Mari, a time when Assyria was already in eclipse.

[2a] For this reading of the place-name (and not the previous rendering: Šarmaneḫ) see Durand, *MARI* 5 (1987), 230.

[3] For the royal epithet *šarru dannu*, common in Akkadian, see the parallel biblical usages *meleḵ ʿaz* (Isa. 19:4) and *ʿoz meleḵ* (Ps. 99:4).

himself. Ten (to) fifteen kinglets are vassals of Hammurabi (literally "follow Hammurabi"), the ruler (*awīlum*) of Babylon; so, too, Rim-Sin the ruler of Larsa; so, too, Ibal-pi-el the ruler of Eshnunna; so, too, Amut-pi-el the ruler of Qaṭna; (and) twenty kinglets are vassals of Yarim-Lim the ruler of Yamḫad. . . .' "[4]

Itur-Asdu's report thus reveals a multipolar system in this region of six middle-range powers, including Mari. The last two kingdoms mentioned by him, Qaṭna and Yamḫad, were in Syria; and Yamḫad seems to have been the strongest of all six at that time—a situation generally reflected in Zimri-Lim's correspondence. Politics and commerce, of course, go hand in hand, and in an inventory of a shipment of tin, four of the same kingdoms appear again, while Eshnunna and Larsa, located at the far eastern end of the arc, are replaced by Ugarit and Hazor at the western end of the arc.[5] Hazor, in Northern Palestine, though within the commercial sphere of Mari, was apparently beyond Mari's ordinary political horizon, that is to say, it was south of Qaṭna, the southernmost kingdom within the sphere of influence of Mari. That Hazor, too, was a kingdom, much like the other powers noted by Itur-Asdu, is reflected in the biblical statement that "Hazor was formerly the head of all those kingdoms" (Josh. 11:10). This refers to the erstwhile status of Hazor, when several vassals in Northern Palestine were gathered around the city.[6] In a much later period Hazor even assembled its vassals against the invading Israelites (Josh. 11:1–5).

What was Itur-Asdu seeking to convey to the tribal chiefs at Tarmanni? Most likely he was trying to persuade them to join in an alliance with Mari. He was implying that it was hopeless for small peoples or political entities to remain unaligned, that is to say, in political limbo, vulnerable and insecure, liable to be set upon and gobbled up by one or other of the powers of the day.

This picture seems to shed new light on an interesting passage in

[4] It is likely, though not certain, from Dossin's treatment of this letter (see above, n. 1), that the text is broken off after the mention of Yamḫad. [I am grateful to Prof. J.-M. Durand for examining the tablet in order to check my proposal that the name of an additional kingdom might have appeared after Yamhad. In his letter of 25 May 1985 Prof. Durand points out that the tablet (no. A. 482) is indeed broken and suggests certain possibilities, but unfortunately this matter remains unsolved.]

[5] On the tin inventory see A. Malamat, *IEJ* 21 (1971), 75–89; and cf. the collation of the text in *ARM* XXIII (1984), No. 556, pp. 528 f., which introduces several improved readings.

[6] See A. Malamat, *JBL* 79 (1960), 12–19.

the Bible which until now has remained rather obscure. In the Book of Numbers the seer Balaam is brought by the king of Moab to curse the Israelites but, instead, God places a blessing in his mouth. In Num. 23:9, he says: . . . *hen ʿāmm lᵉb̲ād̲ād̲ yiškōn ub̲aggôyîm lôʾ yit̲ḥaššāb̲*, which has been variously rendered: "Lo, a people dwelling alone and not reckoning itself among the nations" (RSV); "Lo, a people living by themselves, not accounting themselves as one of the nations" (Chicago American Translation); or "There is a people that dwells apart, not reckoned among the nations" (Jewish Publication Society New Translation). The Hebrew word *bād̲ād̲* has been rendered here, as elsewhere in the Bible, as "alone, apart, separate."[7] According to the commentators, it carries two possible nuances, one of strength—Israel dwelling securely and peacefully (cf. Deut. 33:28)[8]—and the other of exclusiveness—Israel having nothing in common with the other nations and being aloof.[9] The nuance of strength is actually intimated in Midrashic literature, which understands *bād̲ād̲* in Deut. 33:28 and Num. 23:9 as connoting self-reliance and not weakness,[10] which would make little sense in the context of Num. 23.

We can now see that the term *bād̲ād̲* has the sense of "independent, unaligned," regarded as a virtue—the very opposite attitude to that taken by Itur-Asdu. Thus what Balaam was actually seeing in his vision was a self-confident, rather strong nation, entirely independent of other nations. Itur-Asdu's argument now puts this passage into bold relief, despite the fact that, or rather because, it is its very antithesis. In this light, then, we can translate the biblical passage as "Lo, (Israel) is a people encamped in isolation, not considering itself among the (other) nations."[11] To explore just how this political declaration was turned into a theological statement (cf., e.g., Deut. 7:6–7) would require a further study.

---

[7] For the biblical occurrences and the meaning "isolation, separation" see *BDB*, pp. 94 f., and *HAL*[3], p. 105.

[8] Cf., e.g., G.B. Gray, *Numbers* (*ICC*) (Edinburgh 1912), pp. 346 f. for other views as well and recently J. Milgrom, *Numbers* (*JPS Torah Commentary*; Philadelphia 1990), p. 197 and on Balaam as a diviner, pp. 471 ff.

[9] See A. von Gall, *Zusammensetzung und Herkunft der Bileam Perikope* (Giessen 1900), p. 25.

[10] See Sifre, *Wᵉzoʾt Habbĕrak̲a*, 256.

[11] See B.A. Levine, *Numbers*, vol. 2 (AnBi), (forthcoming) on Num 23:9.

22

KING LISTS OF THE OLD BABYLONIAN PERIOD AND BIBLICAL GENEALOGIES*

Biblical genealogies—especially the ethnographic tables in Genesis and the tribal genealogies assembled mainly in the first nine chapters of 1 Chronicles—represent a unique historiographical genre within the literature of the ancient Near East.[1] Only at the start of the Islamic period did Arab chronographers create such broad genealogical tables, encompassing northern and southern Arabian tribes, dwarfing in extent even their biblical archetypes.[2]

An extraordinary document containing the full genealogy of the Hammurapi dynasty (henceforth GHD), recently published by J.J. Finkelstein,[3] prompts a reassessment in this field. The Old Babylonian king list, together with the upper part of the Assyrian King List (henceforth AKL),[4] now provides further insights into the essence

* This article was originally published in W.W. Hallo (ed.), *Essays in Memory of E.A. Speiser* (*JAOS* 88, 1968), pp. 163–171, and remains here practically unchanged.

[1] On genealogies in the Bible in general, see the biblical dictionaries s.v.: e.g., *The Interpreter's Dictionary of the Bible* II, 1962, pp. 362 ff. (R.A. Bowman); *Encyclopaedia Biblica* III, 1958, cols. 663 ff. (Y. Liver; in Hebrew), with bibliographical references there. For the various interpretations of Israelite tribal genealogies, see W. Duffy, *The Tribal-Historical Theory on the Origin of the Hebrew People*, 1944. Cf. also L. Ramlot, Les généalogies bibliques, *Bible et Vie chrétienne* 60 (1964), pp. 53 ff.

[2] The basic treatment of these genealogies in relation with their biblical antecedents is still W. Robertson Smith, *Kinship and Marriage in Early Arabia*², 1903. Cf. also the most recent studies on Arabian genealogies: J. Obermann, "Early Islam," in *The Idea of History in the Ancient Near East*, 1955, especially pp. 242 ff. and 290 ff.; W. Caskel, Die Bedeutung der Beduinen in der Geschichte der Araber, *Arbeitsgemeinschaft für Forschung des Landes Nordrhein-Westfalen*, Heft 8, 1953; *idem, Ǧamharat an-nasab—Das genealogische Werk des Hišām ibn Muḥammad al-Kalbi* I–II, 1966.

[3] The Genealogy of the Hammurapi Dynasty, *JCS* 20 (1966), pp. 95–118 (hereinafter cited by page number only); for specific points see also the bibliographical references there.

[4] The first real comprehension of the upper portion of AKL was achieved by B. Landsberger, Assyrische Königsliste und "Dunkles Zeitalter," *JCS* 8 (1954), pp. 33 ff. and 109 ff. (hereinafter cited only by page number); for two subsequent comprehensive investigations, cf. F.R. Kraus, Könige, die in Zelten wohnten, *Mededelingen der koninklijke Nederlandse Akademie van Wetenschappen* (Afd. Letterkunde, N.R. 28, No. 2), 1965; H. Lewy, Assyria (2600–1816 *B.C.*), CAH I, Ch. XXV (rev. ed.), 1966, pp. 17 ff. For the two full copies of AKL extant, cf. I.J. Gelb, *JNES* 12 (1954), pp. 209 ff.

and structure of biblical genealogies. Moreover, examination of lineage systems among present-day primitive tribal societies, which have been the subject of intense anthropological study in recent years, may give a clearer picture of genealogical patterns in the ancient Near East, in spite of the different historical and sociological contexts, and especially as those societies are of an entirely illiterate nature.[5]

We should note, *a priori*, the parallel and the divergent features in the genealogical schemes of the Bible and the Mesopotamian king lists, for they define the possibilities of comparative discussion. Whereas the king lists are of an obvious vertical construction, biblical genealogies are spread out on a horizontal plane as well, exemplified for instance by the twelve tribes stemming from Jacob. Only the latter, a two-dimensional pattern, can form a true family tree, revealing a genealogical panorama of a single tribe or of an entire group of peoples. The Bible, followed by the Arabian genealogists, often resorts to accommodating female elements, wives or concubines, mothers or daughters, elements which naturally have no place in strictly vertical lineages of societies based on agnatic descent.

Vertical, one-dimensional patterns record only "genealogical depth" and sequence of generations, while the two-dimensional pattern forms points of segmentation; that is, it encompasses nodal eponyms from which stem several descendants who in turn may act as founding ancestors of peoples, tribes and clans, such as Terah, Abraham, Isaac, Jacob and his twelve sons, in the Bible. This segmentation, with its wide range of primary and secondary lineages, is the foremost concept in the genealogical positioning of the individual and in the ascertaining of kinship, whether on a broad ethnographic plane or within a more restricted tribal circle. Hence, the king lists are particularly relevant only to the study of the vertical genealogies in the Bible. However, super-imposition of the two diverging Mesopotamian lineages, Babylonian and Assyrian, renders a somewhat two-dimensional picture, thus enabling us to approach the other genealogical patterns as well.

---

[5] However, a conclusive study of this facet must be left to a combined effort with modern anthropology, for within the present discussion only casual steps have been taken in this direction. Illuminating comparative material may be gleaned from investigations of, for instance, African peoples; cf., *inter alia*, E.E. Evans-Pritchard, *The Nuer*, 1940 (especially Ch. V); M. Fortes, *The Web of Kinship among the Tallensi*, 1949 (Chs. I and II); I. Cunnison, *The Luapula Peoples of Northern Rhodesia*, 1959 (Ch. IV). Cf. also L. Bohanan, A Genealogical Charter, *Africa* 22 (1952), pp. 301 ff.; and E. Peters, The Proliferation of Lineage Segments in Cyrenaica, *Journ. Royal Anthr. Inst.* 90 (1960), pp. 29 ff.

It is now evident that the vertical genealogical compositions in the Bible stem from archetypes current among West Semitic tribes from the Old Babylonian period (and possibly earlier), antedating those of the Bible by hundreds of years. The Babylonian king list under discussion dates to the reign of Ammiṣaduqa (1646–1626 B.C., according to the middle chronology used in the present paper), the penultimate ruler of the Hammurapi dynasty. But Landsberger (cf. n. 4 above) has convincingly shown that even the upper part of AKL, preserved only in the final redaction of the list as a whole, is the work of scribes of the Old Babylonian period, more precisely of the West Semitic dynasty of Shamshi-Adad, an older contemporary of Hammurapi. Moreover, these royal genealogies were composed using a technique similar to that known in the Bible of fictitiously linking historical personages to earlier eponyms, in fact representing names of an artificial character, such as tribes or geographical entities—as demonstrated by Finkelstein concerning GHD, and Kraus for AKL.

What is more, comparison of the Babylonian and Assyrian king lists, headed by essentially identical putative eponyms, indicates a common genealogical tradition, whether historically based or of mere scribal deduction—one most likely shared by early West Semitic tribes in general. A similar consciousness of common ancestors is evident in the genealogical tables of Genesis, many of the peoples living along-side Israel being assigned within the same family tree as Israel itself. The external evidence now lends support to the assumption that the genealogical traditions contained in Genesis reflect beliefs actually current among those peoples, notions which consciously upheld their common ancestry and not the products of fancy or the pride of Israelite scribes. The self-centered Israelite approach is apparent only in its tendency to place the Israelite line at the center of the family tree, whereas the other peoples derive from it as secondary branches. (The Table of Nations in Genesis 10, which does not include Israel at all, is a matter for separate consideration.)

The upper part of AKL is divided into three sections, the first two of which will concern us in the present paper. At the start, seventeen names are given with the concluding formula "total of 17 kings who dwell in tents," followed by ten names summarized by the phrase "total of 10 kings who are ancestors." As Landsberger has proved (pp. 33 f.), this latter group is to be regarded as the "Ahnentafel" of King Shamshi-Adad. In contrast, GHD lists the generations in an uninterrupted line; at the end of the list of fictitious and historical kings, however, three *palû*'s (i.e. "eras" or "dynasties") are given by name (in historical sequence) reading: the *palû* of the Gutians, the *p.* of the Haneans, and the *p.* of the Amorites—to which all the generations listed are to be distributed, as demonstrated by Finkelstein (pp. 103–113).

Yet, to arrive at the very nature of these genealogies and to derive the most instructive lesson for the parallel biblical patterns as well, a structural analysis is called for, comparing the two king lists, Babylonian and Assyrian. Such analysis reveals four successive groups, distinct in their historiographical character and functional aim, which we may here term: (a) the genealogical stock, i.e. the common antecedent generations; (b) what we refer to as the determinative line, i.e. the specific descent of a people or dynasty; (c) the table of ancestors, the actual pedigree of (d) a concrete historical line or dynasty. These, in principle, accord with the structure of the biblical genealogies, yet such segments are not formed into a single continuous line, but are scattered in the Bible.

The genealogical stock

Group (a) includes the names at the top of the two royal lists which derive from a common basis, as Finkelstein has attempted to demonstrate. The two texts differ in order of names and in several major or minor textual variants, which are, in part, the result of faulty transmission. Moreover, the cumbersome names of the first three lines of GHD prove each to be compounded forms of two originally separate names corresponding to pairs of names in AKL. Accepting Finkelstein's analysis, the first nine to eleven names are common to both lists.[6] This is the genealogical depth of many lineages in ancient times, even as in some modern tribal societies.[7]

[6] In AKL, the problematic entries are Emṣu and ḪARṣu (Nos. 7–8) which seem to be variants of a single name corresponding to Namz/ṣū of GHD (No. 8); and Zu'abu and Nuabu (Nos. 11–12), which may or may not be equated with Zummabu and Namḫū of GHD (Nos. 10–11) (see Finkelstein, pp. 98–99). As the last equation (Nuabu-Namḫū) seems especially doubtful, the latter names are possibly to be ascribed to group (b), and would then reveal a standardized pattern of ten generations in the genealogical stock (see below).

[7] For a 10-generation depth among the Bedouin east of Damascus, cf. Caskel, *Die Bedeutung*... (above, n. 2), p. 7; for a constant 11 generations among the Bedouin of Cyrenaica (though their history may be traced as far back as the 11th century

This genealogical stock is an apparently artificial composition of personal names (such as Adamu) and appellatives or even tribal names (the most obvious examples are Ḫanū/Ḫeana and Dit/dānu) and toponyms (such as possibly Madara and Namzū), presented as putative eponyms. Most have definite affinities, whether ethnic or geographical, or even linguistic (especially the GHD forms), with the West Semitic peoples. Such lists may have been transmitted orally among these tribes as mnemotechnic accounts, such as paralleled in modern tribal genealogies; they could even have been some sort of desert chant, as suggested by Finkelstein concerning the first six names (p. 112). The fictitious stock could have easily been absorbed into the general genealogical scheme, mainly because of the fluidity in usage of personal names, tribal names and toponyms, a universal phenomenon especially frequent among West Semitic peoples in the Old Babylonian period.[8] In order to lend an authentic ring to this putative list, it was built around approximately ten generations, as a sort of retrojection of the optimal ten-generation pattern of real lineages, as found in the "Ahnentafeln" of the Babylonian and Assyrian kings, appearing later in both AKL and GHD (see group [c], below).

The character and make-up of this group immediately brings to mind the scheme of the Hebrew line (*tōlᵉdōt*) from Shem to Terah or Abraham (Gen. 11:10–26), surely to be regarded as the genealogical stock of the people of Israel, which was held in common with several other related peoples. Quite a separate matter is the genealogy from Adam to Noah (Gen. 5), comprising the universal ancestors of the antediluvian generations, beyond the realm of actual history. The compiler of GHD was also aware of an earlier era (*palū*), but he saw no need to enter its generations into his list (cf. line 32), they being of no relevance for the historical reality of the West Semitic tribes. Interestingly enough, the biblical name of the progenitor of mankind, Adam, is paralleled by the second name in AKL,[9] and possibly the

A.D.), cf. M. Gluckman, *Politics, Law and Ritual in Tribal Society*, 1965, p. 272 (citing Peters, *op. cit.* [above, n. 5]), and pp. 271–275 for African (quoting several works mentioned above, n. 5) and other tribal lineages of 10- to 12-generation depth.

[8] J.R. Kupper, *Les nomades en Mésopotamie au temps des rois de Mari*, 1957, pp. 215 ff., gives several examples including Numḫā (compare Namḫū, GHD No. 11), a West Semitic tribal and geographical name, as well as an element in personal names.

[9] As alluded to by A. Poebel in the initial treatment of AKL: *JNES* 1 (1942), p. 253. For the personal name Adamu in the Old Akkadian period, see I.J. Gelb, *Glossary of Old Akkadian*, 1957, p. 19, and in the Old Babylonian period, C.J. Gadd, *Iraq* 4 (1937), p. 35.

fourth in GHD. This name may have actually been borrowed from early West Semitic genealogical concepts and applied in the Bible at the beginning of the primordial line, out of etymological considerations; for in Hebrew *ʾādām* is also the generic term for "man," there being a play on the word *ʾᵃdāmā* "ground" in Gen. 2:7—"And the Lord God formed man (*ʾādām*) of the dust of the ground (*ʾᵃdāmā*)." The ante- and postdiluvian lines (i.e. of Adam and of Shem, respectively), symmetrically arranged to a ten-generation depth, are undoubtedly the product of intentional harmonization and in imitation of the concrete genealogical model (cf. Mishnah Aboth 5:2).

Though according to the Massoretic version the line from Shem to Abraham embraces ten generations, there are various indications of possible minor fluctuations in the original scheme of this group.[10] On the one hand, Shem or Abraham, or possibly both, were not initially included within the genealogical stock. The former may have been appended as a heading to join the Hebrew line to the Table of Nations and the primordial accounts in Genesis, Arpachshad having originally headed the list. We may also assume that the list in fact concluded with Terah, to whom the Bible ascribes a line (*tōlᵉdōt*) of his own (Gen. 11:27), whereas his three sons, Abraham, Nahor, and Haran, the father of Lot, were conceived of as the founding ancestors of individual lineages. On the other hand, the Septuagint (cf. also Luke 3:35) inserts an additional link between Arpachshad and Shelah—Kenan, a tradition also reflected in the Table of Nations in the Book of Jubilees (8:1 ff.).

Moreover, the name Arpachshad is linguistically and ethnographically puzzling, and differs from the other names in Shem's line, which are short and comprised of a single name element. We most likely have here a fused form of two names, just as with the initial entries in GHD, the parallel becoming even more obvious if we assume that Arpachshad once stood at the head of the line. Indeed, already in ancient times (cf. Jubilees 9:4; Josephus, *Antiquities* I, 6:4) there was a tendency, shared by modern exegetes, to identify the second element in Arpachshad with Chesed, the Chaldeans.

Like its Mesopotamian archetype, the line of Shem also contains

---

[10] For particulars on this line, which is attributed to the P source, like most of the Pentateuchal genealogical records, cf. the commentaries, especially O. Procksch, *Die Genesis*$^{2-3}$, 1924, pp. 492 ff.; B. Jacob, *Genesis*, 1934, pp. 304 ff.; and U. Cassuto, *From Noah to Abraham*, (English ed.), 1964, pp. 250 ff.

a mixture of appellatives, tribal names, and toponyms, all in the guise of patriarchal eponyms. Among the appellatives we may include Shem, for its meaning in Hebrew, as in the Akkadian cognate, is simply "name," or "reputation," "posterity."[11] Most likely appellative, too, is Peleg, "a division," at least on the basis of the etymology given in the Bible—"for in his days was the earth divided (*niphl^{e}gā*)" (Gen. 10:25), though there has been an attempt to relate the name with *Phalga* on the middle Euphrates, a place name known from Hellenistic times. The outstanding tribal name is Eber, a personification derived from the gentilicon *ʿib̲rī*, "Hebrew" (see below, n. 14), and surely not the other way around. Another possible tribal name is Reu, a compound form of which, Reuel, constitutes a sub-tribe in the genealogy of Edom (Gen. 36 *passim*), as well as of Midian (Num. 10:29; LXX Gen. 25:3).[12]

The three last links in the line of Shem—Serug, Nahor and Terah—stand out as topographical entries, all three signifying locations in the Balikh region and the north-western tributary of the Habur and attested in neo-Assyrian documents as Sarūgi, Til-Naḫiri, and Til-(ša)-Turaḫi.[13] Only the city Nahor/Naḫur was known as an important political center already in the 19th–18th centuries B.C. in texts from Cappadocia, Chagar Bazar and, above all, in the Mari documents, where it appears as a focal point of West Semitic tribes as well. The proximity of the three sites to Haran associates these eponyms with the ancestral home, according to biblical tradition, of the Hebrews; this is the special significance of their insertion within the genealogical stock.

As with the Mesopotamian parallel, here too, putative compilation was facilitated by onomastic and toponymic affiliation, that is, identity of personal, clan or tribal names, and of geographic locations, a phenomenon common enough in the Bible as well. Thus, the name Eber, which in the Israelite mind had a geographic connotation associated

[11] The suggested derivation of Shem from Shumer (with the final syllable silent), reintroduced by S.N. Kramer, *Studia Biblica et Orientalia* III (Analecta Biblica 12), 1959, pp. 203 f., does not seem plausible.

[12] In the latter connection, W.F. Albright, *CBQ* 25 (1963), pp. 5 f., has shown that Reuel is the Midianite clan-name of Hobab, and not the name of his actual father.

[13] Cf., in addition to the commentaries mentioned in n. 10 above, W.F. Albright, *From Stone Age to Christianity*[2], 1957, pp. 236 f., and R. de Vaux, *RB* 55 (1948), pp. 323 f. On Nahor, in the cuneiform sources as well as in the Bible, see A. Malamat, *Encyclopaedia Biblica* V, s.v. cols. 805 ff. (Hebrew). The component *Til-* in these and other place-names of the Neo-Assyrian period, may be an Aramean-Assyrian appendage to older names of sites which had been re-established in this period.

with *ʿēḇer hannāhār*, "beyond the river," where "in days of old your fathers lived" (Josh. 24:2), is found in the Bible also as a clan or personal name (Neh. 12:20; 1 Chron. 5:13; 8:12, 22). Again, Nahor serves both as the eponym of the Nahorites (Gen. 22:20–24), and as the name of the "city of Nahor" (Gen. 24:10). Moreover, this phenomenon is clearly displayed in the account of the genealogy of Cain, relating in the founding of the first city, that Cain "called . . . after the name of his son, Enoch" (Gen. 4:17). But Enoch is also the name of a clan in the tribe of Midian (Gen. 25:4), as well as in the tribe of Reuben (Gen. 46:9). The same is true in many other instances, such as the name Dan, which is eponymic, tribal and topographic, in the last instance applied to the town of Laish after its conquest by the Danites: "And they called the name of their city Dan after the name of Dan their father, who was born unto Israel" (Judg. 18:29).

However, comparison of the Mesopotamian and the biblical genealogical stocks is of special interest concerning the respective eponyms Ḫanū and Eber, both representing actual historic entities well-known even to the later redactors of the lists. The insertion of these eponyms among the antecedent generations undoubtedly represents a prevailing attitude on the antiquity of these tribes, as GHD actually indicates in ranking "the *palū* of the Haneans" earlier than "the *p.* of the Amorites," and implies an awareness of putative relation with subsequent entries. However, this latter does not necessarily have bearing on true ethnic kinship of subsequent generations, as GHD may serve to show. Whereas the Shamshi-Adad dynasty of Assyria in effect likely stemmed from the Hanean tribal association, this does not hold for the Babylonian dynasty, which was closely related with the Amnānu and Yaḫruru tribes, as indicated in its determinative line in GHD (group [b]) and various other sources. Yet, these latter tribes, as is evidenced in the Mari documents, were part of a tribal association other than the Haneans: their frequent rivals, the Yaminites (see below note 17).

Thus, the mention of the eponym Ḫeana (Ḫanū) in the lineage of the kings of Babylon conflicts with actual ethno-historic reality. But the compilers of GHD took no objection to this obvious discrepancy, indicating the actual contrast only by accommodating the determinative Babylonian line (group [b]) within the *palū* of the Amorites, as against the *palū* of the Haneans, which embraces the latter part of the genealogical stock (group [a]), from Ḫeana on.

The above conclusions are instructive concerning the relation between the eponym Eber and the concept "Hebrew." Eber, too, may have in reality been linked with only this branch or that, and did not necessarily envelop *all* the generations following it. Indeed, the empiric use of the term "Hebrew" (which occurs some thirty times in the Bible) is of a definite ethnic nature, applying only to the people of Israel, as has rightly been noted by several scholars dealing with this problem.[14] Moreover, as widely recognized, this term is specifically used to denote the Israelites as such in their confrontation with other peoples (thus against the Egyptians, Philistines and Canaanites). Hence, anyone assuming that the biblical term "Hebrew" embraces a circle wider than the Israelites alone, a view based mainly on the appearance of the eponym Eber six generations prior to Abraham, must bear the *onus probandi*.

The other descendants of Eber, such as the Nahorites or even the "sons" of Lot, were not necessarily considered as actual Hebrews, whether by self-definition or otherwise. The direct grafting to Eber of far-away tribes of the South Arabian region, represented by Joktan and his descendants in the Table of Nations (Gen. 10:25 ff.), is elusive. The only eponym expressly bearing the designation "Hebrew" is Abraham. Much has been speculated regarding the precise meaning of the phrase "Abraham the Hebrew" (Gen. 14:13), but even with all the shades of meaning attributed to this phrase,[15] its major intent is obviously to single out Abraham as the founder of the determinative line (group [b]) of the Israelite genealogy. There is no indication that any other people related to Abraham but not of the direct Israelite line was "Hebrew" (i.e. the "sons" of Keturah, the Ishmaelites and the Edomites).

This state of affairs is similar to the Mesopotamian context: Shamshi-Adad was regarded as a Hanean in contrast to the kings of Babylon, just as the rulers of the local dynasty at Mari actually adopted the

[14] Among others, B. Landsberger, *Kleinasiatische Forschungen* 1 (1930), pp. 329 ff.; de Vaux, *op. cit.* (above, n. 13), pp. 337 ff.; and especially M. Greenberg, *The Hab/piru*, 1955, pp. 91 ff. The various proposed etymologies of the term *ʿibrī*, and its even more intricate relationship with Ḫab/piru-ʾApiru (cf. the bibliography in the last mentioned work), are beyond the scope of the present paper.

[15] The two most recent major studies are W.F. Albright, Abraham the Hebrew, *BASOR* 163 (1961), pp. 36 ff., regarding *ʿibrī*, like Egyptian *ʿApiru*, as a "donkey driver," "caravaneer"; and especially N.A. van Uchelen, *Abraham de Hebreeër*, 1964, which reviews the history of interpretation of our passage, from LXX on, van Uchelen himself stressing the military aspect of the term here, typifying Abraham as a warrior-hero. This same facet is interestingly also often found in the term Ḫana of the Mari documents. E.A. Speiser regards Gen. 14 as a Hebrew adaptation of an Akkadian source, seeing in Abraham a Ḫabiru warrior; see his *Genesis*, 1964, pp. 102 ff.

titulary "king of Ḫana," while the rulers of the Old Babylonian dynasty at Uruk were apparently referred to as kings (of the tribe) of Amnānu, as attested in regard to two of them.[16] Thus finds expression the concept of the specific determinative line. We cannot be far off in assuming that, had we possession of the genealogical tables of the two latter dynasties (i.e. of Mari and Uruk), Ḫanū would most likely be found among the earlier eponyms (group [a]) in both, in spite of the ethnic affinity of the Uruk dynasty. Another parallel use of the terms "Hanean" and "Hebrew" is revealed in their application in a geographical-territorial context, signifying the main areas of ultimate sedentation of these originally nomadic tribes. Thus, the Mari documents refer to the middle Euphrates region as "the land of Ḫana" (*māt Ḫana*), whereas in the Bible the land of Canaan (or a part thereof) is once called "the land of the Hebrews" (Gen. 40:15).

The further genealogical line

Group (b): The determinative line

We include in this group the generations bridging the common genealogical stock with the tables of ancestors; in the Mesopotamian lists these determine the pedigrees culminating in the founders of the West Semitic dynasties in Babylon and Assyria (i.e. Sumuabum and Shamshi-Adad, respectively). Finkelstein has convincingly shown that, while the pedigree of Sumuabum actually starts with Ipti-yamūta (No. 14), the latter's two "ancestors," Amnānu and Yaḫruru (Nos. 12 and 13), serve to determine the national affiliation of the Babylonian line (pp. 111–112). As already noted, these latter were West Semitic, basically nomadic tribes; thus, if we were to label the Babylonian lineage up to Ipti-yamūta, in terms employed by AKL, the phrase "total of 13 kings who dwell in tents" would be most appropriate.

The determinative Babylonian line may illuminate the controversial

[16] I.e., Sīnkāshid and one of his grandsons (either Sīngāmil or Ilumgāmil); see A. Falkenstein, *Baghdader Mitteilungen* 2 (1963), pp. 22 ff. Moreover, an obscure passage in a letter of king Anam of Uruk to Sinmuballiṭ of Babylon (col. III, l. 40—*ibid.*, pp. 58, 62, 70) evidently points to a special connection between Uruk and the Amnānu. However, Falkenstein has raised doubts as to whether the Uruk dynasty truly stemmed from the Amnānu, or for that matter whether it was West Semitic altogether. Cf. also the review of the above by F.R. Kraus, *BiOr* 22 (1965), pp. 287 ff.

subject of the origin and meaning of the term DUMU.MEŠ-*yamina*, i.e. "sons of the South," found in the Mari documents, and there only, as a designation for a broad tribal confederation, the Amnānu and Yaḫruru comprising its main elements.[17] The grafting of the Babylonian table of ancestors to the latter tribes indicates that Yaminite groups had become entrenched in southern Mesopotamia already long before Yaḫdunlim (c. 1825–1810 B.C.) and Shamshi-Adad (c. 1815–1782 B.C.)—the respective founders of the West Semitic dynasties in Mari and Assyria. In Babylon the Yaminites achieved political independence some three generations prior to the above rulers, namely, in the days of Sumuabum (c. 1894–1881 B.C.), whereas at Uruk the special ties of the Amnānu with the ruling dynasty go back to the time of king Sīnkāshid (c. 1865–1833 B.C.; see above, n. 16). Thus, it would seem that the term DUMU.MEŠ-*yamina*, used by the Mari authorities and perhaps even coined by them, may have been applied originally to these tribal units for they had already become a decisive historical factor in the regions to the *south*, from the viewpoint of Mari.[18]

As for AKL, the determinative genealogical line embraces, according to our present analysis, the names from Abazu to Apiashal (Nos. 13–17); that is, the last five generations of "the 17 kings dwelling in tents." In contrast to the parallel section in GHD, the names here in AKL are obscure and not of a tribal character, but rather seem to be proper names. They are unknown from any other source, except for the name Ushpia (No. 16), mentioned in late Assyrian royal inscriptions

[17] On this tribal association and its sub-groups, see Kupper, *op. cit.* (above, n. 8), ch. II: Les Benjaminites. It should be noted that Amnānu and Yaḫruru together are explicitly designated as Yaminites only in *ARM* III, 50, ll. 10–13 (and not in the oft-quoted passage in *ARM* I, 42, ll. 30–31), as is the former alone in Yaḫdunlim's Foundation Inscription, col. III, ll. 6 ff. (in ll. 17 and 21 DUMU-*mi-im* surely represents an abbreviated form of the term Yaminites). See my "Aspects of Tribal Societies in Mari and Israel," *XVe Rencontre assyr. internat.*, Université de Liège, 1967, p. 137, n. 1, for the various readings of DUMU.MEŠ-*yamina*.

[18] Admittedly, the Yaminites as such are referred to throughout the Mari documents as being only in the regions to the north and west of Mari, where they were still pursuing a (semi-)nomadic life. In contrast to important groups of urbanized Yaminites to the south, these gained mention in the documents through their continual conflict with the Mari authorities. On the other hand, A. Parrot, in *Abraham et son temps*, 1962, pp. 45 f., has doubtfully suggested that the name Yaminites indicates that this tribal grouping originated in southern Mesopotamia, from whence it penetrated northward at an early period. The DUMU.MEŠ-*sim'al*, i.e. "sons of the north," were, of course, always located much farther to the north, namely in the upper Habur and Balikh valleys.

as an early Assyrian king who founded the national sanctuary in the city of Ashur.[19] It is doubtful whether Ushpia was inserted in the list, as suggested by Mrs. H. Lewy, in order to indicate the transition from nomadic life to permanent settlement in Ashur, for he is definitely included among the "kings dwelling in tents," and he is not even the last of these. More probably, an early historical Assyrian king was purposely inserted here in the determinative line of AKL in order to lend it further authenticity.

Group (c): Table of ancestors

While in GHD the table of ancestors may be deduced only indirectly, on the basis of the seeming authenticity of the personal names preceding Sumuabum, in AKL this group appears as a separate section concluding with the rubric "10 kings who are *ancestors*" (see above, p. 219). In the latter list, however, the generations are given in reverse order; that is, in ascending generations. In reality, we should detach the first generation from this table, i.e. Apiashal (son of Ushpia), whose name is not West Semitic, in contrast to all the other names in this group, for he also appears earlier in the genealogical list (No. 17) and is repeated here only to tie up with the former section. Shamshi-Adad should then be appended at the end of the table of ancestors as the tenth name, for this pedigree, beginning now with Ḫalē (No. 18), is actually his (see the Table at the end of this article).

Of special note is the fact that the parallel group in GHD, i.e. from Ipti-yamūta to Sumuabum (Nos. 14–23), also includes exactly ten entries. Thus we may assume that the ideal pattern of an "Ahnentafel" was based on a constant genealogical depth of ten generations. From the viewpoint of the genealogical pattern, it was immaterial whether this aim was achieved by means of integrating even fictitious names (such as, possibly, the pair of rhymed names Yakmesi-Yakmeni, Nos. 22–23 in AKL), in the lack of fuller knowledge of actual ancestors; or by means of entries such as Aminu (AKL, No. 26), evidently Shamshi-Adad's brother, not father (who is definitely known as Ila-kabkabu, both from a remark in AKL proper and from other sources), though

[19] See Landsberger, p. 109, n. 206. According to H. Lewy, *op. cit.* (above, n. 4), pp. 18 f., Ushpia reigned before the mid-third millennium B.C., but the dating of this king to the end of the Third Dynasty of Ur or thereabouts seems preferable; cf. W.W. Hallo, *JNES* 15 (1956), pp. 220 f.

Aminu apparently preceded Shamshi-Adad to the throne (Landsberger, p. 34).

The nine ancestors of Sumuabum and of Shamshi-Adad, who lived in the 20th and 19th centuries B.C. at places unknown to us,[20] were tribal chieftains who may even have adopted the title "king," like those in the middle Euphrates region mentioned in the inscriptions of Yaḫdunlim from Mari: "7 kings, fathers (*abū*) of Ḫana" (Disc Inscription, col. I, ll. 15–16); and three Yaminite "kings" named with their regal cities and tribal territories (Foundation Inscription, col. III, ll. 4–10). The actual rulers who reigned in the city of Ashur proper during the period of Shamshi-Adad's forebears were accommodated by the compiler of AKL between Aminu and Shamshi-Adad. The first of these, Sulili, is listed as Aminu's son, a seemingly fictitious linkage with the previous section. These kings, most of whom are attested to in other sources, should be regarded as a line more or less synchronous with the "Ahnentafel" of Shamshi-Adad, and thus not to be included within his actual pedigree (and consequently omitted in the Table at the end of this article).[21]

The above analysis clarifies the underlying structure of the royal Mesopotamian genealogies. Tables of ancestors containing ten generations were appended to the universal stock by means of transitional links—our determinative line. Here, the difference in span of the respective determinative lines is highly instructive, five entries in AKL as against two in GHD (or six as against three if the eponyms Nuabu and Namḫū, respectively, are to be detached from the genealogical stock and joined to the following section; see above, n. 6).

This difference of three generations is not, evidently, incidental but rather the outcome of the structure of the genealogical scheme as described, and reflects the true chronological gap existing between

[20] Only the immediate predecessors of Shamshi-Adad can be assumed to have ruled in the city of Terqa near the confluence of the Habur river; see Landsberger, p. 35, n. 26. This same city may have also been the ancestral home of the Mari dynasty, as indicated by a letter to king Zimrilim urging that the *kispu* rites honoring the manes of his father Yaḫdunlim be performed there (*ARM* III, 40); cf. A. Malamat, Prophecy in the Mari Documents, *Eretz-Israel* 4 (1956), p. 76 (Hebrew).

[21] For an attempted reconstruction of the two parallel lines, cf. Hallo, *op. cit.* (above, n. 19), p. 221, n. 9, which we may accept with some reservation: Apiashal and Sulili, respectively opening and closing the Ahnentafel of Shamshi-Adad (Hallo's left-hand column) should be removed to the top of the line of "real" kings of Ashur (Hallo's right-hand column), following Ushpia (cf. Landsberger, p. 33). Mrs. Lewy's conjecture (*op. cit.* [above, n. 4], p. 20) that Shamshi-Adad's Ahnentafel is in fact to be ascribed to Sulili is hardly acceptable.

the foundation of the two West Semitic dynasties, in Babylon (start of 19th cent. B.C.) and in Assyria (end of 19th cent. B.C.). As Finkelstein has already demonstrated (pp. 109 ff.), the two dynastic lists, in spite of the artificiality of many of the names, rely on chronological-historical traditions and on more or less reliable calculations of generations. The surprising chronological harmony between the two lists is evident from the fact that Shamshi-Adad and his Babylonian contemporary, Sīnmuballiṭ the father of Hammurapi, both occupy the same respective numerical position, that is, the twenty-seventh. However, we have noted above (p. 168) concerning the two dynastic founders, that Sumuabum (No. 23) preceded Shamshi-Adad by some three generations (though he was the fourth king before Sīnmuballiṭ). Now, if the respective scribes of the two lists began their reckoning from one and the same common stock, and since the table of ancestors of the dynastic founders was based on a constant ten-generation depth, the cancelling out of the above chronological discrepancy was achieved by means of appropriate additions to the Assyrian determinative line.

The royal genealogies of Israel

In dealing with the generations subsequent to the basic stock, comparative treatment of the data in the Bible and the Mesopotamian archetypes is a more complicated matter, forcing us, *inter alia*, to reconstruct the biblical lineages from scattered materials, sometimes even resorting to sources of a narrative nature. The determinative lineage defining the people of Israel comprises the series of the three Patriarchs—Abraham, Isaac and Jacob, whereas, e.g., Abraham-Isaac-Esau specifies the Edomites, and the eponyms Haran and Lot, the Ammonites and the Moabites, respectively. But intramural Israelite usage demands an additional eponym following the basic patriarchal scheme, representing one of the twelve tribes, such as Judah, Benjamin, etc., to complete the determinative line. Ultimately, these four generations determine each and every Israelite lineage.

However, these individual lineages, which are to be regarded as the "tables of ancestors," are of a problematic character. On the one hand, the initial generations represent, as a rule, a graduated, intra-tribal classification—sub-tribe, clan, family. On the other hand, the lineages are normally selective, telescoping generations here and there similar to modern tribal genealogies, and thus depriving them of true chronological value.[22] A case in point is the lineage of Moses (third generation from Levi—Ex. 6:16–20) as against that of his younger contemporary Joshua (ninth, or possibly tenth, generation from Joseph—1 Chron. 7:22–27).

For sake of comparison with GHD and AKL, we must ascertain as closely as possible the ideal genealogical model within the corpus of biblical genealogies. There seems to be no more suitable parallel than the lineage of David, founder of the venerable dynasty of Judah, which was surely compiled and transmitted with the utmost care.[23] Whereas David's line of successors is given in 1 Chron. 3, his "table of ancestors" may easily be recognized as a distinct entity among the many branches of the tribe of Judah (see 1 Chron. 2:5, 9–15). The same "table of ancestors" has been appended to the Book of Ruth as well (4:18–22).[24] Both of these sources seemingly derive from an earlier genealogical document, as implied also in the heading "Now this is the line (*tōlᵉdōt*) of Perez" (Ruth 4:18) to the lineage: Perez (the son of Judah)-Hezron-Ram-Amminadab-Nahshon-Salmon (Salma)-Boaz-Obed-Jesse-David.

It is most interesting that, here again, a "table of ancestors" contains exactly ten generations, even though this depth is much too shallow to fill the time-span between the "Patriarchal period" and the time of David.[24a] This discrepancy is also apparent from the fact that Nahshon son of Amminadab is placed in the fifth generation before David, whereas according to biblical tradition he was a tribal head of Judah in the days of the Exodus (cf. Ex. 6:23; Num. 1:7; 2:3; 1 Chron. 2:10), some two hundred-fifty years before David. Moreover, in keeping with the abovementioned principle of gentilic classification,

---

[22] See the recent pointed remarks of D.N. Freedman, in *The Bible and the Ancient Near East* (ed. G.E. Wright), 1961, pp. 206 f., and K.A. Kitchen, *Ancient Orient and Old Testament*, 1966, pp. 54 ff., both citing various examples, especially from the Exodus–Numbers cycle.

[23] A similar practice is found among modern tribal lineages, e.g. the Luapula of Rhodesia where the royal line is preserved at a 9-generation depth, as against the telescoped commoner lineages which embrace only 4 to 7 generations; cf. I. Cunnison, History and Genealogies in a Conquest State, *American Anthropologist* 59 (1957), pp. 20 ff. (especially p. 27).

[24] See the commentaries on Chronicles by J.W. Rothstein – J. Hänel, *Das erste Buch der Chronik*, 1927, pp. 18, 44; W. Rudolph, *Chronikbücher*, 1955, p. 16; J.M. Myers, *I Chronicles*, 1965, pp. 13 f.; and on Ruth by W. Rudolph, *Das Buch Ruth*, 1962, pp. 71 f.

[24a] But note some 20 generations from Levi to Samuel, David's older contemporary, in the fuller, though suspicious, genealogy of Heman in I Chron. 6:18–23 (= 33–38 in the English version).

the compiler of this table resorted in the first two or three generations to eponyms personifying well-known tribal groups within Judah (Perez, Hezron and possibly also Ram).

In short, David's table of ancestors is largely an artificial construction formed on an ideal, traditional model, as befitting royal lineage. David's lineage (group [c]) links up with the eponym Judah in the determinative Israelite line (group [b]), which in turn is tied to the genealogical stock (group [a]), i.e., the line of Shem. Indeed, the entire reconstructed genealogical line, like the continuous Mesopotamian king lists, is brought forth in the New Testament, within the pedigree of Jesus, which was traced back through David (from Abraham to David in Matthew 1:3–6, and from David to Adam, in ascending order, in Luke 3:31–38).

As with the Davidic dynasty, the Bible gives the genealogy of the house of Saul, the first Israelite king, of the tribe of Benjamin. Yet Saul's "table of ancestors" has been preserved only in an incomplete form, and then in two conflicting traditions. His immediate ancestors are included in an appendix to the genealogy of the tribe of Benjamin in 1 Chron. 8:29 ff., with a duplicate, but slightly tampered-with version in 1 Chron. 9:35 ff.[25] The latter gives the line as: Jeïel ("the father of [the city of] Gibeon")-Ner-Kish-Saul. The linkage of the house of Saul with the Israelite settlement in Gibeon is strange in itself, for Saul's family stemmed from the city of Gibeah of Benjamin. This tie is seemingly artificial, as evidenced also in the Massoretic text of 1 Chron. 8, an apparently more reliable version where Ner is lacking among the sons of the "father of Gibeon" (v. 30). Ner appears only in v. 33, at the head of Saul's line.

Another genealogical tradition, fuller and more revealing, opens the cycle of the Saul stories in I Sam. 9:1.[26] Unlike the genealogical lists, and as in narrative and historiographical usage, the sequence of generations here ascends, like the table of ancestors of Shamshi-Adad; that is, "Kish (father of Saul), son of Abiel, son of Zeror, son of Bechorath, son of Aphiah, son of a (Ben)jaminite." Here, the name of Ner, father of Kish and grandfather of Saul, has been omitted, as

---

[25] See the commentaries on Chronicles in the previous note: Rothstein-Hänel, pp. 165 ff.; Rudolph, pp. 80 f.; Myers, p. 62.

[26] In addition to the references in n. 25, where the relation between the two traditions is dealt with, see S.R. Driver, *Notes on the Hebrew Text of the Books of Samuel*², 1913, pp. 68 f.; M.Z. Segal, *The Books of Samuel*, 1956, p. 65 (Hebrew).

against the list in Chronicles and the fragment of the family record of Saul (1 Sam. 14:50–51).[27] It is also difficult here to draw the dividing-line between Saul's actual ancestors and the fictitious eponyms personifying sub-tribal groups within Benjamin. Yet it is almost certain that Bechorath, the fifth generation (including Ner) before Saul, already represents Becher, one of the major Benjaminite clans (Gen. 46:21; 1 Chron. 7:6, 8: and cf. 2 Sam. 20:1).[28] However, Bechorath's father Aphiah, who is otherwise unknown, could hardly be the immediate link with the eponym Benjamin. The unusual formulation "Aphiah, son of (Ben)jaminite (*ben īš yᵉmīnī*)" would indicate that at least one antecedent (the unnamed "Benjaminite") is missing before reaching the determinative line.

A comparative table of the parallel genealogical structures underlying the Israelite and Mesopotamian royal lines[29] is given on page 234.

---

27 This last passage can only read as translated in the King James Version and rightly interpreted by Rudolph, *Chronikbücher* (above, n. 24), p. 81: "And the name of the captain of his (i.e. Saul's) host was Abner, the son of Ner, Saul's uncle; and Kish was the father of Saul; and Ner the father of Abner was the son of Abiel." That is, Abner (and not Ner) was Saul's uncle and the brother of Kish, and Abner and Kish both were sons of Ner and grandsons of Abiel. Any other interpretation would require textual emendation.

28 Thus already B. Luther, *ZAW* 21 (1901), p. 55; and Segal, *loc. cit.* (above, n. 26). One of Becher's sons, Abijah (1 Chron. 7:8), is possibly to be identified with the above-mentioned Abiel (with an exchange of the theophoric element).

29 Another interesting point in GHD possibly bearing on the Bible can only be noted here. Finkelstein has shown that the final passage in GHD, dealing with mortuary offerings for the manes of royal ancestors, etc., gives the raison d'être for the entire document. The text seems to have been inherently involved in the *kispu* ceremonies honoring the past generations of the royal line, held on the day of the new moon (pp. 113 ff., 117). In 1 Sam. 20, it is related that Saul held a feast on the new moon (vss. 5, 18 ff.), while David was to have returned to Bethlehem, his home, to participate in family sacrifices (vss. 6, 29). Could these gatherings, held at ancestral homes, have been the occasion on which genealogical accounts were employed to invoke the names of dead ancestors, as has been assumed for the *kispu* ritual held by the Babylonian and Assyrian dynasties?

COMPARATIVE STRUCTURAL TABLE OF ROYAL GENEALOGIES

	BABYLONIA	ASSYRIA	ISRAEL	
	(Sumuabum) (GHD)*	(Shamshi-Adad) (AKL)	(David)	(Saul)
Group (a) Genealogical Stock	Ara(m/Ḫarḫar) (1)	Ṭudiya (1)	Shem	
	Madara (2)	Adamu (2)	Arpa//chshad	
	Tu(b)ti(ya) (3)	Yangi (3)	(Kenan)	
	(Y)amuta/Atamu (4)	Sa/i/uḫlamu (4)	Shelah	
	Yamqu (5)	Ḫarḫaru (5)	Eber	
	Suḫ(ḫa)la(m)ma (6)	Mandaru (6)	Peleg	
	Ḫeana (7)	Emṣu (7)	Reu	
	Namz/ṣū (8)	ḪARṣu (8)	Serug	
	Ditānu (9)	Didānu (9)	Nahor	
	Zummabu (10)	Ḫanū (10)	Terah	
	Namḫū (11)	Zu'abu (11)		
		Nuabu (12)		
Group (b) Determinative Line	Amnānu (12)	Abazu (13)	Abraham	
	Yaḫrurum (13)	Bēlū (14)	Isaac	
		Azaraḫ (15)	Jacob	
		Ušpiya (16)		
		Apiašal (17)	Judah	Benjamin
Group (c) Table of Ancestors	Ipti-yamūta (14)	Ḫalē (18)	Perez	—
	Buḫazum (15)	Samanu (19)	Hezron	—
	Su-malika (16)	Ḫayanu (20)	Ram	X (a Benjaminite)
	Ašmadu (17)	Ilu-mer (21)	Amminadab	Aphiah
	Abi-yamūta (18)	Yakmesi (22)	Nahshon	Bechorath
	Abi-ditan (19)	Yakmeni (23)	Salma	Zeror
	Ma-am (?)-x-x-x (20)	Yazkur-ēl (24)	Boaz	Abiel
	Šu-x-ni (?)-x (21)	Ila-kabkaku (25)	Obed	<Ner>
	Dad (banaya [?]) (22)	Aminu (26)	Jesse	Kish
	Sumuabum (23)	Shamshi-Adad (27)	David	Saul
Group (d) Historical Line	(Sumula'ē) (24)	(etc.)	(etc.)	(etc.)
	(Zābium) (25)			
	(Apil-Sīn) (26)			
	(Sīn-muballiṭ) (27)			
	(Ḫammurapi) (28)			
	(etc.)			

* (Cf. Finkelstein, p. 114).

ABBREVIATIONS

AÉM	*Archives épistolaires de Mari*
AfO	*Archiv für Orientforschung*
AHw	W. von Soden, *Akkadisches Handwörterbuch*, I–III, Wiesbaden, 1965–81
AIPHOS	*Annuaire de l'Institute de Philologie et d'Histoire Orientales et Slaves*
AJA	*American Journal for Archaeology*
AnBi, AB	Anchor Bible
ANEP	J.B. Pritchard, *The Ancient Near East in Pictures*, Princeton
ANET	J.B. Pritchard, *Ancient Near Eastern Texts Relating to the Old Testament*[3], Princeton, 1969
AnSt	*Anatolian Studies*
AOAT	*Alter Orient und Altes Testament*
AoF	*Altorientalische Forschungen*
ARI	*Assyrian Royal Inscriptions*
ARM, ARMT	*Archives Royales de Mari* (*transcrite et traduite*); see List of *Archives Royales de Mari*, p. 240
AS	*Assyriological Studies*
AT	D.J. Wiseman, *The Alalakh Tablets*, London, 1953
BA	*Biblical Archaeologist*
BaM	*Baghdader Mitteilungen*
BASOR	*Bulletin of the American Schools of Oriental Research*
BBAO	*Berliner Beiträge zum Alten Orient*
BDB	F. Brown, S.R. Driver, C.A. Briggs, *A Hebrew and English Lexicon of the Old Testament*, Oxford, repr. 1959
Bib	*Biblica*
BIN	*Babylonian Inscriptions*, Collection J.B. Nies
BiOr	*Bibliotheca Orientalis*
BK	*Biblischer Kommentar*
BZAW	*Beihefte zur Zeitschrift für die alttestamentliche Wissenschaft*
CAD	*Chicago Assyrian Dictionary*
CAH	*Cambridge Ancient History*, I–II, 3rd ed., Cambridge, 1970–75
CBQ	*Catholic Biblical Quarterly*
CTH	*Catalogue des textes hittites*
EA	*El-Amarna*
EAEHL	M. Avi-Yonah, E. Stern (eds.), *Encyclopaedia of Archaeological Excavations in the Holy Land*, Jerusalem, 1975–78
EAMr	W.L. Moran, *The Amarna Letters*, Baltimore, 1992
EI, ErIs	*Eretz Israel*
FAOS	*Freiburger Altorientalische Studien*
FHWB	J. Friedrich, *Hettitisches Wörterbuch*
FS	Festschrift (Jubilee Volume)
GAG	*Grundriss der Akkadischen Grammatick*, Roma, 1952
GGA	*Göttingische gelehrte Anzeigen*
GLECS	*Comptes Rendus du groupe linguistique d'études Chamito-Sémitiques*
HAL(AT)	L. Köhler, W. Baumgartner, J.J. Stamm, *Hebräisches und aramäisches Lexicon zum Alten Testament*, Leiden, 1967–95
HT(h)R	*Harvard Theological Review*
HUCA	*Hebrew Union College Annual*

ICC	*International Critical Commentary*
IDB	*Interpreter's Dictionary of the Bible*
IEJ	*Israel Exploration Journal*
JAOS	*Journal of the American Oriental Society*
JCS	*Journal of Cuneiform Studies*
JESHO	*Journal of the Economic and Social History of the Orient*
JHS	*Journal of Hellenic Studies*
JJS	*Journal of Jewish Studies*
JNES	*Journal of Near Eastern Studies*
JNSL	*Journal of Northwest Semitic Languages*
JRAS	*Journal of the Royal Asiatic Society*
JSOT	*Journal for the Study of the Old Testament*
JSOTS	*Journal for the Study of the Old Testament, Supplements*
JSS	*Journal of Semitic Studies*
KA	F.H. Weissbach, *Die Keilschrifttexte der Achämeniden*, 1911
KAI	H. Donner, W. Röllig (eds.) *Kanaanäische und aramäische Inschriften*, I–III, Wiesbaden, 1962–64
KAR	*Keilschrifttexte aus Assur religiösen Inhalts*
KS	*Kleine Schriften*
LAPO	*Littératures anciennes du Proche-Orient*
MARI	*Mari Annales Recherches Interdisciplinaires*
MDOG	*Mitteilungen der Deutschen Orient Gesellschaft*, Berlin
MEE	*Materiali Epigrafici di Ebla*
MEIE	A. Malamat, *Mari and the Early Israelite Experience*, Oxford, 1989 (repr. 1992)
MSL	B. Landsberger, *Materialen zum Sumerischen Lexicon*, Roma
NAB	St. Langdon, *Neubabylonische Königsinschriften*, 1912
NABU	*Nouvelles Assyriologiques Brèves et Utilitaires*
N(ew)JPS	*A New Translation of The Holy Scriptures*, Jewish Publication Society
OB	*Old Babylonian*
Or	*Orientalia*
PN	*Personal Name*
PRU	*Palais royal d'Ugarit*
RA	*Revue d'Assyriologie*
RAI	*Rencontre Assyriologique Internationale*
RÉS	*Revue des Études sémitiques*
RHA	*Revue Hittites et Asianique*
RLA	E. Ebeling, B. Meissner . . . D.O. Edzard (eds.), *Reallexikon der Assyriologie*, Berlin-New York
RSO	*Rivista degli Studi Orientali*
RSV	*Revised Standard Version*
SAA	*State Archives of Assyria*, Helsinki
SCME	*Canadian Society for Mesopotamian Studies*, Bulletin
SEL	*Studi Epigrafici e Linguistici*
SJOT	*Scandinavian Journal of the Old Testament*
SVT	*Supplements Vetus Testamentum*
THAT	E. Jenni, C. Westermann (eds.), *Theologisches Handwörterbuch zum Alten Testament*, München-Zürich, 1971–76
ThR	*Theologische Rundschau*
T(h)WAT	G.J. Botterweck, H. Ringgren, H.-J. Fabry (eds.), *Theologisches Wörterbuch zum Alten Testament*, München-Zürich
TUAT	O. Kaiser (ed.), *Texte aus der Umwelt des Alten Testaments*, Gütersloh, 1981–00
UF	*Ugarit-Forschungen*

UT	*Ugaritic Texts*
VD	*Verbum Domini*
VT	*Vetus Testamentum*
WO	*Welt des Orients*
WZ	*Wissenschaftliche Zeitschrift*
WZKM	*Weiner Zeitschrift für die Kunde des Morgenlandes*
ZAW	*Zeitschrift für die alttestamentliche Wissenschaft*
ZDPV	*Zeitschrift des Deutschen Palästina-Vereins*
ZT(h)K	*Zeitschrift für Theologie und Kirche*

LIST OF *ARCHIVES ROYALES DE MARI* (*ARMT*)

ARMT I	G. Dossin, *Correspondance de Šamši-Addu et de ses fils*, Paris, 1950
ARMT II	C.-F. Jean, *Lettres diverses*, Paris, 1950
ARMT III	J.-R. Kupper, *Correspondance de Kibri-Dagan, gouverneur de Terqa*, Paris, 1950
ARMT IV	G. Dossin, *Correspondance de Šamši-Addu et de ses fils* (*suite*), Paris, 1951
ARMT V	G. Dossin, *Correspondance de Iasmaḫ-Addu*, Paris, 1952
ARMT VI	J.-R. Kupper, *Correspondance de Baḫdi-Lim*, Paris, 1954
ARMT VII	J. Bottéro, *Textes économiques et administratifs*, Paris, 1957
ARMT VIII	G. Boyer, *Textes juridiques*, Paris, 1958
ARMT IX	M. Birot, *Textes administratifs de la salle 5 du Palais*, Paris, 1960
ARMT X	G. Dossin & A. Finet, *Correspondance féminine*, Paris, 1978
ARMT XI	M. Burke, *Textes administratifs de la salle 111 du Palais*, Paris, 1963
ARMT XII	M. Birot, *Textes administratifs de la salle 5*, 2e partie, Paris, 1964
ARMT XIII	G. Dossin *et al.*, *Textes divers*, Paris, 1964
ARMT XIV	M. Birot, *Lettres de Yaqqim-Addu, gouverneur de Sagaratum*, Paris, 1974
ARMT XV	J. Bottéro & A. Finet, *Répertoire analytique des tomes I à V*, Paris, 1954
ARMT XVI/1	M. Birot *et al.*, *Répertoire analytique* (*tomes I–XIV, XVIII et textes divers hors-collection*), 1: *Noms Propres*, Paris, 1979
ARMT XVII/1	J.-G. Heintz, *Index documentaire des textes de Mari, Fascicule 1, Liste/Codage des textes, Index des ouvrages de référence*, Paris, 1975
ARMT XVIII	O. Rouault, *Mukannišum: L'administration et l'économie palatiales à Mari*, Paris, 1977
ARMT XIX	H. Limet, *Textes administratifs de l'époque des šakkanakku*, Paris, 1976
ARMT XXI	J.-M. Durand, *Textes administratifs des salles 134 et 160 du Palais de Mari*, Paris, 1983
ARMT XXII	J.-R. Kupper, *Documents administratifs de la salle 135 du Palais de Mari*, I–II, Paris, 1983
ARMT XXIII	G. Bardet, F. Joannès, B. Lafont, D. Soubeyran, P. Villard, *Archives administratives de Mari I*, Paris, 1984
ARMT XXIV	P. Talon, *Textes administratifs de salles "Y" et "Z" du Palais de Mari*, Paris, 1985
ARMT XXV	H. Limet, *Textes administratifs relatifs aux métaux*, Paris, 1986
ARMT XXVI/1	J.-M. Durand, *Archives épistolaires de Mari* I/1, Paris, 1988
ARMT XXVI/2	D. Charpin, F. Joannès, S. Lackenbacher, B. Lafont, *Archives épistolaires de Mari* I/2, Paris, 1988
ARMT XXVII	M. Birot, *Correspondance des gouverneurs de Qaṭṭunân*, Paris, 1993

INDEX

Archives royales de Mari (= ARM) and Other Ancient Near Eastern Sources

BIBLICAL AND POST-BIBLICAL SOURCES

Post Biblical Sources

GENERAL INDEX

STUDIES IN THE HISTORY AND CULTURE OF THE ANCIENT NEAR EAST

EDITED BY

B. HALPERN AND M.H.E. WEIPPERT

ISSN 0169-9024

1. G.W. Ahlström. *Royal Administration and National Religion in Ancient Palestine.* 1982. ISBN 90 04 6562 8
2. B. Becking. *The Fall of Samaria.* An Historical and Archaeological Study. 1992. ISBN 90 04 09633 7
3. W.J. Vogelsang. *The Rise and Organisation of the Achaemenid Empire.* The Eastern Iranian Evidence. 1992. ISBN 90 04 09682 5
4. T.L. Thompson. *Early History of the Israelite People.* From the Written and Archaeological Sources. 1992. ISBN 90 04 09483 0
5. M. el-Faïz. *L'agronomie de la Mésopotamie antique.* Analyse du «Livre de l'agriculture nabatéenne» de Qûṯâmä. 1995. ISBN 90 04 10199 3
6. W.W. Hallo. *Origins.* The Ancient Near Eastern Background of Some Modern Western Institutions. 1996. ISBN 90 04 10328 7
7. K. van der Toorn. *Family Religion in Babylonia, Syria and Israel.* Continuity and Change in the Forms of Religious Life. 1996. ISBN 90 0410410 0
8. A. Jeffers. *Magic and Divination in Ancient Palestine and Syria.* 1996. ISBN 90 04 10513 1
9. G. Galil. *The Chronology of the Kings of Israel and Judah.* 1996. ISBN 90 04 10611 1
10. C.S. Ehrlich. *The Philistines in Transition.* A History from ca. 1000-730 B.C.E. 1996. ISBN 90 04 10426 7
11. L.K. Handy (ed.). *The Age of Solomon.* Scholarship at the Turn of the Millennium. 1997. ISBN 90 04 10476 3
12. A. Malamat. *Mari and the Bible.* 1998. ISBN 90 04 10863 7